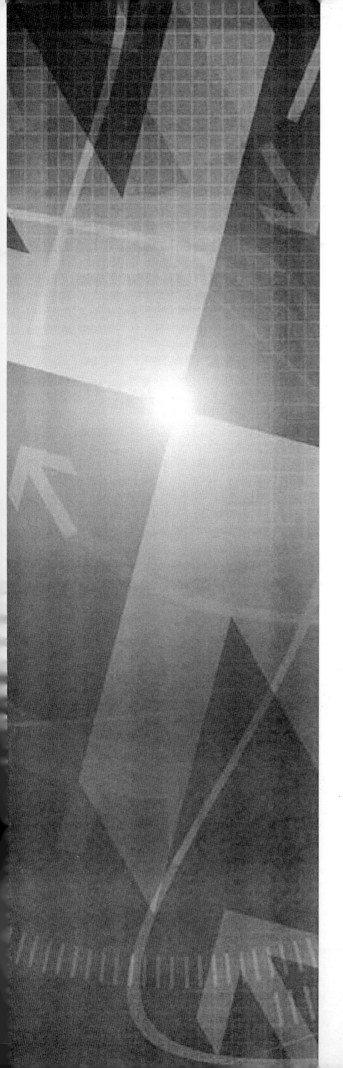

CISI Diploma

Private Client Investment Advice & Management

Edition 3, July 2016

This learning manual relates to syllabus
version 3.0 and will cover exams from
8 December 2016 to 29 June 2017

APPROVED WORKBOOK

Welcome to the Chartered Institute for Securities & Investment's Investment Management study material.

This manual has been written to prepare you for the Chartered Institute for Securities & Investment's Investment Management examination.

Published by:
Chartered Institute for Securities & Investment
© Chartered Institute for Securities & Investment 2016
8 Eastcheap
London
EC3M 1AE
Tel: +44 20 7645 0600
Fax: +44 20 7645 0601

Email: customersupport@cisi.org
www.cisi.org/qualifications

Author:
Julian Ellis Chartered FCSI FPFS CertPFS (DM) Certs CII(MP & ER) & Chartered Wealth Manager and Chartered Financial Planner
Reviewers:
Stephen Curry, BA (Hons) Economics, Reading 1970; MA Business Economics, Reading 1971
Anthony Ward BSc, MCSI, FPFS Chartered Financial Planner

This is an educational manual only and the Chartered Institute for Securities & Investment accepts no responsibility for persons undertaking trading or investments in whatever form.

While every effort has been made to ensure its accuracy, no responsibility for loss occasioned to any person acting or refraining from action as a result of any material in this publication can be accepted by the publisher or authors.

A learning map, which contains the full syllabus, appears at the end of this manual. The syllabus can also be viewed on cisi.org and is also available by contacting the Customer Support Centre on +44 20 7645 0777. Please note that the examination is based upon the syllabus. Candidates are reminded to check the Candidate Update area details (cisi.org/candidateupdate) on a regular basis for updates as a result of industry change(s) that could affect their examination.

The questions contained in this manual are designed as an aid to revision of different areas of the syllabus and to help you consolidate your learning chapter by chapter.

Learning manual version: 3.1 (July 2016)

Learning and Professional Development with the CISI

The Chartered Institute for Securities & Investment is the leading professional body for those who work in, or aspire to work in, the investment sector, and we are passionately committed to enhancing knowledge, skills and integrity – the three pillars of professionalism at the heart of our Chartered body.

CISI examinations are used extensively by firms to meet the requirements of government regulators. Besides the regulators in the UK, where the CISI head office is based, CISI examinations are recognised by a wide range of governments and their regulators, from Singapore to Dubai and the US. Around 50,000 examinations are taken each year, and it is compulsory for candidates to use CISI learning manuals to prepare for CISI examinations so that they have the best chance of success. Our learning manuals are normally revised every year by experts who themselves work in the industry and also by our Accredited Training Partners, who offer training and elearning to help prepare candidates for the examinations. Information for candidates is also posted on a special area of our website: cisi.org/candidateupdate.

This learning manual not only provides a thorough preparation for the examination it refers to, it is also a valuable desktop reference for practitioners, and studying from it counts towards your Continuing Professional Development (CPD). Mock examination papers, for most of our titles, will be made available on our website, as an additional revision tool.

CISI examination candidates are automatically registered, without additional charge, as student members for one year (should they not be members of the CISI already), and this enables you to use a vast range of online resources, including CISI TV, free of any additional charge. The CISI has more than 40,000 members, and nearly half of them have already completed relevant qualifications and transferred to a core membership grade.

Completing a higher level examination enables you to progress even more quickly towards personal Chartered status, the pinnacle of professionalism in the CISI. You will find more information about the next steps for this at the end of this manual.

With best wishes for your studies.

Lydia Romero, Global Director of Learning

It is estimated that this manual will require approximately 200 hours of study time.

What next?

See the back of this book for details of CISI membership.

Need more support to pass your exam?

See our section on Accredited Training Partners.

Want to leave feedback?

Please email your comments to learningresources@cisi.org

Chapter One

Financial Advice Within a Regulated Environment

An exam specification breakdown is provided at the back of this workbook

1. Introduction

In this chapter we will be building on your knowledge, looking in greater detail at the implications of the UK legal and regulatory framework and how this impacts on the provision of private client investment advice.

Some of the terminology and concepts will already be familiar to you in your day-to-day work. We will build upon this knowledge and seek to strengthen your ability to apply the knowledge to real life. We hope that this will give you confidence for your exam.

You must continue reading and extending your understanding of the topics covered through additional study. This workbook does not represent everything you may be expected to know for the exam.

You will see icons or symbols alongside the text. These indicate activities or questions that have been designed to check your understanding and help you validate your understanding.

Here is a guide to what each of the symbols mean:

 Question

This identifies a question that will enable you to check your knowledge and understanding.

 Analyse

This gives you an opportunity to consider a question posed and compare your answers to the feedback given.

1.1 Objectives

The Legal and Regulatory Framework

1. Understand the main provisions of FSMA 2000 and associated secondary legislation and assess their implications for the business operations of the private client adviser.
2. Understand the aims of the European Financial Services Action Plan, and evaluate the effects of Markets in Financial Instruments Directive (MiFID) and Capital Requirements Directive (CRD) on the business systems and controls of the private client adviser.
3. Understand the role, regulatory objectives and functions of the Financial Conduct Authority (FCA) and Prudential Regulation Authority (PRA) and how they affect the control structures of firms.
4. Relate the FCA's Principles and Conduct of Business rules to the processes of advising clients, managing investments and reporting to customers.
5. Apply the rules on 'treating customers fairly' and 'client's best interest' to the process of advising clients.
6. Know the extent of an investment adviser's duty to disclose material information about a recommended investment.
7. Identify 'conflicts of interest' and their potential impact on clients and business operations and understand the compliance requirements that exist to prevent such occurrences.

8. Understand the fiduciary responsibilities of intermediaries, the rights of aggrieved customers and the rules for handling complaints.

9. Understand the principal measures to combat financial crime (insider dealing, market abuse, money laundering [ML]) and evaluate their impact on the firm, the private client adviser and the process of advising and managing private client investments.

2. Financial Services and Markets Act 2000 (FSMA 2000) and the Regulatory Bodies

2.1 Regulatory Framework

Up to 1986, the City and financial institutions had been mainly self-regulating. The ethos was *dictum meum pactum* ('my word is my bond'). However, with the Conservative government of 1979 ushering in an era of home and share ownership to the general public, there was recognition that a more robust regulatory framework needed to be created. This aimed to protect the new shareholders.

The government appointed Professor Gower to report on the issue, and a hybrid system of self-regulation within a statutory framework was created through the Financial Services Act 1986. Through this Act, firms must be authorised in order to conduct investment business.

When Labour came to power in 1997, the industry had seen several calamitous events, all of which undermined both the reputation of the City institutions and the individuals who worked within them. All were highly publicised and well known to the general public, a large proportion of which had been using financial instruments to a greater or lesser degree.

These events included:

* widespread pension mis-selling
* the collapse of Barings
* the Maxwell pension fraud.

The Chancellor announced a radical reform of the financial services industry, which included independence for the Bank of England and the creation of a single statutory regulator. So the Financial Services and Markets Act 2000 (FSMA 2000) came into force on 30 November 2001 (a date otherwise known as 'N2'), and with the Act came the creation of the Financial Services Authority (FSA) in statute law, together with statutory powers, a single ombudsman and a compensation scheme.

2.2 The Regulatory Structure in the UK

After a consultation period, Her Majesty's Treasury (HMT) issued a document in February 2011 called *'A New Approach to Financial Regulation: Building A Stronger System'*. This was enacted by the Financial Services Act 2012. The FSA was divided into two bodies:

* **the Prudential Regulation Authority (PRA)** – established as an operationally independent subsidiary of the Bank of England for prudential regulation and supervision of deposit-takers (ie, banks), insurers and systemically important investment firms

- **the Financial Conduct Authority (FCA)** – responsible for conduct issues across the entire spectrum of financial services. It is also responsible for market supervision and the prudential supervision of firms not regulated by the PRA.

In addition, the **Financial Policy Committee (FPC)** was established in the Bank of England, charged with the primary objective of identifying, monitoring and taking action to remove or reduce systemic risks with a view to protecting and enhancing the resilience of the UK financial system. The FPC has a secondary objective of supporting the economic policy of the government.

In 2013, the Financial Services Authority (FSA) replaced its old risk and supervision business units with a prudential business unit and a conduct business unit (covering consumers and markets) in preparation for the move to the regulatory structure – which took effect from 1 April 2013.

To ensure that the regulatory structure would be in place on 1 April 2013, the FSA moved to a 'twin peaks' model – this meant that banks, building societies, insurers and major investment firms had two groups of supervisors: one focusing on risk and safety and one focusing on conduct. All other firms (ie, those not dual-regulated) were solely supervised by the conduct supervisors.

Stylised Diagram of the Regulatory Framework

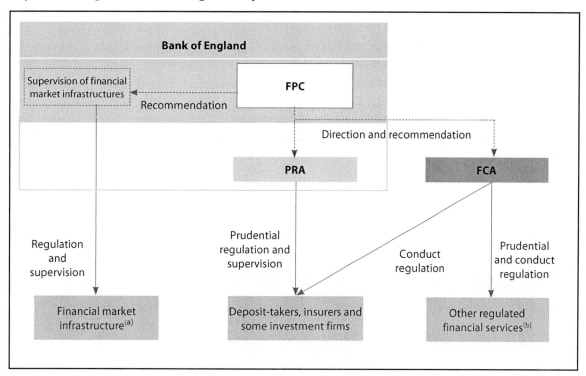

a.   Excludes regulation of trading platforms, which is the responsibility of the FCA.
b.   Includes asset managers, hedge funds, exchanges, insurance brokers and financial advisers.

Source: Bank of England. Quarterly Bulletin 2013 Q1

2.2.1 The Financial Policy Committee (FPC)

The FPC is an official committee of the Bank of England. It focuses on the macroeconomic and financial issues that may threaten the stability of the financial system and economic objectives, including growth and employment.

It is charged with identifying, monitoring and taking action to reduce systemic risks with a view to protecting and enhancing the resilience of the UK financial system.

The FPC makes recommendations and gives directions to the PRA on specific actions that should be taken in order to achieve its objectives. The PRA is responsible for implementing FPC recommendations on a 'comply or explain' basis, and for complying with the FPC's directions in relation to the use of macroprudential tools, specified by HMT legislation. The PRA reports to the FPC on its delivery of these recommendations and directions.

The PRA provides firm-specific information to the FPC, to assist its macroprudential supervision.

2.2.2 The Prudential Regulation Authority (PRA)

The PRA's role is to contribute to the promotion of the stability of the UK financial system through the microprudential regulation of the types of firms set out above. Its general objective is to promote the safety and soundness of PRA-authorised firms, and it will meet this objective primarily by seeking to minimise any adverse effects of firm failure on the UK financial system and by ensuring that firms carry on their business in a way that avoids adverse effects on the system.

For insurance supervision, the PRA has two complementary objectives: to secure an appropriate degree of protection for policyholders and to minimise the adverse impact that the failure of an insurer or the way it carries out its business could have on the stability of the system.

The PRA supervises around 1,700 deposit-takers, banks, building societies, credit unions, insurers and major investment firms that have the potential to present significant risk to the stability of the financial system.

2.2.3 The Financial Conduct Authority (FCA)

The FCA's key aim is to ensure financial markets work well so consumers get a fair deal.

To complement this single strategic objective, the FCA also has three operational objectives. These are:

- secure an appropriate degree of protection for consumers
- protect and enhance the integrity of the financial system
- promote effective competition in the interests of consumers.

These objectives are intended to bring about the following three broad outcomes:

- Consumers get financial services and products that meet their needs from firms they can trust.
- Firms compete effectively, with the interests of their customers and the integrity of the market at the heart of how they run their business.
- Markets and financial systems are sound, stable and resilient with transparent pricing information.

The FCA kept the previous regulator's (the FSA's) policy of credible deterrence, pursuing enforcement cases to punish wrongdoing. Its market regulation will continue to promote integrity and carry on the fight against insider dealing, in which the previous regulator secured 20 criminal convictions since 2009.

The FCA's approach to and style of supervision is different to that of the previous regulator (the FSA). The FCA carries out in-depth structured supervision work with those firms with the potential to cause the greatest risks to their objectives. This means fewer supervisors allocated to specific firms, but allows the FCA greater flexibility to carry out more thematic reviews on products and issues across a particular sector or market. This new approach is underpinned by judgement-based supervisions.

The FCA's integrity objective includes within it the 'soundness, stability and resilience' of the UK financial system. With regard to resilience, the FCA expects firms to maintain high standards in their risk management, having procedures in place to ensure continuity of critical services. Firms are required to comply with standards for resilience and recovery set in this area.

To ensure that the relevant markets work well, the FCA has increased its focus on delivering good market conduct. The FCA's key priorities in delivering good market conduct are:

- a renewed focus on wholesale conduct – in particular inherent conflicts of interest
- trust in the integrity of markets
- preventing market abuse.

The National Audit Office (NAO) is the statutory auditor of the FCA, with the power to carry out value-for-money reviews. HMT can also carry out economy, efficiency and effectiveness reviews.

2.2.4   The Monetary Policy Committee (MPC)

The Monetary Policy Committee (MPC) is a committee of the Bank of England (the Bank). The MPC is set a price stability target by the Chancellor of the Exchequer. This is the inflation target that the MPC is set each year. Currently the target is 2% measured by the 12 month increase in the Consumer Price Index (CPI). The inflation target is confirmed each year in the budget. If inflation moves away from the target by more than one percentage point in either direction the MPC is required to write an open letter to the Chancellor providing an explanation. The MPC is also responsible for setting interest rates. By setting the rate it hopes to meet the inflation target.

The MPC is accountable to the UK Government for complying with its remit as set out by the Chancellor. The Committee's performance and procedures are reviewed by the Oversight Committee of the Court. The Bank is accountable to Parliament through regular reports and evidence given to the House of Commons Treasury Select Committee. The Bank is accountable to the public through the publication of the minutes of the MPC meetings and the Inflation Report.

The MPC is made up of nine members – the Governor, the three Deputy Governors for Monetary Policy, Financial Stability and Markets & Banking, the Bank's Chief Economist and four external members appointed directly by the Chancellor. The appointment of independent members is designed to ensure that the MPC benefits from expertise in addition to that within the Bank itself.

2.3 Regulated Activities and Investments

Under the general prohibition of FSMA 2000, all firms undertaking a regulated activity must be authorised or exempt. Those exempt are:

- Bank of England/central banks/International Monetary Fund (IMF)
- local authorities/charities (deposits only)
- appointed representatives
- recognised investment exchanges (RIEs)
- recognised clearing houses (RCHs).

The list of regulated activities (Regulated Activities Order 2001) for which firms must be authorised (Part 4A Permissions) to transact business has expanded since the original list was created, and includes the following:

- dealing in investments as principal or agent
- arranging deals in investments
- managing investments
- advising on investments
- providing basic advice on stakeholder products
- advising on conversion or transfer of pension benefits
- establishing, operating or winding up a collective investment scheme (CIS)
- establishing, operating or winding up a pension scheme
- sending dematerialised instructions in investments
- safeguarding and administering investments
- accepting deposits
- issuing e-money
- funeral plan providers
- Lloyds – advice on syndicate participation or managing the underwriting of syndicates
- mortgage-related activities
- home reversion and home finance activities
- effecting and carrying out contracts of insurance and insurance mediation
- operating a multilateral trading facility (MTF).

To be clear, the Act also outlines the specified investments within these activities that cover:

- shares
- bonds and other forms of indebtedness, eg, certificates of deposit (CDs)
- certificates representing investments, eg, American depositary receipts (ADRs) or global depositary receipts (GDRs)
- instruments giving entitlements, eg, warrants
- units in a CIS
- options
- futures (excluding those agreed for commercial purposes as opposed to investment/speculative purposes)
- contracts for difference
- rights under a stakeholder pension scheme
- deposits
- long-term insurance (life)

- general insurance
- Lloyds syndicate capacity and membership
- funeral plan contracts
- regulated mortgage contracts
- home reversion plans and home purchase plans eg, equity release schemes
- electronic monies.

As advising on and managing investments is covered, we should remember that it is a criminal offence to carry on investment business in the UK without authorisation, carrying a maximum two-year jail term and/or an unlimited fine. Also, an unauthorised firm cannot enforce an investment agreement and will have to make good any losses to clients and/or pay any profit from contracts entered into when unauthorised.

2.4 Status and Structure of the FCA

The FCA is a private company limited by guarantee, which is owned by the government and wholly financed by the financial services industry via a fee structure.

The FCA is accountable to the Treasury, to which it submits an annual report, and through an annual general meeting (AGM) where the general public, as well as the industry, are invited to review its activities. The FCA is accountable to the Treasury through a variety of mechanisms. The Treasury has the power to appoint or dismiss the FCA's board and chairman. The FCA must carry out an investigation and report to HM Treasury if there has been a significant regulatory failure.

The Treasury has the power to commission reviews and inquiries into aspects of the FCA's operations. Reviews are to be conducted by someone whom the Treasury feels is independent of the FCA, and are restricted to considering the economy, efficiency and effectiveness with which the FCA has used its resources in discharging its functions. Such inquiries may relate to specific, exceptional events occurring within the FCA's range of regulatory responsibilities.

2.4.1 Objectives of the FCA

In July 2013 the FCA published a document titled *'The FCA's Approach to Advancing its Objectives'*. The paper was guidance on how the FCA would approach its statutory objectives, as well as a request for comments on its approach.

The main purpose of the guidance document was to show how the FCA intends to meet its three operational objectives and to explain what firms and consumers can expect from the FCA.

The FCA has three main operational objectives covering protecting consumers, market integrity and promoting effective competition.

Protecting Consumers

The FCA explains in its 'consumer protection objective' how it will secure an appropriate degree of protection for consumers, and what this means to the businesses and markets that it regulates.

Therefore, the FCA aims to:

- ensure customers are treated in a way that is appropriate for their level of financial knowledge and understanding
- be more outward looking by engaging more with consumers and understanding more about their concerns and behaviour
- set clear expectations for firms and be clear about what firms can expect from the FCA
- intervene early to tackle potential risks to consumers before they take shape
- be tougher and bolder, following a strategy of credible deterrence and using new powers of intervention and enforcement.

The FCA has a competition duty to promote effective competition when addressing the consumer protection (or market integrity) objective. What the competition duty means is that it will look to achieve the desired outcomes using solutions that promote competition regardless of which objective it is pursuing.

The FCA will normally choose the most pro-competitive measure that is compatible with its duties as a whole. Consideration of how to apply this in practice will be made on a case-by-case basis.

Market Integrity

The FCA's 'market integrity objective' is to protect and enhance the integrity of the UK financial system. To achieve this, the FCA concerns itself with a number of factors, including:

- the soundness, stability and resilience of the financial markets
- the transparency of the price information process in those markets
- combating market abuse
- the orderly operation of the financial markets
- reducing financial crime in the UK financial system.

To ensure that the relevant markets work well, the FCA has stated that it will focus on delivering good market conduct. It will intervene proactively to make markets more efficient and resilient, improving integrity and choice.

The FCA aims to ensure that market infrastructure is sound and well run, so that users of markets have confidence in the reliability of the pricing processes and are confident that the transactions they enter into are properly executed. To perform this role, the FCA will look at a wide range of behaviour that damages trust in the integrity of markets or threatens consumer protection.

In its supervision of markets, the FCA will look at wholesale conduct, eg, getting involved if it sees poor behaviour that has a wider impact on trust in the integrity of markets, or if inappropriate activity is likely to have negative consequences for retail consumers.

Promoting Effective Competition

The FCA has a 'competition objective' to promote effective competition in the interests of consumers in the markets it regulates. It also has a competition duty to promote effective competition when addressing the consumer protection or market integrity objectives.

The FCA has a number of powers to pursue its competition mandate. It can make rules in support of its objective to promote competition to benefit consumers or take action against firms that it regulates.

2.4.2   FCA Handbook

The FCA and PRA divided the previous Handbook to create their individual handbooks. If printed in their entirety, they are immense, so there are online tools which help firms to create a tailored handbook specific to their particular business, ie, areas of approved activities.

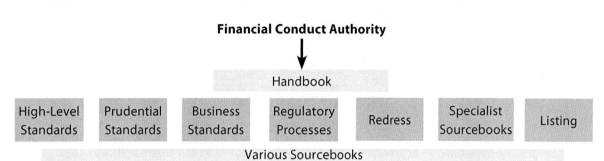

The various Sourcebooks appear in the different blocks of the Handbook and are referenced by their abbreviated reference code. Below are the Sourcebooks which cover the activities of someone who provides investment advice and management to a private client. (It should be noted that, depending on your firm's business model and complexity, this list should not be relied upon as regulatory guidance. You must refer to your compliance department/consultants for direction.)

Handbook Block	Sourcebook	Reference Code
High Level Standards	**Principles for Businesses** The fundamental obligations of all firms under the regulatory system	PRIN
	Senior Management Arrangements, Systems and Controls The responsibilities of directors and senior management	SYSC
	Threshold Conditions The minimum standards for becoming and remaining authorised	COND
	Statements of Principle and Code of Practice for Approved Persons The fundamental obligations of approved persons (APs)	APER
	The Fit and Proper Test for Approved Persons The fundamental standards for becoming and remaining an approved person	FIT
	Code of Conduct The code of conduct for PRA-approved persons	COCON
	Training and Competence The commitments and requirements concerning staff competence	TC
	General Provisions Interpreting the Handbook, fees, approval by the FCA, emergencies, status disclosure, the FCA logo and insurance against fines	GEN

Handbook Block	Sourcebook	Reference Code
	Financial Stability and Market Confidence Sourcebook Guidance to FCA functions under the short-selling regulations	FINMAR
	Fees Manual The fees provisions for funding the FCA, FOS and FSCS	FEES
Prudential Standards	**Interim Prudential Sourcebook for Investment Business** The prudential requirements for investment firms	IPRU-INV
Business Standards	**Conduct of Business Sourcebook** The conduct of business requirements applying to firms with effect from 1 November 2007	COBS
	Market Conduct Code of Market Conduct, price stabilisation rules, interprofessional conduct, endorsement of the Takeover Code, alternative trading systems, what is acceptable market conduct and what is market abuse	MAR
	Client Assets The requirements relating to holding client assets and client money	CASS
Regulatory Processes	**Supervision** Supervisory provisions including those relating to auditors, waivers, individual guidance, notifications and reporting	SUP
	Decisions, Procedures and Penalties The FCA's procedures for taking various actions	DEPP
Redress	**Dispute Resolution: Complaints** The detailed requirements for handling complaints and the Financial Ombudsman Service (FOS) arrangements	DISP
Regulatory Guides	**Enforcement** The FCA's enforcement activity against firms	EG
	Financial Crime Guide Financial crime: a guide for firms	FC
	The Perimeter Guide The Perimeter Guidance manual – covering circumstances when authorisation is required or exempt person status is available	PERG
	The Responsibilities of Providers and Distributors for the Fair Treatment of Customers	RPPD

The Sourcebooks provide six different provisions and these are indicated by a single letter next to the text:

R. Rules – a firm contravening these may be subject to discipline

D. Directions – binding on those to whom they are addressed

P. Statements of Principle for Approved Persons (APs) and binding on all APs

C. Paragraphs which outline behaviour which does not constitute market abuse

E. Evidential provisions, a rule not binding in its own right but which relates to another binding rule

G. Guidance to explain the implications or suggest a possible way to be compliant. A firm cannot be disciplined for failure to follow guidance.

Using this information and being able to navigate the Handbook allows you to look in more detail at the regulations, thus becoming more familiar with regulatory concepts and how this impacts on private client advice.

2.4.3 Powers of the FCA

FSMA 2000 gave the FSA, and its successor the FCA, the power to issue a number of different notices. The regulator has various tools at its disposal designed to enforce the requirements of the rules, regulations and legislation, and these are outlined for firms in SUP, DEPP and EG. Actions can be taken against authorised firms and/or individuals and so it is important that APs are aware of their regulatory responsibilities and what may happen to them if they contravene the rules.

There are a variety of statutory notices which can be issued to firms and/or individuals:

- **Warning notices** – provide details of what the FCA proposes to do and the recipients have the right to make representations as to why the FCA should not take that action
- **Decision notices** – give details of what the FCA will do, but include the right of appeal
- **further decision notice** – agreement has taken place after discussion after the original decision notice. A further decision notice can only be issued with the recipient's consent
- **Notices of discontinuance** – let the recipient know that the FCA, after having previously sent warning and/or decision notices, is taking no further action
- **Final notices** – published on the website. These set out the final actions the FCA will take
- **Supervisory notices** – give details of what action has taken place. These are published and must be preceded by a warning or decision notice.

The first we normally see of these actions against firms is a press release that summarises the details that will be included in the attached final notice. As previously mentioned, the notice will always, where possible, point towards a Principle that has been broken, because the Principles for Businesses are given the status of rules (see Section 4.1 for details of the Principles).

Regulatory Decisions Committee (RDC)

Rather than the FCA enforcement team making decisions which are implemented in the notices listed above, the decisions are made by the Regulatory Decisions Committee (RDC).

The RDC is an independent body. Apart from the chairman, none of the members of the RDC is an FCA employee. The members comprise:

a.   current and recently retired practitioners with financial services industry skills and knowledge, and
b.   other suitable individuals representing the public interest.

This should facilitate an environment whereby independent decisions are made as to whether further action is required in cases where a breach of rules is suspected. The RDC is the body responsible for statutory notices, but it is not responsible for gathering the evidence itself. The FCA enforcement team will bring cases to the RDC, including recommendations for action, with respect to the following areas:

- restriction of regulated activities
- refusal of an application for Part 4A permission
- refusal of AP status
- making a prohibition order
- imposition of a financial penalty, public censure or restitution order.

Any decisions not taken by the RDC will be taken under executive procedures (where the FCA uses statutory powers). An example of this would be the imposition of a requirement on firms to submit regular reports on trading results, management accounts and customer complaints.

When determining whether or not to take disciplinary action, the regulator will consider the full circumstances relevant to the case. However, businesses concerned with the provision of advice or investment management services to private clients should remember the statutory objective of the FCA – to provide appropriate protection to clients.

Disciplinary Measures

1. **Private warnings** – these are issued when formal disciplinary action is not deemed appropriate, but the firm/persons involved should be made aware that they were close to it. Perhaps it was a minor matter or remedial action had already been taken. The FCA requires the recipient to acknowledge receipt of the letter.
2. **Variation of permission** – the FCA may vary the Part 4A permission previously awarded for regulated activities if:
    i.   the firm is failing to satisfy threshold conditions for that activity
    ii. the firm has not conducted the relevant activity for at least 12 months
    iii. it is necessary for the protection of consumers.
3. **Withdrawal of authorisation** – the FCA will consider this action if it is seriously concerned about the firm or its conduct, or if the firm has finished conducting regulated activities.
4. **Withdrawal of approval** – this prevents an AP from continuing in the controlled function that the approval originally related to. The FCA must issue a warning notice to all interested parties on proposal, and then a decision notice on deciding. Any interested party can refer it to the Financial Services and Markets Tribunal (FSMT). Once a final notice is issued, the FCA may publish the decision.
5. **Prohibition of individuals** – the FCA can prevent any individual, approved or not, from undertaking a function in relation to regulated activities, if it appears that the individual is no longer fit and proper. The prohibition order could prevent a person's employment by a firm or simply restrict the functions they may undertake. Similar to withdrawal of approval, the FCA must issue a warning notice and a decision notice. When a final notice is issued, the prohibition can be published. The individual can refer to the FSMT.
6. **Public censure and statement of misconduct** – this will be issued on an AP or a firm if the FCA believes it has contravened a requirement imposed on it by FSMA 2000. A warning notice will be issued prior to the publication of the censure or statement.
7. **Financial penalties** – these will be considered if:
    i.   a firm has contravened a requirement under FSMA 2000
    ii. an AP is guilty of misconduct
    iii. any person has engaged in market abuse
    iv. a company or a director has contravened the listing rules.

Fines are regarded as a considerable deterrent to non-compliant behaviour, especially since they are publicly disclosed. However, the amounts vary depending on the circumstances. Again, warning, decision and final notices are required beforehand.

Anyone receiving a decision notice or supervisory notice has the right to refer the FCA's decision to the FSMT within 28 days, and during this time the FCA can take no action.

2.4.4 Powers of Redress on Behalf of Consumers

The power of the FCA to gain redress for customers is granted through FSMA 2000 and indeed the ability of clients to sue for damages on behalf of themselves.

- S56 FSMA gives the FCA the power to issue a prohibition order.
- S71 FSMA gives an individual the power to sue if he suffers a loss as a result of a breach of the following:
  - S56(6) involves a firm or individual acting in contravention of a prohibition order
  - S59(1) involves a firm allowing an individual to carry on a controlled function without authorisation
  - S59(2) involves a firm allowing a contractor to carry on a controlled function without authorisation
  - S150 allows an individual to sue if he suffers a loss as a result of the firm contravening an FCA rule.

However, it is S397 FSMA (now replaced by S89–94 FSA 2012) which is of particular relevance to the private client adviser. The section covers misleading statements and practices and this makes it an offence to make false, deceptive or misleading statements to induce another person into an investment.

Case Study

A stockbroker tells a potential client that the shares of ABC (a casino company) are very cheap because ABC has just won a contract to provide a casino at Wembley. If the details of the contract were false, S89–94 of the FSA 2012 could be used to punish the stockbroker for making false and misleading statements to persuade a potential client to purchase shares.

While this is a very simple example to demonstrate the point, private client advisers have to be on their guard to ensure that they do not overstate the case for an investment. It should also be noted that the law is there to protect not just existing clients, but also potential clients.

There are, however, three defences against the charge:

1. The person reasonably believed their act would not create an impression that was false or misleading.
2. After certain disclosures to investors, this may have been a method of price stabilisation in line with the FCA's rules.
3. The forecasts were made in line with 'control of information' rules laid down by the FCA. This defence may also include the use of Chinese walls.

2.5　Money Advice Service (MAS)

The MAS is an independent organisation whose statutory objectives are to enhance the understanding and knowledge of members of the public about financial matters (including the UK financial system), and to enhance the ability of members of the public to manage their own financial affairs.

It is paid for by a statutory levy on the financial services industry, raised through the FCA.

3.　European and Other Legislation

3.1　Introduction

The UK, as a member state of the European Union (EU) for over 40 years, played an important part and crucial role in attempting to create a single market across European financial services. Directives issued by the European Parliament are issued to member states for implementation into their own legislation. In the case of the UK, these directives are reflected within this workbook. At the time of writing it is not clear how the result of the EU referendum will impact on the single market for financial services. This will only start to become apparent once Article 50 of the Treaty of Lisbon has been triggered (if it is triggered) at which point negotiations will take place for the UK exit of the Union over a two year period.

Many of the EU directives are applied to the European Economic Area (EEA), which is wider than the EU. Currently, the EU comprises 28 member states, namely:

Austria, Belgium, Bulgaria, Croatia, Cyprus, Czech Republic, Denmark, Estonia, Finland, France, Germany, Greece, Hungary, Ireland, Italy, Latvia, Lithuania, Luxembourg, Malta, Netherlands, Poland, Portugal, Romania, Slovakia, Slovenia, Spain, Sweden and the United Kingdom.

The EEA comprises the EU plus three additional countries (Iceland, Norway and Liechtenstein). Switzerland is not part of the EU or the EEA but it is part of the European single market.

3.2　Financial Services Action Plan (FSAP)

The FSAP was a key component of the EU's attempt to create a single market for financial services.

The European Council, held in Cardiff in June 1998, requested the European Commission to:

'table a framework for action... to improve the single market in financial services, in particular examining the effectiveness of implementation of current legislation and identifying weaknesses which may require amending legislation'.

The cornerstone of the action plan's achievement was the Markets in Financial Instruments Directive (MiFID).

What do you think this means for private clients in the UK?

Clients should be able to purchase products and services from anywhere in the EU and be afforded the same rights irrespective of where the products and services were purchased.

How will this change the role of the financial adviser, if the universe of products and services to choose from increases?

What is the case for harmonisation, and what are the perceived benefits for clients? What opportunities do you believe it affords to firms that offer products and services to clients across the EU? Use the information which follows to consider your response.

3.3   Markets in Financial Instruments Directive (MiFID)

The Investment Services Directive (ISD) issued in 1993 specified that firms had to be authorised in one member state to provide investment services. This single authorisation allowed firms to provide those services in other member states, without the need for further authorisation. This principle is known as 'passporting'.

This directive was superseded in the UK on 1 November 2007 by MiFID, the two principal goals of which are as follows:

1. Extend the scope of the passport to include a wider range of services.
2. Remove the major barrier to cross-border business through application of host state rules to incoming passported firms.

3.3.1   MiFID Core and Ancillary Services

Previously, under the ISD, only a limited number of investment services were included in those that could be passported. Under MiFID this list expanded and in doing so created the core activities which can be passported, namely:

*   investment advice
*   some underwriting activities
*   operating multilateral trading facility (MTF), which are coming online currently
*   activities relating to commodity derivatives
*   portfolio management
*   dealing on own account
*   execution of orders on behalf of clients.

Additionally, there are services that cannot be passported in their own right. In these cases the service must be provided in conjunction with a core service as above.

The services which cannot be passported in their own right are:

- safe custody
- granting credit to investors
- advising on capital structures, mergers and acquisitions
- foreign exchange services
- investment research.

3.3.2   Home State vs Host State Regulation

MiFID makes a distinction between a firm's home state and its host state when engaging in cross-border activities. The home state is that which regulates the firm, and the host state is the EEA territory in which the firm is operating.

If the firm is operating in the host state from its base in its home state, then it is the home state regulations that must be followed. If the firm sets up a branch in the host state, the host state conduct of business rules must be observed for all investment business carried out by the branch in the host state.

In reality, this means that it is not necessary to comply with the rules of 28 different EU states, but only the conduct of business rules, and that these have been harmonised to a greater extent, with the implementation of the MiFID legislation in 2007.

3.3.3   Financial Instruments Covered by MiFID

MiFID applies only to activities in relation to specified financial instruments. These are:

- transferable securities, ie, shares, bonds and other securities giving the right to acquire shares and/or bonds
- units in collective investment undertakings
- money market instruments
- financial futures contracts
- forward interest rate agreements (FRAs)
- interest rate and currency swaps
- options to acquire or dispose of any of the above, including currencies and interest rates
- commodity derivatives including over-the-counter (OTC) commodity derivatives with a cash-settled option other than on default or termination. Other OTC commodity derivatives which are physically settled, which are not for commercial purposes
- credit derivatives
- financial contracts for difference (CFDs).

3.4   Capital Requirements Directive (CRD)

The Capital Requirements Directive (CRD) 'recasts' (amends and restates) the earlier Capital Adequacy Directive (CAD) and Banking Code Directive, and came into force on 1 January 2007. It is applied to banks, building societies and most investment firms.

The premise of the directive is built upon the ISD belief that a customer in the EU should be under no greater risk of a firm becoming insolvent than if they had placed their business with a home state firm.

It is designed to ensure that firms hold adequate resources and have adequate systems and controls to manage both their business and its associated risks. The amount of financial resources will depend on the business carried out, the size of the business, its activities and the risks those activities give rise to. Also factored into this calculation will be scope, products and services. This captures what is referred to as the 'three pillars'.

Quantification of risks arising for financial firms' trading and credit businesses	Series of robust requirements on public disclosure by firms, to encourage a stronger role for market discipline in ensuring that firms hold capital appropriate to their business	Stronger constructive dialogue between regulators and firms on the risks run by the latter, and the level of capital which should be held to support them

4. FCA Principles for Businesses and Statements of Principles

4.1 Principles for Businesses

The FCA has set out 11 Principles for Businesses that apply to every firm conducting a regulated activity. Some Principles apply to all authorised firms regulated by the FCA, and some only apply to firms carrying on specific business, ie, advising clients and/or managing discretionary portfolios (see Principle 9).

These are a general statement of the fundamental obligations of firms under the regulatory system, and also form the foundation for the 'fit and proper' test for firms and individuals.

1.	Integrity	A firm must conduct its business with integrity.
2.	Skill, care and diligence	A firm must conduct its business with due skill, care and diligence.
3.	Management and control	A firm must take reasonable care to organise and control its affairs responsibly and effectively, with adequate risk management systems.
4.	Financial prudence	A firm must maintain adequate financial resources.
5.	Market conduct	A firm must observe proper standards of market conduct.
6.	Customers' interests	A firm must pay due regard to the interests of its customers and treat them fairly.

7.	**Communications with clients**	A firm must pay due regard to the information needs of its clients, and communicate information to them in a way which is clear, fair and not misleading.
8.	**Conflicts of interest**	A firm must manage conflicts of interest fairly, both between itself and its customers and between a customer and another client.
9.	**Customers: relationships of trust**	A firm must take reasonable care to ensure the suitability of its advice and discretionary decisions for any customer who is entitled to rely upon its judgement.
10.	**Clients' assets**	A firm must arrange adequate protection for clients' assets when it is responsible for them.
11.	**Relations with regulators**	A firm must deal with its regulators in an open and co-operative way, and must disclose to the FCA appropriately, anything relating to the firm of which the FCA would reasonably expect notice.

If a firm breaches a Principle it will be liable to disciplinary sanctions, but the onus is on the FCA to show that the firm has been at fault.

 Do these Principles appear to be reasonable expectations of firms' behaviour?

Most people would look at this list and say that the Principles are nothing more than what a customer would expect. However, the FCA has found, over time, that many firms have been in breach of these Principles, in particular Principle 6 (Customers' interests), thus the 'treating customers fairly' (TCF) initiative which began to try and encourage firms to 'do the right thing'.

We look more closely at TCF and acting in a client's best interest in Section 6, but, commonly, those interviewed by the FCA are not able to explain how these Principles are actually met within their business. Try the following exercise.

 Look at the Principles, and try to think of a positive indicator of that Principle being met and a negative indicator demonstrating that the Principle is being breached. Consider the systems and controls you have in place in your own business, and examples of published cases where firms were found to be breaching the Principles.

4.2   Statements of Principle and Code of Practice

The FCA has taken the approach that a firm is typically a collection of individuals, and, because of the importance of some of the roles carried out by some of these individuals, there are certain standards to which they must adhere. So the APER Sourcebook lays out the Statements of Principle for Approved Persons. Additionally, there is a Code of Practice to help assess whether a person's conduct complies with the Statements of Principle.

4.2.1 The FCA's Approach to Approved Persons and Specifying Controlled Functions

The new Senior Managers Regime (SMR) applies to **dual-regulated firms** (except insurers) and certain overseas firms and aims to raise standards of governance and increase individual accountability.

For **single-regulated firms** the FCA specifies all existing Significant Influence Functions (SIFs) (excluding the actuarial controlled functions CF12: actuarial function, CF12A: with-profits actuary and CF12B: Lloyd's actuary).

The FCA also specifies the existing customer function (CF30), which applies to both dual-regulated and single-regulated firms. The FCA will undertake a review on what longer-term changes are necessary to the AP's regime.

The five types of controlled function are:

1. **Governing functions** – these are the persons responsible for directing the affairs of the business. If the business is a company then they will be the directors of that company. If the business is a partnership, then they will be the partners. It is important to remember, however, that the deciding factor is not just whether the person has the title of director – someone who acts as a director, even if they are not formally registered as such (for example, a 'shadow director') will also require PRA/FCA approval because of the influence they exert over the firm.
2. **Required functions** – these are specific individual functions which the PRA/FCA expects every firm to have, if it is appropriate to the nature of the business. For example, every firm should have appointed someone to fulfil the compliance oversight function and the money laundering reporting function. The individual tasked with performing the apportionment and oversight function (CF8) does not need to be an AP.
3. **Systems and controls functions** – these are the functions which provide the governing body with the information it needs to meet the requirements of Principle 3 of the Principles for Businesses.
4. **Significant management function** – this function only occurs in larger firms, if there is a layer of management below the governing body, which has responsibility for a significant business unit, eg, the head of equities, the head of fixed income and the head of settlements. Until recently, several different significant management functions were identified, but now they have been merged into one.

All of the above groups are described by the FCA as SIFs because the persons fulfilling these roles exercise a significant influence over the conduct of a firm's affairs.

5. **Customer-dealing function** – this function involves giving advice on dealing, arranging deals and managing investments. The individuals have contact with customers in fulfilling their role. Examples of customer functions are an investment adviser, the customer trading function and the investment management function.

Customer functions are not SIFs.

The table below sets out Part 1 of the FCA controlled functions (FCA authorised persons and appointed representatives).

Type	CF	Description of controlled function
FCA governing functions*	1	Director function
	2	Non-executive director function
	3	Chief executive function
	4	Partner function
	5	Director of unincorporated association function
	6	Small friendly society function
FCA required functions*	8	Apportionment and oversight function
	10	Compliance oversight function
	10A	CASS operational oversight function
	11	Money laundering reporting function
	40	Benchmark submission function
	50	Benchmark administration function
Systems and control function*	28	Systems and controls function
Significant management function*	29	Significant management function
Customer-dealing function	30	Customer function
FCA significant influence functions		

The table below sets out Part 2 of the FCA controlled functions (PRA authorised persons):

Type	CF	Description of FCA controlled function
FCA governing functions*	1	Director function
	2a	Chair of the nomination committee function
	2b	Chair of the with-profits committee function
	3	Chief executive function
	5	Director of an unincorporated association function
	6	Small friendly society function
	10	Compliance oversight function
	10A	CASS operational oversight function
	11	Money laundering reporting function
	40	Benchmark submission function
	50	Benchmark administration function
	51	Actuarial conduct function (third country)
Systems and controls function*	28	Systems and control function
Significant management function*	29	Significant management function
Customer-dealing function	30	Customer function
*FCA significant influence functions		

Both the PRA and the FCA will be able to refuse the application.

To give an example, if someone is appointed to be both a chief executive and a (board level) executive director, they will only need to apply to the PRA for the chief executive function (CF3). They will not need separate approval for director function (CF1).

4.2.2   Fit and Proper

Individuals working for authorised firms who perform a controlled function (a function relating to the carrying on of a controlled activity) are required to obtain AP status from the FCA.

The FCA will only grant approval to persons whom it deems to be fit and proper (and may withdraw approval if it deems the person no longer fit and proper). If the FCA refuses to grant approval, the matter may be referred to the FSMT.

In assessing fitness and propriety, the most important considerations will be the person's:

*   honesty, integrity and reputation
*   competence and capability, and
*   financial soundness.

AP status must be obtained from the FCA prior to appointment to undertake a controlled function, and the FCA must be informed within seven days if an AP stops performing the controlled function.

Before hiring a new employee, a firm needs to ensure that credit and Disclosure and Barring Service (DBS) checks are undertaken. This will hopefully uncover those who are financially unsound or have previously been involved in fraudulent activity.

Recently, the FCA has made it clear that it will conduct telephone interviews with those applying to perform SIFs. This process has led to a significant increase in the number of applications being declined.

4.2.3   Statement of Principles for Approved Persons

Principles 1 to 4 apply to all APs, and Principles 5 to 7 only apply to those approved to perform SIFs.

Statement of Principle 1

An AP must *'act with integrity'* in carrying out his controlled function.

Statement of Principle 2

An AP must *'act with due skill, care and diligence'* in carrying out his controlled function.

Statement of Principle 3

An AP must observe *'proper standards of market conduct'* in carrying out his controlled function.

Statement of Principle 4

An AP must *'deal with the FCA and with other regulators'* in an open and co-operative way and must disclose appropriately any information of which the FCA would reasonably expect notice.

Statement of Principle 5

An AP performing a SIF must take reasonable steps to ensure that the business of the firm for which he is responsible in his controlled function is *'organised'* so that it can be *'controlled effectively'*.

Statement of Principle 6

An AP performing a SIF must exercise *'due skill, care and diligence in managing'* the business of the firm for which he is responsible in his controlled function.

Statement of Principle 7

An AP performing a SIF must take reasonable steps to ensure that the business of the firm for which he is responsible in his controlled function, *'complies'* with the relevant requirements and standards of the regulatory system.

4.2.4   Code of Practice

The Code sets out descriptions of conduct which, in the FCA's opinion, do not comply with the relevant Statements of Principle. The Code also sets out certain factors which are to be taken into account in determining whether an AP's conduct complies with a particular Statement of Principle.

Some may agree that private client advisers, who are in a position of trust with clients and responsible for their assets, should pay particular attention to perceived breaches of these Principles. It should be noted that this is not a comprehensive list of conduct which does not comply with the Principles, and we would recommend additional reading of the APER Sourcebook.

Principle 1

Deliberately misleading (or attempting to mislead) a client, the firm or the FCA and/or deliberately falsifying documents or misleading a client about performance of investments.

Principle 2

Failing to inform a customer or the firm of material information (eg, risks or charges) in circumstances where he should provide it.

Principle 3

A factor to be taken into account in determining whether or not an AP's conduct complies with this Statement of Principle is whether he, or his firm, has complied with relevant market codes and exchange rules.

Principle 4

Deliberately preparing inaccurate or inappropriate records or returns in connection with a controlled function, eg, performance reports, training records or details of qualifications, or inaccurate trade confirmations.

Principle 5

Deliberately misusing the assets or confidential information of a client or a firm, eg, front running or churning.

Principle 6

Deliberately designing transactions so as to disguise breaches of requirements and standards.

Principle 7

Deliberately failing to disclose the existence of a conflict of interest in connection with dealings with a client.

4.3 Training and Competence

4.3.1 Introduction

In line with the MiFID Article 5 which discusses the knowledge, skills and expertise of employees, the regulator has revised the Training and Competence Sourcebook and it should now be read in conjunction with the SYSC Sourcebook in which it states:

'A firm must employ personnel with the skills, knowledge and expertise necessary for the discharge of the responsibilities allocated to them.' (SYSC 3.1.6)

This covers all firms, and the revised rules relating to training and competence also apply to firms with employees that carry on activities for retail clients, customers or consumers.

4.3.2 Attaining Competence, Appropriate Examinations and Supervision

A firm should not assess a person as competent to carry on any of a specified range of activities until they have demonstrated competence and passed each module of an appropriate examination. Firms must not allow employees to do any of the following, without having passed each module of an appropriate examination:

- certain 'advising and dealing' activities
- acting as a broker fund adviser
- advising on syndicate participation at Lloyd's
- acting as a pension transfer specialist.

Until such time as the employee is deemed competent they must be appropriately supervised, and those supervising employees must have the necessary coaching and assessment skills as well as technical knowledge to act as competent supervisors and assessors.

4.3.3 Maintaining Competence

A firm must review employees' competence on a regular and frequent basis, and take appropriate action to ensure that they remain competent for their roles, and specifically take into account:

- the employees' technical knowledge and its application
- the employees' skills and expertise
- changes in products, legislation and regulation.

4.3.4 Record-Keeping

A firm must make appropriate records to demonstrate compliance with the rules in this Sourcebook, and keep them for the following periods after an employee stops carrying on the activity:

- at least five years for MiFID business, a life policy, a personal pension scheme or a stakeholder pension scheme
- three years for non-MiFID business, and
- indefinitely for a pension transfer, conversion, opt-out or free-standing additional voluntary contributions (FSAVC).

5. Conduct of Business Sourcebook (COBS)

5.1 Introduction

The COBS (Business Standards block) has wider-ranging rules and guidance on a variety of activities, many of which directly affect the way firms deal with private clients. MiFID has had a significant effect on this section of the Handbook. The COBS Sourcebook is a shift of emphasis from detailed rules to principles and high level rules and guidance.

COBS applies to firms carrying on the relevant activities (see Section 5.1.1) from an establishment maintained by them in the UK. COBS also applies to a firm's MiFID business carried on from an establishment in another EEA state, but only where that business is carried on within that state. So for an EEA MiFID investment, COBS rules that relate to MIFID business do so only where that business is carried on from an establishment in the UK.

Another change to COBS from November 2008 was the inclusion of appointed representatives.

Finally, before we look at the detail of the sections of COBS which directly affect advisers, wherever the rules talk about information being transmitted in a durable medium, this means paper or any instrument which allows the recipient to store it unchanged for an appropriate time, ie, on a PC but not the internet unless it is held in a storage area with the ability to retrieve it.

What follows are only highlights from the COBS Sourcebook with some of the issues that you will be expected to know. Reference to our learning material, including the FCA's Handbook, is recommended.

5.1.1 Activities Subject to COBS

The activities covered are:

- accepting deposits
- designated investment business
- long-term insurance business in relation to life policies
- activities relating to the above.

5.2 Client Classification (COBS 3)

Under COBS, clients are generally categorised as:

- retail
- professional, or
- eligible counterparties.

In reality, since these new classifications came into force, it is much harder for retail clients to opt up to professional clients. However, they can be reclassified on a transaction-by-transaction basis.

In all cases, new clients have to be informed of the classification which the firm has given to them, and the greatest level of protection must be afforded to retail clients.

If clients do wish to opt up, they must be able to meet two criteria from a quantitative test to become elective professional clients:

- average trade frequency of > ten per quarter over previous four quarters
- portfolio worth > €500,000
- works, or is involved, in financial sector for > one year in a professional capacity.

Furthermore, the firm must apply a qualitative test, whereby it assesses the expertise, experience and knowledge of the client. Financial firms are treated as 'per se' (Latin: in itself) professional clients.

5.3 Communication with Clients (COBS 4)

You will see more about the concepts upon which these rules are based in Section 6 in relation to TCF and acting in the client's best interest. We need to remember Principles 6 and 7.

Can you remember Principles 6 and 7 from Section 4.1? If not, go back and review them and make sure you are confident that you can relate the Principles to the rules outlined in this chapter.

5.3.1 Fair, Clear and Not Misleading

Underpinning the rules relating to advisers dealing with clients, is *'fair, clear and not misleading'* which is at the core of the financial promotion rules and the information that is sent to clients. Firms must ensure that:

- if the firm's regulator (the FCA) is named and matters are not regulated by them, it says so
- financial promotions which deal with products or services where the client's capital is at risk, must say this
- yield quotes must give a balanced view of both short-term and long-term prospects
- if an investment is complex, it must be clearly explained
- if communications relate to a packaged product, the provider of that product is accurately, fairly and clearly described.

5.3.2 Communicating with Retail Clients

Generally speaking, firms have to make sure they do not disguise, diminish or obscure important items, statements or warnings.

When firms outline past performance, they must make sure that it is not any more prominent than other information, covers at least five years or since launch and shows the effects of charges and commission. With simulated performance, the firm must say that it is simulated and what the simulation is based on. With future performance, it must say on what it is based, and there must be a prominent warning that it is not a reliable indicator of future returns.

All firms should ensure that approval for financial promotions is completed by an appropriate individual.

5.3.3   Information Requirements when Managing Investments

Firms providing portfolio management services must establish a meaningful way of evaluating, and subsequently reporting on, the performance. This should be accessible by the client and should include appropriate benchmarks based on the clients' objectives and the type of investments used. When managing on behalf of retail clients, firms must:

- state the method and frequency of valuations
- detail any delegation of the discretionary portfolio
- state the benchmarks the portfolio is assessed against
- state the types of designated investments and the types of transactions which may be carried out, including any limit details or restrictions on the managers' discretion
- state the management objectives and the level of risk that may be incurred on the client's behalf.

If firms are holding client money or investments for retail clients, they must provide additional details of who may hold them on their behalf, what would happen if the third party became insolvent, if they are likely to be held in omnibus accounts and the safeguards around that.

5.4   Advising and Selling (COBS 9)

Rules on suitability apply when firms make personal recommendations relating to designated investments and when they manage investments. They exist to ensure that firms take all reasonable steps to establish that recommendations, or decisions to trade, are suitable for the client.

Suitability consists of three elements, all of which must be obtained in order to establish suitability:

Suitability does not apply to execution-only business, and if the client is a professional client, firms can assume that the client has the necessary knowledge in this area.

Once suitability is established, the content of suitability reports is not prescriptive but they must at least specify the client's demands and needs, explain why recommendations are suitable for the client's needs, and set out any possible disadvantages of the transaction.

5.5 Dealing and Managing (COBS 2, 9, 11, 12)

An important aspect of the rules for dealing and managing is captured in the SYSC Sourcebook which says that firms must take all reasonable steps to identify conflicts of interest between between the firm and a client, and between one of its clients and another.

5.5.1 Conflicts of Interest (SYSC 10)

Firms are obliged to take all reasonable steps to identify conflicts of interest between:

- the firm, including managers, employees, appointed representatives/tied agents and parties connected by way of control, and a client of the firm, and
- the firm and a client, and between one of its clients and another.

Under these obligations, firms should:

- maintain effective organisational and administrative arrangements, designed to prevent conflicts of interest from adversely affecting client interests
- for those producing 'externally facing' investment research, have appropriate information controls and barriers to stop information from these research activities flowing to the rest of the firm's business, eg, 'Chinese walls'
- if a conflict of interest cannot be managed away, ensure that the general or specific nature of it is disclosed
- prepare, maintain and implement an effective conflicts policy
- provide retail clients and potential retail clients with a description of that policy, and finally
- keep records of those activities where a conflict has arisen.

5.5.2 Chinese Walls

A Chinese wall is an information barrier implemented within a firm to separate and isolate persons who make investment decisions from persons who are privy to undisclosed material information which may influence those decisions. This is a way of avoiding conflict of interest problems. SYSC requires firms to establish 'Chinese walls' if an employee holds information which must be withheld from other parts of the business. Similar to the conflicts policy, the details of this are not prescriptive so smaller firms may have far less detailed policies than larger, more complex firms.

5.5.3 Investment Research and Recommendations

When a firm produces research, it must ensure that it is labelled or described as investment research or is otherwise presented as an objective or independent explanation of the matters contained in the recommendation.

If the recommendation in question is made by an investment firm to a client, it does not constitute the provision of a personal recommendation. In this instance, investment research is defined as research or other information recommending or suggesting an investment strategy, explicitly or implicitly, concerning one or several financial instruments or the issuers of financial instruments. This includes any opinion as to the present or further value or price of such instruments intended for distribution channels or for the public.

5.5.4 Dealing Commission

Under rules about the handling of dealing commission, an investment manager must not accept goods or services in addition to the execution of its customer orders, if it:

- executes its customer orders through a broker or another person
- passes on the broker's or other person's charges to its customers
- is offered goods or services in return for the charges referred to above.

The goods and services related to the execution of trades must be:

- linked to the arranging and conclusion of a specific investment transaction
- provided between the point at which the investment manager makes an investment or trading decision and the point at which the investment is carried out.

If the goods or services relate to the provision of research, the requirements of the rule on the use of dealing commission are met if the research:

- is capable of adding value to the investment or trading decisions
- represents original thought
- has intellectual rigour
- reaches meaningful conclusions.

There are however goods and services which the FCA does not regard as meeting the requirements, and are therefore not permissible:

- services relating to the valuation or performance measurement of portfolios
- computer hardware
- connectivity services such as electronic networks and dedicated telephone lines
- seminar fees
- subscriptions for publications
- travel, accommodation or entertainment costs
- order and execution management systems
- office administrative computer software, such as word processing or accounting programmes
- membership fees to professional associations
- purchase or rental of standard office equipment or ancillary facilities
- employees' salaries
- direct money payments
- publicly available information
- custody services relating to designated investments belonging to, or managed for, customers, other than those services that are incidental to the execution of trades.

Any goods and services purchased through dealing commissions must be disclosed to clients before execution (prior disclosure) and periodically, at least once a year.

5.5.5 Best Execution

The landscape for best execution and a firm's policy is shifting rapidly at the moment with the rise of MTFs, and particularly the entry into the market of retail MTFs. Firms must take all reasonable steps to obtain the best results for clients. Careful consideration must be given to:

- client category
- client order
- instruments involved
- the execution venue.

Price considerations now need to include the cost of the venue, all expenses and clearing and settlement costs.

Firms are required to advise clients of their order execution policies, which will include details of all the venues that are likely to be used and the factors that will affect the choice of venue. This will need to be reviewed at least annually. You do not have to receive explicit client consent, as you only have to advise them of your policy.

5.5.6 Client Order Handling

Comparable client orders must be executed in turn, ie, in the order they were received:

Once a firm has agreed to execute a current client order, it must do so as soon as reasonably practicable.	**BUT** the firm may postpone the order where it has taken reasonable steps to ensure that it is in the best interests of the retail client.

5.5.7 Aggregation and Allocation

Firms can only aggregate their own accounts deals with clients, or aggregate two or more clients orders if:

- it is likely that the aggregation will benefit each of the clients whose orders have been aggregated
- the client has been notified that it may sometimes work to their disadvantage.

The firm must have an order execution policy in place.

5.5.8 Compliance for Investment Managers and Firms Receiving and Transmitting Orders

Firms and senior managers in firms need to have systems and controls and reporting mechanisms to ensure that:

- **investment managers** act in their clients' best interests when placing orders for them
- **firms** receiving or transmitting orders for clients must act in their clients' best interests.

When considering the conflicts that may arise, how might a client be disadvantaged? Could a conflict of interest benefit certain clients?

5.6   Rules on Cancellation and Right to Withdraw (COBS 15)

As part of the product disclosure rules outlined in Section 6.3.1, there will be references to the client's right to cancel if they wish. In all cases, records will need to be retained, indefinitely for pension transfers and free-standing additional voluntary contributions (FSAVCs), five years for life policies or pension cases and three years for any other investments.

Contract	Cancellation period
• a life policy (including a pension annuity, a pension policy or within a wrapper) • a contract to join a personal pension scheme or a stakeholder pension scheme • a pension contract • a contract for a pension transfer • a contract to vary an existing personal pension scheme or stakeholder pension scheme by exercising, for the first time, an option to make income withdrawals	30 calendar days
• a contract for a cash deposit individual savings account (ISA)	14 calendar days
• to buy a unit or share in a regulated collective investment scheme (CIS), (including within a wrapper or pension wrapper) • to transfer a child trust fund (CTF) • to open or transfer an ISA or Junior ISA • enterprise investment scheme (EIS)	14 calendar days
• accepting deposits • designated investment business	14 calendar days

5.7   Reporting to Clients (COBS 16)

5.7.1   Occasional Reporting

The rules on occasional reporting require firms, other than those managing investments, to give adequate disclosure to clients regarding any orders carried out on their behalf. Specifically a firm must:

• provide the client, in a durable medium, with the essential information concerning the execution of the order
• for a retail client, send the client a notice, in a durable medium, confirming the execution of the order and such of the trade confirmation information as is applicable:
   ○ as soon as possible and no later than the first business day following that execution, or
   ○ if the confirmation is received by the firm from a third party, no later than the first business day following receipt of the confirmation from the third party, and
   ○ supply a client, on request, with information about the status of his order.

5.7.2 Periodic Reporting

Firms managing investments are required to provide periodic statements in a durable medium, unless such statements are provided by another person. This should happen at least every six months, but the client can request them every three months. If the portfolio is leveraged, a statement must be sent monthly.

 Why is reporting important for a) clients, and b) the firms?

Obviously for clients it means that they can compare and contrast the performance over a period. It may prompt them to contact the adviser. It provides the firm with information about the performance and allows firms to monitor their activities against other management information (MI), ie, is there a connection between decline or increase in clients depending on the performance of their advisers? Is there a correlation between statement production and increased complaints, or rise in funds under management (FUM) or new client recommendations? Reporting can be a crucial monitoring tool for firms' business activities.

6. Treating Customers Fairly (TCF) and Acting in the Client's Best Interest

6.1 The FCA's Journey with TCF

Principle 6 is the Principle on which the initiative of TCF is founded:

'A firm must pay due regard to its customers and treat them fairly' is the underlying Principle for the TCF initiative. It is the responsibility of the senior management of firms to deliver this.

TCF is not about standardising client services and products across industries. This is why the FCA is not providing detailed rules for businesses, because it will be different for every type of business and business model. Instead, the regulator has focused on the desirable outcomes for customers.

Outcome 1 – Consumers can be confident that they are dealing with firms where the fair treatment of customers is central to the corporate culture.

Outcome 2 – Products and services marketed and sold in the retail market are designed to meet the needs of identified consumer groups and are targeted accordingly.

Outcome 3 – Consumers are provided with clear information and are kept appropriately informed before, during and after the point of sale.

Outcome 4 – If consumers receive advice, the advice is suitable and takes account of their circumstances.

Outcome 5 – Consumers are provided with products that perform as firms have led them to expect, and the associated service is of an acceptable standard and as they have been led to expect.

Outcome 6 – Consumers do not face unreasonable post-sale barriers imposed by firms to change product, switch provider, submit a claim or make a complaint.

6.2   Examples of Consumer Outcomes being Delivered

What firms need to do is consider these outcomes and demonstrate how they deliver them from their business model, to clients. The FCA does however help firms by providing suggestions of what the outcomes may look like.

Outcome 1 – Example

1. Reporting and analysing information from staff appraisals demonstrates that behaviours match the firm's customer-centric culture, as expressed by senior management.
2. The firm analyses staff remuneration. The remuneration policy includes measures around the fair treatment of consumers. Analysis of this demonstrates positive staff behaviours.
3. The firm collates feedback from a representative sample of staff, to understand staff views on customer fairness and to capture any recommendations and improvements. Results indicate that staff are motivated, understand how to treat customers fairly and are positive about the customer benefits that the firm delivers. The firm has established a target for this feedback. The results of this feedback drive change and the firm can evidence these actions.

Outcome 2 – Example

1. The firm has identified points within the product life cycle where the cancellation of a product could result in customer detriment. It is able to demonstrate consistently high persistency levels at these times and if performance varies, reasons are understood and do not indicate consumer fairness issues.
2. The firm has articulated what it expects the customer profile will be for its products and analysis of actual customer profiles indicates that this expectation is consistently being met. If there is variation, the firm establishes why and reasons do not impact on customer fairness. This is tracked over time and trends are monitored.

Outcome 3 – Example

1. When planning a marketing campaign, the firm uses customer panels to check the information is appropriate for the target market. The firm assesses the effectiveness of these panels using post-sale customer feedback. The results demonstrate that customers understand and are able to articulate what they have bought, know the action that they need to take and are aware of the benefits and risks of taking action. This has helped the firm to establish that communications are fair, clear and not misleading.
2. The firm has documented plans in place setting out the timing, purpose and means of planned customer contact activity. It has a record showing evidence of customers consistently receiving appropriate, timely communications, allowing them to make informed decisions.

Outcome 4 – Example

1. A central specialist team assesses the quality of advice. They apply a sound approach, checking the evidence that has been gathered and the appropriateness of the recommendations made. These assessments indicate very low levels of poor advice and when these do occur, prompt action is taken to improve performance.
2. The firm reviews the mix of advised sales by product type and provider, and checks the degree of concentration of sales to identify any potential sales bias. These reviews show an appropriate mix of products and providers, and the firm can demonstrate no sales bias exists.
3. The firm expects a certain percentage of recommendations to be made for products that do not attract commission in the normal course of business. The actual proportion of such recommendations is tracked at an adviser level and is in line with expectations.

Outcome 5 – Example

1. The firm has set standards for the quality and speed of service, has communicated these to customers, and monitors delivery of these standards. Results demonstrate that standards are being met. If there are any variations, the firm understands why and these do not indicate customer fairness issues.
2. Product performance is as customers have been led to expect, or if not, the firm takes appropriate action to improve it and/or customers are kept informed of reasons why. In practice, this can involve measuring performance against the terms of the product and comparing performance to alternative products, benchmarks or competitors over an appropriate period of time.

Outcome 6 – Example

1. Any barriers can be justified and are in line with customer expectations (eg, exit fees are understood by the customer and are only applied in the stated circumstances). The firm measures the application of barriers to ensure they are applied fairly.
2. The reasons for and volumes of complaints received are in line with expectations. The firm conducts root cause analysis and takes corrective actions where appropriate. Feedback about the complaint process indicates there are no barriers to making and resolving complaints.

6.3   Know Your Customer (KYC)

It is important that, in the regulated environment, advisers are as certain as they can be that they have done a good job for clients. Advisers who are unable to evidence the collection of sufficient KYC data will find it difficult to show that they have acted in the client's best interests, even if they have.

As there is no set structure for obtaining this information, it is the skill of the adviser in ascertaining the client's particular circumstances that is most important. The client must feel trust in the same way as the skilled adviser demonstrates empathy. During the course of initial discussion to establish suitability of a portfolio or product, an adviser must gather the following:

- **personal information** – name, address, date of birth, marital status, dependents and health
- **employment** – occupation, employer's details and benefits or details of self-employment

- **income** – from all sources
- **expenditure** – all outgoings including debt or credit card repayments
- **assets** – property, valuables, savings, investments
- **liabilities** – such as mortgages, loans and credit cards
- **objectives** – what the client is hoping to achieve
- **attitude to risk** – how much risk they are prepared to tolerate.

6.3.1 Product Disclosure (COBS 13 and 14)

When firms and advisers provide advice or personalised information about packaged products to a customer, they must provide written details of the key features of the product they are recommending.

The production of this document must be to the same standard as any marketing material with two elements:

- key features of the product (key investor information document – KIID)
- product illustration (key features illustration – KFI).

The KIID describes the product in the order of the following headings:

- **'Its aims'** – a brief description of the product's aims
- **'Your commitment'** or **'Your investment'** – what a retail client is committing to or investing in, and any consequences of failing to maintain the commitment or investment
- **'Risks'** – the material risks associated with the product, including a description of the factors that may have an adverse effect on performance or are material to the decision to invest
- **'Questions and answers'** – the principal terms of the product, what it will do for a retail client and any other information necessary to enable a retail client to make an informed decision.

The KFI must cover:

- the premium or investment
- any guaranteed benefits, ie, sum assured
- a projection of the final benefit, based on the FCA-specified assumed growth rate
- the effect of charges.

Clients have often overlooked the extent or importance of a particular need, and it is then the responsibility of the adviser to point this out, as the professional in this situation. We cannot prevent clients from choosing to ignore this, but advisers need to show that they have recognised issues and have highlighted them to the client and that the client has decided not to take up the recommendations. This all forms part of the details of the ongoing relationship, and is evidence of 'acting in the clients' best interests' at all times.

6.3.2 Retail Distribution Review (RDR)

On 1 January 2013 the rules following the Retail Distribution Review (RDR) came into force. Their purpose is to:

- improve the clarity with which firms describe their services to consumers
- address the potential for adviser remuneration to distort consumer outcomes, and
- increase the professional standards of advisers.

The approach for implementing the RDR means that it applies to advised sales for a defined range of retail products, but does not apply to non-advised business – such as execution-only and discretionary. However, firms that carry out discretionary management and provide advice as part of that service are still covered by the RDR requirements.

The requirements widened the scope of investment products that can be advised on within the scope of the regime for retail investment products.

A firm must not present itself to a retail client as acting independently unless the only personal recommendations in relation to retail investment products it offers to that retail client are based on a comprehensive and fair analysis of the relevant market and are unbiased and unrestricted.

Advisers who are not 'independent' are classified as 'restricted'. They must describe this restricted service to consumers, with a short description to help consumers understand the service that is being provided to them.

Restricted advice is where an adviser can only recommend certain products, product providers or both. Therefore, they might only offer products from one company, or just one type of product. They could also focus on one particular market.

A firm must disclose in writing to a retail client, in good time before the provision of its services in respect of a personal recommendation or basic advice in relation to a retail investment product, whether the advice will be independent or restricted advice.

A firm that provides independent advice in respect of a relevant market that does not include all retail investment products must include in its disclosure to the retail client an explanation of that market – including the types of retail investment products that constitute that market. If a firm provides restricted advice, its disclosure must explain the nature of the restriction. If a firm provides both independent advice and restricted advice, the disclosure must clearly explain the different nature of the independent advice and restricted advice services.

Disclosure must be made in a durable medium or through a website. A firm is able to provide the disclosure by using a services and costs disclosure document or a combined initial disclosure document.

If a firm provides restricted advice and engages in spoken interaction with a retail client, the firm must disclose orally, in good time before the provision of its services in respect of a personal recommendation, that it provides restricted advice and the nature of that restriction.

Advisers will not be able to be remunerated from the product provider when making a personal recommendation to a consumer. They must charge the consumer for the advice and service that they are providing. It is for the adviser and the consumer to agree the charge, prior to the service being provided by the adviser.

The adviser is prohibited from receiving 'trail commission' on any new business carried out with consumers, including existing clients, as of 1 January 2013. But the adviser will be able to receive trail commission on advice provided before 31 December 2012 on legacy business.

A client can pay the adviser separately for the service, or the charge for the service can be deducted from the amount that is being invested.

6.3.3   Management Information (MI)

Controls and formal procedures should be used to avoid keeping everything 'in their head'. MI is very important in analysing trends, helping to forecast the future and solving and identifying problems.

MI could cover customers, calls, visits, meetings and much more. MI is not just about numbers – the views of a locum, customer feedback or complaints can also form an important part of MI.

The FCA looks at MI (evidence of process, the logic behind it and that it is being implemented and measured) and ensuring that it is being challenged.

MI can come in many different forms – some common types are:

*   new business register
*   business persistency
*   training and competence records
*   file reviews
*   customer feedback
*   compliance reports.

It may be appropriate to consider a risk-based approach, where areas of service are monitored more closely when they involve riskier products or solutions.

Standard information may be analysed differently. For example, to gauge what it shows about the fair treatment of customers, rather than the firm's financial performance.

Negative feedback or MI can often reveal more about the firm and its culture than compliments will.

 What kind of MI do you think a group could collect to support the premise that it was treating customers fairly?

Obviously this will depend on the nature of the business and what is proportional to that business.

Can you think about examples that you would use to demonstrate that the customers' outcomes were manifestly being delivered from within an organisation?

7.   Complaints-Handling

7.1   Right to Complain under FSMA

Even if legal action is available, it may be impractical or burdensome for smaller investors to pursue a claim against a firm through the courts. In consequence, FSMA 2000 obliges the FCA to impose requirements on firms to ensure the fair handling of complaints. It also obliges the FCA to set up a body to consider claims against a firm by its customers. This body is the Financial Ombudsman Service (FOS).

7.2   Internal Complaints Handling Procedures

A firm must have in place and operate appropriate and effective internal complaint handling procedures (which must be written down) for handling any expression of dissatisfaction, whether oral or written, and whether justified or not, from or on behalf of an eligible complainant about the firm's services. This must be readily available for customers or potential customers to see at every branch or office of the firm.

In general, the internal complaints-handling procedures should provide for:

- receiving complaints
- responding to complaints
- the appropriate investigation of complaints, and
- notifying eligible complainants of their right to go to the FOS, where relevant.

In particular, a firm's procedures must make provision for:

- appropriate staff to investigate the complaint
- the employee to have the authority to settle complaints (or have ready access to someone who can), and
- the response by the firm to address the complaint adequately and to offer appropriate redress.

 How are customers or potential customers informed of your internal complaints procedure? How does your firm organise its complaints-handling?

We must remember that one of the customer outcomes of TCF is the ability of customers and clients to be able to make a complaint. Eligible complaints can be oral or written. Is every member of staff aware of the procedure to ensure that complaints are handled correctly and in a timely manner?

7.3   Eligible Complainants

An eligible complainant is a person who is, or has been, a customer, or is a potential customer of the firm, and is:

- a private individual, or
- a microenterprise (fewer than ten employees, and an annual turnover or balance sheet below €2 million), or
- a charity which has an annual income of less than £1 million at the time of the complaint, or
- a trustee of a trust which has a net asset value of less than £1 million at the time of the complaint.

A claim of financial loss may relate either to actual loss or to possible future loss (eg, as a result of a mis-sold pension or endowment policy). However, complaints solely about investment performance will not be eligible for review by the FOS, as they are deemed to be ineligible for compensation (caveat emptor) unless it is accompanied by the suggestion that the performance is due to incompetence or poor systems and controls, and this can be shown.

7.4   Record-Keeping and Reporting

Records regarding complaints must be kept for a minimum of three years (five years for MiFID business), and must include the name of the complainant, the substance of the complaint and details of the correspondence.

The FCA requires twice-yearly reports on the number of complaints, broken down into categories, the number of closed complaints, and those outstanding at the end of the period. These reports are made public, so customers and potential customers can see the complaints against the firm.

7.5   Role of The Financial Ombudsman Service (FOS)

The FOS operates independently of the FCA, with a board of directors appointed by the FCA (subject, in the case of the chairman, to Treasury approval). The FOS and its staff are not Crown agents, but are immune from civil actions. They must prepare an annual report for the FCA, on the discharge of its functions.

7.5.1   Procedure and Jurisdiction

The FOS will only accept cases where the complainant has first approached the firm concerned. The FOS has two jurisdictions:

Compulsory Jurisdiction

The FOS will only consider a complaint under compulsory jurisdiction regarding regulated and ancillary activities of authorised firms. Through the FOS, and in accordance with FSMA 2000, resolution must be sought via investigation and must be determined by what is 'fair and reasonable'.

Voluntary Jurisdiction

In essence, this will operate in a similar manner to the compulsory jurisdiction. The main elements are:

* the firm must be a 'willing participant'
* the complainant must be eligible
* the complaint is with regard to business not covered by compulsory jurisdiction and in respect of lending money secured on land, or financial services activities covered by a different scheme previously in existence
* although voluntary, the parties must still submit to any investigation deemed necessary by the FOS.

7.5.2   Redress

The FOS will decide the amount and type of any award. There may be:

* a money award as compensation, and
* a direction to take appropriate action.

The maximum money award is £150,000. The amount of the award may include a contribution towards the complainant's costs. If the FOS considers that an award larger than the maximum would be fair, it can recommend (but not require) the firm to pay the balance.

The decision of the FOS is binding on firms if it is accepted by the complainant.

However, if the complainant is dissatisfied with the outcome, they may seek a remedy in a court. As already outlined, firms must have explained to customers that they have the right to approach the FOS, and must enclose details of how to do this, normally using the booklet that the FOS produces on how to use their services.

7.6   Financial Services Compensation Scheme (FSCS)

The regulator has also set up the FSCS, which deals with compensation claims from eligible claimants in the event of default by:

- a UK-authorised firm
- an appointed representative, or
- an incoming passported EEA firm.

Those who have protected claims are also able to seek compensation from the FSCS. Protected claims are claims made in respect of deposits, insurance and investment business. Protected investment business means designated investment business, the activities of the manager/trustee of an authorised unit trust and the activities of an authorised corporate director (ACD)/depository of an investment company with variable capital (ICVC).

Those that are **not** specifically mentioned as eligible complainants for compensation via the FSCS are:

- authorised firms (other than a sole trader firm, a credit union or a small business whose claim arises out of a regulated activity for which they do not have a permission)
- overseas financial services institutions
- supranational institutions, governments and central administrative authorities
- provincial, regional, local and municipal authorities
- large companies or large mutual associations.

7.6.1   Structure and Compensation Payable

The FSCS is funded by the financial services industry through an annual levy paid by every firm registered with the FCA.

The level of compensation is limited and the FSCS will only pay out for actual financial loss. It also depends on the product and when the claim was made. The current limits are outlined below:

- **deposits** – first £75,000 per person per firm (£150,000 for a joint account) and £1 million protection limit for temporary high balances over £75,000
- **investments** – first £50,000 per person per firm
- **home finance (including mortgage advice)** – first £50,000 per person per firm

- **insurance business** – unlimited; 90% of the claim with no upper limit. 100% protected for compulsory insurance, liability subject to professional indemnity insurance or certain claims for death or incapacity.

Candidates can find more detailed information and updates on the FSCS website: www.fscs.org.uk.

8. Firms' Responsibility for Combating Financial Crime

Financial crime threatens both the FCA's consumer protection and market integrity objectives. The FCA is ready to take action in relation to financial crime risk in the sectors or markets it regulates. The policies and procedures that firms must have in place to help combat financial crime have an impact on clients. It is important to remember that these policies are there to deter those trying to commit financial crime, or at least make it harder for them to attempt to target firms for the purposes of crime.

8.1 Insider Dealing

Insider dealing can be defined as the deliberate exploitation of information by dealing in securities, having obtained that information by virtue of some privileged relationship or position. This is unfair on other market participants who will, in turn, lose confidence in the operation of the relevant market. The legislation on insider dealing is contained in Part V of the Criminal Justice Act 1993 (CJA 1993).

8.1.1 Who is an Insider?

A person who is in possession of price-sensitive information because:

1. they are an inside source, or
2. they have access to the information by virtue of their employment, position or profession, or
3. they have received information, directly or indirectly from a person who is either of 1) or 2).

8.1.2 Offences under CJA 1993

1. **dealing** in price-affected **securities** on the basis of **inside information**
2. **encouraging** another person to do so. This is an offence even if the other person does not deal
3. **disclosing** the inside information, unless no dealing is expected.

These offences can only be committed by an individual, but, of course, encouraging a company to deal could be deemed to be an offence.

8.1.3 Securities Listed in CJA 1993

- shares
- debt securities (including gilts)
- warrants

- depositary receipts
- options on securities
- futures on securities
- contracts for difference on securities or an index based on a basket of securities.

A professional intermediary is a person carrying on a business dealing in securities, and may not be knowingly party to any criminal activity.

8.1.4 Defences

There are three general defences against the charge of insider dealing:

1. did not expect to make a profit
2. information was sufficiently widely held
3. would have dealt without the information.

In addition, there are three special defences against a charge of insider dealing to ensure that legitimate market activities are not curtailed:

1. acted in the course of normal market making
2. market information – it was reasonable for the person to deal despite having the information
3. acting in accordance with 'price stabilisation' rules.

The FCA is empowered under FSMA 2000 to prosecute under CJA 1993. The maximum penalties are:

- **Crown Court** (conviction on indictment) – seven years' imprisonment and/or an unlimited fine
- **Magistrates Court** (summary conviction) – six months' imprisonment and/or a £5,000 fine.

As an alternative to a prosecution for insider dealing, the FCA may take civil action under the market abuse regime.

 What are the ways that a firm can protect itself from insider dealing, either on its own shares or by its employees?

8.2 Market Abuse

8.2.1 Offences

There are seven offences under the Market Conduct sourcebook (MAR)

1. Insider Dealing
2. Improper Disclosure
3. Misuse of Information
4. Manipulating Devices

5. Dissemination
6. Manipulating Transactions
7. Misleading Behaviour/Distortion

Regular market user (RMU) definition – would a hypothetical reasonable person, familiar with the market in question, regard the behaviour as acceptable in the light of all the relevant circumstances?

8.2.2   Examples

To help you understand the offences, here is an example of each offence:

1. **Insider Dealing**
   Already covered in Section 8.1.

2. **Improper Disclosure**
   X, an analyst employed by an investment bank, telephones the finance director at B plc and presses for details of the profit and loss account from the latest unpublished management accounts of B plc.

   X is guilty of the offence of encouraging market abuse.

3. **Misuse of Information**
   Z, an employee of D plc, is aware of contractual negotiations between D and a customer. Transactions with that customer have generated over 10% of D's turnover in each of the last five financial years. Z knows that the customer has threatened to take its business elsewhere, and that the negotiations, while ongoing, are not proceeding well.

   Z sells their shares in D plc.

   Z is guilty of the offence of misuse of information.

4. **Manipulating Transactions**
   Effecting transactions which:

   1. give, or are likely to give, a false or misleading impression as to the supply of, or demand for, investments or as to the price of one or more qualifying investments, or
   2. secure the price or one or more such investments at an abnormal or artificial level.

   A fund manager's performance is measured on the basis of the value of the portfolio at a particular time. The fund manager buys a large quantity of one of the holdings just before that time, to drive the price up.

   The fund manager is guilty of market abuse.

5. **Manipulating Devices**
   Effecting transactions or orders to trade, which employ fictitious devices or any other form of deception.

6. **Dissemination**

Dissemination of information, by any means, which gives a false or misleading impression as to a qualifying investment, by a person who knew, or could reasonably be expected to have known, that the information was false or misleading. This includes the following (nb, includes 'pump and dump' and 'trash and cash'):

- false trade reporting If reckless
- misleading information on bulletin boards
- journalists can be accused of writing misleading articles

7. **Misleading Behaviour**

Behaviour likely to give a regular user of the market a false or misleading impression as to the supply of, demand for, or price or value of, a qualifying investment, including:

- moving commodities
- moving empty cargo ships.

8.2.3   Penalties for Insider Dealing and Market Abuse

Insider dealing is a criminal offence but could be prosecuted as market abuse which is a civil offence. The maximum penalty for the criminal offence is an unlimited fine and up to seven years in prison, whereas for market abuse it is an unlimited fine but no custodial sentence. Insider dealing as a civil offence under the FSMA 2000 requires a lower burden of proof than the criminal offence covered by CJA 1993 making it, in theory, easier for the authorities to gain a successful outcome.

8.3   Money Laundering

Defined as the process by which criminals attempt to hide and disguise the true origin and ownership of the proceeds of their criminal activities, thereby avoiding prosecution, conviction and confiscation of the criminal funds.

There is a significant amount of legislation which firms need to be aware of, but most will leave the interpretation to the Money Laundering Reporting Officer (MLRO). However, it should be noted that senior managers of firms take ultimate responsibility for their firms complying with legislation and ensuring they are doing everything they can to avoid being used to launder money.

8.3.1   Stages of Money Laundering

- **placement** – introducing the criminal funds to the financial system
- **layering** – moving money in a series of complex transactions to mask its origins
- **integration** – removing the money for the benefit of the ultimate beneficiary, who appears to hold clean funds.

8.3.2   Offences

The most serious offences under the Proceeds of Crime Act (2002) are:

*   concealing
*   arranging
*   acquisition, use and possession
*   failure to disclose
*   tipping off
*   assistance (this covers concealing, disguising, transferring, acquiring or using the proceeds of crime if the person knows or suspects that the proceeds came from serious criminal misconduct).

Maximum penalty – 14 years imprisonment and/or an unlimited fine, or both.

8.3.3   Joint Money Laundering Steering Group (JMLSG) Guidance

It is the Joint Money Laundering Steering Group (JMLSG) Guidance that most firms will build their internal procedures upon. However, they must be using a risk-based approach which is proportionate to their client base and their business model. This is designed to ensure that it creates hurdles for those who are trying the break the law, but it is not overly burdensome for honest clients or out of step with other firms of a similar size.

The guiding principles are:

*   obtaining proof of client identities and verifying these
*   staff training and understanding of the issues
*   recognition that individual staff are responsible for reporting suspicious activity
*   summarising the group's approach to assessing and managing ML and terrorist financing risks
*   summarising the firm's procedures for appropriate identification and monitoring checks
*   summarising the appropriate monitoring of policies and procedures.

 The JMLSG Guidance places a lot of emphasis on the firm's KYC policy. Why do you think this is?

In the event of an investigation, firms will be required to provide details of their clients and money received from them. These records, coupled with the further in-depth information you should collect as part of KYC, may well hold vital information. Remember, ML involves the funds from any criminal activity and that includes tax evasion. Senior managers have to be satisfied that they have robust internal procedures and that all advisers are adhering to them.

Chapter Two
Investment Taxation

An exam specification breakdown is provided at the back of this workbook

1.   Introduction

In this chapter we will be building on your existing understanding of the UK tax system, specifically looking at income tax, capital gains tax (CGT) and inheritance tax (IHT).

Much of this will be familiar to you already, not just from your work but from your own personal tax situation. This will provide a good base to build on to look at some of the areas from a more theoretical basis which will help in your examination.

This chapter is also closely linked with Chapter 5, which looks at financial instruments and products. One of the key features of these instruments and products is their tax treatment.

You must continue reading and extending your understanding of the topics covered through additional study. This workbook does not represent everything you may be expected to know for the examination.

You will see icons or symbols alongside the text. These indicate activities or questions that have been designed to check your understanding and help you validate your understanding.

Here is a guide to what each of the symbols mean:

Question

This identifies a question that will enable you to check your knowledge and understanding.

Analyse

This gives you an opportunity to consider a question posed and compare your answers to the feedback given.

1.1   Objectives

Income Tax

1. Understand the role of Her Majesty's Revenue & Customs (HMRC) and the structure of the UK Self-Assessment tax system.
2. Understand when and how income tax is applied to earnings, interest and dividends and, in some cases, capital gains.
3. Be able to calculate simple tax computations.
4. Apply the main rules relating to allowable deductions, Personal Allowances and reliefs, marriage and civil partnerships and their breakdown, and the tax liabilities of minors.
5. Understand the tax treatment of different kinds of investments and the taxation of income arising on overseas investments.
6. Evaluate the tax-efficiency of an investment asset within the wider context of suitability for an individual customer.

Capital Gains Tax

7. Understand the principles of CGT and when and how it arises.
8. Understand the main CGT exemptions and reliefs available including main residence, exempt assets and exemption limits applicable for individuals, trusts and estates.
9. Understand the main disposal rules for CGT, including special rules that apply to disposals on death and between spouses/civil partners.
10. Know the calculations applicable to assets purchased prior to and post 31 March 1982.
11. Be able to calculate taxable gains on an individual's net gains for a fiscal year.
12. Understand due dates for paying CGT and the use of CGT deferral.

Inheritance Tax

13. Understand the liability to IHT and the effects on IHT liability of chargeable lifetime transfers and transfers on death.
14. Understand IHT exemptions and reliefs, excluded assets, potentially exempt transfers (PETs) and gifts with reservation.
15. Understand the rules governing the administration of estates, Grant of Probate and registration of probate.
16. Be able to value assets for probate and lifetime transfers.
17. Be able to calculate IHT liability based on a straightforward example.
18. Understand the relationship between the valuation of assets for CGT purposes and valuation of assets for IHT-related chargeable lifetime and estate transfers.

Offshore Tax

19. Understand the tax treatment of onshore and offshore funds.
20. Evaluate the suitability of an offshore investment for a UK-domiciled individual.

1.2   Exam Information Sheet

An information sheet will be provided in your exam, giving the main tax rates and allowances:

Tables of Rates and Allowances (£)	2016–17
Personal Allowance	11,000
Income Limit	100,000
Married Couple's Allowance:	
older spouse born before 6/4/1935	8,355
Earning less than and	11,000
partner income limits	11,001–43,000
Personal Savings Allowance:	
basic rate (taxed at 0%)	1,000
higher rate (taxed at 0%)	500
Dividend Allowance (taxed at 0%)	5,000

Bands of Taxable Income Rate	
	Earned Income
£0–£11,000	0%
£11,001–£43,000	20% (Basic)
£43,001–£150,000	40% (Higher)
Over £150,000	45% (Additional)

Capital Gains Tax	
Annual exemption (individuals)	£11,100
Over £11,100	10%/20%*
Residential Property	18%/28%*
(*income subject to HRT)	

Inheritance Tax	
Threshold	£325,000
Over £325,000	40%

Companies Tax	
Full Corporation Tax Rate	20%
Small Companies Rate	20%

2. Residence and Domicile

2.1 Introduction

In this section, we will concentrate on three main taxes that impact on investment decisions: income tax, CGT and IHT. However, it is also important to consider the individual and their status, as this can affect the rules applied for each type of tax.

Broadly, there are two status concepts that we need to be aware of:

- resident
- domiciled.

 Before we go on to define them, consider what you think the rules are for each, and which tax do they impact the most?

2.2   Residence

Since 6 April 2013 a Statutory Residence Test (SRT) has applied to determine an individual's residence status for UK tax purposes, including Income Tax, CGT, IHT and Corporation Tax.

The usual way to establish residency in the UK depends on how many days a person spends in the UK in the tax year (6 April to 5 April the following year).

To establish residency under the SRT, a person is subject to three tests. Firstly, the automatic overseas test will determine if an individual is automatically non-resident. Secondly, the automatic UK test will determine if an individual is automatically resident, Thirdly, if they meet neither of the above, then the Sufficient Ties Test (STT) is applied.

Each tax year must be considered separately and the tests applied to it in order. Once an individual meets an automatic test later tests do not have to be considered.

2.3   The Residence Test

Whether a person is a UK resident usually depends on how many days they spend in the UK in the tax year.

An individual is automatically non-resident if either:

- they spent fewer than 16 days in the UK (or 46 days if they haven't been classed as UK resident for the three previous tax years), or
- they work abroad full-time (averaging at least 35 hours a week) and spent fewer than 91 days in the UK, of which no more than 30 were spent working.

An individual will be automatically resident if either:

- they spent 183 or more days in the UK in the tax year, or
- their only home was in the UK – they must have owned, rented or lived in it for at least 91 days in total – and spent at least 30 days there in the tax year.

The STT determines residency based on a combination of the amount of time spent in the UK with the number of ties a person has.

When a person moves in or out of the UK, usually the split-year treatment is applied. This means that the tax year is usually split into two – a non-resident part and a resident part. UK tax is paid on foreign income based on the time they were living here.

2.4   Domicile

The status of domicile is a more permanent one than that of residence. Broadly speaking, an individual is domiciled in a country where they have their permanent home. However, an individual can often retain their domicile for the whole of their life, even if they live abroad. Although it is possible to have dual nationality or dual residence, it is not possible to have dual domicile.

An individual will initially take on a domicile of origin, which is acquired at birth and normally (in England and Wales) is that of the father's domicile. Illegitimate children, or those who are born after the death of their father, take on their mother's domicile. The domicile follows that of the relevant parent until age 16.

It is possible to try to establish a domicile of choice by moving to a new country with the intention of living there permanently. There are no strict rules for acquiring this change of domicile; instead a number of separate factors are taken into account, such as voting in the new country, establishing a business there, making a locally valid will there or acquiring citizenship or nationality.

One clear and strict rule about domicile in the UK is that of being 'deemed domicile'. HMRC will deem an individual UK-domiciled if they have been resident in the UK for 17 out of the previous 20 tax years.

The tax most affected by domicility status is IHT. Any individual who is UK-domiciled or deemed UK-domiciled is liable for IHT on their worldwide property. If someone is non-UK domiciled, they are only liable to IHT on their UK property. You can see from this why it is important for HMRC to be able to deem someone domiciled in the UK!

2.5   Liabilities of UK Residents

Broadly speaking, if an individual is classed as a UK resident, they will have to complete a Self-Assessment tax return. HMRC will tax that individual on all of their income, both earnings and investment income, no matter where in the world it originated.

If an individual is resident in the UK but is not UK domiciled, that individual is entitled to claim the 'remittance basis' of taxation. This means that they are still taxed like other UK residents on their income and gains arising in the UK. They are also taxed on any income or gains they remit to the UK (ie, bring in to the UK from overseas). However, they are not taxed on their foreign income and gains, which remain outside the UK.

Individuals who claim the remittance basis lose their entitlement to UK personal tax allowances, for both income tax (see Section 3.5.3) and CGT (see Section 4.2.5). They also have to pay a remittance basis charge of £50,000 if they have been resident for at least 12 out of the previous 14 and £90,000 if resident in 17 out of the previous 20 tax years.

Those who have less than £2,000 unremitted foreign income and/or gains if they are not brought into the country are not affected by this change. These individuals will still have to pay UK tax on any foreign income and/or gains they remit to the UK.

3. Income Tax

3.1 Types of Tax

In the UK, there are different types of taxes:

- **Direct taxes**, which are imposed directly on the taxpayer.
  Examples of direct taxes are:
  - Income Tax
  - Capital Gains Tax (CGT)
  - Inheritance Tax (IHT)
  - Corporation Tax
  - National Insurance (NI).

- **Indirect taxes**, which are paid indirectly as part of the price of goods or services.
  Examples of indirect taxes (and there are many of them) are:
  - Value-Added Tax (VAT)
  - Stamp Duty Land Tax (SDLT)
  - Stamp Duty Reserve Tax (SDRT)
  - excise duties.

In this chapter, we will concentrate on some of the main direct taxes, and how these are collected by HMRC, whose role it is to ensure the correct tax is paid at the correct time.

 What do you think are the three main ways that direct taxes are collected from individuals?

Taxes are collected by HMRC:

- through Self-Assessment
- by deduction at source through Pay As You Earn (PAYE), and
- by deduction at source on savings and investment income.

3.2 Self-Assessment

The Self-Assessment system of collecting tax was introduced in the UK for the 1996–97 tax year. It is generally for those with more complex tax affairs – the self-employed, company directors and those liable to higher rate tax on investment income. It is not an additional tax, just a simplified method for those people who used to have to complete several tax forms previously, and who may have been paying tax on different types of incomes at different times (even in different years!). The process gives the taxpayer the option of calculating their own tax payments, if they wish. It is estimated that just under ten million people are affected.

The direct taxes that individuals pay under Self-Assessment are income tax (on all types of income), Class 4 National Insurance contributions and capital gains tax.

3.2.1   Filing Dates

We have already mentioned that the Self-Assessment process gives a taxpayer the option of calculating their own tax payments, but they can opt for HMRC to do the calculation for them. Either way, there are strict calendar deadlines to be met, which are tighter if the taxpayer would like HMRC to complete the tax calculation. There are also different deadlines for filing tax returns online, or by paper.

Currently, the key dates are:

- **31 October** (following the tax year to which the return relates)
  - This is the deadline for filing on paper, and getting the HMRC to calculate the tax due in time for payment the following 31 January. For example, the deadline for filing a paper return in relation to 2016–17 tax year is 31 October 2017.
- **31 January** (following the tax year to which the return relates)
  - This is the deadline for filing online. By following the online process, the amount of tax owing will automatically be calculated. For example, the deadline for filing an online return in relation to 2016–17 tax year is 31 January 2018.

Normally tax returns are sent out by HMRC on 6 April, the first day of the new fiscal year. However, it is possible they could be sent later, particularly if HMRC is informed about a change of circumstances for an individual. If this is the case, and the return is not received before 31 July following the tax year to which it relates, the individual has three months from the date of issue to file their return on paper. If they choose to file online, the deadline for filing is three months from the date of issue or 31 January, whichever is the later.

3.2.2   Payments on Account

Once the tax liability has been calculated, it has to be paid. Rather than receive ad hoc payments, HMRC operates a system where the tax due is paid over three dates. The first two payments are known as 'payments on account', with the third being the 'balancing payment'.

The dates of these are:

- **31 January**   First payment on account
- **31 July**   Second payment on account
- **31 January**   Balancing payment

This can sometimes appear a bit complex, as HMRC adopts a 'current year' system which could mean, for example, that the first payment is due in the tax year that the trading year for a self-employed individual ends. This could mean that the first payment is due before the end of the trading year.

For example, John Lewis runs his own plumbing firm, JL Pipes, which has a trading year that ends on 31 March. For the 2016–17 tax year, his first payment on account is due on 31 January 2017, two months before the end of his trading year.

As a result of this, an estimated value has to be used. This estimated value for the first payment on account is always half of the previous tax year's final due amount. The second payment on account is therefore the second half of this amount. The balancing payment will then result in more tax being paid to HMRC (if the tax due has increased) or could lead to a credit if the individual's tax bill has reduced.

Returning to the situation for JL Pipes, in 2014–15 John paid a total income tax bill of £22,000. For 2015–16 his first payment on account, paid on 31 January 2016, is therefore £11,000. The second payment on account, paid on 31 July 2016, is also £11,000. Later in the year, John's accountant tells him that the total is £26,000. As he has only paid £22,000, he needs to pay a balancing payment of £4,000 on 31 January 2017 in respect of tax due from 2015–16. On this date, of course, he must also pay the first payment on account for the 2016–17 tax year, which will be half of the total amount due for 2015–16. Half of £26,000 means that £13,000 will be due alongside the balancing payment.

? Try this one yourself, before checking your answers below.

Kelly is a self-employed consultant. Her income tax liability for the 2015–16 tax year was £8,400, of which she has paid £6,200 on account. What amount(s) is she due to pay on 31 January 2017?

She still has £2,200 to pay as a balancing payment for the 2015–16 tax year. In addition, she will pay her first payment on account for the 2016–17 tax year, which will be £4,200 (half of the overall 2015–16 liability). So that's £6,400 in total.

3.2.3 Interest, Surcharges and Penalties

When the deadlines described above are not met, HMRC can levy interest. This is charged from the date the tax was due, usually 31 January or 31 July. The current rate of interest charged (since September 2009) is 3.0%. To be fair to HMRC, it also pays interest on overpaid tax, which has been set at 0.5% since September 2009.

A 5% surcharge is levied on tax remaining unpaid 30 days after a balancing payment is due, with a further 5% surcharge levied if the tax remains unpaid five months after the due date. Any tax that remains unpaid after the end of the period of 11 months beginning with the penalty date is again subject to a late payment penalty equal to 5% of the unpaid tax. These surcharges are in addition to the interest that is accrued.

There are also automatic fixed penalties, for example of £100 for any return not submitted by 31 January. A further £100 is due for any return still outstanding six months later. It should be noted that the fixed penalties cannot exceed the amount that remains outstanding at the return due date.

Finally, there are also variable penalties HMRC may levy on individuals, eg, for failing to keep records and documents needed to complete a tax return.

3.3 Pay As You Earn (PAYE)

Most employees in the UK do not have to complete a Self-Assessment tax return, as their tax is collected via PAYE. This means their employer must deduct income tax and National Insurance contributions from their pay, and forward the relevant amounts to HMRC.

An employer will know the correct amount to deduct, as HMRC allocates a PAYE code to each employee. This consists of:

- **A number**
  - This indicates the amount of tax-free income (usually) the employee is entitled to.
  - The last figure is always removed, and so you have to multiply by ten to quantify the full 'tax-free' amount.
- **A letter**
  - This indicates the type of Personal Allowance entitlement.
  - There are different letters used to denote the different types of allowances an individual may be entitled to. The most interesting is a 'K code', as that indicates the individual has no tax-free income – the number given representing additional notional income.

Example

A PAYE code of 1100L equates to an annual tax-free income of £11,000, one-twelfth of which would be treated as non-taxable income by an employer each month. The 'L' in the code is the most common, as it represents those eligible for the basic Personal Allowance.

The PAYE system covers many payments including:

- wages and salaries
- fees
- bonuses and commissions
- holiday pay
- pensions
- payments under profit sharing schemes
- statutory sick pay, statutory maternity pay, statutory paternity pay and statutory adoption pay.

3.4   Personal Savings Allowance and Dividend Allowance

On 6 April 2016, the Personal Savings Allowance (PSA) and Dividend Allowance (DA) were introduced. Although they are called Allowances they are not in fact allowances but nil rate tax bands.

- Until 5 April 2016, **interest payments** (savings income), tax was normally deducted at source at 20%. But from the 6 April 2016, interest is paid gross and individuals now receive a Personal Savings Allowance (PSA). The PSA is £1,000. But if any of an individual's income falls within the higher income bracket, this is reduced to £500. For an additional-rate tax payer the PSA is reduced to nil. Also the £5,000 starting rate for savings still continues as a nil rate band of tax separate from the PSA. The £0–£5,000 0% starter-rate band for saving income (interest) is reduced if non-savings income exceeds the Personal Allowance. If non-savings income exceeds £16,000 (2016–17) the 0% band is eliminated entirely.
- **Until 5 April 2016, dividend payments** (dividend income) were paid net of a **10**% tax credit. (Unlike interest payments, the amount of this tax credit was notional and it was not physically paid to HMRC.) Higher-rate taxpayers paid additional tax on grossed-up dividends at 22.5%, while additional rate taxpayers paid at 27.5%. The change effectively means a reduced rate of tax for basic rate taxpayers but increased marginal rates for higher and additional rate taxpayers.

- From 6 April 2016 dividends no longer include a tax credit. Instead, there is a tax free **Dividend Allowance** of £5,000 and after that all dividends will be taxed at 7.5% on dividend income within the basic rate band, 32.5% and 38.1% (on dividend income in the higher and additional rate bands).

Marriage Allowance

If tax eligible income is less that £11,000 (in tax year 2016–17), Marriage Allowance lets a husband, wife or civil partner transfer up to £1,100 of their Personal Allowance to their partner. The Marriage Allowance can be claimed if all the following apply:

- The couple are married or in a civil partnership
- The claimant's annual income is £11,000 or less, plus up to £5,000 of tax-free savings interest
- Their partner's annual income is between £11,000 and £43,000
- The individual or their partner was born on or after 6 April 1935.

3.4.1 Individual Liabilities

An individual is still taxed on their overall personal situation. As a result, it may be possible that more tax may be due. Although both the PSA and the DA are called allowances, they are in fact nil rate tax bands. The total interest and dividends regardless of whether they fall within the allowance are still added to a person's income to calculate their tax bracket. There is no tapering of the PSA. So, if a person has £1 of income in the higher rate tax band, they will lose £500 of their PSA.

3.5 Income Tax Calculation

Now we have looked at how tax is collected, we will concentrate on calculating an income tax liability. In the Private Client Investment Advice & Management (PCIAM) exam you are required to meet the objective of being able to calculate simple tax computations.

There are six steps to an income tax calculation.

 Before looking at the six steps listed below, what do you think they involve, and in what order?

1	Calculate an individual's gross income for the year.
2	Deduct certain allowable amounts from the gross income.
3	Deduct Personal Allowances.
4	Calculate the amount of any payments for which higher rate tax relief is given.
5	Tax the remaining income at the appropriate rates.
6	Give credit for any tax paid at source, and deduct any tax reducers.

We will look in more detail at each step, and incorporate the following case study as we work our way through each step. From 2016–17 onwards, all individuals will be entitled to the same Personal Allowance, regardless of the individuals' date of birth. This allowance is subject to the £100,000 income limit. The individual's Personal Allowance is reduced where their income is above this limit. The allowance is reduced by £1 for every £2 above the limit.

Case Study

Sandra Evans, aged 62, earns £46,500 per year, and 5% of that is deducted by her employer as a pension contribution. She also pays £300 per month into a personal pension plan (PPP).

She no longer has a company car, but her company provides her with private medical insurance, which has a taxable value of £800.

In 2016–17 her building society pays £2,000 interest and she receives £3,000 in dividends. Sandra also invested £10,000 in a VCT in June 2016.

3.5.1   Step 1: Calculate the Gross Income

Case Study

Sandra has gross earnings of £46,500. In addition she receives:

*   interest of £2,000
*   dividends of £3,000

Sandra's gross income for 2016–17 was therefore £46,500 + £2,000 + £3,000 = **£51,500.**

3.5.2   Step 2: Deduct Certain Allowable Amounts

HMRC lets certain allowable amounts be deducted from gross income before tax is applied. Possibly the best known of these are pension contributions paid under the 'net pay' arrangement, eg, personal contributions to company schemes.

To continue the pension theme, contributions to old style retirement annuity contracts (RACs) can also be deducted here. These are still paid gross, mainly due to most pension providers running their RACs on outdated computer platforms that are hard to convert to the more modern system for an investor to receive basic rate tax relief at source.

Other examples of allowable amounts are:

*   share purchases and loans to companies, involving loans to small 'close' companies or loans to buy shares in them
*   partnership investment, where tax relief is available to a partner who pays interest on a loan used to benefit a partnership
*   payment of IHT, where interest is allowable if it is paid on a loan used to meet an IHT liability. The relief is restricted to one year from taking out the loan.

Case Study

Sandra's employer deducts 5% as a pension contribution. This equates to:

*   £46,500 x 5% – £2,325

This is an allowable deduction from Sandra's gross income of £51,750, to leave £49,425.

Of this gross income, Sandra's non-savings income was £44,175 (£46,500 – £2,325).

3.5.3 Step 3: Deduct Personal Allowances

All UK residents, regardless of age (yes, this does include a newborn baby), are eligible for the basic Personal Allowance. In 2016–17, this allowance is £11,000. Although we are all entitled to this amount, not all of us have a tax code of 1100L, mainly due to enjoying 'benefits in kind' which are given a taxable value that is deducted from the standard Personal Allowance.

The Personal Allowance can be enhanced or reduced. There is a Marriage Allowance, whereby a non-taxpayer can transfer £1,100 (2016–17) of their Personal Allowance to their spouse or civil partner. However, the transferor must earn less than £11,000 and the recipient must earn between £11,001 and £43,000.

On the other hand, the Personal Allowance is reduced for incomes, after outgoings, in excess of £100,000. Personal allowance is clawed back at £1 for each £2 of income in excess of this income limit, until it is eliminated entirely. The combination of higher-rate tax and clawback represent an effective 60% rate of tax.

Case Study

Sandra is entitled to Personal Allowance of £11,000. However, this will be reduced by £800 to take her taxable benefits-in-kind. Her taxable income will therefore be:

*   £49,175– £10,200 (£11,000–£800) = £38,975

Although this is the correct calculation for the taxable income, a good habit to get into is to take the Personal Allowance off the non-savings income first. This is due to the order income is taxed in, which is explained more in Step 5.

Sandra's non-savings income is £44,175. Her revised Personal Allowance of £10,200 would therefore be taken off this to reach the amount £33,975. The other income amounts of £2,000 (interest) and £3,000 (dividends) are added to this to arrive at the total taxable income of £38,975.

3.5.4 Step 4: Calculate any Amounts where Higher Rate Relief is Given

There are two primary situations where this happens, and they work in the same way. The two situations are:

*   contributions to pensions plans, where basic rate tax relief is given at source, and
*   Gift Aid contributions to charities.

If an individual makes these contributions during a tax year, the amount paid should be grossed up (by dividing by 0.8). The gross amount is then added to the statutory limit where taxable income is taxed at the basic rate (basic rate extender – which in 2016-17 is £32,000).

The effect is that more of the individual's other income will be taxed at the basic rate rather than the higher rate, therefore effectively providing 'higher rate tax relief'.

Case Study

Sandra is paying £300 pm to a PPP. This means a gross contribution of £375 (£300/0.8) is being invested on her behalf each month.

For this stage of the income tax calculation, we can extend the basic rate tax band for her by:

- £375 x 12 = £4,500

Sandra's basic rate band will therefore be extended to £36,500.

3.5.5   Step 5: Tax the Income

We've finally reached the point where the taxable income is taxed! It is important that the income is taxed in the correct order and at the correct rate.

The correct order for the tax calculation is always:

1. earned income, then
2. savings income, then
3. dividend income, and finally
4. chargeable gains on life assurance policies.

These rates for the 2016–17 tax year are as follows:

	Non-taxpayers	Starting rate taxpayers	Basic rate taxpayers	Higher rate taxpayers	Additional rate taxpayers
Non-savings income	0%	N/A	20%	40%	45%
Savings income	0%	0%*	20%	40%	45%
Dividend income	0%	N/A	7.5%	32.5%	38.1%
Chargeable gains on life assurance policies	0% (20% tax paid in fund, non-reclaimable)	N/A	0% (20% tax paid in fund)	20%	25%

* The starting rate of 0% to savings income only applies in whole or part if there is insufficient taxable non-savings income to absorb the starting rate band (£5,000 for 2016–17), ie, an individual's non-savings income, before Personal Allowance, is less than £16,000 (2016–17).

In Step 3 we established that it was a good idea to deduct the Personal Allowance from the non-savings income. That is because the order in which income is taxed, is also the order in which allowances are deducted (ie, from non-savings income first, then savings income etc).

Case Study

We have established that Sandra has an increased basic rate band of £36,500. This leads to the following computation:

Type of income	Amount	Tax rate	Tax due
Non-savings income	£33,975 (Step 3)	All at 20%	£6,795.00
Savings income	£500 £1,500	At 0% (PSA see 3.4) At 20%	£0.00 £300.00
Dividend income	£3,000	All at 0% (DA see 3.4)	£0.00
	£38,975		**£7,095.00**

Just to clarify, if Sandra hadn't been paying the personal pension contributions, she would have had the standard basic-rate band of £32,000. As a result, £4,500 more of her non-savings income would have been taxed at 40%. However, her £300 per month PPP contribution translates into a gross annual payment of £4,500 and therefore an increased basic rate band, leaving less income taxed at the higher rate.

3.5.6   Step 6: Give Credit for Tax Paid at Source and Deduct Tax Reducers

We now need to consider whether the individual could benefit from any tax reducers. These are simply amounts that can be deducted from the final tax bill. Tax reducers are not deducted from income so do not have any effect on tax bands or clawback levels. The common examples are:

- **Married Couple's Allowance**
  - This is now only available if either spouse (or civil partner) was born before 6 April 1935.
  - It provides relief at 10% of a fixed statutory amount that is updated each tax year (£8,355 for 2016–17 if older spouse was born before 6 April 1935).
  - For couples married before 5 December 2005, the MCA belongs to the husband, although it can be transferred to the wife.
  - For couples married or registered on or after 5 December 2005, the MCA is allocated to the higher earner. Couples subject to the old rules can elect for these new rules to apply to them.
  - The allowance is a tax reducer.

- **Enterprise investments schemes (EIS)** – an investment in an EIS attracts tax relief at 30% of any contribution paid, up to a limit of £1,000,000 per tax year.
- **Seed Enterprise Investment Scheme (SEIS)** – an investment in a SEIS attracts tax relief at 50% of any contribution paid, up to a limit of £100,000 per tax year.

- **Venture capital trusts (VCTs)** – an investment in a VCT attracts tax relief at 30% of any contribution paid, up to a limit of £200,000 per tax year.

As EIS, SEIS and VCTs are all tax reducers, to benefit from the relief the claimant must have a tax liability which can be reduced.

Case Study

We have established that £7,095.00 is the expected **total** tax liability for Sandra.

As she is paid £10,000 into a VCT, Sandra is eligible to a tax reduction of £3,000 (£10,000 at 30%).

Therefore, her tax bill for the year will be £7,095 – £3,000 = £4,095.

4. Capital Gains Tax (CGT)

4.1 Definition

CGT is a tax on gains arising from the disposal of certain capital assets. We will look at what constitutes 'gains' later, but will start by defining disposals and chargeable assets.

4.1.1 Disposals

The most common disposal for CGT purposes is the sale of a chargeable asset. However, there are other examples of disposals that could give rise to a CGT liability, such as:

- gifting an asset
- exchanges of property
- loss or destruction of an asset (personal injury claims are specifically exempt)
- a capital sum received for a surrender of rights.

4.1.2 Exempt Assets

Chargeable assets for CGT are harder to define. Indeed, the easiest approach is to list some of the key 'exempt assets', in other words those that **do not** create a CGT liability on disposal. The main ones for our purposes are:

- an individual's principal private residence
- private motor vehicles
- gilts and most corporate bonds (excluding convertibles)
- assets held in individual savings accounts (ISAs) and child trust funds (CTFs)
- pension investments
- most life policies, when in the hands of the original owner
- National Savings Certificates and Premium Bonds
- chattels (tangible moveable objects) where the value at disposal does not exceed £6,000

- a chattel which is deemed a 'wasting asset' (basically, an expected life of less than 50 years)
- betting and lottery winnings
- foreign currency, when for own personal use outside the UK
- shares in VCTs
- shares in EISs, as long as they have been held for at least three years
- personal injury compensation.

In addition to the above, most UK residents are allowed use of an annual exemption, which, in 2015–16 and 2016–17, covers the first £11,100 of gains. This is a 'use it or lose it' exemption, meaning that no unused element of the exemption from one tax year can be carried forward to the next tax year.

Chargeable assets:

- property
- land
- buildings
- leases
- shares and investments
- antiques
- jewellery
- possessions of more than £6,000 in value
- business assets such as premises, goodwill and trademarks.

4.2 CGT Calculation

Just as we saw for the income tax calculation, there are now six steps to the CGT calculation. This has been simplified in recent years by the removal of indexation and tapering relief and the introduction of a flat rate of CGT, and so the calculation is a couple of steps shorter than it used to be!

 Again, before looking at the six steps listed below, what do you think they involve and what is the correct order for calculating a possible CGT liability?

1	Determine the disposal proceeds.
2	Deduct the acquisition cost.
3	Deduct any purchase and sale costs, and any enhancement costs incurred.
4	Set off any allowable losses.
5	Deduct the annual exemption.
6	Calculate the tax at a flat rate of 10% (18% for residential property) or 20% (28% for residential property) if income is subject to higher rate tax.

Again, we will look in more detail at each step, and incorporate the following case study as we work our way through each step.

Case Study

Jon Carter, aged 46, has a taxable income of £80,000 per year. In August 2016 he sold a holiday home that he purchased in 2001. The sale price was £245,000, and the purchase price £140,000.

Jon has kept all of his paperwork and has calculated that the total cost of the purchase in 2001 was £2,600. The costs involved with the sale have amounted to £3,800.

During his time as owner of the property, Jon spent £21,000 on an extension in 2005. He also calculates that he spent £10,000 over the years maintaining the property to a good standard.

Jon has other investments, some of which have performed poorly. He sold some shares in November 2014, making a loss of £12,000. He has also sold units in a unit trust, incurring a loss of £4,300 in 2016–17.

4.2.1   Step 1: Determine the Disposal Proceeds

The amount treated as the disposal proceeds is usually simply the sale proceeds. However, HMRC has to be satisfied that the sale is on a fully commercial basis. If it might not be, the market value of the asset at the time of the disposal will be used.

The 'market value' approach will be used when the disposal is not deemed to be at 'arm's length'. This mainly occurs on two occasions, namely:

- a disposal between individuals with a close connection (ie, close relatives), and
- a disposal that is deliberately at undervalue or a gift between friends. The parties do not have to have a close connection in this situation for the market value to be used.

Case Study

Jon sold the property on the open market and received a fair commercial price. The disposal proceeds are therefore set at £245,000.

Disposal proceeds	Acquisition cost	Other costs	Losses	Annual exemption	Gain to be taxed
£245,000					

4.2.2   Step 2: Deduct the Acquisition Cost

The acquisition cost is usually the purchase price, as long as the asset was purchased on a commercial basis. If not, the above rules about market value apply.

If the asset was acquired as a gift, the market value at the time of the gift is used.

An important date to remember for CGT purposes is 31 March 1982. This was when, in a previous regime, the value of all assets was rebased. Therefore, where an asset was acquired before 1 April 1982, the asset's cost is deemed to be the market value at 31 March 1982.

Case Study

Jon also purchased the property on the open market and paid a fair commercial price. His purchase was after 31 March 1982 The acquisition cost is therefore set at £140,000.

Disposal proceeds	Acquisition cost	Other costs	Losses	Annual exemption	Gain to be taxed
£245,000	(£140,000)				

4.2.3   Step 3: Deduct any Costs Incurred when Purchasing and Selling

Incidental costs involved in the purchase and sale of an asset (such as legal fees, estate agent fees, stamp duty and auctioneer's fees) are deductible.

Costs involved in **enhancing** the asset (but not general maintenance) can also be deducted.

Note that no deductions are allowed for incidental costs of acquisition or enhancement expenditure before 31 March 1982, when values were rebased.

Case Study

Jon can deduct the £2,600 cost on purchase, the £3,800 cost on sale and the £21,000 cost of the extension. He cannot deduct the £10,000 maintenance cost.

The total deduction at this stage is therefore: £2,600 + £3,800 + £21,000 = £27,400

Disposal proceeds	Acquisition cost	Other costs	Losses	Annual exemption	Gain to be taxed
£245,000	(£140,000)	(£27,400)			

4.2.4   Step 4: Set Off any Allowable Capital Losses

Losses incurred can be offset against gains made. Initially, a loss must be set off fully against any gains made in the same tax year. This is the case even if the subsequent overall gain is reduced to a figure below the annual exemption amount for that tax year.

If the gains are insufficient to absorb the loss, the remaining loss can be carried forward to subsequent years until it is fully used. There is no time limit for this carrying forward – it is indefinite. When offsetting a loss against a gain in a different tax year, it would only be necessary to use sufficient losses to reduce the gain to the annual exemption amount.

Losses brought forward from 1996–97 onwards must be used before losses brought forward from earlier years.

Losses on disposal of exempt assets cannot be offset against gains.

Case Study

Jon has made a loss of £4,300 in this tax year, which must be offset against the gain he has made this tax year. He then has the choice as to whether he wants to use the £12,000 loss made in 2013–14, although given the amount of gain he made on the sale of the holiday home it is likely he will.

Disposal proceeds	Acquisition cost	Other costs	Losses	Annual exemption	Gain to be taxed
£245,000	(£140,000)	(£27,400)	(£16,300)		

4.2.5 Step 5: Deduct the Annual Exemption

The annual exemption is £11,100. It should be noted that this cannot be transferred between spouses.

The annual exemption that trustees are entitled to is half that allowed to individuals, so currently it is £5,550. The allowance can be used against the gain that will be charged at the highest rate.

Case Study

Jon will use the annual exemption to bring his gains down to the minimum.

Disposal proceeds	Acquisition cost	Other costs	Losses	Annual exemption	Gain to be taxed
£245,000	(£140,000)	(£27,400)	(£16,300)	(£11,100)	**£50,200**

4.2.6 Step 6: Tax the Gain

From 6 April 2016, capital gains are taxed at 10% corresponding to basic rate income tax or 20% for higher and additional rate income tax bands except on residential property (and carried interest). For residential property the rates are 18% and 28%. Principal private residence are generally exempt from CGT.

1. See how much of the basic rate band is already being used against your taxable income.
2. Allocate any remaining basic rate band first against gains that qualify for Entrepreneurs' Relief – these are charged at 10%.
3. Next allocate any remaining basic rate band against your other gains. These are charged at 10% (for residential property 20%).
4. Any remaining gains above the basic rate band are charged at 20% (for residential property 28%). Trustees pay 20% (28% for trustees disposing of residential property).

Case Study

Jon Carter is a higher rate income tax payer, so the 28% CGT rate will be used when he sells his holiday flat.

The gain to be taxed is £50,200 x 28% = £14,056.

So, from the sale of Jon's holiday flat for £245,000, he stands to pay a CGT bill of £14,056.

4.3 Payment of CGT

As we mentioned in Section 3, capital gains are reported to HMRC as part of the Self-Assessment system.

 Returning to the case study of Jon Carter that we have just used to illustrate the CGT calculation process, he sold the holiday home in August 2016. What do you think is the deadline for his CGT of £14,056 to be paid to HMRC?

Any CGT payable is due on 31 January following the end of the tax year in which the gain was made. As a result, Jon is due to pay the CGT liability by 31 January 2018.

4.4 Additional Information

This next section covers some of the CGT related information that you may need to be aware of.

4.4.1 Interspouse (and Inter-Civil Partner) Transactions

As the value of assets gets rebased on disposal, it is tempting for couples, married or registered, to swap the ownership between them on a regular basis, thereby minimising any potential gains in the value of the asset. This temptation has been recognised by HMRC and, as a result, there are special rules for disposals between spouses or civil partners.

A disposal from one spouse to another does **not** give rise to a chargeable gain, unless the disposal takes place after the tax year of separation but before divorce (in which case the 'market value' rule mentioned earlier would apply).

When the asset is eventually disposed of by the receiving spouse, the tax liability is based on the acquisition cost incurred by the first spouse. The transfer between spouses is known as a 'no gain no loss' disposal.

This facility can be used to transfer assets from a higher rate taxpaying spouse to a lower rate taxpaying spouse (10%). The facility can also be used as a tax planning opportunity, by ensuring that both spouses fully use their annual exemptions before paying any CGT between them.

4.4.2   CGT on Death

There is no CGT on the disposal of assets following the death of an individual. The beneficiaries are deemed to acquire the assets at the market value at the date of death.

4.4.3   Chattels

Chattels are tangible moveable property, such as furniture. We noted earlier that these are exempt from CGT if the value (not the gain) at disposal does not exceed £6,000.

Chattels sold for more than £6,000 are therefore not exempt from CGT. However, it is possible to limit the gain to 5/3 x (sale price – £6,000) if the result of this calculation is less than the actual gain.

 Dominic purchased a painting for £1,000, and he later sold it for £9,000. What gain is assumed for CGT purposes?

Using the above equation leads us to:

- 5/3 x (£9,000 – £6,000)
- 5/3 x (£3,000) = £5,000
- As this is less than the actual gain of £8,000, this amount can be used by Dominic.

4.4.4   People with Multiple Homes

Just to clarify, individuals can elect which of their residences is to be treated as their 'main residence' and therefore be exempt from CGT. The election must be made within two years of the acquisition of the additional residence. If no election is made, HMRC can decide which property should be treated as the main residence.

Married couples (or civil partners) who are living together can only claim the exemption for one of their properties.

As noted in 4.2.6, disposals of additional houses or flats, including buy-to-let, incurs a higher rate of CGT.

4.4.5   Shares

Shares of the same type and class can be purchased at different times, creating issues for determining the order of purchase and acquisitions.

Disposals of shares, or indeed of units in unit trusts, are identified with acquisitions in the following order:

- acquisitions on the same day
- acquisitions within the following 30 days (preventing the use of 'bed and breakfasting')
- acquisitions in the share pool (which aggregates all other acquisitions not covered above. The average share price of the shares in the pool will be used).

Example

Julie has a shareholding in ABC plc, which she acquired as follows:

- 6,000 shares on 2 September 1998 purchased for £5,000
- 4,000 shares on 26 May 2002 purchased for £4,200
- 2,000 shares on 22 July 2016 purchased for £1,400

Following some bad news that impacted on the non-systematic risk of the share (see Chapter 7), Julie sold 8,000 shares on 1 July 2016 for £2,800.

The sale and repurchase in July 2016 are grouped together:

- Proceeds of 2,000 shares (£2,800 x 2,000/8,000)   =   £700
- Cost of the 2,000 shares   =   (£1,400)
- Loss   −£700

Share pool

- Proceeds of 6,000 shares (£2,800 x 6,000/8,000)   =   £2,100
- Cost (see below)   =   (£5,520)
    −£3,420

Chargeable loss   −£4,120

Share pool

	Number	Cost
		£
Purchase 2/9/98	6,000	5,000
Purchase 26/5/02	4,000	4,200
	10,000	9,200
Disposal 01/07/16 (9,200 x 6,000/10,000)	(6,000)	(5,520)
Balance carried forward	4,000	3,680

In this case, Julie has a chargeable loss to set against gains, of £4,120.

4.4.6 Shares of Negligible Value

There are occasions where share prices fall so far that they are deemed to have a 'negligible value'. In these situations, HMRC will treat these shares as being disposed of, despite the fact that they haven't physically been sold. This will allow an investor to crystallise a loss.

HMRC publishes a list of shares which it accepts have become of negligible value – www.gov.uk/guidance/negligible-value-agreements-to-30-june-2014#history. This includes some old investment trusts, a few football clubs and some well-known companies such as World of Leather, Marconi and Northern Rock.

4.5   CGT Reliefs

These are different to CGT exemptions in that a gain may be wholly or partly relieved against CGT.

4.5.1   Entrepreneurs' Relief

This was introduced in April 2008 to replace business taper relief.

It can be claimed when an individual disposes of a business, or part of a business. The relief covers the qualifying gains that an individual makes during their lifetime.

For disposals since 6 April 2011 the lifetime limit has been £10 million. This limits the tax to 10% on qualifying assets.

Qualifying gains are:

- a disposal of the whole or part of a business run as a sole trader
- the disposal of shares in a trading company, where the individual has at least a 5% shareholding and is also an employee of the company
- the disposal of a share in a partnership by a partner.

The asset must have been owned for at least one year before disposal.

4.5.2   Business Asset Rollover Relief

This is a form of CGT deferral, which can be claimed by both incorporated and unincorporated businesses when they sell assets used in the business and buy other assets for the business.

There are a number of conditions for this relief to be available, including:

- the business must be trading, and
- the new assets must be purchased in a period starting one year before, and ending three years after, the disposal of the old assets.

This relief allows a business to expand, for example, into new (possibly larger) premises before selling its existing property, and defer the CGT from the sale of its existing property.

4.5.3   Reinvestment Relief into EIS Shares

This relief works along similar lines to Business Rollover Relief.

It is used by investors when making a gain on the disposal of an asset. If they invest that gain into shares that qualify under the EIS, the CGT is deferred.

As with business rollover relief, the investment must be made in a period starting one year before, and ending three years after, the disposal of the asset subject to CGT.

4.5.4   Holdover Relief

This is effectively a form of CGT deferral again, being able to 'hold over' the gain on gifts of certain assets. When this relief is claimed, no CGT becomes payable at the time of the gift, but the acquisition cost to the receiver (the donee) of the gift is reduced by the amount of held-over gain.

This relief can only be given if both the donor and donee jointly claim it, and the donee is resident in the UK (see Section 2 of this chapter for details, if needed).

The relief is available on gifts of trading assets, which are:

- assets used in the trade of the donor by the donor's personal company
- shares and securities of trading companies, provided they are not quoted on a recognised stock exchange or they are those of the donor's personal company (ie, the donor has at least 5% of the voting rights).

Hold-Over Relief is also available on transfers to trusts that attract an immediate charge to IHT (chargeable lifetime transfers [CLTs] more of which in Chapter 6).

5.   Taxation of Investment Vehicles

5.1   Introduction

In the previous two sections of this chapter we looked at the basics of income tax and capital gains tax. In this section we will examine how these taxes impact on the major investment products and vehicles as well as examining both the liability for the investor and the liability incurred within the investment vehicle/product.

This will not be a detailed explanation of each product, as that is covered in more detail in Chapter 5. We will stick to just the taxation aspects, using a similar format throughout to help you compare each (where possible).

Throughout the explanations:

- 'TP' stands for taxpayer
- 'BRTP' stands for basic rate taxpayer
- 'HRTP' stands for higher rate taxpayer
- 'ARTP' stands for additional rate taxpayer.

There is a starting rate of tax for savings if a person's income from savings is £5,000 or less. However, to be eligible for this starting rate the person's total income must be £17,000 or less. The starting rate of tax applies to interest.

5.1.1 Bank and Building Society Savings Accounts

Since 6 April 2016

	Income Tax	Capital Gains Tax
Tax situation of the product	Paid gross	N/A
Tax situation for the investor Personal Savings Allowance	• BRTP £1,000 • HRTP £500 • ARTP £0 • BRTP 20% • HRTP 40% • ARTP 45%	• N/A (the only return received is income, there are no capital gains)
Action by HMRC, and Self-Assessment. Interest received on cash held in an ISA will continue to be tax-free. Starting rate for savings allowance up to £5,000.		

5.1.2 National Savings and Investments (NS&I)

This product group is a bit more complicated, as NS&I operates different products with different tax implications.

Tax-free products	Products that are taxable but paid/credited in full (without deduction of tax at source)
• Direct ISA	• Income bonds
• Cash ISA	• Investment account
• Premium bonds	• Easy access account
• Fixed-interest savings certificates	• Direct saver
• Index-linked savings certificates	• Guaranteed growth bonds
• Children's bonds	• Guaranteed income bonds
	• Pensioner bonds

Some of these products are not currently available for new investment.

5.1.3   Government Gilts

	Income Tax	Capital Gains Tax
Tax situation of the product	Income (savings income) normally paid gross	N/A
Tax situation for the investor: Personal Savings Allowance	• BRTP £1,000 • HRTP £500 • ARTP Nil • BRTP 20% • HRTP 40% • ARTP 45%	• Gilts are exempt from CGT
Other details of note: Any accrued interest on the sale proceeds of gilts is liable to Income Tax if the individual's total nominal holding of gilts exceeds £5,000. Also exempt from stamp duty.		

5.1.4   Corporate Bonds

	Income Tax	Capital Gains Tax
Tax situation of the product	• Paid gross	N/A
Tax situation for the investor: Personal Savings Allowance	• BRTP £1,000 • HRTP £500 • ARTP Nil • BRTP 20% • HRTP 40% • ARTP 45%	• Sterling corporate bonds are exempt from CGT (ie, if they meet the definition of a 'qualifying corporate bond') • If exempt, profits are tax-free, but losses are not allowable • Most bonds issued by companies on or after 1 April 1996 will be 'qualifying' due to new rules introduced in the Finance Act 1996, including relevant discounted securities, but not convertibles
Other details of note: Some corporate bonds are issued as 'deeply discounted securities', where the issue price is less than the amount payable on redemption, by more than 15% or more than 0.5% per year. Profits on the disposal or redemption of these securities will be taxed as income, as opposed to capital gains.		

5.1.5 Company Shares

	Income Tax	Capital Gains Tax
Tax situation of the product	• Paid gross	N/A
Tax situation for the investor	After Dividend Allowance of £5,000 • BRTP 7.5% • HRTP 32.5% • ADRP 38.1%	• Liable for CGT • See Sections 4.4.5 and 4.4.6 for details
Other details of note: Dividends received on shares held in an ISA will continue to be tax free.		

5.1.6 Investment Trusts

	Income Tax	Capital Gains Tax
Tax situation of the product	• Paid gross	• Exempt on disposals made within the investment trust
Tax situation for the investor	After Dividend Allowance of £5,000 • BRTP 7.5% • HRTP 32.5% • ADRP 38.1%	• Liable for CGT • See Sections 4.4.5 and 4.4.6 for details
Other details of note:		

5.1.7 Unit Trusts and Open-Ended Investment Companies (OEICs)

The tax situation of these collective products depends on the asset make-up of the products.

If at least 60% of them are interest bearing. Bond funds are treated differently from direct holdings of bonds. Basic rate tax is deducted at source, but reclaimable if not liable; and they are not exempt from CGT on gains made on fund holdings by the individual investor.

	Income Tax	Capital Gains Tax
Tax situation of the product	• Paid gross	• Exempt
Tax situation for the investor: Personal Savings Allowance	• BRTP £1,000 • HRTP £500 • ARTP Nil • BRTP 20% • HRTP 40% • ARTP 45%	• There is a CGT liability on disposal (despite the fact the underlying assets may be CGT free or exempt)
Other details of note:		

If less than 60% of the assets are interest-bearing:

	Income Tax	Capital Gains Tax
Tax situation of the product	• Paid gross	• Exempt on disposals within the fund
Tax situation for the investor	After Dividend Allowance of £5,000 • BRTP 7.5% • HRTP 32.5% • ADRP 38.1%	• Liable for CGT • See Sections 4.4.5 and 4.4.6 for details
Other details of note:		

5.1.8 Exchange-Traded Funds (ETFs)

	Income Tax	Capital Gains Tax
Tax situation of the product	• Paid gross	• Exempt on disposals within the fund
Tax situation for the investor	After Dividend Allowance of £5,000 • BRTP 7.5% • HRTP 32.5% • ADRP 38.1%	• Liable for CGT
Other details of note: ETFs do not create a stamp duty charge on purchase.		

5.1.9 Individual Savings Accounts (ISAs and Junior ISAs)

An ISA isn't a product as such, but a tax wrapper that can be used to make an existing investment vehicle or product more tax efficient.

For ISAs, refer to Section 5.1.1, where the investment vehicles currently incur an income tax liability. Attaching the ISA wrapper to these vehicles removes the income tax liability, making them tax-free.

For stocks and shares ISAs, refer to Sections 5.1.3–5.1.8, where there is an income tax and CGT liability for an investor. Attaching the ISA wrapper to these types of investment vehicles removes the income tax and CGT liability for the investor completely.

5.1.10 Child Trust Funds (CTFs)

	Income Tax	Capital Gains Tax
Tax situation of the product	• Tax-free	• Exempt
Tax situation for the investor	• No liability	• Exempt
Other details of note: CTFs are exempt from the rule that states a parent is taxable on a child's investment income of more than £100, if the capital came from the parent.		

5.1.11 Derivatives (Futures and Options)

	Income Tax	Capital Gains Tax
Tax situation of the product	• No income produced	• N/A
Tax situation for the investor	• No income produced	• Liable for CGT

Other details of note: In very rare circumstances, transactions may be treated by HMRC as a trading activity and therefore be liable to income tax.
If a tax avoidance scheme uses futures or options to produce a return that is effectively guaranteed, the profit is subject to income tax (under ITTOIA).

5.1.12 Enterprise Investment Scheme (EIS)

	Income Tax	Capital Gains Tax
Tax situation of the product	• Tax–free	• N/A
Tax situation for the investor	After Dividend Allowance of £5,000 • BRTP 7.5% • HRTP 32.5% • ADRP 38.1%	• CGT free as long as shares held for three years • CGT deferral relief possible (see Section 4.5.3 for details)

Other details of note:
- Investment into an EIS receives tax relief at 30% up to a maximum contribution of £1 million per tax year. This relief is given as a tax reducer.
- Income tax relief is withdrawn if shares are disposed of within three years.
- It is possible to carry back investments to a previous tax year, to receive tax relief in that previous year (as long as the overall maximum limit of £1 million is not exceeded).

5.1.13 Seed Enterprise Investment Scheme (SEIS)

	Income Tax	Capital Gains Tax
Tax situation of the product	• Tax-free	• N/A
Tax situation for the investor	After Dividend Allowance of £5,000 • BRTP 7.5% • HRTP 32.5% • ADRP 38.1%	• CGT free as long as shares held for three years • CGT deferral relief possible (see Section 4.5.3 for details)

Other details of note:
- Investment into an SEIS receives tax relief at 50% up to a maximum contribution of £100,000 per tax year. This relief is given as a tax reducer.
- Income tax relief is withdrawn if shares are disposed of within three years.

5.1.14 Venture Capital Trusts (VCTs)

	Income Tax	Capital Gains Tax
Tax situation of the product	• Tax-free	• Exempt
Tax situation for the investor	• Tax-free	• CGT free with no minimum holding period

Other details of note:
- Investments into a VCT receive tax relief at 30%, up to a maximum investment limit of £200,000 per tax year. This relief is given as a tax reducer.
- Income tax relief is withdrawn if shares are disposed of within five years.

5.1.15 Personal Pension Plans (PPPs)

	Income Tax	Capital Gains Tax
Tax situation of the product	• Tax-free	• Exempt
Tax situation for the investor	• Any income taken from a pension fund is taxable at the individual's highest marginal rate	• Exempt

Other details of note:
- Contributions to a PPP benefit from tax relief at source, meaning a net investment made by an individual is grossed up immediately at the basic rate by the provider.
- Higher rate tax relief is available by extending an individual's basic rate band by the gross contribution.

5.1.16 Qualifying Life Assurance Products

	Income Tax	Capital Gains Tax
Tax situation of the product	• Income paid within the fund (equivalent to 20% when combined with CGT)	• CGT paid within the fund (equivalent to 20% when combined with income tax)
Tax situation for the investor	• Non-TP can't reclaim • BRTP has no further liability • HRTP has no further liability • ARTP has no further liability	• Exempt when in the hands of the original owner

Other details of note:
- There are a number of rules that check to see whether a life assurance plan is 'qualifying' or not. The most basic of these is that contributions must be paid at least annually, which clearly rules out single premium life assurance products.

5.1.17 Non-Qualifying Life Assurance Products

	Income Tax	Capital Gains Tax
Tax situation of the product	• Income paid within the fund (equivalent to 20% when combined with CGT)	• CGT paid within the fund (equivalent to 20% when combined with income tax)
Tax situation for the investor	• Non-TP can't reclaim • BRTP has no further liability • HRTP has a further liability of 20% of the chargeable gain following a chargeable event • ARTP has a further liability of 25% of the chargeable gain	• Exempt when in the hands of the original owner

Other details of note:
- An investor is allowed to take annual payments of up to 5% of the original investment with no immediate liability to income tax, regardless of their tax status.
- This can be done for a maximum of 20 years (ie, effectively the investor is having their capital returned in chunks). However, the withdrawals do not have to be consistent as the allowance is cumulative, meaning an investor may be able to withdraw a lot more than 5% of the original investment if they have not taken any previous withdrawals.
- If an investor takes more than the 5% allowance, there may be a personal income tax liability if the gain, when added to their other income for the year, makes them a higher rate taxpayer (remember Section 3.5.5 listing the order that income is taxed, with 'chargeable gains' the last item).
- When an investor cashes in their investment, a calculation is made to determine the chargeable gain and see if there is a further liability for the investor.
- In both of these situations, an investor who is still in the basic rate band can use 'top slicing' to help them remain in that band and create no further liability. Top slicing is of no use to an investor who is already a higher rate taxpayer before the chargeable gain is added to their income.
- A simple comparison example of this process is given below.

Top Slicing Example

Matt and Ben are twins. Matt earns £30,000 pa after the deduction of his Personal Allowance, whereas Ben earns £31,180 pa after the deduction of his Personal Allowance. They both took out investment bonds eight and a half years ago, each investing £100,000.

They have both been taking 5% of this original investment at the start of each year as they have been told there will be no tax to pay on it immediately. The bonds are now both worth £67,000 and they have decided to encash them.

Matt	Ben
<ul><li>Cash-in value £67,000</li><li>Add withdrawals of 9 x £5,000 = £45,000</li><li>Less original investment (£100,000)</li><li>Chargeable gain = £12,000</li><li>The gain has been made over eight full years and so can be 'sliced' by eight</li><li>£12,000 ÷ 8 = £1,500 slice</li><li>This is added to the top of Matt's taxable income for the year of £30,000, making a total income for the year of £31,500</li><li>This is below the basic rate band for 2016–17 of £32,000 and so Matt has no further liability</li></ul>	<ul><li>Cash-in value £67,000</li><li>Add withdrawals of 9 x £5000 = £45,000</li><li>Less original investment (£100,000)</li><li>Chargeable gain = £12,000</li><li>The gain has been made over eight full years and so can be 'sliced' by eight</li><li>£12,000 ÷ 8 = £1,500 slice</li><li>This is added to the top of Ben's taxable income for the year of £31,180, making a total income for the year of £32,680.</li><li>This is £680 above the basic rate band for 2016–17 of £32,000 and so this amount is taxed at an additional 20%</li><li>£680 x 20% = £136</li><li>We then need to multiply this back up by the number of full years the bond was in force for</li><li>£136 x 8 = £1,088</li><li>Ben will have an additional tax liability of £1,088 following the encashment of his bond</li></ul>

5.2   Overseas Investments

The main attraction of offshore products, many of which are available to UK investors, is that they are usually established in low-tax countries, so the investment should roll up more or less free of tax. This is known as 'gross roll-up'. However, this fact alone does not mean that an offshore product is automatically better than an onshore product.

5.2.1   Offshore Sterling Deposit Accounts

These are generally situated in tax havens such as the Channel Islands or the Isle of Man. As we said in Section 2 of this chapter, UK resident taxpayers are taxed on the arising basis. As a result, whether the interest earned is brought into the UK or not, a UK resident is taxed at the same rate as on UK savings income: 20%, 40% or 45%.

There is no particular benefit for a UK resident to invest in offshore deposit accounts.

5.2.2   Offshore Life Policies

These are issued in countries such as Luxembourg, the Republic of Ireland, the Channel Islands and the Isle of Man. As mentioned already, the perceived advantage is 'gross roll-up' due to the tax position of the fund. This could be a significant advantage over the long term.

As all offshore policies issued after 17 November 1983 are deemed to be non-qualifying, the chargeable gain is fully assessed to tax at 20%, 40% or 45% following a chargeable event. If the individuals total taxable income is £17,000 or less for the year then no tax will be payable. Just as with onshore bonds, top slicing can be used to calculate the liability.

Time apportionment relief is available for periods of residence outside of the UK, based on the percentage time the investor was non-UK resident during the term of the policy. However, this still means that the whole of the gain is chargeable if the policyholder was a UK resident for the whole of the policy term.

A quick comparison of onshore and offshore bonds for a higher rate taxpaying UK resident is therefore:

Onshore		Offshore	
Gain in fund	£100,000	Gain in fund	£100,000
Less tax at 20% in the fund	(£20,000)	Investor's tax at 40%	(£40,000)
Net gain	£80,000	**Net gain**	**£60,000**
Investor's additional tax at 20%	(£16,000)		
Net gain	**£64,000**		

Of course, the investor hopes that the tax efficient fund growth in the offshore bond will more than compensate for the difference in personal tax treatment.

5.2.3   Offshore Funds

Again, offshore funds are generally set up in territories where there is little or no tax, such as Luxembourg, the Republic of Ireland, the Channel Islands and the Isle of Man. They may be suitable for certain investors, in particular those who are non-UK resident, as offshore income and gains are free of tax.

For tax purposes, offshore funds are divided into reporting (previously known as distributor) and non-reporting (previously non-distributor) funds.

Dividends from reporting funds are treated as gross income and are taxed at the standard dividend rates of 7.5%, 32.5% or 38.1%. Gains from these funds are subject to CGT, with the calculation based on standard CGT principles and with the investor being able to use the CGT annual exemption to keep a gain to a minimum.

For non-reporting funds, the idea is that most income is accumulated and that little or no dividends are paid. The gain on disposal is calculated using CGT principles, but the gain is actually liable to income tax (not CGT) at the investor's highest marginal rate. The CGT annual allowance cannot be used to limit this income tax liability.

Reporting funds are generally preferable for most UK investors due to CGT rates being more favourable than income tax rates. Also, because the income is received gross, non-taxpayers benefit.

However, non-reporting funds do have the advantage of income being accumulated in a low tax environment and so the investment should grow faster. They are sometimes used by UK residents to roll up income and only realise the profits when they become non-UK resident.

6. Inheritance Tax (IHT)

6.1 Definition

IHT is charged on certain transfers of property or value – it is therefore not just a death duty!

The individual who makes the transfer is known as the donor (or transferor). The individual who receives the transfer is known as the donee (or transferee).

Going back to a topic we covered in Section 2 of this chapter, the concept of domicility is crucial for IHT liabilities.

 Thinking back, how does an individual's domicile status impact on their IHT liability?

Donors who are domiciled, or deemed domiciled, in the UK are subject to IHT on their worldwide property. Donors who are non-UK domiciled are subject to IHT on their UK property only.

6.2 IHT Rates

There are three rates of IHT, which are linked to the prevailing nil rate band (NRB). In 2016–17 the NRB is £325,000. The rates are:

- £0–£325,000   0% (for any cumulative value of transfers)
- Over £325,000   20% (for chargeable lifetime transfers)
- Over £325,000   40% (for transfers on or within seven years prior to death subject to taper relief).

If at least 10% of the deceased's estate is left to charity, a reduced rate of 36% applies.

6.3   Types of Transfer

There are four types of transfer that a donor can make.

 Before looking at the answers below, what do you think these are?

The types of transfer are:

- exempt
- potentially exempt
- chargeable
- transfers on death.

We will go on to look at each of these in more detail.

6.3.1   Exempt Transfers

These are simply transfers that are not taxed. The following table lists the main exempt transfers, along with relevant details and whether the transfer is exempt if made during the lifetime of the donor only, or during their lifetime and on their death.

Type	Monetary amount (if applicable)	Relevant details
Interspouse (and inter-civil partner)	• Unlimited if donee is a UK domicile • If donee is non-UK-domiciled in UK there are special rules which were changed in April 2013	• This exemption can be applied both during lifetime and on death. • Spouses have to be married and not 'common law'. • Transfers are exempt, even if the spouses no longer live with each other (different to CGT rules).
Annual exemption	• £3,000 per tax year	• This is just a lifetime exemption. • If the whole £3,000 is not used in a tax year, the balance can be carried forward for one year only.
Small gifts	• £250 to any person in any one tax year	• This is just a lifetime exemption. • It can be used a number of times, to different donees. • It **cannot** be used in conjunction with the annual exemption as part of a larger gift.

Type	Monetary amount (if applicable)	Relevant details
Normal expenditure	• No limit	• This is just a lifetime exemption. • After making the gift, the donor should be able to maintain their ordinary standard of living. • The expenditure must be regular, or if the first in a series, clear evidence of an intention must be ongoing. • Payments must be made out of taxable income and not, for example, inheritances, lottery winnings, capital from share sales or proceeds from life assurance bonds.
Gifts on marriage/civil partnership	• £5,000 from each parent • £2,500 from grandparent or greater- grandparents • £1,000 from any other	• This is just a lifetime exemption.
Gifts for education and maintenance	• 'Reasonable provision'	• This is just a lifetime exemption. • Payments are exempt until the child's 18th birthday, or on ending full-time education (if later). • Illegitimate, step and adopted children are included.
Gifts to charities and political parties	• Unlimited	• This exemption can be applied both during lifetime and on death.
Gifts for the national benefit	• Unlimited	• This exemption can be applied both during lifetime and on death. • This includes gifts to museums, libraries, universities, the National Trust and Housing associations.
Death on active service	• Entire estate	• The estates of members of the armed forces are tax-free, if they die because of wounds received or diseases contracted while on active service.

6.3.2 Potentially Exempt Transfers (PETs)

A PET is a lifetime transfer by a donor to:

• another individual
• a bare trust
• a disabled trust.

Up until 21 March 2006, transfers into interest in possession and accumulation & maintenance trusts were also treated as PETs. Since this date, they are now regarded as CLTs (see Section 6.3.3).

No tax is charged at the date of the PET, and the transfer does not even have to be reported to HMRC. If the donor survives seven years, the transfer becomes fully exempt and is excluded from any IHT calculation.

If the donor dies within seven years of making the transfer, the tax due can be tapered down based on how long the donor lived after making the transfer. The tapering table shown below is based on the tax due, not the value of the PET itself. The donee is liable to pay any tax due.

Years between transfer & death	Percentage of tax due
Up to 3	100%
More than 3 but not more than 4	80%
More than 4 but not more than 5	60%
More than 5 but not more than 6	40%
More than 6 but not more than 7	20%
More than 7	Exempt

 George gifted £100,000 to his daughter, Zoe, in April 2011, to help her buy her first house. He died in June 2016, leaving an estate of £500,000 which is split equally between George's five nephews. What is Zoe's IHT liability, if any, on the amount she received?

The answer is that she is not liable for any tax, as the gift falls below the NRB (and transfers are measured in chronological order, so the gift of £100,000 is the first amount set against the NRB). Of course, if George had survived another couple of years, the gift would have become exempt and would not be included in the IHT calculation at all.

It is important to note from this example that, although the tapering table was unused, there is still a possible advantage in that IHT is chargeable on the value of the PET at the date it was made, not the date of death, effectively putting a ceiling on the value of the gift.

It is possible to use the value of the property transferred at the date of death, if it has fallen since the date of the original transfer. This rule does not apply to chattels deemed to be 'wasting assets' (ie, having a useful life of 50 years or less).

6.3.3   Chargeable Lifetime Transfers (CLTs)

These are transfers that are not exempt or potentially exempt. The most common transfers are lifetime gifts to trusts, other than to bare trusts and trusts for a disabled person (which we have already established are PETs) and transfers to a company.

Tax on CLTs is payable at 20% on the excess above the NRB at the time of the transfer with a further 20% payable on death. There will be no further tax to pay if the donor then survives seven years. If they do not, additional tax will be due, based on the higher death rate, although any tax already paid will be offset, and the same tapering table used for PETs can be utilised.

The rules that apply to PETs about the value of the transfer being based on the date of transfer and not the date of death also apply to CLTs. In addition, the 'reduction in value' rule also applies.

6.3.4   Transfers on Death

IHT is chargeable on the death of an individual, with the tax chargeable as if the deceased had made a transfer of value equal to the value of his or her estate immediately before death. The taxable estate is the individual's assets, less their liabilities. These assets might include the value of life policies payable on the death of the individual.

There are also certain types of assets that are excluded, including:

- assets situated outside the UK (for a non-UK domiciled individual)
- unit trusts and OEIC holdings if the beneficial owner is a non-UK domicile.

6.3.5   Gifts with Reservation

A gift with reservation is a gift which is not fully given away by the donor, so the donee either receives the gift with conditions attached, or the donor retains some benefit. Examples where this occurs include gifting the deeds of a house but continuing to live there without paying a market rent, or gifting the ownership of a work of art but still having the work in the donor's property.

The consequences of making a gift with reservation are not very tax-efficient and may, in fact, result in a double IHT charge. The gift is treated as a transfer of value at the time it is made, which may be immediately chargeable or become chargeable on the death of the donor within seven years. However, the gift never actually leaves the donor's estate and so, on their death, it is added back into the estate on the basis of its value at death.

An extension of this concept is that of Pre-Owned Assets Tax (POAT). This is an income tax charge on the benefit individuals receive by having low-cost enjoyment or use of certain assets they used to own, or free/low cost enjoyment of certain assets for which they provided the funds to purchase. This charge came into effect in April 2005, but can apply to such arrangements put in place, all the way back to March 1986.

By paying the POAT income tax charge, the individual avoids possible IHT on the transaction. It is therefore sometimes a tough judgement call to decide whether to elect for the asset involved to be subject to IHT on death by opting out of POAT, or to remain paying the POAT income tax charge.

6.4   Cumulation Principle

This is a crucial aspect that applies to the calculation of IHT, whether chargeable during a donor's lifetime or on death. As we have already seen, transfers that are potentially exempt remain in the IHT calculation process for seven years. If the cumulative value of all PETs exceeds the NRB on the donor's death, IHT will be due on the excess. This is when the tapering relief comes into play, although it should be remembered that PETs are set against the NRB in chronological order so, conceivably, the PET that leads to the NRB being exceeded will be the most recent one and therefore the taper relief may be limited.

As far as CLTs are concerned, again all CLTs over a seven-year period are added together, with tax immediately payable once the NRB is exceeded.

A transfer drops out of the cumulation once it is more than seven years old. However, even transfers that have dropped out may still be relevant for a PET made within seven years of the original transfer. This is one of the most complex areas applying to IHT and means that it is possible that CLTs made up to 14 years before a donor's death may be included in the cumulation process. There wouldn't be any tax to pay on these old CLTs themselves, but by being included in the cumulation it is more likely the estate will fall (partly or wholly) above the NRB and be liable to tax.

6.5   Transfer of the Nil-Rate Band

The NRB can be extended for married couples/people in civil partnerships. The change was based on the fact that the NRB on the first death was often wasted because all or most of the property was transferred to the surviving spouse/civil partner. These transfers would fall under the interspouse exemption anyway.

Where the second death occurrs after 8 October 2007 (and the couple were married/in a civil partnership at the time of the first death) the percentage of any unused prevailing NRB can be carried forward and applied to the NRB at the time of the second death. This amount is then added to the standard prevailing NRB at the time of the second death.

It is probably easiest to see how this works via an example.

Example _____

Laurence and Anne were married in 1961. Laurence died in January 2002 when the NRB was £242,000. He left £60,500 to his son, and the remaining estate of £400,000 to Anne. She died in June 2016 when the NRB was £325,000.

At the time of Laurence's death, 25% of the prevailing NRB of £242,000 was used by non-exempt transfers:

- £60,500 ÷ £242,000 x 100 = 25%

This means that 75% was unused, as the remainder of the estate was passed under the interspouse exemption. Anne therefore 'inherited' this unused percentage.

As a result, on her death in 2016, her NRB was increased accordingly:

- £325,000 (NRB) x 75% = £243,750

This is added to the standard NRB to make a total NRB for Anne on her death of:

- £325,000 + £243,750 = **£568,750**

This increase applies even if the surviving spouse (Anne in this case) had remarried by the time of her death. However, there is an upper limit of 100% by which the NRB can be increased, so the NRB can never be more than double that prevailing at the date of the second death.

6.6 IHT Transactions

We mentioned at the start of this chapter that IHT is charged on certain transfers of property or value. A 'transfer of value' is a reduction in the donor's estate. Therefore, an interest-free loan that is repayable on demand or on death is not treated as a transfer of value. Neither is a commercial transaction where full consideration is received, even if this transaction was a 'bad bargain' (ie, not the best the individual could have negotiated). It should be noted that commercial transactions between family members or business partners are closely scrutinised to ensure they are truly commercial!

The 'loss to the estate' amount might not be the same as the actual value of a gift. An example commonly used, for some reason, is that of an individual owning two expensive vases. Together they may be worth £100,000, but individually they are only worth £20,000. If one vase is gifted away by a donor, the loss to the estate is not the £20,000 single value of the individual vase, but £80,000 as the estate is worth £80,000 less after the gift has been made.

The 'related property' rules are important here, as an individual's assets may be related to similar assets held by their spouse or civil partner. The rules ensure that, when measuring an individual's transfer of value for IHT purposes, account must be taken of these similar assets held by a spouse or civil partner as they are effectively treated as being one asset. This has particular relevance where spouses/civil partners own shares in the same unquoted company, as their joint shareholding is looked at to establish the extent of the loss to the estate on gifting shares away.

6.6.1 Interaction between IHT and CGT

There is considerable interaction between IHT and CGT.

A valuation for IHT is not always the same as a valuation for CGT, because for IHT it is the loss to the estate that is measured, whereas for CGT it is the asset that is valued. However, if an asset is valued for IHT on the death of an individual, the same value is used for CGT purposes. This is then treated as the beneficiary's acquisition cost.

If a disposal attracts an immediate charge to IHT, eg, setting up a discretionary trust, CGT Hold-Over Relief can generally be claimed as discussed earlier in Section 4.5.4 of this chapter. If no holdover relief is claimed, any IHT liability paid can be deducted when calculating the gain, providing the IHT was paid by the donor.

No CGT Hold-Over Relief will be available for exempt or potentially exempt transfers.

Earlier, in Section 6.3.5, we talked about gifts with reservation, and their lack of effectiveness for IHT purposes. It should be noted that, although such gifts never leave the donor's estate as far as IHT is concerned, they would be regarded as being disposals of assets for CGT.

6.7 IHT Reliefs

Just as we looked at reliefs that can apply to CGT, we will now briefly look at the reliefs that can apply to IHT. The three main ones we will look at are:

- Quick Succession Relief (QSR)
- Business Property Relief BPR)
- Agricultural Property Relief.

6.7.1 Quick Succession Relief (QSR)

QSR is available where property in the deceased's estate has passed to them by a chargeable transfer in the five years before their death. Therefore, the property has been valued for IHT purposes and QSR is an attempt to limit the same property being fully chargeable twice in quick succession.

The relief is given by reducing the tax payable on the deceased's estate, by referring to the amount of tax payable on the earlier chargeable transfer, the benefit that passed to the deceased on that transfer, and the period between the transfer and the death.

6.7.2 Business Relief (BPR)

This is a relief for transfers of business property, designed to try to ensure that family businesses (for example) are not crippled by having to pay an IHT bill.

BPR is claimed at two rates. The relief is **100%** for:

- interests in unincorporated businesses, such as sole traders or partnerships
- shareholdings of any size in unquoted and Alternative Investment Market (AIM) companies.

The relief is 50% for:

- controlling shareholdings in fully listed companies
- land, buildings, plant or machinery used wholly or mainly for the purpose of a business controlled by the donor (or if the donor was a partner).

BPR is only available if the donor owned the property for at least two years.

There are some assets that do not qualify for BPR, including:

- businesses that consist wholly, or mainly, of dealing in securities, stocks or shares, land or buildings, or making or holding investments
- if the property concerned is subject to a binding contract for sale at the time of the transfer.

6.7.3 Agricultural Property Relief

This relief is available for the transfer, during lifetime or death, of agricultural property in the UK, Channel Islands or Isle of Man. Agricultural property includes agricultural land, growing crops and farm buildings, but not the animals or equipment. (A way to think of this is if you could pick up the land and turn it over, anything that doesn't fall qualifies!)

Agricultural Property Relief is also claimed at two rates. The relief is 100% for:

- owner-occupied farms
- land that is let on a grazing licence
- property that is let on a tenancy beginning on or after 1 September 1995.

The relief is 50% for interests of landlords in most other let farmland.

The property must have been occupied by the donor for agricultural purposes for the previous two years, or have been owned by the donor for seven years and occupied by someone else for agricultural purposes for that time. As with BPR, the relief cannot apply to property that is subject to a binding contract for sale.

If both Agricultural Property Relief and BPR are available, Agricultural Property Relief is given first. Often assets in a farming business will qualify for BPR even if they did not qualify for Agricultural Property Relief.

6.8 Administration of Estates

The IHT payable on the estate of a deceased person is the liability of the legal personal representatives. The actual tax is due six months after the end of the month in which death occurs.

The quick settlement of IHT is important for the legal personal representatives, as they cannot obtain Grant of Representation to administer the estate until they have accounted for the deceased's assets and paid the IHT due.

If the deceased had made a will, they would have appointed executors to administer their will. If no will exists and the deceased is said to have died intestate, the court will appoint administrators. In order to administer the will, the executors or administrators must be recognised by the court in a document called a Grant of Probate (for executors) or Letter of Administration (for administrators). The court will not issue this document until IHT has been paid.

Historically, personal representatives may well have been forced to take out a loan in order to pay the tax, as they could not access the deceased's assets until the tax was paid. Nowadays, some banks and building societies accept instructions from personal representatives to pay the IHT by electronic transfer out of the deceased's accounts. It should be noted that this facility is not universal, and so IHT loans are still used and remain relevant.

If the deceased individual has a will set up to divide the estate between an exempt beneficiary, such as a charity, and a non-exempt beneficiary, the estate is divided before the tax calculation so that the tax burden is on the non-exempt beneficiary.

6.8.1   Disclaimers and Deeds of Variation

There are two ways in which the terms of the will (or intestacy) can be varied after death that are effective for IHT purposes.

Disclaimers

Providing the property has not already been accepted, the beneficiary can, within two years of death, complete a written disclaimer. Providing there is no consideration in money or money's worth in return for so doing, this will not be a transfer of value for IHT purposes, and the property will pass to the beneficiaries entitled under the will (or intestacy).

For example, a parent who is entitled to receive property from a deceased parent's estate could disclaim this inheritance, safe in the knowledge that under the terms of the parent's will the property would then pass to their children. They have therefore passed the property down a generation without incurring an additional IHT liability.

Deeds of Variation

Similarly, a deed of variation could be used to vary the terms of the will or intestacy for family or tax reasons. These are also known as 'deeds of family arrangement'.

The deed must be made within two years of death and, unlike the disclaimer, can actually divert property to any person or persons nominated by the person giving away their interest in the estate. For example, a potential inheritance from a parent could be diverted to a favourite charity of the beneficiary's choice. This would be effective for IHT purposes as if the deceased had left the money to charity in their will originally.

There are some conditions required: there must be no consideration in money or money's worth; and all beneficiaries giving away their inheritance must be over 18 and of sound mind and must sign the deed. If more IHT is payable as a result of the deed of variation, the legal personal representatives must also sign the deed.

6.8.2   Powers of Attorney

While a power of attorney is not a trust, the role of an attorney is similar to that of a trustee since they act on behalf of and for the benefit of another.

An attorney cannot give away the donor's property unless there is specific permission granted in the deed.

There are two types of power of attorney that can make gifts in limited circumstances.

Enduring Powers of Attorney (EPA)

This is where the donor gives to someone else the power to manage their financial affairs. EPA's are only valid if they were signed before the 1 October 2007. The attorney can use the power immediately if that is what the donor desires. More typically, the donor makes it clear that the power is only to be used if they become mentally incapable of handling their own affairs in the future. A power of attorney is normally revoked if the donor becomes mentally incapable but under the Enduring Powers of Attorney Act 1985, a new type of power was permitted which continues when the donor becomes mentally incapable.

Under Section 3 of the Enduring Power of Attorney Act, an attorney can make gifts or create trusts from the donor's money if it is a reasonable gift of a seasonal nature or at a time of anniversary of a birth or marriage to persons related to or connected to the donor or to a charity to which the donor made, or might be expected to make, gifts.

Any other gifts are not allowed without court approval.

Lasting Power of Attorney (LPA)

The Mental Capacity Act 2005 created a new type of power of attorney called Lasting Power of Attorney (LPA). This replaced the EPA from the 1st October 2007 and covers welfare matters as well as financial decisions. Existing EPAs continue to have effect, but new EPAs can no longer be created.

Health and Welfare Lasting Power of Attorney

This LPA gives an attorney the power to make decisions about things like:

*   daily routine (eg, washing, dressing, eating)
*   medical care
*   moving into a care home
*   life-sustaining treatment.

It can only be used when the donor is unable to make their own decisions.

Property and Financial Affairs Lasting Power of Attorney

This LPA gives an attorney the power to make decisions about money and property, such as:

*   managing a bank or building society account
*   paying bills
*   collecting benefits or a pension
*   selling the donor's home.

It can be used as soon as it is registered, with the donor's permission.

The position regarding gifts is almost identical to Enduring Powers of Attorney; therefore, any IHT planning gifts would require permission from the Court of Protection.

6.8.3   Paying IHT on Lifetime Transfers

IHT on lifetime transfers is primarily charged on the donor, but it could also be paid by the donee. The tax is normally due six months after the end of the month of the transfer, except for transfers made between 5 April and 1 October, when the IHT is due on 30 April the following year.

When a donor dies within seven years of making a PET or chargeable transfer, any tax due is payable by the donee within six months after the end of the month of death.

7.   Tax Planning

7.1   Introduction

Tax planning is clearly an important element of providing investment advice, but it has been correctly said that the 'tax tail shouldn't wag the advice dog'! Basically, tax is an important area of advice, but certainly not the only area.

With this in mind, the following sections set out some fairly simple tax planning strategies, conscious of the fact that each approach must be suitable for specific individual circumstances.

7.1.1   Income Tax

Each person is taxed individually in the UK, and the vast majority of UK residents benefit from at least the basic Personal Allowance. It makes sense that the full Personal Allowance is used, as this is effectively a tax-free band. There is scope, therefore, for couples to allocate the ownership of income-producing assets in the most tax-efficient way. Ignoring other considerations, it is not tax-efficient for a higher rate taxpayer to earn interest from a savings account when their non-taxpaying spouse is earning no income at all.

Even children under 18 have their own tax allowance. Grandparents and other relatives (although generally not parents, due to the '£100 income rule') may consider placing money in an income-producing investment in the name of the child.

Where an individual runs their own business, it is possible they may be able to employ a spouse (although the spouse will have to prove they have done some work to deserve the salary paid!). Often, when couples use this route, the salary is kept to just under the primary threshold (£155.00 a week in 2016-17) for employer and employee National Insurance contributions.

Tax-free, or at least tax-efficient, plans can be attractive to many taxpayers. It is hard to see an argument against people using their ISA allowance each tax year. Although the advantages are relatively less attractive with the introduction of the Personal Savings Allowance, and the exemption from income tax of the first £5,000 of dividend income. Obviously, from a risk perspective, stocks and shares ISAs are not suitable for everyone.

NS&I certificates, either fixed or index-linked, provide tax-free returns and so are particularly attractive for higher rate taxpayers. However, they are non-income-producing and so might not be suitable. Although there are no current issues available, existing index-linked issues can still roll over at the end of their term.

Other investments may be regarded as non-income-producing as far as the income tax system is concerned, but can provide regular returns for investors. An example of this is the 5% allowance from life assurance bonds. These are not tax-free, rather they are tax-deferred until a chargeable event occurs but, with clever planning, this chargeable event can be delayed to a time when the investor is a basic rate taxpayer and therefore has no further liability.

Many individuals swear by the tax-efficient nature of pension contributions, as they are the only current UK investments that provide tax relief on contributions at an individual's highest marginal rate. The amount that can be contributed is subject to an annual limit and there is also a lifetime limit. After the age of 55, the investor can take 25% of the fund tax-free, but the remainder will be subject to income tax when income is taken. Even so, for the majority of investors, pension contributions are tax-efficient if the investors are willing to suffer access restrictions. They are particularly efficient if the investor is subject to higher and additional rate tax while contributing, but basic rate in retirement.

Other tax-efficient investments, at the riskier end of the scale, are EISs and VCTs. Both offer tax relief on contributions, provided as tax reducers (30% for EIS and VCT contributions). However, they are highly risky investments and the tax savings may not be worth the large possibility of the investment failing completely!

7.1.2 Capital Gains Tax (CGT)

Very few private individuals actually pay any CGT, and that is not just because of the credit crunch! This is because the annual exemption, currently £11,100, is usually enough to absorb gains, particularly if this limit is taken into account when disposing of assets. A few strategies to mitigate a CGT liability follow:

1. As with income tax, it makes sense to spread the ownership of non-exempt assets between family members to make use of the maximum number of annual exemptions.
2. For investments that can be easily segmented, it is possible to phase encashments over a number of tax years to use more than one Annual Allowance. Even just encashing one segment in March of a tax year, and leaving the next encashment until after 6 April, will mean that two Annual Allowances have been utilised.
3. Many, possibly more sophisticated, investors deliberately realise paper losses so that they can be set against future gains. As covered in the CGT chapter, this may happen without even having to sell shares if they are on HMRC's 'negligible value' list.
4. Although the act of 'bed and breakfasting' has largely been removed due to the share identification rules, it is still possible for investors to realise gains within the annual exemption and then repurchase a similar (not identical) investment. This has the other advantage of increasing the base cost of the investment. Alternatively, they can repurchase an identical investment within a tax shelter such as an ISA or pension fund.
5. The timing of a CGT payment can also be taken into account. As we saw in the CGT chapter, CGT is due on 31 January after the tax year when the gain was made. A disposal on 5 April 2016 would therefore lead to the CGT being due on 31 January 2017. Delaying the disposal by just one day, to 6 April 2016, would have delayed the due date of CGT by one full year, until 31 January 2018.
6. It is also important to remember the CGT deferral opportunities offered by reliefs such as Hold-Over Relief, Business Rollover Relief and Reinvestment Relief into EIS shares.

7.1.3 Inheritance Tax (IHT)

Since the change made to the IHT rules in October 2007, allowing any unused NRB to be carried forward by a spouse/civil partner, the large market in trusts that generated a similar benefit has diminished. There is still a market for these type of 'will trusts' for unmarried/unregistered individuals.

Most IHT planning focuses on reducing the value of an individual's estate through the use of lifetime gifts. Some of these gifts could be exempt, such as falling under the Annual Allowance limit, the small gifts limit or the gift limits on marriage. Even gifts that are not exempt may well become exempt when the donor survives seven years, so it is important to start the process early and when in good health.

Gifts can also be made on a regular basis and will be exempt if they come under the 'normal expenditure' rules. This can provide a good way to reduce an estate.

Because not everyone is in the position to gift property away (or, even if they are in the position, they may not have the desire to do so), IHT planning often revolves around finding a way to pay a potential IHT bill. The most common route is that of a joint life second death whole of life policy. It is crucial that this type of plan is written under trust to avoid the policy's benefit falling into the deceased's estate and actually making the IHT situation even worse!

For donees who have received a PET that falls above the NRB, a special decreasing term assurance plan known as a gift *inter vivos* policy can cover their potential liability.

For the potential recipients of an estate that is in danger of falling above the NRB due to a previously gifted PET, a seven-year level term assurance plan can be used to cover their potential liability. After seven years, the PET will fall out of the cumulation calculation and therefore the IHT liability on the estate should fall.

These are some of the more basic approaches taken to IHT planning – it can become a very complicated world with providers trying to utilise identified loopholes which, invariably, HMRC then endeavour to remove. As with many elements of financial services, it is a constantly changing area and will undoubtedly remain so in the future.

Chapter Three
Financial Markets

An exam specification breakdown is provided at the back of this workbook

1. Introduction

In this chapter we will be examining the relevance of market-related factors that can influence investment decisions, processes and advice.

Some of the terminology and concepts will already be familiar to you. We will build upon this knowledge and introduce different concepts with which you may be less familiar. We hope that this will give you confidence for your examination.

You must continue reading and extending your understanding of the topics covered through additional study. This workbook does not represent everything you may be expected to know for the examination.

You will see icons or symbols alongside the text. These indicate activities or questions that have been designed to check your understanding and help you validate your understanding.

Here is a guide to what each of the symbols mean:

 Question

This identifies a question that will enable you to check your knowledge and understanding.

 Analyse

This gives you an opportunity to consider a question posed and compare your answers to the feedback given.

1.1 Objectives

World Financial Markets

1. Understand the relative size of world equity markets and predominant asset sectors within each market.
2. Know the key features of the global government and corporate bond markets.
3. Understand the relative benefits, risks and costs of investing in developed and emerging markets.
4. Understand and differentiate between exchange-traded, over-the-counter (OTC) and alternative markets.
5. Apply the principles of asset and liability matching when managing investments in different currencies.
6. Understand how indices are constructed, and the purposes and limitations of using them.

UK Markets

7. Understand the main organisations and processes for transacting, clearing, settling and safekeeping domestic financial securities.
8. Know the methods by which domestic securities are issued and brought to market.
9. Be aware of the purposes and requirements for issuing contract notes.
10. Understand the applicability of Value Added Tax (VAT), stamp duty and Stamp Duty Reserve Tax (SDRT) to transactions in financial services.
11. Understand the purposes and operation of nominee companies.

2.   World Financial Markets

2.1   Size of the World Market

The size of the world stock market is difficult to pin down exactly. Determined by market capitalisation, it changes constantly as shares are traded on the various exchanges around the globe. At the end of 2015, the world stock market was worth in excess of $69 trillion.

It would be difficult to compare the derivatives market since it is calculated using face or nominal values, many of which cancel each other out, as opposed to the real values used for valuing the stock market.

As you would imagine, there are a large number of stock markets around the world, some very large like the New York Stock Exchange (NYSE), others much smaller like the Malta Stock Exchange, where only 23 shares are listed.

We shall now look at the main exchanges around the world in turn, and examine their comparative sizes and predominant sectors.

2.2   United States of America

We start our world tour here, since the United States not only boasts the world's largest stock exchange (NYSE), but is also the home of another stock exchange that is larger than our own – the National Association of Securities Dealers Automated Quotation System (NASDAQ).

2.2.1   New York Stock Exchange (NYSE)

Name of Stock Exchange	Market Value (Dec 2015) $m	Total Annual Share Turnover (Dec 2015) $m	Market Value (Oct 2010) $m
New York Stock Exchange	17,786,787	17,477,291	12,826,262

The origin of the NYSE can be traced to 17 May 1792, when the Buttonwood Agreement was signed by 24 stockbrokers outside of 68 Wall Street, New York under a buttonwood tree.

The NYSE is now operated by NYSE Euronext, which was formed by the NYSE's 2007 merger with the fully electronic pan-European stock exchange based in Paris, called Euronext.

The NYSE is one of the few exchanges that still conduct trading on the floor of the stock exchange, although most orders are now sent through to the floor electronically using a system known as superDOT (Super Designated Order Turnaround system).

On the trading floor, the NYSE trades in a continuous auction format, where floor traders operating out of one of the 1,500 booths can execute stock transactions on behalf of investors. To execute their transactions, they will gather around one of the exchange's 17 trading posts where a specialist broker in that stock, who is employed by an NYSE member firm, acts as an auctioneer in an open outcry auction. The specialists do, on occasions (in fact approximately 10% of the time), facilitate the trades by committing their own capital. This can maintain an orderly market when there is a shortage of buyers and sellers. However, unlike London Stock Exchange (LSE) market makers, they are not obliged to make a market in the shares regardless of market condition. Once a trade has been made, the details are reported on the 'tape' and sent back to the broker who notifies the client who placed the order.

The NYSE is the largest stock market in terms of market capitalisation, and trades the shares of about 2,800 companies. As you can imagine, all stock market sectors are represented on the NYSE, although since companies in the US can only list on one domestic stock exchange, most technology companies choose to list on NASDAQ.

2.2.2 National Association of Securities Dealers Automated Quotations System (NASDAQ)

Name of Stock Exchange	Market Value (Dec 2015) $m	Total Annual Share Turnover (Dec 2015) $m	Market Value (Oct 2010) $m
NASDAQ	7,280,752	12,515,349	3,653,047

Unlike the NYSE, NASDAQ is a non-centralised screen based quote driven market. There is no physical dealing floor since all business is transacted by market makers who display two way pricing on some 3,100 companies via computers linked to a worldwide network some half a million strong. It is larger than the NYSE in terms of number of companies traded and daily turnover.

The NASDAQ is typically known as a high-tech market, attracting many of the firms dealing with the Internet or electronics. Accordingly, the stocks on this exchange are considered to be more volatile and growth-oriented. On the other hand, the companies on NYSE are perceived to be better established.

Whether a stock trades on the NASDAQ or the NYSE is not necessarily a critical factor for investors when they are making investment decisions. However, because both exchanges are perceived differently, the decision to list on a particular exchange is an important one for many companies. A company's decision to list on a particular exchange is also affected by the listing costs and requirements set by each individual exchange. The maximum listing fee on the NYSE is $250,000, while on the NASDAQ the maximum is $155,000. The maximum continual yearly listing fees are also a big factor – they are $500,000 and $125,000 respectively.

2.3 Japan

2.3.1 Japan Exchange Group (JPX)

Name of Stock Exchange	Market Value (Dec 2015) $m	Total Annual Share Turnover (Dec 2015) $m	Market Value (Oct 2010) $m
Tokyo Stock Exchange	4,894,919	5,540,696	3,469,039

The Japan Exchange Group (JPX) is the third largest in the world, by market capitalisation.

The Tokyo Stock Exchange was established on 15 May 1878, and issued government bonds to former samurai. By the 1920s, when Japan experienced rampant growth in the economy, trading stocks over bonds, gold, and silver currencies became the norm. The exchange was shut down in 1945 and reopened in 1949 under the guidance of American authorities. The Tokyo and Osaka Stock Exchanges merged in 2013 to become the JPX. Today, the JPX lists 3,515 companies.

Stocks listed on the JPX are separated into one of three sections:

*   the First Section (for large companies) comprising about 70% of companies
*   the Second Section (for mid-sized companies) comprising about 20% of companies
*   the 'Mothers' section (for high-growth start-up companies) comprising less than 10% of companies.

As you can imagine, banks, electrical and motor manufacturers are dominant on this exchange.

2.4 China

China has three exchanges: the Shanghai Stock Exchange (SSE) with 1,006 listed companies, the Hong Kong Stock Exchange with 1,830 listings and the Shenzhen Stock Exchange. All of the exchanges are governed by the China Securities Regulatory Commission (CSRC). The Shenzhen Stock Exchange has 1,700 listed companies.

Name of Stock Exchange	Market Value (Dec 2015) $m	Total Annual Share Turnover (Dec 2015) $m	Market Value (Oct 2010) $m
Shanghai Stock Exchange	4,549,288	21,342,843	2,803,493

The SSE was founded on 26 November 1990.

The exchange lists two different types of stocks: A and B shares. The difference between the two stocks is the currency that they are traded in. The A shares are traded in the local renminbi yuan currency, whereas the B shares are traded in US dollars. Traditionally, A shares were not available to foreign investors, but in 2003 the Chinese authorities allowed selected foreign institutions to buy A shares, having already opened the B share market to Chinese investors. The majority of the stocks listed on the exchange are A shares. There are 953 A shares and 53 B shares listed on the market.

Name of Stock Exchange	Market Value (Dec 2015) $m	Total Annual Share Turnover (Dec 2015) $m	Market Value (Oct 2010) $m
Hong Kong Stock Exchange	3,184,874	2,125,888	4,679,387

There are 1,830 stocks listed on the Hong Kong Stock Exchange. The index for the Hong Kong exchange is called the Hang Seng, and it was introduced in 1969. The Hang Seng index consists of the 33 largest companies traded on the exchange and represents around 70% of the value of all stocks traded. As you may expect, financial, technology and telecoms companies dominate in terms of market capitalisation.

2.5 Europe

2.5.1 Euronext

Name of Stock Exchange	Market Value (Dec 2015) $m	Total Annual Share Turnover (Dec 2015) $m	Market Value (Oct 2010) $m
Euronext	3,305,901	2,076,722	2,988,977

As mentioned earlier, Euronext is based in Paris although it has subsidiaries in Belgium, Holland, Portugal and the UK. It consists of six cash equities exchanges and six derivatives exchanges, all traded using an electronic order driven trading system.

Euronext was formed on 22 September 2000 following a merger of the Amsterdam Stock Exchange, Brussels Stock Exchange, and Paris Bourse, in order to take advantage of the harmonisation of the European Union (EU) financial markets.

In December 2001, Euronext acquired the shares of the London International Financial Futures and Options Exchange (LIFFE), which continues to operate under its own governance.

In 2002 the group merged with the Portuguese stock exchange, Bolsa de Valores de Lisboa e Porto (BVLP), renamed Euronext Lisbon.

In 2011, Deutsche Börse attempted to merge with NSYE Euronext but, despite both companies being in favour, the deal was blocked by the EU in 2012.

In December 2012, Intercontinental Exchange (ICE) announced plans to acquire NSYE Euronext and this was completed in 2013. Subsequently, ICE listed the renamed Euronext separately in 2014.

2.5.2 Deutsche Börse

Name of Stock Exchange	Market Value (Dec 2015) $m	Total Annual Share Turnover (Dec 2015) $m	Market Value (Oct 2010) $m
Deutsche Börse	1,715,800	1,555,549	1,392,727

The Frankfurt Stock Exchange has over 90% of turnover in the German market. Trading takes place on exchange floors throughout Germany, and on an electronic order driven platform called Xetra.

2.5.3 London Stock Exchange (LSE)

The LSE is the most important exchange in Europe, and one of the largest in the world. It lists over 2,450 companies together with over 300 on Börse Italiana, which the LSE acquired in 2007, making the LSE the most international of all the exchanges.

For comparative purposes here are the figures for the LSE.

Name of Stock Exchange	Market Value (Dec 2015) $m	Total Annual Share Turnover (Dec 2015) $m	Market Value (Oct 2010) $m
London Stock Exchange	3,878,744	2,651,354	3,597,617

2.6 Consolidated List of Major Worldwide Stock Markets

For completeness, here is a list of the ten largest stock markets by market capitalisation:

Name of Stock Exchange	Market Value (Dec 2015) $m	Total annual share turnover (Dec 2015) $m
New York Stock Exchange	17,786,787	17,477,291
NASDAQ	7,280,752	12,515,349
Tokyo Stock Exchange	4,894,919	5,540,696
Shanghai Stock Exchange	4,549,288	21,342,843
London Stock Exchange	3,878,774	2,651,354
Shenzhen Stock Exchange	3,638,731	19,611,249
Euronext	3,305,901	2,076,722
Hong Kong Stock Exchange	3,184,874	2,125,888
Deutsche Börse	1,715,800	1,555,549
TMX Group (Canada)	1,159,928	1,184,828

3. Emerging Markets

3.1 Introduction

The term 'emerging markets' can be defined in different ways:

- markets in those countries described by the World Bank as low or middle income, and
- markets with a stock capitalisation of less than 2% of the total world market.

3.2 Benefits of Investing in Emerging Markets

- **Faster economic growth** – developing nations tend to grow at a faster rate than those countries that are well developed as they try to catch up in terms of living standards and, in the process, develop their infrastructure and financial systems.
- **Savings rates** are usually higher in underdeveloped countries. Foreign direct investment will have a positive benefit on the economy, leading to rapid economic growth. This will lead to a rapid growth in profits.
- **Inefficient pricing** – it is possible to exploit pricing anomalies in underdeveloped economies, where analysis and research on companies are not so well advanced.
- **Industry representation** – there may be the opportunity for investors to gain exposure to different types of industry, not possible in other well developed countries.
- **Attractive valuations** – historically, emerging markets have traded at a discount to developed nations.
- **Low correlation of returns** – historically, there has been a low correlation between the fortunes of developed and emerging markets. This provides the investor with an opportunity for diversification.

3.3 Drawbacks of Investing in Emerging Markets

- **Restrictions on foreign ownership** – some underdeveloped countries impose restrictions on foreigners owning shares in certain companies.
- **Foreign exchange restrictions** – due to restrictions imposed by the emerging nation, it may not be possible to repatriate funds to the UK once the investor has disinvested.
- **Taxation** – while double taxation agreements are in place with most if not all developed nations, there may be local taxes imposed by developing nations that are not covered by existing treaties, thereby adding to the tax burden.
- **Additional costs may be incurred** – for example commission on foreign currency, costs of transferring the money, nominee costs and possibly translation or legal costs.
- **Lack of transparency** – there is likely to be a lower quality and transparency of information from emerging markets compared to countries that are well developed.

3.4 Risks of Investing in Emerging Markets

- **Political** – emerging markets tend to be less politically stable. This could have a devastating effect on foreign investment. For example, new laws could be passed which outlaw the holding of certain investments by foreign persons, inhibit the ability to repatriate funds or impose high levels of taxation.
- **Volatility** – emerging markets are more volatile than developed ones and are prone to banking or other crises. Lack of information can result in a 'herding' of foreign investment into a small number of companies, which will see a sharp rise, but this could be followed by an equally sharp fall if foreign investment is withdrawn from one of these companies in the future.

- **Liquidity** – emerging markets are more concentrated, ie, less liquid than developed markets. Investments are generally less marketable and therefore tend to trade with much wider spreads.
- **Capital** – custody and settlement may be far more difficult to arrange, and the potential for fraud may be increased with less developed regulatory protection and problems with translation. Understanding a contract in English can be difficult enough without the added complication of interpreting complex terms in a foreign language.
- **Currency risk** – emerging markets tend to have weaker currencies, which are far more susceptible to sudden movements following the withdrawal of foreign investment. Any loss incurred on the exchange rate will reduce, and could exceed, the potential gains on the investment capital.

Example

John invests £50,000 in an emerging market, Westonia. The investments have done well for him but the political climate is changing, an election is due and the people in the know think that the opposition will seek to restrict the withdrawal of foreign investment should they get to power. John decides to encash his investments, which are falling in value due to the political uncertainties, and he escapes with a gain of 10% on his initial investment. However, he now has to repatriate the funds and is staggered to discover that the pound is now 30% stronger against the local currency than it was when he invested his capital in Westonia. He makes an overall loss of 20%.

Asset and Liability Management

The definition of asset and liability management: a risk management technique to earn an adequate return, while maintaining a comfortable surplus of assets beyond liabilities. This now takes into consideration a number of variable factors such as interest rates, currency exchange rates, earning power and a degree of willingness to take on debt. This is also called surplus management.

The early origins of asset and liability management date to the high interest rate periods in the mid-to-late 1970s and early 1980s in the United States. Previously, a bank could, for example, borrow money for a year at 5% and lend the same money at 5.5% to a highly rated borrower for five years. This appeared to be a good transaction for the bank, but with it came risk. When the time came for the bank to refinance its loan, interest rates may have risen and it may have had to pay a higher rate on the new financing than the fixed 5.5% it was earning on the loan. There was a potential mismatch between assets and liabilities, a mismatch that could be shown in the market value (immediate) method of accounting, but not so immediately in the accruals method of accounting.

This was not such a problem before the 1970s, as interest rates in developed countries were relatively stable, so losses due to asset-liability mismatches were negligible. With yield curves generally upward-sloping (a 'normal' yield curve), banks could exploit the market by borrowing short and lending long.

In the 1970s and into the early 1980s, a period of volatile interest rates ensued. Many firms, which had been used to operating on the accruals accounting basis, did not recognise the risks they were taking until it was too late and the loss itself had been accrued. Many large firms went to the wall.

In response to this, managers of financial firms focussed on asset-liability risk. The focus was not so much on whether the value of assets might fall, or the value of liabilities might rise, it was more on the fact that capital might be depleted by a narrowing of the difference between assets and liabilities. In essence, we are talking about a cash flow risk here, as the capital of most financial institutions is small relative to their assets or liabilities, so a small change in assets or liabilities can be translated into large percentage changes in capital. We only have to look at the situation over recent years, and the 'credit crunch', to see this in practice.

A number of different techniques were used to analyse the risks, and became known as asset-liability management (ALM). These included techniques such as gap analysis and duration analysis, which worked well if both assets and liabilities comprised fixed cash flows.

A more expansive technique is that of 'scenario analysis' where several interest rates are specified for the following five or ten years. Many different scenarios would be examined, anticipating very different behaviours throughout the entire yield curve. Assumptions would then be made as to how assets and liabilities would perform under each scenario. Based upon these assumptions, the performance of a firm's balance sheet could be projected for each scenario. If the projected performance was particularly poor under certain scenarios, the firm could adjust assets or liabilities (or both) to address the situation.

ALM has evolved greatly since the 1980s. The growth of the derivatives market has helped facilitate a variety of hedging techniques (eg, a utility company's hedging of gas prices can be presented as a form of ALM). There has also been a major development in the securitisation market, allowing firms to directly address asset-liability risk by removing assets or liabilities from their balance sheet. Again, we have witnessed the fallout from this securitisation development during the credit crunch.

The scope of ALM has also increased, which is why we are including it in this section. Along with interest rate exposures and liquidity risk, ALM techniques are being adopted to address foreign exchange risk so that the situation described above of John's investment in Westonia can be avoided by corporations.

4. The UK Markets

4.1 Introduction

The LSE is a recognised investment exchange (RIE) and, as such, is answerable to the Financial Conduct Authority (FCA). The LSE has a responsibility to:

'ensure that the operation of each of its markets is orderly and provides proper protection to investors, and to promote and maintain high standards of integrity and fair dealing'.

Its main responsibilities include:

- providing a primary and secondary market for equities and fixed interest securities
- supervising member firms
- regulating the market
- recording all deals
- disseminating price-sensitive information received via its Regulatory News Service (RNS).

4.2   Member Firms of the LSE

All member firms are broker dealers. As such, they can act in one of two capacities:

- Act as agent on behalf of the customer where they take a commission (broker).
  - ○ Here they will receive an order from a non-member client and will arrange the trade with another member firm for a commission.
  - ○ Alternatively they may have an order to purchase, and a matching order to sell, from another client. They can act as agent to an agency cross-transaction, charging a commission to both parties but offering the same price to both parties.
- Act as principal where they trade their own book (dealers).
  - ○ They will be selling shares held on the firm's own books to the client.

Market makers provide liquidity to the market by making a two-way price (bid offer spread), using a screen-based system to display their prices. Broker dealers can see the prices being offered and place their orders based on the quoted prices.

Most of the equity dealing is conducted via a range of electronic systems hosted by the LSE, as follows:

4.3   Stock Exchange Electronic Trading Service (SETS)

The Stock Exchange Trading Service (SETS) is an electronic order driven service trading FTSE 100, FTSE 250 and the FTSE Small Cap Index constituents, as well as other securities.

Additional functionality following changes in the rules under MiFID (Markets in Financial Instruments Directive), means that SETS now also provides market maker support for all stocks deemed to be liquid under MiFID definitions.

It allows buyers and sellers to be matched, thus avoiding the need to go through a market maker who would charge a spread.

Order Book

The following types of order are permissible:

- **At best** – this specifies the number of shares to be bought or sold, and is executed immediately at the best possible price. The main problem that can occur is if the market for the stock is very thin (illiquid), the spread may widen considerably, particularly at either end of the trading day. The bargain is, however, being executed whatever the price and may therefore secure a very poor price for the client.
- **Limit** – these are the only orders which remain on the screen. The client will specify the number of shares required to be bought or sold and the maximum (purchase) or minimum (sale) price they are prepared to accept.
- **Execute and eliminate** – these orders have a quantity and limit price. If it cannot be filled in its entirety, then the deal can be partially filled but the remaining part of the deal is abandoned.
- **Fill or kill** – these orders may be limited to a particular price, and if not filled in full, then the entire deal is abandoned. It is possible to leave the price open, in which case the order will rely on the depth of the order book.

- **Market** – this is an 'at best' order which is held on the order book during an auction call period. These deals are given top priority for matching at the end of the auction period, according to the time they were submitted.
- **Iceberg** – these orders allow market participants to enter large orders onto the order book with only a certain specified portion of the order visible to the market. The order must have details of the total size of the order and the specified amount to be made visible. Once the peak is entirely dealt with, the system automatically keeps reintroducing orders until the entire amount is dealt.
- **Hidden limit orders** – these are limit orders where both the price and volume are hidden. Unlike iceberg orders where the peak is continually refreshed and displayed, participants will have no idea if there is any remaining order or not. They are only available for large orders meeting certain threshold conditions.
- **Hidden pegged orders** – these orders allow participants to peg their order to the best bid, offer or mid-price.

An example of an order book follows:

Buy			Sell		
Price	**Time**	**Volume**	**Price**	**Time**	**Volume**
360	11:10	4,000	361	11:18	3,000
360	11:15	2,000	361	11:24	2,000
359	11:06	1,000	362	11:04	5,000
359	11:08	2,000	362	11:09	3,000

 What would the order book look like if a limit order to sell 8,000 at no worse than 360p was submitted at 11:25?

The answer follows:

Buy			Sell		
Price	**Time**	**Volume**	**Price**	**Time**	**Volume**
359	11:06	1,000	360	11:25	2,000
359	11:08	2,000	361	11:18	3,000
			361	11:24	2,000
			362	11:04	5,000
			362	11:09	3,000

The order would have been partially filled with 6,000 shares being sold at 360, leaving 2,000 shares on the order book.

The order book can be seen by any market participants, and a yellow strip on the SETS screen will display the best prevailing buy and sell prices for each security. Orders that are put through the order book must be executed at best price. Both member firms are given notification of the trade once it is settled, and the deal is automatically reported to the LSE.

Only LSE firms and SETS participants (members of EU exchanges authorised to conduct SETS trades) can input orders.

A central counterparty (CCP) service exists for all deals executed on SETS, which enables trades to be conducted anonymously and guarantees trades, removing counterparty risk. Participants can now use either LCH.Clearnet Ltd or SIX x-clear AG as their CCP for SETS trades.

Trades are normally settled through the CREST system, operated by Euroclear UK & Ireland.

Orders outside the order book are permitted, providing that they are satisfied by the best bid or offer price on the order book. If they cannot be settled at that price, they must be settled at the volume-weighted average price or better.

All deals on SETS are settled on a **T+2** basis, ie, two business days after the date of trade.

4.4   Stock Exchange Automated Quotation (SEAQ) system

Unlike SETS, SEAQ is a **quote driven** screen based system for trading.

This means that member firms can act as market makers and compete with each other by making two prices in stocks in the hope of attracting business from other members (known as broker dealers). Since all market makers must quote real-time two-way prices in all market conditions and act as willing counterparties to trades, they are often required to commit their own capital when there is a lack of market liquidity.

SEAQ is for the following securities:

- fixed interest market, and
- AIM (alternative investment market) securities not traded on SETS or SETSqx.

The quotes must appear between the mandatory period of 8:00am and 4:30pm, and apply to any deal no greater than the historic size of the average institutional trade in the shares, known as normal market size (NMS). This is shown on SEAQ as the minimum quote size (MQS).

Throughout the day, the best prices are shown by the yellow strip and are referred to as the 'touch'. This is the price at which a broker dealer is obliged to transact, subject only to size, in order to fulfil 'best execution' requirements. Deals outside the NMS would need to be negotiated with the broker-dealer. The minimum permitted price change is called the 'tick size' (generally 0.1p, 0.25p, 0.5p or 1p depending on the price and liquidity of the share).

If the best bid price is equal to the best ask price, it is called a 'choice price'.

If the bid price is greater than the ask price, it is called a 'back' or a 'backwardation'.

The SEAQ system offers a screen that changes colour depending on the last price movement of the security: blue for an upward price movement, red for a downward movement and green for an unchanged price.

Remember that SEAQ is a quotation system, not a dealing system. If a firm wants to deal, it must telephone the firm and arrange the transaction.

In order to ensure a transparent market, all trades conducted within the mandatory quote period are reported to the LSE by market makers within three minutes. This is known as 'trade reporting'.

The LSE publishes the size and price of trades up to six times NMS on SEAQ immediately, a process known as 'publication'. Trades greater than six times NMS have delayed reporting for one hour. Very large trades (over 75 times NMS) can be withheld from the market for up to five days, to enable the market maker to unwind a large position without the market going against him. Market makers can deal anonymously through specialist firms known as inter-dealer brokers (IDBs) in order to facilitate this. They can also borrow stock from stock borrowing and lending intermediaries (SBLIs) to help preserve market liquidity.

4.5 SETSqx

The Stock Exchange Electronic Trading Service – quotes and crosses (SETSqx) is the trading platform used for securities that are less liquid than those on SETS. It replaced SEAQ for all Main Market securities in 2007. It is a hybrid system combining elements of SETS and SEAQ.

SETSqx combines the features of the SEAQ market maker model, and supports it with some additional electronic order book functionality.

How does it work?

- Market makers must provide continuous prices throughout the trading day, and have obligations which are similar to those on SEAQ. The mandatory quote period is slightly different and they have the option to participate in the electronic auctions.
- In addition to trades being executed through market makers, there are four auctions 'uncrossings' that take place daily at 8:00am, 9:00am, 11:00am, 2:00pm and 4:35pm. During these auctions, the system works like the order book, and matches as many orders as possible.

At other times during the day, the system continues to work as a quote driven system.

Because of the limited liquidity in the securities traded on SETSqx, iceberg and market orders are not supported, although different types of limit orders are.

4.6 Trading in Gilts

Gilts are traded in a similar way to the quote driven trading of equities. Broker dealers are permitted to deal both as principal and agent, very much like their equity counterparts. For example, the rules for trade reporting of gilt deals are the same as for equity deals.

The main difference is in the way gilt market makers operate. Gilt-edged market makers (GEMMs) undertake to the Debt Management Office (DMO) to make two-way prices in a range of securities in any conditions, not to the stock exchange.

GEMMs report daily to the FCA in terms of their financial stability, and are not under an obligation to display daily prices on SEAQ (in fact this system is used very little for gilts).

As SEAQ is rarely used in the gilt market, a broker will need to phone around to establish the best price for the size of deal. A firm that is not a GEMM will need to take all reasonable steps to make sure that the transaction price is better than the best price available from a registered market maker.

GEMMs have a choice as to whether to deal in non-index-linked gilts only, index-linked gilts only, or both.

Inter-dealer brokers (IDBs) are set up as separate companies, although they can be subsidiaries of broker/ dealers. Their role is to act as a matching agent for market makers who wish to undo their positions with them, and maintain confidentiality. They do this by settling as principal, thereby maintaining the anonymity of the market makers involved. Keeping this secretive theme, prices displayed on IDB computer screens are not available to brokers or clients, just to market makers. It should be noted that IDBs also operate in equity quote driven markets, such as SEAQ, which we have described earlier.

The normal settlement timing for trades in gilts is **T+1**, ie, one business day after the trade date.

4.6.1 The Gilt Repo Market

'Repo' is short for 'sale and repurchase' agreement. One party agrees to sell gilts to another party, but with a formal agreement to buy equivalent securities from them at an agreed price and on a specific date. It is therefore a form of secured borrowing, with the gilt itself used as collateral.

The interest rate generated by the difference between the sale and repurchase prices is the repo rate.

All participants in the gilt market are free to utilise repo transactions.

A 'reverse repo' occurs when gilts are purchased first, with an agreement to sell back in the future. This allows market participants to go short in the market.

Agreements to repurchase at a specific date are known as 'term repos'. There are also 'open repos' where there is no set redemption date, and contracts roll over on a daily basis until one of the parties decides to cancel the deal. There are also 'overnight repos' which, unsurprisingly, apply to any repo where the settlement date is the next day.

4.6.2 Gilt Strips

'STRIPS' is the acronym for 'Separately Trading Registered Interest and Principal Securities', meaning certain gilts can be stripped into their individual cash flows of interest and principal payments. They are explained further in Chapter 5.

Only a GEMM, the DMO or the Bank of England can strip or reconstitute a strippable gilt, although, once done, anyone can trade or hold strips.

4.7 Trading in the UK Fixed Interest Market

This market includes local authority bonds, listed corporate bonds and some eurobonds, but excludes gilts. As a result, it is smaller and deemed less important than the gilts market.

The DMO is not involved in this market. Market makers are registered with the LSE, which imposes the dealing obligation for market makers to buy and sell up to a marketable quantity of stock at a firm price. This marketable quantity is determined by the LSE. Apart from the absence of the DMO, the overall operation of the market is very similar to that for gilts.

The rules for trade reporting are the same as for gilt and equity deals.

The normal settlement timing for trades in the UK fixed interest market is **T+2**, ie, two business days after the trade date.

The electronic Order book for Retail Bonds (ORB) was established by the LSE on 1 February 2010 to provide a more liquid and transparent market in retail bonds.

EU regulations distinguish between wholesale (typically denominations of £50,000 or greater) and retail (usually £1,000, some £5,000 or £10,000).

At the moment most corporate bonds are wholesale. The secondary market for retail bonds is fragmented, usually over-the-counter; therefore, most private investors use corporate bond funds rather than dealing directly.

The ORB provides a similar facility to that which is used for share trading for a select number of gilts, supranational organisations and UK corporate bonds.

Investors can enter orders on the order book either directly, if a sophisticated investor, or via a broker who offers direct market access (DMA).

Dedicated market makers also provide two-way prices.

The market operates with an opening auction phase between 8:00 and 8:45am and closes at 4:30pm.

Most corporate bonds are traded in lot sizes of £1,000. The standard lot size for gilts is £1; the 'tick' size is 1p for both.

4.8 American and Global Depositary Receipts

4.8.1 American Depositary Receipts (ADRs)

An American Depositary Receipt (ADR) is a dollar-denominated negotiable instrument issued by a depositary bank in respect of non-US-listed shares that have been lodged with the bank.

These were originally designed to enable US investors to invest in overseas shares without the high dealing costs and delayed settlement associated with overseas investment. However, they are now also used by UK institutional investors wishing to purchase UK-listed shares, therefore avoiding stamp duty. Stamp Duty Reserve Tax is paid on creation of the ADR but not on subsequent dealing.

Up to 20% of a company's voting share capital may be converted into ADRs and many UK companies have used ADRs as a means of raising capital. Sometimes more than one share is deposited to make up one ADR, for example, one ADR = ten shares.

ADRs are denominated in US dollars. Dividends are paid to the holding bank in the currency of the overseas company and paid to the holder of the ADR in dollars.

ADRs are traded on the NYSE, NASDAQ and are also traded in the UK through SEAQ.

4.8.2 Global Depositary Receipts (GDRs)

Depositary receipts (DRs) issued outside the US are known as global depositary receipts (GDRs). Again, shares are deposited in a bank which issues the GDR.

GDRs are often listed on the Luxembourg Stock Exchange, the Frankfurt Stock Exchange and on the LSE, where they are traded on the International Order Book (IOB).

4.8.3 International Order Book (IOB) and International Retail Service (IRS)

International Order Book

The IOB, offered by the LSE, offers easy and cost-efficient access for traders looking to invest in fast-growing economies, eg, in Central and Eastern Europe, Asia and the Middle East via depositary receipts.

The service is based on an order driven electronic order book similar to SETS, but with the added option for member firms to display their identity pre-trade by using 'named orders', offering greater visibility in the market.

Deals are quoted in US dollars with trading available from 8:00am until 3:30pm.

The market has grown rapidly since its inception in 2011, with Gazprom, Sberbank, Samsung and Lukoil amongst the most heavily traded on the LSE.

International Retail Service (IRS)

The IRS is a service provided by the LSE that allows UK investors to trade in overseas stocks quoted in sterling without having to worry about exchange rates through the CREST system. This allows shares to be held in dematerialised form. Not all international equities are listed on the IRS. There are currently around 350 large cap equities available, primarily European and US companies.

	International Order Book	International Retail Service
Market type	Order driven	Quote driven
Securities Traded	ADRs/GDRs	US and European blue chip equities
Currency	US dollars	Sterling
Market Makers	No	Yes (committed principals – CPs)
Settlement	Euroclear Bank	CREST depositary interests (CDIs)
Trading	8:00am–3:30pm Opening/closing auctions; continuous trading in between	8:15am–5:00pm (Mandatory quote period for most European stocks 8:15am–4:00pm)

4.9   Settlement

We will now look briefly at the clearing and settlement procedures for UK domestic financial securities.

The process of clearing and settlement involves a number of stages:

Confirmation

The details of the deal are confirmed. This involves both sides of the transaction being compared to ensure they match.

Clearing

The LSE allows a choice of CCP for trades on SETS and SETSqx market. This can be either LCH.Clearnet Ltd or SIX x-Clear AG. It does not matter whether the trading counterparty is using the same or a different CCP.

Settlement

The securities are transferred into the name of the new owner, against payment. This system whereby the securities are only transferred against simultaneous payment is known as 'delivery versus payment' (DvP). The converse of this is that the buyer will not release the cash unless it is against the simultaneous transfer of the securities. From this perspective, it is described as 'cash against delivery' (CAD). This system of settlement provides security for both the seller and the buyer of the securities.

A system for delivery **free of payment** is also available.

Settlement Periods

The UK markets operate a rolling settlement system. For UK equities and corporate bonds, the settlement period is T+2 (trade date plus two business days) and gilts are settled T+1. Trades that settle on the next working day are described as 'cash settled'.

4.9.1   CREST

The CREST settlement system is used for UK and Irish securities markets. It settles transactions in equities, corporate bonds and commercial paper, gilts and Treasury bills and money market instruments, certificates of deposit (CDs) and a range of international securities, and can facilitate settlement in pounds, US dollars or euros.

CREST offers investors the opportunity to hold their shares in dematerialised form (where there is no certificate issued evidencing ownership, just an electronic record), either in their own name within CREST, or in the name of their nominee company. Additionally, deals can be settled through CREST, and paper certificates held outside the system.

How Does the CREST System Work?

- **Structure**
  Members have securities in accounts in CREST (much in the same way as we have money in a bank account). There are different types of members depending upon their technical ability to interface with the system. Individuals wishing to hold stocks in CREST are known as CREST-sponsored members, but can only do so through an institution that has the technical ability to interface with CREST, known as a CREST member (eg, a stockbroking firm). The individual beneficial owner will appear on the company register as the recorded legal owner of the shares that it has in its CREST accounts. Balances are dynamic, ie, they continually change as settlement occurs.

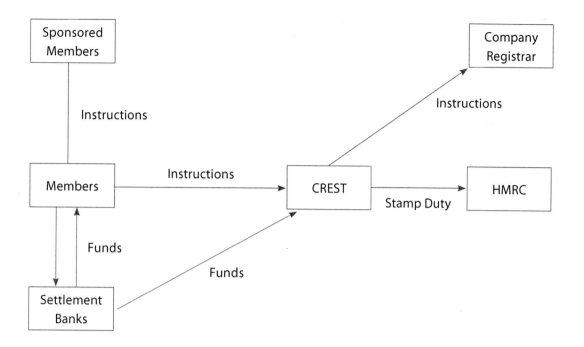

- **Settlement Banks**

  Each member must have a contractual arrangement with their bank, guaranteeing the settlement of their CREST transactions up to an amount known as a debit cap (think of it as akin to an overdraft limit). CREST records each member's obligations (purchases/sales) on a cash memorandum account (CMA) on a real time basis throughout the day. At the end of the day, the net position has to be settled by the member's settlement bank with CREST. Settlement banks maintain liquidity balances with the Bank of England specifically for the settlement of CREST liabilities. The amount of unused facility (credit) at any point during the day is known as the **'headroom'**. Using our overdraft analogy, it is the unused portion of our overdraft limit.

- **Company Registrars**

  Company registrars are required under the Companies Act to maintain a list of their shareholders. As trades settle, CREST issues register update requests (RURs) to the company registrars, instructing them to update their shareholder register. It may take companies a little while to update their records, so it is worth noting that ownership legally passes at the point of payment, even if the records are not updated until later in the day.

- **Revenue Authority**

  CREST acts as collector of transfer tax (stamp duty) for the relevant tax authorities.

The CREST Process in Order

Trade date:

- The trade and price are agreed through the exchange.
- Each member (the buying and selling members) creates a settlement instruction, and sends it to CREST.

On or just after the trade date:

- CREST compares both settlement instructions and ensures that the details are correct and match.

Settlement date:

- CREST sends details of the trade to its single settlement engine (SSE) for settlement.
- The SSE checks that the seller has sufficient securities, that the buyer has sufficient headroom and that the buyer's bank has sufficient liquidity with the Bank of England.

If so the transaction is settled:

- The securities are simultaneously moved from the selling member's account to the buying member's account.
- Funds are transferred from the buying settlement bank to the seller's settlement bank.
- The CMA of the buyer is debited and the CMA of the seller is credited.
- The SSE sends confirmation that the trade has settled to CREST.
- CREST sends a RUR to the company registrar, to update the register of shareholders.

Each business day, between 5:00am and 4:30pm, CREST attempts to settle transactions. This can be done as long as the transaction has reached its settlement date and there are sufficient resources available to allow the transaction to settle.

5. How UK Securities are Issued

5.1 Gilts

The market in UK government bonds (gilts) is managed by the DMO, an executive agency of the Treasury.

The DMO manages the government's public sector net cash requirement (PSNCR), which is the difference between government revenue and government expenditure. The DMO issues new gilts each week, by auction. The gross gilt issuance in the financial year 2015–16 was £127.7 billion. This is down from the peak in 2008–9 of £227.6 billion.

Auction Process

- Large investors submit competitive bids at the price and quantity of stock required.
- If successful, they pay the price they bid.
- Individuals can submit 'non-competitive bids' for amounts up to £500,000 nominal (market makers can bid non-competitively for no more than 0.5% of the gilt on auction). If successful they are allocated the stock at the average price of all accepted bids.
- 'When issued' trading is allowed on the stock exchange. This occurs between the announcement of the auction, and when the gilts are actually issued, ie, at the auction itself.
- Once a gilt is issued, it can be traded in the secondary bond market.

Rarely, but occasionally, gilt auctions fail. The first failure of a gilt auction since 2002 occurred on 25 March 2009.

> *LONDON (Reuters) – Britain suffered its first failed government bond auction since 2002 on Wednesday, after bids fell more than £100 million short of the £1.75 billion the government was trying to raise.*
>
> *Gilt prices initially tumbled, but market strategists said the result did not suggest Britain was facing an incipient funding crisis as it prepares to issue a record amount of gilts this year and next to fund extra spending through the recession.*
>
> *Instead, they blamed opaque Bank of England gilt-buying plans for the fact the UK DMO could not find enough bidders for the 2049 gilt at an auction, where there would usually be heavy demand from pension funds and insurers.*

If this happens, the stock becomes a 'tap stock' and it is then released slowly when the price reaches predetermined levels.

When the demand for a gilt is high, the DMO can issue further blocks of a particular gilt. These are known as tranches.

Syndicated Offers

With a syndicated offer, the DMO, on behalf of the government, appoints a group of banks to manage the sale of a gilt on its behalf. A lead manager and co-lead managers are appointed, who advise and market the gilt to investors.

Potential investors are approached to find out how much of the issue they are prepared to buy, and at what price. From this information, a book of demand is constructed. The book closes, and the issue is priced when the lead manager agrees that the size and quality of the book meet the issuer (DMO's) objectives. The gilts are then allocated to the investors.

Syndicated offers had only been used once before 2009. This method was used for an offer in June 2009, and the DMO now uses this extensively as it facilitates the issuance of very long-dated conventional and index-linked issues.

5.2   How Equities are Issued

There are two types of company: private limited companies and public limited companies (plcs).

Only plcs can issue shares to the general public and have their shares publicly traded on a recognised stock exchange. In practice, only a proportion of plcs choose to do so. Some choose to be listed on the LSE's AIM, rather than seek a full listing.

5.2.1   Full Listing

There are strict criteria, known as listing rules, for private companies to gain a full listing.

These rules are laid down by the FCA, which acts as the competent authority for listing, referred to as the UK Listing Authority (UKLA). In this capacity, it also maintains the official list detailing all the companies listed on the LSE.

These rules include the following requirements (NB: minimum sums in first two bullet points are trivial nowadays, and have no significance in terms of scale required for a listing. Companies can have a Premium or Standard listing. The former have more stringent governance requirements, over and above that required by EU legislation):

- Market capitalisation of at least £700,000 with at least 25% of shares freely available to the public (known as the free float).
- Market value of any bonds to be listed must be at least £200,000.
- There cannot be any restrictions on the sale of the shares (this is to avoid the situation of family companies who sometimes place a restriction on selling shares in the company).
- No-one can have more than 30% of the voting rights.
- There must normally be three years of audited accounts available.
- The directors must have appropriate experience and expertise.
- There are slightly less stringent rules for companies in certain sectors, eg, scientific research based activities, providing they have the requisite three years trading experience.
- Pre-vetting of the prospectus by the UKLA.

5.2.2   Listing on AIM

Gaining admission to the AIM is far less onerous, since the minimum capitalisation level, free float and trading record are not required. As a result, most AIM companies are in their early stages of development, having the intention of seeking a full listing at a later date.

The requirements for seeking a listing on aim are as follows:

- A **nominated adviser (NOMAD)** must be appointed. Their role is to advise directors of their responsibilities under AIM rules, and the content required in the prospectus that they must issue, in order to be admitted to AIM.
- A **nominated broker** must also be appointed. Other than providing information about the company to interested parties, their role is primarily to make a market and facilitate trading in the shares of the company.

5.2.3   New Issues Methods

If the company wishes to raise more capital through their listing or admission, this is done via an Initial Public Offering (IPO).

These are four types of IPO, which are also known as marketing operations. These are fixed price offer, tender offer, offer for subscription and placing. The fifth method of achieving a listing – known as an 'introduction' – raises no new capital.

Offer for Sale

- The company sells its shares to an issuing house. These do not necessarily have to be new shares. For example, family shareholdings could be offered to the public in this way.
- The issuing house then invites applications from the general public, based on a detailed prospectus known as an offering document. For an AIM share listing, a less detailed prospectus is necessary, but there must be a warning about investing in smaller company shares. The prospectus is prepared by the directors, but assessed by an independent sponsor (usually either a solicitor or an accountant).

- The independent sponsor must also provide a letter to the UKLA, confirming working capital adequacy. This normally accompanies the prospectus.
- An advert will also be placed in a national newspaper detailing the flotation. This is known as a formal notice.
- The offer price will be slightly higher than the price paid to the company.
- The offer can be on either a fixed or tender price basis.

Fixed Price Offer

- The price is fixed just below the price at which the offer is expected to be fully subscribed, in order to ensure an active secondary market.
- Potential investors subscribe for a particular number of shares at the fixed price.
- If, as is usually the case due to the price setting criteria, the issue is oversubscribed, the shares are allocated by either a scaling down or by a random selection from the applications received, as detailed in the offer document.

Pricing the offer is a difficult task, since there is a delicate balance between encouraging an active secondary market while avoiding an excessive oversubscription, which may indicate that the company has not raised as much capital as it could have done. In addition, market sentiment could change between the date of the offer and the closing date for applications. For this reason, some companies may prefer to issue the shares on a tender basis.

Tender Offer

- Rather than fixing a price, invitations for tenders are sought from prospective shareholders.
- Normally a minimum price is stipulated, and investors subscribe for a given number of shares at a price they are prepared to pay.
- When the offer is closed, a strike price is determined. This will normally be set with a view to achieving an active secondary market, and all bidders at or above this price will be satisfied.
- All successful bidders pay a uniform striking price, unlike an auction.

Although this form of offering is more attractive in terms of achieving the best result for the company, the administrative complications involved have made this a less popular option in practice.

Offer for Subscription

- This is rarely used nowadays, as it does not permit the secondary sale of existing shares. It is mainly used for new investment trusts.
- A detailed prospectus and advertisement are required for a full listing, but nowadays they are usually published electronically on the company's or sponsor's website, with hard copies also available.
- An issuing house fully underwrites the issue for an agreed commission, ensuring the company sells all the shares on offer. Usually this is conditional upon the company achieving a minimum subscription level.
- This kind of IPO can also be offered on either a fixed or tender price basis.

Placing (Selective Marketing)

- The company markets the issue via a broker, an issuing house or other financial institution.
- The shares are then placed to selected clients (hence the alternative term for a placing: 'selective marketing').

- The advantages of this method are as follows:
  - The prospectus does not need to be so detailed.
  - Underwriting is not required.
  - Advertising is not required, unless a full listing is proposed.
  - As a result, this is a cheaper alternative for the company seeking a listing.

Most AIM companies will issue their shares using this method.

5.2.4 Introduction

Companies can also achieve a listing on the LSE by means of an introduction. These are not IPOs since no new capital is raised. This method is available to those companies already listed on an overseas exchange or demutualised companies like former building societies. The benefit of a full listing is to make the shares more accessible to UK investors, which could aid any capital-raising activities which may be required in the future.

6. Indices

6.1 Introduction

Indices are a very useful way of comparing the value of a variable over different points in time.

The way they work, is by choosing a point in time, known as the base period, and giving the value of the variable at that time an arbitrary value. For simplicity, this is usually a round number such as 100 or 1,000. Future changes to the index value of the variable can then be compared with the base value or subsequent values, to indicate trends over a period of time or signal movements against the trend.

Index numbers are very useful for comparing how the value of a basket comprising many different items changes over a period of time. These indices are called composite indices. Both the Retail Price Index (RPI) and the Consumer Price Index (CPI) are examples of composite indices, which indicate the level and growth (or reduction) of inflation in the UK economy.

The level of these indices will be interpreted by the market in terms of economic outlook, which may have profound implications for both bond and stock prices. In addition, there will be a tangible effect on the value and coupon of certain index-linked securities, eg, index-linked gilts.

6.2 Stock Market Indices

There are over 3,000 market indices worldwide, some of which track the performance of a single market, and others which cover a sector, region or combination of markets.

Stock market indices have many uses:

1. acting as a barometer for the market
2. aiding portfolio measurement

3. assisting with asset allocation decisions
4. acting as the basis for certain other investment products, eg, index tracker funds, exchange-traded funds, index derivatives or structured products.

We will examine the use of indices in terms of portfolio performance and review in Chapter 7.

6.2.1 Types of Equity Index

There are many different methods of constructing an index, eg, geometric, arithmetic, weighted or unweighted. We will look at the three most commonly used methods below, but before doing so, let us consider the thought processes which should be followed before constructing an index from scratch.

When considering how to construct an index, the following points should be borne in mind:

- which markets or sectors to track
- the basis for inclusion of its constituents
- how to combine or average the relative prices of the various constituents
- whether and how to weight these constituents
- how changes to constituents are going to be handled
- whether to include or exclude dividend income.

There also needs to be consideration for the potential user of the index, as follows:

- Does it satisfy the needs of investors?
- Is it taken from a broad enough base?
- Can it be replicated for portfolio performance measurement, or by product providers for index-related products?
- Are there any restrictions on holding any constituents?
- Is it transparent in terms of composition and calculation?

The three most commonly used indices are as follows:

Price Weighted Arithmetic Indices

These indices assume that an equal number of shares are held in each of the constituents. It follows that those constituents with the higher share price will have a greater impact on the overall index value compared with those constituents with a lower share price.

While this type of index is relatively easy to administer, the disadvantage of weighting in favour of the more expensive stocks is considerable. In addition, there is no account taken of the number of shares in issue of each constituent, which may make the index unrepresentative of the true market performance.

A price weighted arithmetic index is an index where the constituents are weighted in proportion to their price per share. This means that the higher the share price the greater the impact it will have on the overall index value compared to those with a lower share price. No account is taken of the number of shares in issue of each constituent which may make the index and representative of the true market performance.

Example

If the index consisted of two stocks one of which was worth £9 and the other £1, although the constituent with £9 has substantially fewer shares in issue it will have a greater impact on the index. The index in this case would be £5 (£9 + £1)/2. If the £9 stock increased by 10% (to £9.90) and the £1 stock decreased by 50%, (to 50p) the index would move to £5.20.

This makes a price-weighted arithmetic index unsuitable as a performance measurement benchmark, or as a market barometer.

 Can you think of an example of a price-weighted arithmetic index?

The Dow Jones Industrial Average (DJIA) is a price-weighted arithmetic index, and has survived despite the shortcomings highlighted above.

Unweighted Geometric Indices

With these types of index, the geometric mean is used to calculate the value of the index.

 What is the difference between arithmetic and geometric mean?

Arithmetic mean is what most people understand by the word 'average' in that a set of numbers are added and the sum is divided by the count of numbers in the set, **n**.

The geometric mean is similar, except all the numbers in the set are multiplied and then the nth root of the product is taken.

Example

Take two numbers, 2 and 8.

The **arithmetic mean** is 2 + 8 = 10 divided by 2 = 5

The **geometric mean** is the square root of 2 x 8 =16 which is 4.

The disadvantages of this type of index are as follows:

*   It always understates the price rises and overstates the price falls, compared with a price-weighted arithmetic index.
*   It collapses if the value of a constituent falls to zero, since anything multiplied by zero is zero!

For these reasons, unweighted geometric indices should not be used to measure portfolio performance or as a market barometer.

Can you think of an example of an unweighted geometric index?

An example of this type of index is the FT30.

Market-Value-Weighted Arithmetic Indices

The constituents of these types of index are weighted in terms of their relative market capitalisation. In addition, the constituents are usually drawn from a broad base of the market being represented.

This makes them the more suitable for performance measurement, asset allocation and for pricing index related products. They still have a disadvantage in that if dominated by a handful of large cap companies, they may not offer the diversity needed for comparison with portfolio performance, or an index-based product.

 Can you think of an example of a market-value-weighted arithmetic index?

Examples would include the FTSE 100, S&P 500 and the Hang Seng.

Free Float Indices

The 'free float' is the proportion of a company's securities available to outside investors. It usually excludes shares held by strategic investors or government holdings in large privatised companies. Some overseas companies limit the amount of shares available to non-resident investors. FTSE adjust weightings in their indices according to the free float. This makes the indices more useful as a measurement of performance since it reflects more closely what fund managers can actually buy.

Capped Indices

The FTSE capped 5% index series are based on the underlying constituents of the FTSE 100 and the FTSE All-Share index. Companies that have a market capitalisation of more than 5% are capped. This allows investors to monitor the impact of reducing the size of the largest companies within these two flagship indices. The FTSE All-Share index is also available capped at 4%.

6.2.2   Limitations of Using Equity Indices in Portfolio Measurement

- They do not take into account the effect of costs and taxation.
- Most track price movement and do not include dividend reinvestment. If total returns are quoted, often the dividend is assumed to be reinvested at the ex-dividend (XD) date, and not the interest payment date.
- They assume that the investor is fully invested in constituent companies at all times.
- There is a 'survivorship bias', ie, only the companies that have continued to meet the criteria of the index remain in it, whereas other companies that have failed to meet the criteria or that have declined and then been swallowed up by other firms will have left the index. This may not replicate the situation in a real portfolio.
- The weighting by market capitalisation often leads to a high covariance portfolio, where favoured sectors are overly represented in the index, leading to potential instability should the bubble burst.

We will look at the main stock market indices in greater detail in Chapter 7.

7.   Contract Notes

The rules regarding contract notes are to be found in the FCA Handbook – Conduct of Business Sourcebook (COBS) 16.2.1R.

With the exception of where you are managing investments for retail clients, the contract note must be sent out to them 'in a durable medium' as soon as possible, and no later than the first business day following that execution.

COBS 16 Annex 1R details the information which must be included in the contract note, where applicable:

*   the identification of the firm
*   the name or other designation of the client
*   the date of trade
*   the time of trade
*   type of order (eg, limit order or market order)
*   the venue identification
*   the instrument identification
*   the buy or sell indicator
*   the nature of the order if not buy or sell
*   the quantity
*   the unit price
*   the total consideration
*   the total sum of the commissions and expenses charged
*   the rate of exchange obtained (where currency conversion is required)
*   the client's responsibilities in relation to settlement of the transaction (eg, time limit for payment or delivery)
*   if the client's counterparty was the firm itself, in the firm's group, or another client of the firm, the fact that this was the case, unless the order was executed using a system which facilitates anonymous trading.

 Can you obtain a contract note? Look for the features we have mentioned. How does it compare with others you have seen?

COBS also states that firms must retain copies of contract notes for a minimum period of five years for MiFID business or three years for non-MiFID business.

7.1   Stamp Duty

Stamp duty used to apply to a conveyance, transfer or a lease of land, as well as transfers on shares. Since 1 December 2003, these are now subject to Stamp Duty Land Tax.

For instruments executed on or after 1 December 2003, stamp duty only applies to transfers of stock and marketable securities, and to certain transfers of interest in partnerships.

- Tax is payable on the transfer of shares at 0.5%.
- It is usually only paid by the buyer.
- It is rounded to the nearest £5.
- It is not charged on gilts, public authority securities, UK corporate bonds, bearer stocks, transfers to registered charities and foreign registered securities, including most ETFs, and AIM securities.

From 13 March 2008, instruments transferring stock or marketable securities with consideration of less than £1,000, and therefore previously chargeable with £5 stamp duty, became exempt. Most do not need to be presented to HMRC for stamping, and may be sent directly to the company registrar.

7.2 Stamp Duty Reserve Tax (SDRT)

Stamp Duty Reserve Tax was introduced in 1986 to deal with transactions in shares where a transfer form had not been executed. Paperless transactions are outside the scope of stamp duty. SDRT is a transaction tax charged on 'agreements to transfer chargeable securities', unlike stamp duty, which is charged upon documents. The rate is also 0.5% and the same conditions listed above for stamp duty also apply to SDRT, apart from the rounding of SDRT to the nearest 1p.

SDRT now accounts for the majority of taxation collected on share transactions effected through the UK's Exchanges. The majority of this taxation is collected automatically through the CREST system, although payments are also collected for transactions that are effected outside of CREST (referred to as 'off-market' payments), or inputted incorrectly through CREST. This is done either by way of a cheque or the Clearing House Automated Payment System (CHAPS). This process eliminates the need for a document, ie, stock transfer form. However, if a paper transaction is drawn up and duly stamped, the transaction will fall within the stamp duty regime, and the SDRT charge is cancelled.

7.3 Panel on Takeovers and Mergers (POTAM)

In order to cover the running costs of the Panel on Takeovers and Mergers (POTAM), a £1 levy is imposed on all sterling contracts of 'equities' where the consideration exceeds £10,000. This is imposed on both the purchases and sales.

7.4 Value Added Tax (VAT)

Commission

A stockbroker's commission is exempt from VAT.

Investment Management Fees

These are generally **subject to VAT**.

Offset Charging Schemes

Some brokers offer a scheme where they charge the client the full rate of commission (with no VAT payable) and offset these commissions against the annual management fee (which is subject to VAT). This reduces, or could even eliminate, the VAT payable by the client over the year.

7.5   Nominee Companies

Nominee companies are formed by banks or other fiduciary organisations (one that holds assets in trust for a beneficiary). They are typically wholly owned subsidiaries (separate legal entities) that do not trade.

Assets that are held separately from those belonging to the financial organisation, and in trust for clients, cannot be sold by a liquidator and the proceeds used to repay the firm's debts, should the firm become insolvent.

Financial institutions set up nominee companies with the sole purpose of holding clients' assets separately from their own (segregating the assets) to give clients maximum protection under English law. Shares and other securities owned by clients are legally registered in the name of the nominee company, (which becomes the legal owner) but the beneficial ownership remains with the client.

This aids in administering portfolios and speeds up trading.

Nominee companies maintain accounts, which may be 'designated' or 'pooled'. If a client's securities are held in a designated account, they are separately identifiable from those of the firm's other clients. If they are held in a pooled account, although there will clearly be detailed records showing which clients own what, there may be one large holding registered, covering the individual holdings of a large number of underlying clients.

Given that the function of a nominee company is to register and administer holdings of shares and other securities on behalf of clients, it is often involved in administrative tasks, such as:

* collection of dividends
* preparation of annual consolidated tax vouchers
* advising clients of corporate actions and seeking their instructions
* arranging transfers when a share is purchased or sold.

Chapter Four
Trusts and Trustees

An exam specification breakdown is provided at the back of this workbook

1. Introduction

In this chapter we will be examining the principles and key features of trusts and the law governing their creation and management.

Some of the terminology and concepts will already be familiar to you. We will build upon this knowledge and introduce different concepts with which you may be less familiar. We hope that this will give you confidence for your examination.

You must continue reading and extending your understanding of the topics covered through additional study. This workbook does not represent everything you may be expected to know for the examination.

You will see icons or symbols alongside the text. These indicate activities or questions that have been designed to check your understanding and help you validate your understanding.

Here is a guide to what each of the symbols mean:

 Question

This identifies a question that will enable you to check your knowledge and understanding.

 Analyse

This gives you an opportunity to consider a question posed and compare your answers to the feedback given.

1.1 Objectives

Trusts and Trust Legislation

1. Know the key features of trusts – arrangement, participants, types, documentation.
2. Know the different types of trust and what each is designed to achieve.
3. Understand the key provisions of the Trustee Act 2000 and how these relate to the investment powers of trustees and the trust deed.

Taxation of Trusts

4. Understand the concept of a chargeable lifetime transfer and be able to assess the Inheritance Tax (IHT) consequences of different scenarios relating to interest in possession.
5. Know the requirements for charitable status, how charities are taxed, and the purpose and rules of Gift Aid.

2. Trusts and Trust Legislation

2.1 History of Trusts

The law of trusts developed in the Middle Ages around the time of the Crusades. Over the centuries since the introduction of Roman law, England had developed a fairly detailed set of rules which the population was obliged to abide by. This was known as common law – common since the rules had to be adhered to by everyone.

The courts enforced common law by following decisions and principles laid down in previous cases very closely. While this served a useful purpose for settling the majority of disputes, at times, the application of the rigid and inflexible rules that had developed through the courts led to problems when dealing with more unusual circumstances. In the 14th century, a system was introduced whereby anyone who found the application of common law to be unfair or 'inequitable' could apply to the king. The king soon delegated his powers to the Lord Chancellor who then established the Court of Chancery. The cases brought before the Court of Chancery were not decided on common law but according to the judge's sense of justice. Over time, the law of equity evolved with its very own rules, principles and procedures.

Wealthy landowners would go away to fight for the king for several years. Rather than leave their property unoccupied, they sometimes transferred it to a relative. This was done on the strict understanding that the relative and their family could live on the land in return for looking after it, but when the wealthy landowner returned, they would have to transfer it back. As you can imagine, after many years of enjoying the property, some of these relatives reneged on their side of the deal on the return of the (formerly) wealthy landowner!

Under common law, the legal title was in the relative's name so the courts could not recognise any right to the property from the former owner. A device known as the 'use' was developed to avoid this happening. This enabled the wealthy landowner to convey the legal title to the relative but at the same time oblige the relative to hold the land for the use of another (the wealthy landowner in this case). While this arrangement was not recognised in common law, it was a moral obligation and therefore enforced in equity by the Court of Chancery.

The use was the forerunner of the modern trust as we know it today.

2.2 What is a Trust?

While there is no statutory definition of a trust, the following summarises the key elements which should be present:

- an individual (settlor)
- gifts certain assets (the trust property)
- to be managed by a third party (trustee)
- in accordance with defined objectives (the trust deed)
- for the benefit of certain people (beneficiaries).

2.3 Trust Creation

Trusts can be created by a variety of means including orally, by deed, by will, by statute or, as we shall see later, in secret. We will now look at the methods most commonly used by settlors, in turn:

2.3.1 Creation by Deed

This is the most common method of creating a trust. There is no prescribed format but most solicitors and trust corporations will have tried and tested templates that can easily be adapted to suit the settlor's particular requirements.

The deed will specify the following:

- the trust property
- the names of the trustees
- the names of the beneficiaries
- the name of the protector (if there is one)
- the powers of the trustees
- the rights of the beneficiaries.

It must be signed by the settlor and is usually also signed by the trustees to confirm their acceptance.

Trusts can also be created over life policies very simply by filling out the life office's trust form.

2.3.2 Creation by Will

A trust can be expressly stated in the will or arise because of a gift to a minor. Even if the will does not include provisions to set up a trust, the executors are effectively holding the entire estate on trust for the beneficiaries until they can fully distribute it.

Clearly, a will trust will not come into operation until after the testator has died. Therefore, the trust may not receive any assets until many years after the will is prepared. There is also the possibility that the will may be revoked prior to death, such that the trust never comes into operation.

Some wills avoid the need and possible expense of setting up trusts by giving permission to the parents of any minors to provide a valid receipt for property left to their children.

2.3.3 Creation by Statute

There are many trusts created or implied by statute.

The following are two examples of such trusts:

- **Section 33 Administration of Estates Act 1925** – this provides for the creation of a trust for sale on intestacy. This has been altered by Section 5 of the Trusts of Land and Appointment of Trustees Act 1996, the effect of which is that personal representatives now have a power, but not a duty, to sell land held within the estate.
- **Section 36 Law of Property Act 1925** – if a legal estate is held by two or more persons as joint tenants, it is held in trust.

2.4 Legal Requirements for a Valid Trust

2.4.1 The Three Certainties

In order to create a valid express trust, **three certainties** are required:

1. **Certainty of intention** – words must be used indicating an intention to create a trust. The equitable maxim 'equity looks at the intention not the form' means that no particular form of words is used but the court will look at the words used in light of all the circumstances. 'On trust for' would be sufficient in this regard.
2. **Certainty of object** – it must be clear for whom the trust is intended. This could be a simple case of naming the beneficiaries 'A & B in equal shares absolutely' or for a class of people 'any of my children who survive me'.

Case Study

In a case called **McPhail v Doulton (1971)** the rule was tested thoroughly where a will included a gift to the employees of a certain company, and their relatives and dependents. The test that was put forward by the House of Lords was to ask the question: 'can a trustee tell with certainty, in relation to any hypothetical individual who presents himself before the trustee, whether he is a member of that class?'

In **this** case it was possible to ascertain whether any person presenting themselves was either an employee, a relative or a dependent, so the trust was valid for certainty.

As we shall discuss later, charitable trusts need not fail for uncertainty of object.

3. **Certainty of subject matter** – it must be established, with clarity, what property is to be held on the express trust. If the subject matter is not certain, the whole trust fails (although hopefully, if the settlor is still alive, they would be able to clarify the position).

2.4.2 Rules against Perpetuities and Accumulations

It has long been considered to be against public policy to allow property to be retained in trust for an indefinite length of time. Similarly, it was decided in Thelluson v Woodford (1799) that if trustees were allowed to accumulate income indefinitely, then in theory, the trust fund would grow with compound interest and could eventually contain a significant proportion of the national wealth. This seems extraordinary now, but it was clearly of great concern at the time!

The rules against perpetuities are contained in the Perpetuities and Accumulations Act 2009, which states that the ultimate interest in a settlement must vest within 125 years, but the 80-year limit still applies to trusts set up before April 2010.

The perpetuity rule does not apply to gifts to charities or pension schemes.

A trust can accumulate over its lifetime so again a maximum of 125 years. However, this applies to trusts set up after the 6 April 2010. For trusts executed prior to then (including will trusts) the previous accumulation periods remain:

1. the life of the settlor
2. 21 years from the death of the testator or settlor
3. the minority of any persons living at that time (ie, until they are 18)
4. the minority of any persons entitled under the settlement.

2.4.3   Constitution of the Trust

Depending on what type of property is involved, certain formalities need to be satisfied before the property is validly transferred, and the general principle is that 'equity will not perfect an imperfect gift'. Thus, in the case of land, there needs to be a deed, and in the case of shares, Sections 182–183 of the Companies Act 1985 provides that in general, a share transfer form must be executed and delivered with the share certificates, followed by entry of the name of the new owner in the company books.

2.5   Parties to a Trust

As we have already discussed, every trust has a settlor, trustees and beneficiaries. Some trusts also have a protector. We will look at each of these participants in turn.

2.5.1   Settlor

The settlor is the person who sets up the trust by transferring money or other property to trustees to hold upon the terms of the trust they are seeking to establish. The terms of the trust will be laid out in a trust deed for gifts during the settlor's lifetime (*inter vivos*) or in the will on death.

The placing of property into trust is effectively a gift of the assets, which means that the settlor no longer has any control over them. However, some settlors find this unpalatable and therefore many modern trust deeds include provisions which reserve certain powers for the settlor. Commonly the settlor will wish to reserve the power to appoint and remove trustees, but they can go further and reserve the power to appoint investment managers or, more unusually, retain the investment powers completely.

On a practical point, settlors need to be careful not to retain too much control, since the courts could set aside the trust as a sham in such circumstances. This would mean that the trust is ignored for tax purposes and therefore any potential tax benefits of setting up the trusts would be lost. This is far more common with offshore trusts where it may be possible for the settlor to also be a beneficiary.

 Who do you think may be a settlor?

In fact, any legal entity that is capable of owning or transferring property could be a settlor, which could include an individual or a corporation.

2.5.2 Trustees

The trustees are the legal owners of the trust property and on appointment the property will be vested in them by the settlor. This process is known as 'constituting the trust'.

The original trustees are appointed by the trust deed, sometimes called a 'settlement'. The original trustees of will trusts are appointed in the will. If someone dies intestate (without a valid will) the administrators will be the trustees of any trust set up as a result.

 Who do you think may be appointed a trustee?

Anyone capable of owning a legal interest in property may be appointed as a trustee, which means that they have to be over 18 and of sound mind (*sui juris*). This also includes corporate entities known as trust corporations, empowered by their memorandum and articles to act as a trustee. Most major banks have subsidiaries who perform this function, eg, Barclays Bank Trust Company.

How Many Trustees are Allowed?

There can be any number of trustees although most trusts will have between two and five.

If the trust contains land, in order to give a valid receipt for the proceeds of sale, there must be at least two trustees (unless one is a trust corporation) and no more than four.

Duties of Trustees

As we have seen, the job of the trustee is to hold the trust property for the benefit of the beneficiaries in accordance with the trust provisions.

The role carries with it the following principal general duties:

- **Comply with the terms of the trust** – the trustee must be familiar with the terms of the trust and comply with the duties and powers contained in the trust instrument. Any failure in this duty could be in breach of trust and the trustees would have to make good any losses which have arisen as a result of negligence.
- **To take control of the trust property** – the trustee must ascertain the assets of the trust and ensure these are vested in the names of the trustees. For example, they will need to make sure that any shareholdings are registered in the names of the trustees. Failure to do so could result in loss or misappropriation, which would also be a breach of trust for which the trustee would be liable.
- **Act impartially between the beneficiaries** – trustees must act in the best interests of the beneficiaries, but importantly must also act impartially between all the beneficiaries. As we will discuss later, some beneficiaries only have an interest in the income arising in a trust, and others may just have an interest in the capital. When considering which investments to purchase on behalf of a trust, the trustees must have regard to the interests of all beneficiaries and not be biased one way or another.

- **Duty to keep accounts** – a trustee must keep clear and accurate accounts of the trust, and provide them to beneficiaries on request. There is no duty to have these audited, but the trustee can choose to do so.
- **Duty to provide information** – a trustee must produce information and documents on request of the beneficiaries.
- **Duty of care** – in addition to the above general duties, there has always existed an overarching duty of care that covers all the actions of a trustee. While this has developed over the years from common law, it has now been complemented by the statutory duty of care imposed by Part 1 of the Trustee Act 2000.
- **Common law duty of care** – this has been developed from case law over the years, and interestingly (for us) most of the important cases were concerned with investment related issues.
  - **Speight v Gaunt (1883)** – a trustee should conduct trust affairs in the same way a prudent man of business would conduct his own. This case centred on the use of agents, in this case a stockbroker, who defaulted on his duties. However, the trustee was not found liable since he had been prudent in seeking expert help.
  - **Re Whiteley (1886)** – in relation to investment, a trustee should use the same diligence as that wich a man of ordinary prudence would take in the management of his own affairs, or the affairs of someone for whom he felt morally bound to provide.
  - **Re Luckings Will Trusts (1968)** – this concerned the management of a majority interest in private company shares within a trust. A majority shareholder would be prudent to seek more information than an ordinary shareholder; indeed he may seek a seat on the board. If he did not do so, he would be lacking in his duty of care.
  - **Bartlett v Barclays Bank Trust Company (1980)** – again, this case concerned the management of a private company and the court followed the ruling in Re Luckings Will Trusts but also said that a higher duty of care is expected of a professional trustee who specialises in trust management.
- **Statutory duty of care** – the Trustee Act 2000, which came into effect on 1 February 2001, established a new statutory duty of care for trustees. This is found in Part 1, which is reproduced below:
  Whenever the duty under this subsection applies to a trustee, he must exercise such care and skill as is reasonable in the circumstances, having regard in particular:
  a. to any special knowledge or experience that he has or holds himself out as having, and
  b. if he acts as trustee in the course of a business or profession, to any special knowledge or experience that it is reasonable to expect of a person acting in the course of that kind of business or profession.

As you will see, this legislation imposes a general standard of care as to what a reasonable man would do in the circumstances but supports the ruling in Bartlett v Barclays Bank Trust Company for professional trustees and those with specialist knowledge or experience.

Limitations of the Statutory Duty of Care

The statutory duty of care will only apply to the following:

a. exercising the powers of investment
b. acquisition of land
c. using agents, nominees or custodians
d. insurance of trust property.

Furthermore, it is possible (under Schedule 1 Section 7 of the Trustee Act 2000) to exclude the statutory duty of care in the trust instrument.

However, the common law duty of care will apply to each and every exercise of the trustees' powers, therefore it will continue to be of great relevance and importance to the activities of trustees.

Exemption Clauses

In addition to being able to exclude the statutory duty of care, trust instruments have, for some time, commonly included exemption clauses whereby the settlor agrees to exonerate the trustees from any liability for negligence. In Armitage v Nurse 1998, an exemption clause of this type was considered by the courts, and it was held that exemption clauses were valid for any breach of trust in the absence of dishonesty. As you can imagine, you will not see many modern trust deeds managed by solicitors and professional trustees without this clause inserted!

Powers of Trustees

The trust deed will commonly confer additional powers to the trustees. These could be specific investment powers or, if there is a life policy held in trust, the power to pay premiums, make claims, exercise options and switch funds.

All trustees must act unanimously in the exercise of their powers.

The Trustee Act 1925 also conferred statutory powers on trustees with regard to the power to apply income (Section 31) or capital (Section 32) to beneficiaries.

Trustee Act 2000

As we shall see later, the Trustee Act 2000 conferred new statutory powers of investment on trustees.

In addition, the Act gave trustees a statutory power to delegate day-to-day duties to an agent, including the powers of investment. The Act requires the trustees to set out a policy statement stating how the investment management functions should be managed in the best interest of the trust.

The Act also created an express professional charging clause for non-charitable trusts which allows the payment of fees to a trustee appointed in a professional capacity where there is no charging clause in the deed.

 What do you think the position is for laypersons acting as trustees?

The general rule is that trustees cannot benefit from their position, therefore laypersons are not allowed to charge for acting as a trustee, but can claim reasonable 'out of pocket' expenses.

The Act also gave the trustees the power to insure 100% of the trust property.

2.5.3 Beneficiaries

The beneficiaries are the persons or objects for whose benefit the trust is created. Beneficiaries can either be named in the trust instrument ('my children Jenny and Sarah in equal shares') or described by a class ('all my children in equal shares'). Clearly the latter approach would provide extra flexibility if a settlor was intending to have more children. In certain cases, the trustees may be given the power to exercise discretion as to who benefits from the trust.

There are various types of beneficial interest:

Absolute vested interest – the beneficiary has a full equitable ownership, which cannot be taken away. There are three conditions which must be satisfied for an interest to be vested, and these are that:

1. the identity of the beneficiary is known
2. any conditions are satisfied, and
3. the respective shares are known.

If any of these conditions are not satisfied, the interest is known as a 'contingent interest'.

Life interest – a beneficiary (called the life tenant) is entitled to the income on the trust property but not the capital. An immediate right to the income is called an 'interest in possession'. Where there are successive life interests, the person who is not enjoying the immediate right to the income has an 'interest in remainder'.

Remaindermen – these beneficiaries will receive the capital of the trust fund on the death of the life tenant. Until that time their interest is known as an 'interest in reversion (or reversionary interest)'.

Example

Dave settles money on Julia for life, then to Phillippa for life, and then to Freddie providing he reaches the age of 21 (he is four at present).

Julia has an interest in possession, which is vested.

Phillippa has an interest in remainder, which is vested since there are no conditions.

Freddie has an interest in reversion, which is contingent on him reaching 21 years of age.

A beneficiary cannot control the trustees but they do have a personal right to enforce the trust and ensure that the trustees carry out its provisions.

In certain circumstances the beneficiaries can terminate the trust.

This is known as the rule in **Saunders v Vautier (1841)**. The conditions that must be present for them to successfully call for an end to the trust are that:

1. all the beneficiaries are ascertained
2. there is no possibility of further beneficiaries
3. they are all of full age and capacity, and
4. the beneficiaries are unanimous.

This rule can be expressly excluded in the trust instrument.

2.5.4   Protector

Protectors are much more common in offshore trusts than in England and Wales, and their most common role is to veto the proposals of trustees. Unlike trustees, they do not have trust property vested in their name.

The scope of the protector's powers are set out in the trust instrument and these can be either reactive or proactive:

Reactive – the protector reacts to the actions of a trustee, eg, to distribute money to a beneficiary.

Proactive – the protector takes the initiative and instigates an action, eg, to remove a trustee.

Like trustees, anyone who is *sui juris* can be a protector, including a corporate body.

Practical Point

Clearly, the more power given to the protector, the more cumbersome the administration of the trust could become. However, appointing a protector may give the settlor the desired peace of mind that someone will be able to oversee the activities of the trustees, hence the term often used to describe this role is 'settlor's comfort'.

2.6   Classification of Trusts

As we have seen, equity developed the law of trusts. Many different and difficult situations have arisen over the years, requiring the court to recognise and deal with them appropriately. This has left us with many different types of trust, which are recognised by the courts as discussed below.

Express Trust

An express trust is one where the terms are expressly set out, usually in writing but for personal property this could be by a clear declaration. This could be by way of a lifetime settlement, by will or on intestacy. In the latter case this is also known as a statutory trust.

Implied Trusts

Implied trusts are created as a result of what the law infers as being a person's intention. There are two main types of implied trusts: resulting and constructive.

Resulting Trust

An implied resulting trust could arise following a transfer of property from A to B without any indication that a gift was intended or has taken place. The property would be held in a resulting trust for A, as on B's death the property would revert (be transferred back) to A. Similarly, A could transfer property to B to hold for C's lifetime. If there is no instruction as to what is to happen to that property on C's death the property would be held in a resulting trust for A, as on C's death the property would return to A (or A's estate if he too had died).

Constructive Trust

A constructive trust is one that is imposed by law, usually to remedy inequitable, unconscionable, improper or unjust conduct. An example would be where someone acts as trustee 'de son tort', ie, that he acts as though he is a trustee and receives an item of trust property or makes a profit at the expense of a trust. In these circumstances he is legally deemed to be holding the property and profit on constructive trusts for the benefit of the beneficiaries and is accountable to them for them.

Another example of where a constructive trust will be imposed is where there is a 'secret trust'.

Example _____

More about secret trusts

These trusts take effect though the operation of the will. The intention of a secret trust is to obtain confidentiality. The beneficiaries, and the terms of the trust, can remain secret. There are strict rules which must be followed in order for these trusts to be valid. There are fully secret trusts and half secret trusts.

With fully secret trusts, the will may appear to leave property absolutely to individual A. However, at some point during their lifetime, the testator must have communicated either orally or in writing (or by sealed letter to be opened upon the testator's death) with A, who agreed to hold the property in trust for another or others.

Half secret trusts are where the trust is partially expressed in the will. The word 'trust' can appear in the will but not the terms of the trust or the intended beneficiaries. The purpose of these trusts is again to retain confidentiality but also to prevent possible fraud by the legatee. An example of such a trust would be 'to Jayne on the terms I have previously communicated to her'. The rule with regard to the communication of half secret trusts is different to that of fully secret trusts in that the communication (written or oral) and acceptance must take place either before or at the same time as making the will.

Automatic Resulting Trust

Automatic resulting trusts also arise through the operation of law.

If one person transfers property or funds to another for a specific purpose, this creates a trust relationship between them. The recipient is under an obligation to carry out that purpose.

Example of an Automatic Resulting Trust

In Barclays Bank v Quistclose Investments (1970), Rolls Razor was deeply indebted to Barclays. It needed further additional sums to be able to pay a dividend which it had declared. Rolls Razor borrowed funds from Quistclose in order to satisfy the dividend declared. The terms of the loan were such that the funds would only be used for the sole purpose of paying the dividend. The loan was paid into an account with Barclays, and Barclays was given notice of the arrangement.

However, between the time that the loan was advanced and the dividend was paid, Rolls Razor went into liquidation. Barclays Bank claimed that it was entitled to exercise a set-off of the money in the account against the debts that Rolls Razor owed to Barclays. Quistclose claimed that the money had to be returned, as the purpose for which it had been lent had now failed and was incapable of being fulfilled (as Rolls Razor was now in liquidation).

The House of Lords (with the leading judgement being given by Lord Wilberforce) unanimously held that the money was held by Rolls Razor on trust for the payment of the dividends; that purpose having failed, the money was held on trust for Quistclose. The fact that the transaction was a loan, did not exclude the implication of a trust. The legal rights (to call for repayment) and equitable rights (to claim title) could co-exist. Barclays, having notice of the trust, could not claim the money to set off against the debts of Quistclose. Similarly, the liquidator of Rolls Razor could not claim title to the money, as the assets did not form part of the beneficial estate of Rolls Razor. This was a landmark case and henceforth, these types of trusts are often described as Quistclose Trusts.

This ruling was backed up by Lord Millet in a later case which went to the House of Lords, namely **Twinsectra v Yardley (2002)**.

3. Types of Trust

We will discuss the taxation aspects of the most commonly used trusts later, but in the meantime let us consider the main features, benefits and possible uses of the following trusts.

3.1 Bare Trust

A bare trust is where the trustee holds the trust property for a single beneficiary who is 18 or over (England and Wales) or 16 or over (Scotland) and has full mental capacity. The beneficiary, who holds the whole of the equitable interest may, under Saunders v Vautier (1841), call for the legal interest from the trustee which will give them absolute ownership property held in trust, and therefore end the trust.

One example of this would be a life policy on trust for Jimmy (an adult) absolutely. In this case, the trustee's duty is just to claim the proceeds from the life office and pay it over to Jimmy.

Resulting Trusts and Constructive Trusts (see section 2.6, earlier) are usually bare trusts.

 In what circumstances do you think bare trusts would be an appropriate solution?

Bare trusts are particularly useful for grandparents who wish to pass on assets to their grandchildren or set aside money for their school fees or university education. As we discussed earlier, the named beneficiary has an 'absolute entitlement' to the assets that are placed in trust, but they will be held in the name of the trustee until the child reaches the age of 18.

This could be useful for settling assets that the beneficiary could not hold directly, eg, stocks and shares (because minors cannot contract to buy and sell them).

An absolute trust for a minor is commonly referred to as a bare trust, and is what most investors understand by a bare trust. Technically, they are not a bare trust in the strict sense because the beneficiaries are under 18 years of age, and cannot terminate the trust until they are 18. Further, the trustees have active investment and management duties. Nevertheless, this chapter follows usual practice in referring to them as bare trusts.

On reaching the age of 18, the beneficiary will be able to call on the assets. The trustees will have no discretion as to whether to comply with this request. As we shall see later, the income on a bare trust is deemed to be that of the beneficiary who will be able to use any unused Personal Allowance to mitigate, or avoid completely, any income tax on the income arising within the trust fund. For parents, this type of trust is not so attractive, since any income over £100 would be deemed to be that of the parents for income tax purposes. For grandparents however, this rule does not apply.

Any growth on the assets held in trust will be outside the estate of the settlor and, providing the settlor survives seven years from the date of creating the trust, there will be no inheritance tax to pay.

The disadvantage of bare trusts is the lack of flexibility – the beneficiary can get their hands on the funds at 18, which may not be desirable (for the settlor!).

3.2   Interest in Possession Trust

An interest in possession is the right to receive an income from the trust fund, or use of the trust assets.

Interests in possession are sometimes established in a will, and are a potentially useful way of providing a safe income for dependants of the settlor, while ensuring that some assets are saved in order to be passed on at a later date.

Legislation enacted in 2006 changed the tax treatment of these trusts, and new interest in possession trusts are now treated in much the same way as discretionary trusts for IHT purposes. As such, while an interest in possession trust may well still be a viable option, some settlors will wish to investigate other possibilities, particularly discretionary trusts which provide greater flexibility.

3.2.1 Power of Appointment (or Flexible) Trusts

Trusts can be fixed-interest trusts in as much as once they are set up, the beneficial interests cannot normally be altered. However, it is also possible to set up a trust where the trustees are given a 'power of appointment' to appoint or vary beneficiaries or vary the terms of the trust.

The class of potential beneficiaries can be drafted very widely, giving the trustees maximum flexibility. This can cater for any changing family or personal circumstances like marriage breakdowns or bankruptcy.

There will be a default beneficiary who has a right to the income (ie, an interest in possession) and possibly capital if the trustees do not appoint any of the other beneficiaries.

 Can you think of a situation where this arrangement could be particularly useful?

These types of trust are commonly used for life assurance policies written in trust. This gives the settlor power to change beneficial interest and appoint new trustees during their lifetime.

There are, of course, other advantages in setting up a life policy under a trust. These are as follows:

- The proceeds are, subject to certain conditions, paid outside of the deceased's estate and therefore avoid any potential IHT charge.
- The trust funds can be paid to the trustees without the need for Grant of Representation (outside probate). This means that the proceeds can be paid by the insurance company within a matter of days after production of the death certificate.

3.3 Discretionary Trust

Discretionary trusts, along with bare trusts, have become the family trust of choice. In a discretionary trust, no beneficiary has a right to the income – the trustees have the power to accumulate, and distributions will be at their discretion.

The trustees have discretion in two ways:

1. They can select which beneficiary or beneficiaries from a class of beneficiaries receive payments of either income or capital.
2. They can decide the amount of trust income or capital each beneficiary receives.

An example would be 'on trust for such of my children or grandchildren as the trustees shall, from time to time, appoint'.

 What do you think are the potential uses of a discretionary trust?

The main advantage of discretionary trusts is their flexibility. Again, this can cater for changes in circumstances, like possible future divorce of a child, remarriage of the surviving spouse, or the threat of bankruptcy to any beneficiary. Discretionary trusts are also useful to guard against spendthrift beneficiaries who will not be able to have access to the capital and who will only benefit from the income if the trustees so decide. Placing funds in a discretionary trust can also mean that potential beneficiaries can continue to receive means-tested benefits, which would otherwise cease. For example, this type of trust could prove very useful for providing for beneficiaries who have learning difficulties.

The settlor can guide the trustees, normally by leaving a 'letter of wishes' with the will. Although not binding, this could be a useful steer for the trustees in exercising their discretion during the lifetime of the trust.

There are certain IHT disadvantages of discretionary trusts, although as we shall see later, since 22 March 2006, these are now shared with interest in possession trusts created after that date. Clearly these taxation implications need to be weighed up against the benefits of greater flexibility and control.

3.4   Accumulation Trust

Trustees can accumulate income within the trust and add it to the trust's capital. They can also pay income out, as with discretionary trusts. These are not to be confused with the old accumulation and maintenance trusts that stopped in 2006.

3.5   Charitable Trust

Charitable trusts are a type of **purpose trust** in that they promote a purpose and do not primarily benefit specific individuals. In the UK, charitable trusts are regulated by the Charities Commission.

A charitable trust must be of a charitable nature, for the public benefit and wholly and exclusively **charitable**. For tax purposes, Her Majesty's Revenue & Customs (HMRC) states that the definition of a 'charitable trust' is a trust established for charitable purposes only.

Under the Charities Act 2006 there are 13 purposes:

1.   the prevention or relief of poverty
2.   the advancement of education
3.   the advancement of religion
4.   the advancement of health or the saving of lives
5.   the advancement of citizenship or community development
6.   the advancement of the arts, culture, heritage or science
7.   the advancement of amateur sport
8.   the advancement of human rights, conflict resolution or reconciliation or the promotion of religious or racial harmony or equality and diversity
9.   the advancement of environmental protection or improvement
10. the relief of those in need, by reason of youth, age, ill health, disability, financial hardship or other disadvantage
11. the advancement of animal welfare
12. the promotion of the efficiency of the armed forces of the Crown; or the efficiency of the police, fire and rescue services or ambulance services
13. Any other purposes charitable in law.

In fact the purposes defined in the Charities Act 2006 are very similar to those used previously but with greater detail on what constitutes 'other purposes beneficial for the community'. The last category meant that everything that was previously considered charitable remained so.

Prospective charities must apply to the Charity Commission to claim charitable status and thereby the tax benefits connected with a charity.

3.5.1   The Benefits of Being a Charitable Trust

Generally speaking, charitable trusts are subject to the same rules as private trusts, but they enjoy a number of advantages over private trusts, some of which are particularly relevant when considering the management of investments on behalf of the trustees.

The Perpetuity Rule

We discussed earlier that the perpetuity rule prohibits settlors from tying up their property indefinitely. Charitable trusts are the exception to this rule, since they will be valid even though they may last for an infinite period of time.

Tax Advantages

As you would expect, charitable trusts and charities enjoy significant tax advantages, and this is the main motivation for bodies seeking charitable status.

The investments of charities are:

* exempt from income tax
* exempt from CGT on disposals by the trust
* exempt from stamp duty.

In addition:

* no capital gains tax is payable on gifts by individuals to charity (this is an exempt disposal)
* no IHT is payable on outright gifts by individuals to a charity
* charities benefit from a mandatory 80% business rate relief for the premises that they occupy; the further 20% is discretionary and may be awarded by the local authority to whom the rates are payable
* gifts to charitable trusts may qualify for income tax relief under Gift Aid (or a payroll-giving scheme) as described in the following section.

3.5.2   Gift Aid

Gift Aid is basically tax relief on money donated to UK, EU, Norway and Iceland charities and community amateur sports clubs.

HMRC treats donations as if the donor had already deducted basic rate tax from them. The charity can then reclaim this tax to increase the value of a donation.

The Gift Aid scheme was introduced in 1990. It enables UK-resident individuals and companies to give gifts of money to charity tax-efficiently.

The scheme now can apply to any donation, whether large or small, regular or one-off.

How it Works

Charities take the donation, which is money that has already been taxed – and reclaim basic rate tax from HMRC on its gross equivalent – the amount before basic rate tax was deducted.

Basic rate tax is 20%, so this means that a gift of £10 using Gift Aid is worth £12.50 to the charity.

Higher rate taxpayers can claim the difference between the higher rate of tax (40%) and the basic rate of tax (20%) on the total (gross) value of the donation to the charity on their Self-Assessment forms. Similarly, additional rate taxpayers can claim back the difference between 45% and 20%.

Example

Peter is a higher rate taxpayer. He donates £100, but the total value of his donation to the charity is £125. In addition, he can claim back 20% of this (£25) for himself. He will need to make this claim via his Self-Assessment tax return.

Gift Aid Rules

Donations will qualify for tax relief as long as they are not more than four times the amount of tax the donor paid in the tax year (6 April to 5 April).

To satisfy the Gift Aid conditions donors must:

- give the charity a Gift Aid declaration, which should include:
  - their name
  - their home address
  - the charity's name
  - details of the donation, stating that it is a Gift Aid donation
  - confirmation that they have paid UK tax – to cover the tax the charity will reclaim.

A declaration can be made to cover individual donations or a series of donations, and can cover donations made during a specified period or to cover all future donations. They can also be backdated for up to four years prior to the date of the declaration.

3.5.3 Limitations of Becoming a Charity

There are restrictions on what charities can do. These are determined by the Charity Commission both in terms of purpose and operations. This is primarily to ensure that all money raised, and any surpluses, can only be distributed in accordance with the charitable objectives of the organisation. It is essential to think carefully before applying to become a registered charity.

- Charity trustees cannot be paid, other than for reasonable expenses. This could restrict the professional assistance the organisation might otherwise be able to engage.
- Charity law also demands that trustees avoid any situation where charitable and personal interests might conflict.
- Charities aren't allowed to undertake political campaigning.
- Being a charity restricts the type of trading activities the organisation is allowed to undertake.

4. The Investment of Trusts

4.1 Investment Duties in Equity

Case law through the years has provided a clear framework as to what is expected in equity. In this context 'equity' in the legal sense means 'fairness'. Historically, it was administered by the Court of Chancery, in opposition to the strict rules of common law. Not to be confused with shares!

Trustees are expected to conduct investment business to the standard of a prudent person in business. If the trustee is a trust corporation, that company owes a higher standard of care (Bartlett v Barclays Bank Trust Company [1980]).

In Nestle v National Westminster Bank (1993), the court had to decide upon the balance the trustee has to achieve, as regards the interests of the life tenant and the remaindermen.

This led to some general guidelines:

1. It was not a wise policy to change investments too frequently.
2. A trustee with power of investment should undertake periodic reviews of the investments held in trust. These reviews should be undertaken at least annually.

4.2 Investment Powers in the Trust Deed

The trustees must observe the powers granted in the trust deed. The trustees must ensure that they understand the meaning of the powers and conform to them strictly.

Modern trust deeds often confer wide powers of investment on the trustees, eg, 'invest as if absolutely entitled'. The trust deed could also give permission to retain hazardous or wasting assets. However, many old trust deeds do not confer any powers of investment on trustees. In the absence of investment powers in the trust instrument, the trustee will have to rely on the investment powers laid down by statute.

4.3 Statutory Investment Powers

The Trustee Investment Act 1961 defined three ranges of investment which limited the proportion of a trust that could be invested into different types of investment. The two limited and risk-averse ranges were both known as the 'narrow range' which were essentially fixed interest securities. The riskier investments were known as 'wide range investments' which were primarily equities. The Act laid down strict rules as to the percentage split of the portfolio with regard to these ranges. If the trustees had power to retain assets, there was also a special fund in which these assets were held until disposal.

Although at the time this was welcome legislation, it has been found to be too restrictive in the modern era of portfolio management. The Trustee Investment Act 1961 has now been repealed in the most part, and replaced by the Trustee Act 2000.

As we have already seen, Part 1 of this Act introduced a statutory duty of care for trustees.

However, the most important aspect of this legislation, from our perspective, is contained in Part 2 of the Act. This details a new power of investment which is summarised as follows:

- Trustees now have the right to invest in anything as if they are 'absolutely entitled', subject to the 'standard investment criteria'.
- Standard investment criteria includes:
  - the suitability of the type of investment for the type of trust (eg, age of beneficiaries and life tenancy)
  - whether the particular investment selected is the most suitable of its type. The assessment of suitability will include considerations as to the size and risk of the investment, the balance between income and capital growth, and will include any relevant ethical considerations as to the kind of investments appropriate for the trust.
- The standard investment criteria cannot be excluded by a settlor in the trust instrument or by including wide powers of investment in the trust instrument.
- There is a need to review investments from time to time to see if they need to be varied. Although the Act does not stipulate how frequently this must take place, the case of Nestle v National Westminster Bank must be borne in mind.
- There is also a need to diversify the investments of the trust to the extent that is appropriate to the circumstances of the trust.
- Trustees are permitted to invest in freehold or leasehold land in the UK (but not overseas). Under the Trustee Investment Act 1961, there was a minimum unexpired term of 60 years for leasehold property, but this has been removed. Property can be bought for:
  - investment
  - occupation by the beneficiary
  - or for any other reason.
- Since the trustees have powers of an absolute owner, they will also have the power to mortgage.
- A trustee must seek advice before setting up a trust fund, or on review, unless the trustee does not think it is necessary in the circumstances (not defined in the Act but is considered to cover situations where there are only small sums to invest). The advice must be from a person whom the trustee reasonably believes to be qualified. This duty to seek advice also applies to express powers given in the trust instrument, not just the statutory investment powers.
- Trustees are also bound by their duty of care, to act fairly between all beneficiaries entitled to income and capital.
- The general power of investment does not apply to pension trusts, authorised unit trusts or certain charitable trusts.

5. The Taxation of Trusts

5.1 Income Tax

Trustees are subject to tax under Self-Assessment and they need to register the trust with HMRC by 5 October of the tax year after the trust is set up (or when it makes gains or income if later) in a similar way to the self-employed.

They need to complete Self-Assessment tax returns (in this case a trust and estate tax return). As with other Self-Assessment tax payers, trusts have to make interim payments on account.

All trustees are jointly liable for any outstanding tax, and are personally liable for any penalties which may be incurred. The income tax treatment of trusts varies depending upon the circumstances and nature of the trust.

5.1.1 Income Tax Payable by the Settlor

There are certain occasions when, no matter what type of trust (other than trust for 'vulnerable' beneficiaries, which includes disabled persons and bereaved minors), the income is deemed to be that of the settlor and is taxed accordingly (even though it may not have been distributed to him).

This applies in two circumstances:

- when either the settlor, their spouse or civil partner retains an interest in the trust (but this does not include widow, widower or separated spouse or equivalent for a civil partner)
- where the trust is for the benefit of a minor unmarried child of the settlor.

The settlor can reclaim any tax payable on trust income from the trust. As it is taxed as income of the settlor who has to pay it, it will, in effect, been paid twice. But since the rate of tax is likely to be higher than that paid in the trust, it is not good tax planning for this situation to arise.

We will look at each of the main types of trust in turn.

5.1.2 Bare Trusts

Income arising within the trust is deemed to be that of the beneficiary, who must include it in his Self-Assessment forms and pay tax on it personally. He will be able to use his Personal Allowance against this income.

5.1.3 Interest in Possession Trusts

In these types of trust, the beneficiary will have a right to the income as and when it arises.

Tax is payable within the trust on income at the same rates as for an individual paying basic rate tax, ie, 7.5% on dividends and 20% for all other income. However, the trust is not entitled to a Personal Allowance.

There is no higher rate tax within the trust. The trustees are responsible for paying the tax. But if the income is paid to the beneficiary, the beneficiary will have to include the income in their tax return and may be liable to additional tax on receipt of trust income, if this takes the beneficiary into the higher rate or additional band. In view of the above, trustees will often mandate the income directly to the beneficiary.

The beneficiary will receive a tax voucher showing the net income after expenses, and this will be broken down into the sources of income, ie, savings, dividends and other income. Management expenses do not reduce the tax payable by the trustees, but may reduce the higher rate tax payable, since they are deducted from the income to be declared by the beneficiary.

The beneficiary will receive a tax voucher showing the net income after expenses, and this will be broken down into the sources of income, ie, savings, dividends and other income.Management expenses do not reduce the tax payable by the trustees, but may reduce the higher-rate tax payable, since they are deducted from the income to be declared by the beneficiary.

5.1.4   Discretionary or Accumulation Trusts

- Trustees are responsible for paying tax on income received by discretionary trusts or accumulation. The first £1,000 is taxed at the basic rate. Non-dividend income is taxed at 20% and dividend income at 7.5%.
- If the settlor has more than one trust, this £1,000 is divided by the number of trusts they have. However, if the settlor has set up five or more trusts, the basic rate band for each trust is £200.
- Where the trust income is over £1,000 then tax is payable at 45% on non-dividend income, and 38.1% on dividend income.
- Trustees do not qualify for the Dividend Allowance introduced in 2016. (For the tax year 2015–2016 the first £1,000 were not subject to additional tax as the tax credit covered them and dividends above that were taxed at 30.56%.
- Tax relief is given on certain allowable expenses, to be set against income (but not investment adviser's fees which must be charged to capital).

If income is accumulated (not paid out), then there is no further tax to pay. However, if income from a discretionary trust is distributed, it carries a 45% tax credit irrespective of the source of that income in the trust (dividend or savings income).

Non-taxpayer	Basic rate taxpayer	Higher rate taxpayer or additional rate taxpayer
Can reclaim some or all of the tax suffered.	Can reclaim 25% of the income falling within the basic rate band.	No further tax to pay.

This can result in a further charge to income tax on the trustees. This is because they will have paid less tax to HMRC than the 45% tax they are vouching to the beneficiary (as a result of the fact there may be dividend income taxed at 38.1%). Since they are providing a tax voucher potentially enabling a beneficiary to reclaim 45% tax (if they are a non-taxpayer), HMRC could be out of pocket. To avoid this situation occurring, the trustees had to pay the extra tax from the trust when income is distributed.

5.2 Capital Gains Tax (CGT)

Capital gains tax is assessed on the trustees of UK resident trusts in a very similar way to that of individuals who are higher rate taxpayers (already covered in Chapter 2 of your studies). Tax payable by trustees decreased from 28% to 20% in 2016–17 (except in the case of residential property which remains at 28%). This applies irrespective of the income of the trust or beneficiaries, except for bare trusts. Tax is due by 31 January in the year following the end of the tax year of disposal.

However, there are a few notable differences when dealing with trusts:

5.2.1 Annual Exemption

The normal CGT annual exemption available for trustees is half of that available to an individual. Since 6 April 2015 this has been £5,550.

However, the trust exemption has to be shared between any trusts set up by the settlor since 6 June 1978, to a minimum of one-fifth per trust.

> **Warning**
>
> Care must be taken here, since the settlor may have a personal pension or a life policy set up in trust which he must include, even if these trusts cannot give rise to a CGT liability. However, occupational pension schemes and former retirement annuities are not included.

Bare trusts and trusts for disabled persons (when the trusts for the vulnerable tax treatment is not applicable) are entitled to the same annual allowance as an individual, ie, £11,100.

Annual Exemption Amounts for Trusts

To summarise, this is how much each trust would be entitled to if there had been more than one trust set up by the same settlor since 6 June 1978.

One Trust	Two Trusts	Three Trusts	Four Trusts	Five Trusts or more	Trust for the disabled
£5,550	£2,775 each	£1,850 each	£1,387.50 each	£1,110 each	£11,100

5.2.2 Holdover Relief

The creation of a trust by the settlor is a disposal for CGT purposes and the market value of the assets at the date of creation of the trust will be used to calculate the amount of any gains payable by the settlor. However, it may be possible to claim holdover relief to avoid a potential tax liability arising at that time.

Holdover relief is a form of CGT deferral where the donor of gifts of certain assets can effectively hold over the gain so that no CGT becomes payable at the time of the gift, but the acquisition cost of the receiver is reduced by the amount of the held over gain. This means that the receiver acquires the assets at the original acquisition cost to the donor. This relief has to be claimed jointly and only applied to certain assets.

From **22 March 2006**, holdover relief is available under most circumstances, for **any assets** placed into trust. In this case, only the settlor would need to claim the relief and advise the trustees accordingly.

> **Warning**
>
> This relief will not be available for bare trusts or trusts which include a minor unmarried child of the settlor (unless this is a trust for a disabled person). Since 9 December 2003, holdover relief has not been available for transfers into a trust, where the settlor, their spouse or civil partner has or may acquire an interest. If this relief is given, and within the clawback period (a period of six years from the end of the year of assessment in which the trust is set up) the settlor either obtains an interest or makes arrangements to obtain an interest at a later date, the relief can be clawed back by HMRC.

In addition, holdover relief may be claimed when trustees transfer assets to beneficiaries. Under these circumstances, the relief must be claimed jointly by the beneficiaries and the trustees. The beneficiaries will effectively acquire the assets at the trustees' acquisition cost, which may enable them to defer the disposal to use their individual annual exemption or partially dispose of the assets each year, again using their individual annual exemptions, to potentially avoid a CGT charge altogether.

5.2.3 Deemed Disposals

In addition to actual disposals within the trust, a charge to CGT may also arise on other occasions within a trust. An example of this would be if an interest in possession ends on the death of a life tenant, and the property passes to the remainderman. For pre-22 March 2006 trusts, since CGT does not generally become payable on death, this often results in a free uplift of values.

> **Warning**
>
> If holdover relief is claimed by the settlor when transferring assets into the trust, these held over gains would normally be chargeable to CGT on the death of the life tenant. Also, if the end of the life tenancy occurs as a result of an action other than death, for example remarriage of the settlor's wife, this would be a deemed disposal by the trustees, and chargeable to CGT.
>
> For lifetime trusts created on or after 22 March 2006, there is generally no CGT uplift on the death of the life tenant.

Another example of a deemed disposal is where a beneficiary becomes absolutely entitled to trust property on achieving a contingency, eg, 21st birthday. Once the beneficiary has become absolutely entitled, the trustees will be holding the assets as bare trustees.

It may be helpful to consider each of the main types of trust in turn.

5.2.4 Bare Trusts

Any gains are treated as the beneficiary's gains and any liability will be payable by them. Any subsequent transfer of assets to the beneficiary will be disregarded for CGT purposes.

Bare trusts for minors continue to have CGT advantages, even if the trust was set up by a parent. Unlike other forms of trust, the gains on bare trusts for minors, if the parent has settled the assets, are chargeable to the minor, not the parent. This means that they will have their full annual exemption available and not the lower trust annual exemption. They are also less likely than the settlor to need their annual exemption for other purposes.

5.2.5   Interest in Possession Trusts

To summarise what was discussed above, the position on the death of a life tenant is as follows:

Pre-22 March 2006 Trusts
- No CGT on death of life tenant – free uplift in acquisition values.
- Held over gains are chargeable on the death of the life tenant.

Example

Jimmy created an Interest in Possession Trust in 1994 with an asset which he had owned for 20 years, valued at £100,000. The value of the asset at 31 March 1982 was £50,000. The gain of £50,000 was held over to the trustees.

The life tenant died on 21 January 2014 and the asset was worth £300,000 at that date.

The gain of £200,000 will not be chargeable to CGT, but the trustees will now be liable for the held over gain of £50,000.

Trusts commencing on or after 22 March 2006
- No CGT on death of life tenant – no uplift in acquisition values
- Held-over gains are chargeable on the death of the life tenant.

In addition, if the trustees allow a beneficiary to occupy a property held in the trust for their main residence, it should be possible to claim principal private residence exemption provided holdover relief was not claimed when the property was placed in trust.

5.2.6   Discretionary Trusts

Pre-22 March 2006 Trusts
- Holdover relief could be claimed by the settlor for business assets or family company shares only.

Trusts Commencing on or After 22 March 2006
- Holdover relief can be claimed by the settlor for all assets.
- Holdover relief is not available where the settlor has, or may acquire, an interest.
- Transfers to beneficiaries are deemed disposals for CGT purposes but holdover relief is available to the trustees in the same way as it was available to the settlor.

5.3 Inheritance Tax

The Finance Act of 2006 drastically changed the tax treatment of trusts.

The creation of a trust is a transfer of value for IHT purposes: the amount of the gift will be assessed as the reduction in the value of the donor's estate, not necessarily the market value.

Once again, we will look at the main types of trust and consider the IHT implications of each one in turn.

5.3.1 Bare Trusts

- The creation of a bare trust is a potentially exempt transfer (PET).
- The trust will only be taxable if the settlor dies within seven years.
- If the beneficiary dies, the trust will be included in his estate for IHT purposes.

5.3.2 Discretionary Trusts

The IHT rules for discretionary trusts now also apply to most lifetime interest in possession trusts.

There are three elements:

Creation of the Trust

- This will be a chargeable lifetime transfer with tax payable at 20% if it takes the settlor's cumulative total over the nil-rate band (NRB).
- If the settlor dies within seven years, there may be further tax to pay. If this is between three and seven years, taper relief may apply.

Periodic Charges (also known as the Principle Charge)

- Apply to the trust, not the settlor.
- Will apply whether or not the settlor is alive or dead.
- This will occur on every ten-year anniversary of the trust creation.
- The charge is 30% of the current lifetime rate (presently 20%). This makes the maximum charge 6% of the value of the trust fund.
- The seven-year IHT cumulation of the settlor immediately before the creation of the trust is taken.
- Any capital distributions within the previous ten years also need to be taken into account.

Exit Charge (also known as the Proportionate Charge)

- This charge applies to capital leaving the trust.
- Taxed at 30% of the effective rate from the start of the trust, or if it is after ten years, the effective rate from the last periodic charge.
- If there was no IHT to pay on creation due to the amount being within the NRB, the effective rate would be nil so there would be no exit charge.
- It is then time apportioned by the number of complete successive quarter years since the last periodic charge (expressed as n/40ths).

Example

John made a transfer of £248,000 to a discretionary trust on 1 October 2000, when the NRB was £242,000. John had made no other gifts prior to setting up the trust. A capital payment of £33,000 was made from the trust to a beneficiary in January 2003.

The value of the trust on 1 October 2010 was £405,000.

No charge on creation since two annual exemptions plus the NRB cover the amount.

No exit charge on capital payment since effective rate was nil.

Periodic Charge

Value of the trust at 10th anniversary	£405,000
plus capital disbursement of	£33,000
total amount subject to IHT	£438,000
less current NRB	£325,000

leaves taxable amount of £113,000 tax at 20%: £22,600

Effective rate: £22,600 ÷ £405,000 = 5.58%

Tax charge: £405,000 x 5.58% x 30% = £6,780 (payable by the trustees from the trust fund)

(Note: alternative method: £113,000 x 6% = £6,780 arrives at the same answer.)

Further example: A further capital payment of £30,000 is made from the trust to a beneficiary on 21 April 2016.

Exit Charge

30% of the effective rate from the last 10th anniversary: 5.58 x 30% =1.674%.

£30,000 capital distributed on 21 April 2016: £30,000 x 1.674% = £502.20.

Time apportionment: 1/10/10 to 21/04/16 = 5 years 6 months = 22 quarter years = 22/40.

£502.20 x 22/40 = £276.21 payable by the recipient.

5.3.3 Trusts for Minors

Rules were introduced by the Finance Act 2006 to replace accumulation and maintenance trusts. Two types of trust were created by the death of a parent. These allow the accumulation of income but do not incur the full application of the periodic or exit charge rules.

Trusts for Bereaved Minors

- May be created on the death of a parent (by will or on intestacy) or under the Criminal Injuries Compensation Scheme.
- Must provide an absolute interest at 18.
- Until then, trust treated as child's for IHT purposes (like pre-2006 interest in possession trusts).
- No periodic charge or exit charge at 18.

18 to 25 Trusts

- May be created on the death of a parent (by will or on intestacy) or under the Criminal Injuries Compensation Scheme.
- Must provide an absolute entitlement by the age of 25.
- Trust treated as child's for IHT purposes until 18.
- Exit charge payable on absolute entitlement based on the period since the beneficiary's 18th birthday.

Chapter Five
Financial Instruments and Products

An exam specification breakdown is provided at the back of this workbook

1. Introduction

In this chapter, we will be building your product knowledge so that you have a good understanding of the different types of investment asset classes, financial instruments and products and schemes available in the UK.

To help you with your examination, we suggest that you use this chapter to bring your existing knowledge up-to-date for those areas that you are familiar with, and use it to fill in those gaps in your knowledge where you may not be dealing with particular types of product on a day-to-day basis.

You must continue reading and extending your understanding of the topics covered through additional study. This workbook does not represent everything you may be expected to know for the examination.

You will see icons or symbols alongside the text. These indicate activities or questions that have been designed to check your understanding and help you validate your understanding.

Here is a guide as to what each of the symbols means:

Question

This identifies a question that will enable you to check your knowledge and understanding.

Analyse

This gives you an opportunity to consider a question posed and compare your answers to the feedback given.

1.1 Objectives

To pass the exam you will need to be able to differentiate between:

- investment asset classes
- financial instruments
- other products and schemes available in the UK.

In particular, you should ensure that for each product or instrument you know its:

- key features
- potential for risk and reward
- advantages and disadvantages to investors
- product pricing and availability
- any special taxation considerations
- any redemption and penalty features that may apply.

You should also know the various products well enough to be able to answer a question that asks you to compare and contrast different products.

2. Bank and Building Society Savings Accounts

2.1 Current Accounts

Current accounts are now offered by banks and most building societies. They are instant access accounts through which the majority of us conduct our day-to-day banking requirements. There is typically no charge for a basic current account as long as it runs in credit, although most banks and building societies now also offer a range of current accounts for which the customer pays a fee to receive a package of added benefits. Some pay interest, although rates tend to be very low.

They are the base account for a range of additional products and services:

- cheque book
- overdrafts
- standing orders and direct debits
- debit cards
- telephone and internet banking facilities
- credit cards.

2.2 Savings Accounts

Savings accounts come in a number of forms, such as branch based, postal, telephone operated, and internet-only versions.

The amounts of interest payable on these products is often (but not exclusively) linked to the cost to the bank or building society of operating that product. For example, a branch-based account requires high street style premises and a relatively large number of staff whereas the other extreme is an internet-only account which can be run from head office by a limited number of staff. As internet-only accounts are cheaper to run, they often pay better rates of interest than branch-based accounts.

Interest payable sometimes gives an indication of risk and the bank or building society's need for additional capital, as was seen recently in the credit crunch. Higher rates can tend to indicate higher risk to the depositor (eg, if the bank is not covered by the UK Financial Services Compensation Scheme [FSCS]).

Instant or easy access accounts, as the name implies, means that depositors can withdraw their money without having to give any notice of their need to withdraw funds. These accounts typically offer the lowest rates of interest. They are particularly useful for holding a reserve of cash for emergencies.

Notice accounts require investors to give a minimum number of days' notice before being able to withdraw funds. In exchange for the notice arrangement, the accounts pay a higher rate of interest. Notice periods vary between financial institutions, but usually start with a minimum of 30 days needing to be given, with 60, 90 and 120-days' notice accounts also being quite common. Investors usually have the ability to forgo the notice period and obtain immediate access to their money, but there will be a financial penalty such as a loss of interest.

Term accounts are those that pay a set rate of interest and run for a set period, normally one, two, three, four or five years, and, normally, the longer the period, the better the rate. There will always be a penalty for withdrawing early and this can be prohibitive.

Regular savings accounts often offer relatively high interest rates to savers who are prepared to commit to save an amount each month. The amount which needs to be paid into the account is usually between £10 and £500 per month and time limits usually apply, in that the high rate of interest applies for, say, up to twelve months, at which point the account typically reverts to an immediate access account earning a lower rate of interest. This means that although the rate of interest may be attractive, it usually only applies to a relatively small amount of money for a short time and therefore doesn't earn the saver much in real terms.

Savings bonds are also being offered by many banks and building societies. With these products, investors tie up their savings for a given period, say one, three or five years, and earn a fixed rate of interest for the life of the bond. Additional deposits and withdrawals may be heavily restricted or not allowed at all. These products are often available for limited periods only.

Depending on the type of savings account, interest may be paid at the end of the term, annually or more frequently. Interest rates may be variable, fixed or tiered, where the more you invest, the higher the rate of interest you earn. Access to some savings accounts is dependent upon having a minimum amount to deposit and some are also limited to a maximum. Since April 2016 banks and building societies have paid interest gross.

As a rule of thumb, better rates of interest can be obtained by tying money into a savings product for a minimum period, but savers should be careful to consider the position should they need to access their money before this period ends. Some accounts don't allow for access before the end of the agreed period, and the saver may find they are worse off than if they had merely used an instant access account, if they have to pay penalty costs for early withdrawal.

A prudent investor will always ensure that sufficient money is kept accessible to cover emergency needs, and that penalties are not incurred.

| Exam Tip! | The weekend financial pages of various newspapers provide a useful summary of current best rates. |

3.   National Savings and Investments (NS&I)

National Savings and Investments (NS&I) are considered to be one of the safest types of investment because they are guaranteed by the UK government.

In addition, they can be purchased either online, over the telephone, through post offices or by post.

NS&I aims to set its interest rates at a level where inflows balance withdrawals, so its investments do not typically offer very attractive returns. In the current market they do offer a degree of security not necessarily offered by equivalent investments.

You will need knowledge of NS&I products for your examination, together with an idea of current rates.

<table>
<tr><td>Exam Tip!</td><td>A helpful 'Quick Guide for Financial Advisers' is available on the NS&I website www.nsandi.com under the Adviser Centre section, which you may wish to consider downloading as part of your revision programme.</td></tr>
</table>

3.1 National Savings Premium Bonds

Product Characteristics	Tax Status/Suitability for Investors	Terms/Penalties for Early Surrender
• Lump sum or monthly investment. • No income paid. • Prizes paid each month ranging from £1 million to £25. • Investments may be for between £100 (£50 for monthly standing orders) and £50,000. • Rate from 1 June 2016: prize fund calculated at 1.25%.	Prizes are tax-free: • No income tax or capital gains tax payable.	• Bonds can be encashed at any time without loss of capital.

3.2 National Saving Certificates (NSCs)

Product Characteristics	Tax Status/Suitability for Investors	Terms/Penalties for Early Surrender
• Lump sum investments earning a guaranteed rate of interest over the term of the investment. • Available for two- and five-year terms. • Fixed interest and index-linked issues. • Investors can purchase both the two- and five-year term certificates, if available. • Investments may be for between £100 and £15,000 per issue. **Not currently on general sale (June 2016), but available for maturing certificates.**	Tax-free: • No income tax or capital gains tax payable.	• NSCs can be encashed early with the loss of 90 days' interest. With index-linked certificates, you will lose all index-linking in the year of encashment. • Investors will be offered alternatives when their certificates mature and these should be considered carefully. If no action is taken they may continue at a lower rate of interest.

3.3   Guaranteed Growth Bonds

Product Characteristics	Tax Status/Suitability for Investors	Terms/Penalties for Early Surrender
• Lump sum term investment available for one, two, three and five year terms. • Guaranteed fixed rate of interest, if held for the full term. • Interest added to the bond annually. • Invest any amount between £500 and £1 million. **Not currently on general sale (June 2016) but available for maturing bonds.**	• Interest is taxable but paid gross.	• 90 days' interest on any amount withdrawn early.

3.4   Guaranteed Income Bonds

Product Characteristics	Tax Status/Suitability for Investors	Terms/Penalties for Early Surrender
• Lump sum term investment available for one, two, three and five year terms. • Guaranteed fixed rate of interest, if held for the full term. • Interest credited to a bank account of your choice monthly. • Invest any amount between £500 and £1 million. **Not currently on general sale (June 2016) but available for maturing bonds.**	• Interest is taxable but paid gross.	• 90 days' interest on any amount withdrawn early.

3.5   Children's Bonds

Product Characteristics	Tax Status/Suitability for Investors	Terms/Penalties for Early Surrender
• Previously called Children's Bonus Bonds. Terms changed September 2012. • Matures once it reaches its first five-year anniversary on or after the child's 16th birthday. • Online, phone and post account. For children under 16 years. Parents, grandparents, great-grandparents can invest. • Minimum balance £25, maximum £3,000 in each issue. • Fixed rate of interest. Five year term. • Current issue is No. 35 paying 2.50% AER, tax-free.	• Tax-free for parents and child.	• Penalty of 90 days' interest.

3.6   Income Bonds

Product Characteristics	Tax Status/Suitability for Investors	Terms/Penalties for Early Surrender
• Lump sum investment. • Minimum investment £500, maximum £1 million. • Variable rate of interest. From 6 June 2016 1.00% gross. • Income is payable into a bank account of the investor's choice, 5th of each month.	• Interest is taxable but paid gross. • Investors will need to declare interest on their tax return. • This provides investors with a 'cash flow' advantage.	• Bonds can be encashed at any time, without notice and without any penalty.

3.7   Direct Saver Account

Product Characteristics	Tax Status/Suitability for Investors	Terms/Penalties for Early Surrender
• Savings account. • Withdrawals online or by phone. • Minimum balance £1, maximum £2 million. • Variable rates of interest, from 6 June 2016 0.8% (gross/AER). • Available to anyone aged 16 or over.	• Interest taxable but paid gross.	• Not applicable.

3.8   Investment Account

Product Characteristics	Tax Status/Suitability for Investors	Terms/Penalties for Early Surrender
• Postal only savings account from May 2012 (no passbook). • Minimum balance £20, maximum £1 million. • Variable rates of interest, from 1 July 2016 0.45% gross/AER. • Available to anyone aged 16 or over. Grandparents can open an account for younger children.	• Interest taxable but paid gross.	• Not applicable.

3.9   Other Currently Available Products

Direct ISA – tax-free cash ISA, online and by phone.

Those products, currently not available to new investors, generally offer renewals on maturing sums to existing investors for similar periods but at different rates.

3.10   Guaranteed Equity Bonds

From time to time, NS&I issue guaranteed equity bonds, the returns on which are linked to the performance of the FTSE 100 index. The last issue (Issue 18) was over a five-year term, giving the growth in the FTSE 100 up to a maximum of 40%.

If the FTSE 100 index grows over the term, investors benefit from that growth (not dividends). If it falls, investors still receive 100% of their original investment. In January 2015, all issues were fully subscribed and new money could not be subscribed to them.

4. The Advantages and Disadvantages of Cash Investments

When considering the types of investments that may be suitable for a client, it is important to consider the advantages and disadvantages from the client's perspective. These products are probably quite familiar to you, so try the following exercise.

 Analyse

Think of as many advantages and disadvantages of cash investments as you can. When you have a list, compare it to the answers below.

Suggestions – Advantages and Disadvantages of Cash Investments

Advantages

- They provide a high level of security for the investor's money (Deposit Protection Scheme).
- The capital on deposit is not exposed to investment risk.
- Immediate access accounts provide a good home for holding short term emergency monies.

Disadvantages

- The real value/purchasing power of the capital may be eroded by inflation.
- Returns are often low.
- Uncertainty of income for the investor. If the interest rate is variable, it will fall and rise with interest rates generally.
- There is no potential for capital growth.

5. Government Debt (Gilts)

The difference between the amount of money that the government spends and the amount of money that it collects through taxes is known as the Public Sector Net Cash Requirement (PSNCR). A significant proportion of this shortfall is funded through the issue of gilt-edged securities (gilts).

A gilt, put very simply, is effectively a tradeable (securitised) IOU from the UK government, acknowledging that the government owes the owner of the gilt some money. In common with most situations when money is lent by one party to another, interest is payable on the borrowing and the borrowing has to be repaid. When we talk about gilts, the interest payment is described as the 'coupon' and the repayment of the borrowing is described as the redemption of the gilt. The amount repaid at the redemption date is described as the **nominal value**.

5.1   The Feature of Gilts – Different Types

The government issues two main types of gilts:

*   conventional gilts
*   index-linked gilts.

Conventional Gilts

These are the simplest type of gilt issued by the UK government and comprise just over 75% of all the gilts that are in issue. They pay a fixed rate of interest (coupon), which is payable half yearly. On maturity, the owner of the gilt will receive the final coupon and the redemption value.

Convention in the market is to quote gilt prices as the price an investor has to pay to purchase £100 of nominal (redemption) value and is a 'clean' price excluding any accrued interest. Accrued interest is quoted separately as + or − a certain number of days. The current market price at the time the investor buys the gilt may be more than or less than £100.

If the current market price of a gilt is above £100, the gilt is described as trading 'above par' and the investor will make a capital loss on the gilt when it is redeemed. If the current market price of the gilt is below £100, the gilt is described as trading 'below par'. The investor will buy the gilt for less than £100 and will therefore make a capital gain when the gilt is redeemed at maturity.

Gilts are described in terms of the percentage coupon they pay and the maturity date, so a gilt issued by the government paying a 4% coupon and maturing in 2022 would be described as:

> 4% Treasury gilt 2022

The amount of coupon paid is the quoted percentage of the nominal value of the gilt and not of the purchase price. An investor paying £118 for £100 nominal of gilt will therefore receive a coupon payment of £4 per year (4% x £100), split into two equal instalments of £2 each.

Differently named gilts have been issued over the years. Recent issues have been named 'Treasury Stock', but previous issues have been named 'Exchequer Stock', 'Conversion Stock' 'Consolidated Stock' and 'War Loan'. Although the name indicates the purpose or features of the original issue of the stock, there is now little practical significance in the name as they are all obligations which HM Treasury is liable to repay.

Index-Linked Gilts

In addition to conventional gilts, the UK government has, since 1981, been issuing index-linked gilts. They now account for almost 25% of all the gilts in issue.

The quoted coupon is typically quite low, but is increased in line with how much inflation has increased over the time since the gilt was originally issued. The coupon payments are therefore 'real' rates of return and the income from these gilts is inflation proofed.

A similar process applies to the redemption value. This too is increased in line with how much inflation has increased since the gilt was issued, and protects the investor's capital against inflation, although it is not growing in real terms.

To use the technical term, the coupon payments and redemption value are 'uplifted'. The measure of inflation used to calculate the uplifting is the Retail Price Index (RPI), not the Consumer Price Index (CPI) which is now used as the Bank of England inflation target and is often quoted by the government and media.

It would be logical for the inflation uplifting to take account of the increase in inflation for the exact period from the date of issue to the date of payment of the coupon/redemption proceeds. Unfortunately this is not the case. For gilts issued before 2005, the allowance for the inflation uplifting is calculated with an eight-month time lag. For those issued after 2005, a three-month time lag is used (see facing page).

Example Calculation

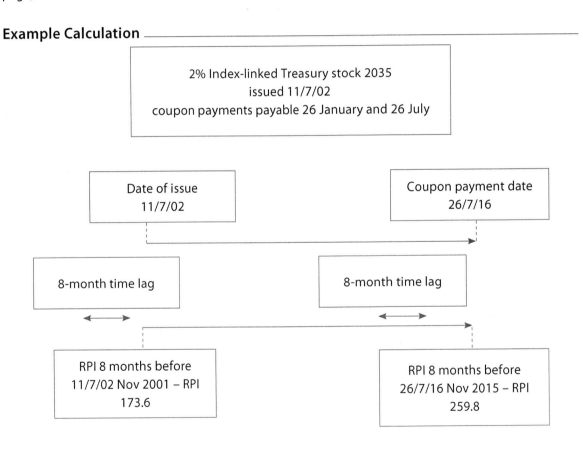

Formula for calculating the July 2016 coupon payment:

$$\frac{2\%}{2} \times \frac{259.8 \text{ (RPI 8 months prior to coupon payment)}}{173.6 \text{ (RPI 8 months prior to issue)}} = 1.4965\%$$

Assuming our investor owns £15,000 gilts, the coupon payment would be:

$$\frac{£15,000}{£100} \times 1.4965 = £224.47$$

Exam Tip!	In addition to the exam paper, you will be given a supplementary information pack containing a copy of the Debt Management Office (DMO) Gilts Daily Price List. The examiner often comments that students don't use this information effectively. You should familiarise yourself with the information contained in this list. Your tutor will give out a copy and go through the contents with you on your course.

Since 2005, index-linked gilts have been issued with a shorter time lag of three months, and the methodology for calculating the coupons and redemptions values is significantly different from the above.

The newer methodology uses an index ratio to measure the growth in inflation since the gilt was originally issued.

Exam Tip!	You need not concern yourself with calculating an index ratio. In practice they are published on the DMO website www.dmo.gov.uk following the publication of the RPI each month. For the exam you will find them on your Gilts Daily Price List.

Example Calculation

> 1 1/8% Index-linked Treasury gilt 2037
> issued 21/2/2007
> coupon payments payable 22 May and 22 November

$$\text{Interest payment for } 22/5/16 = \frac{1.125 \text{ (Coupon)}}{2} \times 1.28746 \text{ (index ratio } 22/2/16) = £0.72419$$

Floating Rate Gilts

Although there are currently none in issue, the government has, in the past, issued some floating rate gilts, paying a variable coupon comprising a margin above (or below) a reference rate such as the London inter-bank bid rate (LIBID). The coupon payable is reset periodically in line with market rates.

With regard to the coupon, in the past there have also been issues where there were:

- **floors** – a minimum level of coupon that is paid
- **caps** – a maximum level of coupon that is paid
- **collars** – in which the coupon floats dependent on market rates between a floor and a cap.

The coupon payments on these gilts were paid quarterly, and as the coupon moved in line with market interest rates, they tended to trade close to par value.

5.2   Break-Even Inflation Rates

The break-even rate represents the average rate at which inflation must be over the remaining life of an index-linked gilt for the investor to see equal returns by buying the inflation-linked gilt as opposed to having bought a conventional gilt of similar maturity date. This will depend on the investor's tax rate as the inflation uplift of the index-linked repayment is free of capital gains tax (CGT).

If inflation rises above the break-even rate, the index-linked gilt will provide a better return. If inflation falls below the break-even rate, the index-linked gilt will provide a lesser return.

5.3   Issues by Local Authorities

In addition to the central government raising finance through the issue of bonds, local government has the power to do the same.

In the past, local authorities issued bonds to raise money to finance the building of infrastructure in our cities. There is no legal constraint on local authorities still doing so, but it has been actively discouraged since the 1980s when we started to see a much more centralised approach to economic control.

Since December 2004, Transport for London (itself designated as a local authority) has raised funds through the issue of local authority bonds, to finance improvements in the transport infrastructure. In 2011, it raised £600 million to help finance the Crossrail project.

The return on these instruments tends to be higher than that on gilts, as the risk is perceived to be higher. They are not government guaranteed in the same way as gilts.

The types of bonds that local authorities can issue include the following:

- **Yearlings** – these are short-term debt instruments issued with maturities of either one or two years, issued in minimum denominations of £1,000 nominal.
- **Local Authority Stocks** – these are very similar to gilts, in that they are longer-term bonds, paying a fixed coupon semi-annually.
- **Fixed Loans/Local Authority Mortgages** – these instruments are known as local authority bonds or mortgages, and are issued for a set term during which the local authority pays the holder interest. Terms typically range from one to six years and rates vary depending on the issuing authority. They constitute a lump sum investment where no additions or withdrawals are allowed, and the capital is repaid at the end of the term.

5.4   Redemption Dates and the Use of Sinking Funds

Most gilts have a specified redemption date. Some, however, are different in style.

Double-Dated Gilts

In the past, the government has issued double-dated gilts, for instance 7¾% Treasury Loan 2012–15. There are no such issues among current gilts. The government can choose to redeem these gilts on any day between the first and final maturity dates, providing it gives at least three months' notice.

When it chooses to redeem will depend on whether these gilts represent cheap or expensive borrowing for the government. As rates were lower in the market place when 2012 arrived, the government redeemed the gilt at the earliest opportunity because it could re-borrow the money at lower rates. If rates are higher in the markets, the government is likely to redeem these gilts at the latest possible date.

Undated Gilts

There are also a small number of undated gilts in issue, some of which date back as far as the 19th century. Technically the redemption of these bonds is at the government's discretion, after a specified date, which has long since gone. The government recently announced the repayment of some of these undated stocks and this may see the whole sub-sector finally flushed out in due course if market yields stay low.

Sinking Funds

A sinking fund makes a provision for the repayment of the capital outstanding under a bond, and therefore reduces the default risk of the bond.

They usually work in one of two ways:

- A counterpart fund can be established, where the issuer of the bond puts money aside each year in readiness for redemption.
- Alternatively, the issuer may repay a set proportion of the bond at set intervals. For example, 1/15th of a bond's issue may be redeemed every year for fifteen years.

The method of selecting the bonds to be redeemed will be specified in the terms of issue, and may be by way of lottery, whereby serial numbers of the bonds to be redeemed are drawn at random. If, however, it is agreed in the terms of issue that the bonds will be redeemed at par and the bonds are trading at less than par value in the markets, the issuer may choose to purchase bonds in the market with a total par value equal to the amount that is to be redeemed.

There is usually a period during the initial life of a bond where the sinking fund does not operate. In the example above, for instance, the bond may be a twenty-year issue with no redemptions during the first five years, and 1/15th of the bond is redeemed annually thereafter.

The existence of a sinking fund may reduce the risk associated with a particular bond.

5.5   Gilt Pricing and Accrued Interest

We have seen so far that gilts are priced per £100 of nominal or redemption value, but the gilts market also adopts a 'clean' and 'dirty' pricing system.

If an investor wishes to buy a gilt, they will be quoted the clean price. The clean price is the price that is quoted in the financial press.

When they actually come to pay for the gilt, they will pay the dirty price. This comprises the clean price plus an allowance for accrued interest. For the majority of time that gilts are traded, the dirty price will be more than the clean price.

This is how it works:

Seven business days before the coupon payment is due, the identity of the registered owner of the gilt is established, and the coupon payment for the whole half-year is paid to that investor on the coupon payment date.

The owner of a gilt, who sells it between coupon payments, will be entitled to interest which will be paid to the new holder on the next coupon date. When buying a gilt, the purchaser must therefore compensate the seller for the interest that was accrued during the seller's period of ownership.

The following diagram illustrates the point.

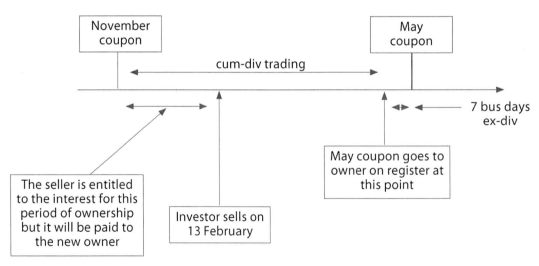

The clean price plus (or minus) the accrued interest, makes up the dirty price.

During the cum-div trading period, the accrued interest is added to the clean price to compensate the seller for the interest accrued, which will be paid to the new holder.

During the ex-div period, the accrued interest is deducted from the clean price to make up the dirty price. If a gilt is sold during this period, the purchaser will have owned the gilt for a few days before the coupon payment is made. As such, they will be entitled to the accrued interest for the number of days that they owned the gilt, before the coupon payment date. As the coupon for the whole half-year will be paid to the seller, the seller must rebate the purchaser the accrued interest that the purchaser is entitled to. The purchaser therefore pays the clean price for the gilt, with the value of the accrued interest owed to him by the previous owner, deducted from the cost.

Accrued Interest Calculation Example

Julia sells a 5% Treasury stock 2025 on 27 November (settlement on 28 November). The clean price is £128.6 and the coupon payment dates for this particular gilt are 7 March and 7 September. What is the dirty price paid to Julia by the purchaser of the gilt (assume no commissions etc)?

Step 1: Calculate the number of actual days that Julia has owned the gilt since the last coupon payment date

8 September (day after coupon payment date) to 28 November (settlement days) = 82 days

Step 2: Calculate the number of actual days in the coupon period (Assume from March 2015; redeemed 7 March 2025)

Sep	=	23 (8th – 30th)
Oct	=	31
Nov	=	30
Dec	=	31
Jan	=	31
Feb	=	28
Mar	=	7 (1st – 7th)
Total	=	181

Step 3: Calculate the proportion of the half-yearly coupon payment for which the purchaser must compensate Julia

$$£100 \times (5\% \times 1/2) \times 82/181 = £1.13$$

Step 4: Calculate the dirty price

£128.6 (clean price) + £1.13 (accrued interest) = £129.73

5.6 Calculation and Interpretation of the Flat Yield

Yields are a measure of return expressed as a percentage of the purchase price of the investment. You should know how to calculate and interpret three types of yield in relation to gilts. The first of these is the flat yield.

Formula:

$$\textbf{Flat yield} = \frac{\textbf{annual coupon (gross)}}{\textbf{price (clean)}} \times \textbf{100}$$

The flat yield, which is also known as the running, interest or income yield, merely looks at the income received by way of coupon, and expresses it as a percentage of the amount paid for the gilt. It is useful for an investor seeking income and not expecting to hold the gilt until maturity.

The flat yield has however, a number of drawbacks:

* It only takes into account the return by way of coupon, not capital, and is therefore an incomplete measure of return. If the gilt is held to redemption the investor may also make a profit or loss on their capital depending on whether the purchase price was above or below £100.
* If the investor is a taxpayer, they will be liable to pay income tax on the coupon received. This measure also ignores the investor's tax status.

? Using the formula above, calculate the flat yield for the following gilt. You can check your answer below.

A Treasury gilt is paying a 5% coupon and is priced at £128.6

A Treasury gilt paying a 5% coupon and priced at £128.6 would give a flat yield of:

5/128.6 x 100 = 3.89%

5.7 Calculation and Interpretation of the Gross Redemption Yield

The gross redemption yield is a far more accurate way to calculate the return on a gilt, because it takes both the income and potential capital gain (or loss) at maturity into account.

A simple way of calculating this is as follows:

5% Treasury gilt 2025
Clean price £128.6

Step 1: Calculate the flat yield

£5/£128.6 x 100 = 3.89%

Step 2:   Calculate the annual per cent return on the profit or loss element

£128.6 (current price) – £100.00 (redemption value) = £28.6

Divide the profit (or loss) by the number of years until redemption – £28.6/10 = –£2.86 per annum

Divide this by the current price – £2.86/£128.6 x 100 = –2.22%

Step 3:   Total the return from both parts of the calculation:

+3.89%
<u>–2.22%</u>
<u>+1.67%</u>

Although this above example demonstrates the concept, in reality the calculation is more complex and incorporates the time value of money. In practice, a financial calculator will give a more accurate result. In conclusion, stocks priced below par have a gross redemption yield which exceeds gross flat yield. Conversely, stocks above par (common nowadays) produce a gross redemption yield below gross flat yield.

The gross redemption yield is also referred to as the 'yield to maturity'.

For the examination, income yields and gross redemption yields are calculated for you on the Gilts Daily Price List.

5.8   Calculation and Interpretation of the Net Redemption Yield

The net redemption yield takes the gross redemption yield a step further and calculates the after-tax redemption yield for an investor, taking into account their personal tax status.

The tax status of gilts is:

*   profits on redemption are exempt from CGT
*   coupon payments are subject to income tax.

The return from the coupon must therefore be reduced by the amount of tax payable, to give an investor's after-tax return.

Using the example above:

Step 1:   Calculate the flat yield   £5/£128.6 x 100 = 3.89%

Step 2: Reduce this by the tax rate of the investor

Tax Status	BRTP (20%)	HRTP (40%)	45% Tax Rate
Gross flat yield	3.89%	3.89%	3.89%
Less tax payable	−20%	−40%	−45%
Net flat yield	3.11%	2.33%	2.14%

Step 3: Add the annual return from the capital profit or loss element, to calculate the net redemption yield

Tax Status	BRTP (20%)	HRTP (40%)	45% Tax Rate
Net flat yield	+3.11%	+2.23%	+2.04%
Loss to redemption	−2.22%	−2.22%	−2.22%
Net redemption yield	+0.89%	+0.01%	−0.18%

In this example, in one case, the yield is actually negative and a more accurate calculation will be achieved on a financial calculator. Nevertheless, it illustrates the tax inefficiency of this stock for an additional rate taxpayer.

5.9   The Yield Curve

In bond markets, much reference is made to the yield curve.

The yield curve is a graphical representation of the gross redemption yields (yields to maturity) for government bonds, plotted over a range of maturities. When the yield for each maturity has been plotted on the graph, a line of best fit is drawn through the points, and the yield curve, also known as the term structure of interest rates, is created.

The shape of the yield curve changes over time, and for the exam, you will need to know the shapes and theories explaining them. Although there are many different theories, the shape of the 'real world' yield curve is always likely to be influenced by a combination of these factors, although some factors may be more significant in different situations.

The Normal Yield Curve

The normal yield curve is upward sloping, to the right, as per the following diagram, although it can be down sloping (inverted), horizontal (flat), humped or a mixture of shapes along different parts of the curve.

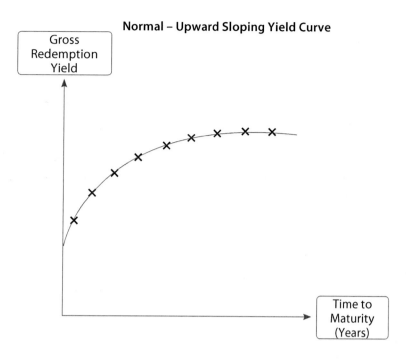

Normal – Upward Sloping Yield Curve

Some of the main theories that explain the possible shapes of the yield curve are explained below.

Liquidity Preference Theory

This theory suggests that an investor who invests in longer-dated bonds has to wait longer for their money to be repaid to them and therefore take additional risk which requires a greater return. It therefore explains the shape of the upward sloping normal curve.

Shorter-dated bonds return the investor's money sooner and therefore represent a lower risk, and the points plotted on the yield curve for these are correspondingly lower.

Pure Expectations Theory

This theory states that long-term yields are the geometric average of expected short-term rates. The yield curve therefore becomes a reflection of market expectations of interest rates.

When the yield curve is inverted, as seen in the following diagram, short-term interest rates are higher than long-term rates.

Given the inverse relationship between bond prices and interest rates, if the market expects yields at the longer end of the curve to increase, interest rates are likely to increase and bond prices will fall. The theory predicts that in anticipation of this movement, bond traders will sell long-dated gilts.

If market expectations are that long yields will fall, interest rates will fall, bond prices will rise in which case the theory predicts that bond traders will buy long-dated gilts.

There is often an inverted yield curve just before a recession, because interest rates tend to be reduced to kick-start the economy and investors buy at the long end of the yield curve in order to profit from the anticipated fall in bond yields and corresponding rise in bond prices.

NB: the bond market is actually a collection of different bond markets and this is highlighted in times of market stress when higher quality issues become disassociated from lower quality issues as investors seek low risk bonds as a safe haven (eg, AAA rate government issues) and shun poorer quality issues. When discussing the yield curve, it should be noted that you need to understand which yield curve is being referred to. In the UK this will normally be the UK gilt yield curve as shown on a gilts daily price list.

Inflation expectations also have a bearing on the prices of bonds – although this is much more significant at the longer end of the curve. If it is anticipated that there will be a period of high inflation, then the real value of the return obtained from the bond will fall the longer it is held. Consequently the yield needed to reward investors for holding the bond to maturity needs to be higher for longer maturity bonds.

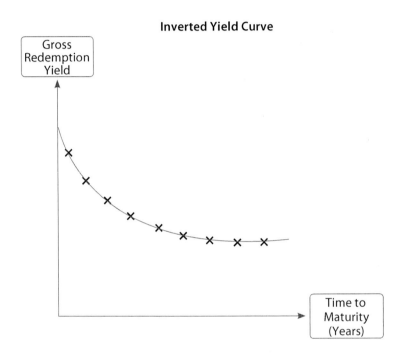

Segmentation Theory (or Preferred Habitat)

This theory considers the short, medium and long-dated bonds on the curve to belong to different markets, with differing forces of supply and demand to take into account.

Pension funds, for instance, have a preference for investing in longer-dated gilts to match their liabilities, whereas banks and insurance companies have a need to maintain liquidity in their investments, and therefore have a preference for investing at the short end of the curve. You may sometimes see discontinuities or anomalies in the curve where there is a gap between two such influences or a change from an influence in one part of the curve to a different influence in another part of the curve.

Government and Central Bank Policy

In order to control the economy, governments and central banks use the supply of and demand for government bonds as a tool for stimulating or cooling economic growth. At the most basic level, governments initially tended to borrow from investors in order to fund particular activities or shortfalls: from 1997 to 2000 the UK government reduced the amount of gilts outstanding and on the face of it, its total debt. What used to be known as the Public Sector Borrowing Requirement (PSBR) was rebranded the PSNCR. However, since 2000, vastly more has been spent by the government than has been generated by the economy, and as a result the government has increased borrowing by issuing more gilts.

A central bank may offer to buy back its debt, and although this has previously been done on a regular basis using funds in existence, the UK and US governments have used this method recently to boost their economies in what has been called quantitative easing (QE). This has differed significantly from the usual government bond buy-backs in that the governments in question have electronically created more of their own currency to pay for the bonds they are buying back, and on a massive scale, giving rise to fears of high (or even hyper) inflation. While theoretically purchasing bonds should push down the yield curve (which it has at the shorter end), the expectation of future high inflation as not yet impacted on the longer end of the curve, where yields are close to record low levels.

5.10   Other Determinates of the Yield Curve

Taxation

As seen earlier, the coupon on gilts is liable to income tax, but any capital gain on a gilt is free of CGT. For higher rate taxpayers, it is more beneficial to invest in gilts paying a lower coupon and generating a capital gain on maturity. Due to present low interest rates, most conventional gilts sell above par and they are therefore tax inefficient. This increases the attraction of index-linked gilts, particularly for higher rate taxpayers.

Bond investment strategies like equity investment strategies revolve very much around market timing and security selection. Market timing techniques involve predicting changes in interest rates and yields, which result in the prices of bonds falling or rising, and security selection techniques involve looking for underpriced and overpriced securities.

Anomaly Switching

A low risk, low return bond investment strategy is anomaly switching. This involves switching or swapping one bond for another where the characteristics of both bonds will be very similar (maturity, coupon and credit rating), but there is a price or yield differential. The rationale is that similar bonds should be similarly priced and if they are not, an arbitrage opportunity arises.

The expensive bond is sold and the cheap bond purchased. When the anomaly in the market is worked through, the transaction is effectively closed out. These investment opportunities are short-term, as the forces of supply and demand in the market act quickly to realign bond prices. If a bond is undervalued due to a short term anomaly, demand for the bond will cause the price to rise, eliminating the opportunity. If the price of a bond is too high (ie, overvalued), investors will sell the bond, depressing the price and bringing it down to a more realistic level.

Policy Switching

This involves switching investment from one bond to another, but this time the bond's characteristics are quite different. Something is expected to happen in the market, which will change the price of one bond relative to another, for instance a credit rating change. This type of switching is a higher risk, higher return strategy.

Log on to a financial website such as the market data section of Bloomberg and have a look at the current shape of the yield curve.

It is higher risk because, unlike anomaly switching, it involves a movement along the yield curve; taking a view on the direction of interest rates.

5.11   Bonds and Duration

Interest rates have an influence on bond prices due to market forces, ie, if an investor can receive a 3% return on cash, why would they buy a bond with the same level of risk only to receive a 2.8% yield? Therefore, if interest rates available on cash change, bonds have to remain competitive investments by offering a similar yield after accounting for risk differences between the two (nb, bond dealers tend to talk about yields rising/falling not prices falling/rising). As interest rates have an effect on the bond market:

*   If interest rates go up   –   bond yields go up   –   bond prices go down.
*   If interest rates go down   –   bond yields go down –   bond prices go up.

This volatility in bond prices translates into risk for an investor. The problem is that not all bond prices change by the same amount if interest rates change.

As a general rule, all other things being equal:

*   **Longer-dated bonds are more volatile than shorter-dated bonds.**
    Consider two different bonds. One has ten years until maturity and the other has only a few months to go until maturity. Interest rates increase. As a result, both bonds are less attractive than they were the previous day, compared with cash.

    The price of both bonds will fall. The price of the longer-dated bond will fall by a higher amount, because the reduction in the price needs to compensate buyers for receiving what is now perceived to be a less attractive coupon for a longer period. The price of a short-dated bond only has to alter a small amount to compensate the investor for a short period of holding the investment before they receive the redemption proceeds and are free to invest elsewhere.

    As bonds approach maturity, the price at which they change hands gets closer and closer to par value (£100) due to this effect. This is known as 'pulling to redemption'.

- **Low coupon bonds are more volatile than high coupon bonds.**
  The coupon payments are cash flows into the account of the investor, followed by the redemption payment. If two bonds have the same time to redemption, the one which represents the greater risk is the one with the lower coupon payments as a greater proportion of your cash is being returned a long way in the future. The higher coupon bond is paying a larger proportion of the total cash flows much sooner, and although the biggest cash flow still comes at redemption, the fact that it pays more cash back to the investor sooner means that it represents less of a risk.

As a rule of thumb, we can see that investors seeking to minimise risk (price sensitivity) should be buying higher coupon bonds with shorter maturity dates, but which of the following bonds is the most volatile:

- a low coupon bond with a short time until maturity?
- a high coupon bond with a long time to maturity?

To know which, we would need to some more details in order to calculate specifically which is more volatile.

A measure called 'Macaulay's Duration' (also sometimes known as 'relative duration' or just duration) measures the sensitivity of the price of a bond to a change in interest rates. It is the weighted average time to the receipt of the returns from holding a particular bond.

You aren't required to be able to calculate duration for the exam, but you need to know the determinants of the calculation. It is useful to have a look at how the calculation is done, and its components.

Example

> **5% Coupon Bond**
> **3 years until maturity**
> **Gross Redemption Yield 7%**

Year of payment	Cashflow	Calculate Present Value	=	Present Value x Time in years until payment	=
T1	£5	$£5/1.07^1 =$	£4.67	4.67 x 1 =	4.67
T2	£5	$£5/1.07^2 =$	£4.37	4.37 x 2 =	8.74
T3	£105	$£105/1.07^3 =$	£85.71	85.71 x 3 =	257.13
Totals			**£94.75**		**£270.54**

Final Step: 270.54/94.75 = 2.86 years

So we see in this example that the average weighted time taken to receive the returns from this bond is 2.86 years.

Using Macaulay's Duration

The bond with the highest duration is the bond whose price will move the most, for a given change in interest rates.

The Determinants of the Calculation

The calculation takes into account the:

- **coupon rate (which determines the size of the cash-flows)** – the higher the coupon, the lower the duration – there is an inverse relationship between the two.
- **time to maturity** – an increase in maturity will increase duration and vice-versa. Duration varies directly with the time to maturity. As the remaining life of a bond reduces, so does duration.
- **yield (which determines the present value of each cash-flow)** – if the yield increases, the present value of each cash-flow will decrease. As the present value of each cash-flow is multiplied by time, proportionally the values in the future are reduced at a greater rate, thereby lowering duration. There is an inverse relationship between the two.

In technical terms, duration is the weighted average of the timing of the bond's cash flows, using the present values of those cash flows as weights.

In more general terms, it can be thought of as the elasticity of bond prices with regard to interest rates, or a measure (in time) of how quickly a bond will repay its true cost.

Bond Investment Strategy using Duration

A successful bond trader will look to alter the duration of their bond portfolio over time depending on expectations of the economy and interest rates.

If a bond manager is expecting a bull market (prices of bonds rising), it is likely they will adjust their portfolio so that the overall duration of the portfolio is longer. Thus it will contain more bonds with prices that will increase when interest rates fall.

Conversely, if a bond manager is expecting a bear market (prices of bonds falling), it is likely they will adjust their portfolio so that overall duration of the portfolio is shorter. Thus it will contain fewer bonds with prices that will decrease heavily when interest rates rise.

This technique is known as 'duration switching' or rate 'anticipation switching' (see Section 5.10 on policy switching).

Modified Duration

If we had a list of bonds and calculated the Macaulay's duration for each, we would be able to identify the bond price that will move the most when interest rates change.

What the measure doesn't do is quantify by how much a bond price will change.

This is where 'modified duration' comes in. In technical terms, it calculates the percentage change in the price of a bond for a 1% change in interest rates.

The formula for calculating it is:

$$\text{Modified duration} = \frac{\text{Macaulay's duration}}{(1 + \text{GRY})}$$

So, for the above example:

$$\frac{2.86}{1.07\%} = 2.67\%$$

Interpretation

For every 1% point change in interest rates, the bond's price will alter up/down by 2.67%.

Usefulness as a Measure of Price Volatility

Modified duration gives an approximation of the amount a bond's price will change, and is only useful for small changes in interest rates.

The formula we have seen suggests that there is a straight line relationship between changes in interest rates and bond prices. In the example above, we said that for every 1% change in interest rates, the bond's price will change by 2.67%.

Convexity

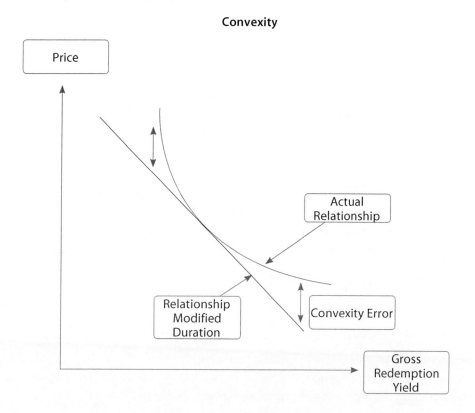

In practice, this is not the case. The actual relationship between yield and price is convex as shown on the above diagram. Convexity is beyond the scope of the syllabus, so it is not covered in detail in these notes. Suffice to say that because of the concept of convexity, modified duration will:

- overestimate the fall in a bond's price, and
- underestimate the rise in a bond's price.

5.12 Gilt Strips

The acronym STRIPS stands for Separately Trading Registered Interest and Principal of Securities. The stripping of a gilt involves taking a standard interest bearing gilt and splitting it into its individual cash flows, ie, coupons and redemption, which can then be bought and sold separately.

Let's look at an example:

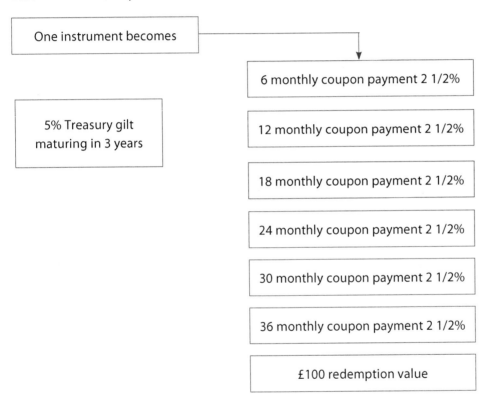

Each instrument then becomes a zero coupon instrument which doesn't pay the investor any interest during the period it is held. The holder merely receives the nominal value of the strip on maturity.

Strips have a duration equal to the term of the single cash payment.

Strips trade at a discount to their face value until maturity.

Advantages of Investing in Gilt Strips

- Single cash flows can be matched against known future liabilities.
- There is no reinvestment risk when investing in strips. (Reinvestment risk is the risk that an investor is unable to reinvest a coupon paid out, at the same rate of coupon as the original gilt.)

5.13 Trading Government Debt

There is a very active market in gilts, which operates through a system of gilt-edged market makers (GEMMs).

GEMMs are appointed by the DMO and have a number of rights and responsibilities, one of which is to quote two-way prices throughout the trading day for all gilts, thereby providing liquidity to the market.

The system is dissimilar to that where equities are bought and sold, in that there is no centralised market place as such, and the GEMMs can choose the system by which they make their prices known to the market.

They deal continuously with major professional investors such as institutional investors and custodians.

Private investors can access the gilt market by purchasing through a stockbroker or a bank or can also use the DMO gilt purchase and sale service, an execution-only postal service operated on behalf of the DMO by Computershare.

An investor purchasing or selling through a stockbroker is likely to incur higher commission charges than if they use the DMO service, but there are advantages:

- Stockbrokers will find the best price available for the investor's purchase or sale, organise all the paperwork and may be able to provide advice on the transaction.
- The investor will also know the price at which they have completed the trade. With the DMO service, this will not be set until the application has been received and actioned.
- In addition, the trade will settle T+1, whereas the DMO service settles on a T+3 basis.

5.14 Reasons for Investing in Government Debt

To consolidate all you have learnt about gilts, think of and list five reasons for investing in UK government debt. There are some suggestions below, with which you can compare your answers.

Six reasons to invest in gilts (UK government debt):

1. they are guaranteed by the British government and with a credit rating close to AAA and therefore considered to be a very secure investment (virtually free of default risk)
2. they provide a regular, stable income
3. index-linked gilts provide an inflation-protected real return
4. any capital gain is tax-free
5. they can be held within an ISA also providing a tax-free income, although the tax-free status of the ISA means that the capital gains exemption is not useful if a profit is made, and
6. their prices tend to be considerably less volatile than those of equities.

6. Corporate Debt

6.1 The Features and Redemption Terms of Different Types of Corporate Debt

One of the main distinguishing features between gilts and corporate bonds is that investors who purchase corporate debt face a greater risk that the company issuing the bond will fail to pay the coupon payments and/or the redemption value. This risk is described as credit risk. This is discussed in Section 6.2 on credit ratings.

Companies tend to issue bonds with more features, when compared to bonds issued by a government. For instance, they may issue convertible bonds and secured bonds, both of which are explained in detail below.

Other distinguishing features include:

Deeply Discounted/Zero Coupon Bonds

As the names imply, these are bonds that pay either a very low coupon or none at all. These bonds trade at a discount to par value, and the investor's return is tied up in the capital gain made at redemption.

Warrants

Bonds may be issued with sweeteners attached, such as a warrant. Warrants give holders the right to buy new shares in a company at a pre-agreed price at a fixed date in the future. A warrant can be detached from the bond that it is issued with, and be traded separately in the market. (They are covered in some detail in the chapter on derivatives.)

Eurobonds

Eurobonds could perhaps be more accurately described as international bonds. You should be aware that they are not specifically bonds issued in euros or in Europe!

Technically, they are bonds issued in a currency other than the currency of the home country, so for instance, a bond issued in Japanese yen in America would be a eurobond, as would a bond issued in euros in the UK. They often involve three different international aspects:

- issuing company
- currency of issue
- country of issue.

They are not limited to one domestic market, but are usually traded in several financial centres. They are mainly unsecured in nature and tend to be issued in bearer form.

Interest is usually paid annually against the presentation of the relevant coupon to an appointed paying agent, without the deduction of tax (ie, no withholding tax). This does not mean that they are tax-free, merely that investors should declare their income from the instruments in the jurisdictions in which they are liable to pay tax.

Bullet Redemption

The majority of bonds are issued on terms which require the issue to be redeemed on one set redemption date. This is known as 'bullet redemption' or 'balloon redemption'. This means that although annual interest payments are made by way of the coupon, the repayment of the full principal loan is made all in one go as opposed to being amortised over a period of time.

Foreign Bonds

These are bonds in the home currency of the country where they are issued, but they are issued by an overseas company. An example would be a bond issued in sterling in the UK, but issued by an American company.

These bonds have names that are linked to the country of issue, so, for example, a bond issued in sterling in the UK by a foreign company is known as a 'bulldog'. A bond issued in Japanese yen in Japan by a foreign company is known as a 'samurai'. There are many more examples.

Callable Bonds

Callable bonds may be redeemed at the issuing company's option, usually on or after a particular date during the term of the issue. One reason a company may call a bond and redeem it early, is if interest rates are lower in the market than under the terms of the issued bond. A call provision would enable it to redeem the more costly bond early, and potentially re-borrow the money at lower rates.

Puttable Bonds

A bond with a put provision enables an investor to insist that a bond is redeemed early at a pre-specified rate. Given the relationship between interest rates and bond prices, this operates to the investor's benefit should interest rates rise, as it effectively acts as a floor on the price/value of the bond.

Coupon Structures

As we have seen, coupons are often fixed. They may also be variable and linked by way of a margin above or below a reference rate.

Another coupon structure is a stepped coupon. As the name implies, the coupon rises at preset intervals over the life of the bond. This is advantageous for the company, in that it provides it with cheaper funds during the early years of the borrowing.

6.2   The Structure and Relevance of Credit Ratings in the Evaluation Process

Given that corporate bonds are subject to credit risk and that most private investors don't have sufficient knowledge or expertise to be able to adequately assess the credit risk on individual bonds, there needs to be a system that looks at this aspect for them.

When a corporate bond is issued, the issuing company will pay for one or more of the credit rating agencies to evaluate the credit risk attached to the bond, and rate the bond accordingly.

The rating is a standardised and concise way of communicating the opinion of the credit ratings agency on the ability of the issuing company to be able to meet its financial obligations, ie, pay the coupons and redemption proceeds when they fall due. It does not constitute a recommendation to buy the bonds.

Ratings are given for each individual bond issue. Different bonds issued by the same company may have different ratings. This is because two bonds issued by the same company can have very different terms and conditions. A secured bond, for example, is likely to have less credit risk than a bond issued by the same company without the benefit of any security. The two bonds are likely to have different credit ratings.

The rating agencies consider a range of information, including financial performance, operating policies, risk management strategies, business environment, levels of assets and liabilities, strength of the management team, the sector and environment in which the company operates and more.

 Analyse

In recent times, the credit rating agencies have been the subject of much criticism. Find out what the criticisms are, and the current position.

Ratings agencies have received criticism (mostly in times of economic stress) that their methods of analysis are too inflexible and that ratings have not necessarily given a true picture of the credit risk posed by a bond, either due to their system being slow to react to real world events, or through having a conflict of interests as they are remunerated by the companies whose debt they rate.

This having been said, even if the actual rating is not changed, a bond may receive a 'negative outlook' warning which alerts the market to the fact that the rating may be downgraded in the near future.

In addition, investors always take the final responsibility on the principle of caveat emptor (buyer beware). This can be seen in operation in the bond market. It has, for example, been possible to find a AAA rated bond issued by a large well-known institution, trading on yields more comparable to those available on bonds many notches lower in the credit ratings system. This is due to the market pricing in the information and views it has on the issuing company and effectively ignoring the published credit ratings. A bond that is initially classified as investment grade but, on review, is reclassified as non-investment grade is known as a fallen angel.

It should therefore be borne in mind that while they remove a lot of the work for investors, published credit ratings are not the only source of information which should be considered when investing in bonds and, although they are generally considered to be of lower risk than equities, default risk can change rapidly in times of market stress. In extreme cases, the volatility of some bonds at the lower end of the credit ratings scale may become just as volatile as equities.

Credit ratings are split between investment grade (BBB–/BBa3 and above) and non-investment grade (BB+/Ba1 and below). The lower the rating, the higher the risk the investor takes and therefore the higher a return or coupon the market will demand. The threshold at which investment grade becomes non-investment grade is significant, because many banks and fund managers are not allowed to hold non-investment grade bonds in their portfolios. The fact that non-investment grade bonds are also colloquially known as junk bonds gives an indication of how generalised the view of non-investment grade bonds can sometimes be.

Standard & Poor's	Moody's	Fitch	
AAA	Aaa	AAA	Investment grade bonds
AA+	Aa1	AA+	
AA	Aa2	AA	
AA–	Aa3	AA–	
A+	A1	A+	
A	A2	A	
A–	A3	A–	
BBB+	Baa1	BBB+	
BBB	Baa2	BBB	
BBB–	Baa3	BBB–	
BB+	Ba1	BB+	Non-investment grade/high yielding/junk bonds
BB	Ba2	BB	
BB–	Ba3	BB–	
B+	B1	B+	
B	B2	B	
B–	B3	B–	
CCC	Caa		
CC	Ca	CCC	
C	C		
		DDD	
D		DD	
		D	

6.3 Convertible Bonds

A convertible bond is a bond with an embedded option allowing the bondholder to convert their bond into a pre-specified fixed number of shares in the company issuing the bond. They are often described as a hybrid security because they are part debt and part equity.

Whether or not the bondholder chooses to convert will depend on the share price in the market at the time they are able to convert. Imagine a bond in which the bondholder can choose to have their nominal value (£100) repaid, or can convert this into 20 ordinary shares in the company issuing the bond. This would be the equivalent of paying £5.00 for each share.

- If the share price in the market is above £5.00 at the point where conversion becomes possible, it is profitable for the investor to convert and receive the higher value shares.
- If the share price in the market is lower than £5.00, it is not profitable for the bondholder to convert.

If we ignore commission charges for the purposes of this example, the investor would be better off by redeeming the bond at £100 and buying the shares in the market at below £5.00.

This choice has a value for the holder of the convertible bond (and comes at a cost!), because they offer the investor the opportunity to participate in the upside of the equity if share prices rise, and provide the downside protection of a bond.

You will find that if you compare the prices of a straight bond issued by a company and a convertible bond, the convertible bond will be trading at a higher value. The higher cost of the convertible is made up by paying for both parts of the bond, the straight bond and the embedded conversion (call) option.

They are also advantageous for companies, in that by adding the sweetener of the conversion rights, they will probably be able to pay a lower coupon, thereby reducing their borrowing costs, although on conversion the equity in the company will be diluted.

There are a number of calculations you should be aware of when analysing convertibles.

Consider the calculations for the following example:

> Conversion ratio = 50 shares per £100 nominal of the stock
>
> The market price of the convertible is £126
>
> The ordinary share price is £2.15
>
> The ordinary share dividend is 2.5 pence per share
>
> The conversion rights expire in December 2018

Conversion Price

The conversion price is the cost of purchasing each share through converting. The formula is:

$$\text{Conversion price} = \frac{\text{market price}}{\text{conversion ratio}}$$

In our example therefore:

$$\text{Conversion price} = \frac{£126}{50} = £2.52$$

Conversion Premium (or Discount)

This calculation identifies the extra cost to an investor of accessing the shares through converting, compared with purchasing the shares at the current price in the market.

$$
\begin{aligned}
\text{Conversion premium} &= \text{conversion price} - \text{share price} \\
&= £2.52 - £2.15 \\
&= £0.37
\end{aligned}
$$

The investor in our example pays £0.37p more for the shares via the convertible than they would if they purchased them in the market. This amount may be expressed as a monetary amount or as a percentage premium compared to the current share price.

Percentage premium calculation:

$$£0.37 / £2.15 \times 100 = 17.2\%$$

Exam Tip! Questions on past papers have included calculations and required candidates to analyse the considerations around converting. Remember, if an investor converts before expiry, there is the loss of income under the bond element to consider and loss of option value. How does this compare with the dividend income paid, if the shares are owned? This is not a consideration if converted at expiry.

6.4   Capital and Interest Cover

We have looked in some detail at the different types of bonds and their characteristics. This particular section looks at ways of evaluating how safe an investor's capital and interest income is for a particular bond.

To understand this section, you will need to know the priority order for repayment of those owed money by a company, should it go into liquidation.

Priority order for repayment:

Liquidators' fees
Fixed charge holders
Preferential creditors
Floating charge holders
Unsecured creditors
Subordinated creditors
Preference shareholders
Ordinary shareholders

Capital Cover

Capital cover calculates the number of times that the value of a company's assets covers the repayment of a particular priority debt. The higher the cover, the lower the risk, should the company get into difficulties.

To begin the calculation, you will need to know the amounts outstanding to the various categories of creditors. We will use the following example:

- £10 million 5% mortgage debenture
- £20 million 6% unsecured loan stock
- £5 million 5% (net) cumulative preference shares
- £20 million £1 nominal ordinary shares
- £30 million ordinary share capital reserves.

Step 1: Rank these liabilities into the order in which they will be repaid, should the company go into liquidation.

Step 2: Calculate the cumulative amount of debt for each level.

Step 3: Divide the total assets available to cover the debt, by each cumulative level.

Liabilities/Security	Amount	Cumulative Amount of Debt	Capital Cover
5% Mortgage debenture	£10m	£10m	£85m/£10m = 8.5x
6% Unsecured loan stock	£20m	£30m	£85m/£30m = 2.8x
5% Preference shares	£5m	£35m	£85m/£35m = 2.4x
Ordinary share capital including reserves	£50m	£85m	£85m/£85m = 1x
Total	**£85m**		

Total Assets ÷ Cumulative Debt

Capital Priority Percentages

This calculation shows the percentage of the company's assets that would have to be used to repay each priority level.

Liabilities/Security	Amount	Cumulative Amount of Debt	Capital Cover	Capital Priority Percentage
5% Mortgage debenture	£10m	£10m	£85m/£10m = 8.5x	£10m/£85m x 100 = 11.8%
6% Unsecured loan stock	£20m	£30m	£85m/£30m = 2.8x	£30m/£85m x 100 = 11.8 – 35.3%
5% Preference shares	£5m	£35m	£85m/£35m = 2.4x	£35m/£85m x 100 = 35.3 – 41.2%
Ordinary share capital including reserves	£50m	£85m	£85m/£85m = 1x	£85m/£85m x 100 = 41.2 – 100%
Total	**£85m**			

Cumulative Debt / Total Assets x 100

Interest Cover

The interest cover calculation takes the profits that a company has made, and looks to see how many times it covers the interest liability on a particular priority debt. Using the example from above again:

- £10 million 5% mortgage debenture
- £20 million 6% unsecured loan stock
- £5 million 5% (net) cumulative preference shares
- £20 million £1 nominal ordinary shares
- £30 million ordinary share capital reserves
- Profit before interest and tax £10 million.

Step 1: Rank the interest bearing liabilities into the order in which they will be repaid, should the company go into liquidation.

Step 2: Calculate the cumulative amount of interest payable for each level.

Step 3: Divide the total profits available to cover the interest, by each cumulative level.

Liabilities/Security	Gross Interest Payable	Cumulative Amount of Gross Interest	Interest Cover
5% Mortgage debenture	£500K	£500K	£10m/£500K = 20x
6% Unsecured loan stock	£1.2m	£1.7m	£10m/£1.7m = 5.9x
5% Preference shares	£250k	£1.95m	£10m/£1.95m = 5.1x
Total	**£1.7m**		

PBIT ÷ Cumulative interest payable

6.5   Security and Borrowing Powers

Debentures

A company can (broadly) borrow in one of two ways to raise finance for its needs. It can borrow the money from a bank by way of loan or overdraft, or alternatively it can issue bonds, known as corporate bonds.

As we mentioned previously, one of the main distinctions between gilts and corporate bonds is that there is increased credit risk when investing in corporate bonds. One of the ways in which this risk can be reduced, therefore making the issue more attractive to prospective investors, is for the terms and conditions of the issue to include some form of security or collateral covering the bondholder, should the issuer default.

This gives the bondholders a right to sell the collateral (charged assets) to repay the bond debt, should the company fail to pay either the coupons or capital redemption. Secured bonds are often referred to in the UK as debentures. Bonds that have no security attached tend to be described as unsecured loan stock. It should be noted that in the US a 'debenture' has the opposite meaning in that it is unsecured loan stock.

There are two types of charge on assets that a company can give:

- **Fixed Charge** – A fixed charge gives the bondholder a right over a specific company asset, such as its land and buildings or plant and machinery. The company is not allowed to sell the charged asset without first obtaining the permission of the bondholders.
  Should the issuing company default, the bondholders can take possession of the charged asset and sell it to obtain repayment.

- **Floating Charge** – Floating charges give bondholder a right over a 'class' of the company's assets or assets generally, as opposed to rights over a specific asset.
  The company is allowed to buy and sell these assets as normal, until a crystallising event, such as a default, occurs. At the point of crystallisation, the specific assets that the bondholders have a right to is defined, and the company no longer has the power to sell them.

6.6 Building Society PIBS and Perpetual Subordinated Bonds

Permanent Interest Bearing Shares (PIBS) are a special type of share issued by building societies that pay a fixed rate of interest, normally half-yearly. Although they are a type of fixed-interest security, the rate of interest is higher than that paid on gilts and many corporate bonds due to the increased level of risk from both credit risk, volatility (as they are permanent, ie, undated they can be very volatile when interest rates change) and the fact that they are not covered by the FSCS. They are comparable in many ways with subordinated irredeemable loanstock, hence the fact that the same type of stocks issued by a now demutualised building society are known as a perpetual subordinated bonds or Perps (sometimes PSBs).

There is a secondary market in PIBS and Perps, and they can be bought and sold in much the same way as equities on the London Stock Exchange (LSE). This market can sometimes be illiquid resulting in wide spreads and, depending on the issue, it is usually only possible to trade in round lots of £1,000 nominal value, or sometimes higher (similar to corporate bonds).

The interest payable on a PIB is subject to income tax.

Some are callable, which makes them less attractive to the investor, and therefore requires a higher relative yield.

7. Corporate Equity

7.1 Features of Ordinary Shares and Types of Dividend

The ownership of shares means that the owner is a member of the company and confers upon the shareholder a number of rights. In this section the terms 'shares' (UK) and 'stock' (USA) are used interchangeably.

Ordinary shares are the most common form of shares issued by companies in the UK.

They represent permanent capital for a company. The company does not have to redeem the shares, although investors are free to sell their shares to other investors.

Typically, shareholders have no security, although they do usually have voting rights (normally one share, one vote) and can vote at company meetings on matters such as the appointment of directors and auditors, approval of proposed dividends and takeovers.

Dividend payments to ordinary shareholders are discretionary on the part of the company, and can only be paid out of profits and distributable reserves after the preference shareholders have received their dividend in full. Most blue chip companies in the UK pay out dividends either quarterly or semi-annually. This usually takes the form of one or three interim dividends and a final dividend which can be viewed as a balancing payment. Dividends are usually declared with the announcement of the company's interim/half-yearly results, and the final dividend at the announcement of the company's full year-end results. However, payment of the dividend may be delayed for some time after it is declared, although the date on which it is to be paid is usually declared at the same time as the amount.

Prior to this 2016–17 tax year, dividends were usually quoted in terms of pence payable per share. Since 6 April 2016, dividends are usually quoted in terms of payable per share and as the amount that the shareholder will receive gross of tax.

Ordinary shares are considered to be the risk capital of a business, in that they are the last to be paid in the event that the company is wound up (there is typically nothing left in the pot to pay the ordinary shareholders if a company goes into liquidation!). This is the risk taken for being a part owner of the company and having the right to share in the profits of the company.

There are a number of variations on the standard ordinary share:

Non-Voting Ordinary Shares/'A' Shares

As the name implies, owners of these shares do not have the right to vote at company meetings. In all other respects they are identical to ordinary shares.

They have typically been issued by founders of companies, particularly family companies, where the existing shareholders do not want to give away any control.

Shareholders are increasingly reluctant to purchase non-voting shares and they are likely to be traded at a discount to the voting shares, despite being entitled to the same level of dividend.

Similarly, a company can issue shares with restricted voting rights.

Deferred Shares

These are shares whereby the holders are not entitled to the payment of a dividend until a condition has been met, such as:

- a specific amount of time must have elapsed since the shares were issued
- the profits have to exceed a certain level
- other classes of shareholders have to have been paid a predetermined level of dividend, before the owners of these shares can be paid.

Golden Shares

These are shares with special voting rights. They may allow the holder to outvote other shareholders in specific circumstances, giving an effective power of veto and often giving the ability to block any one shareholder from acquiring more than a certain proportion of ordinary shares.

They have been issued by companies that the government has privatised, and are held by the government, giving to them effective control over the nationalised company. This prevents events such as takeovers and controlling holdings going abroad, on the basis that these industries are of national importance. (This has subsequently been ruled illegal by the EU!)

Another use of golden shares would be family companies that wish to give a trusted, impartial outsider sufficient powers to help resolve conflicts without involving them in running the company.

Redeemable Ordinary Shares

Companies are allowed to issue redeemable ordinary shares, which may be bought back by the company, at either the option of the company or the shareholder, on a date specified at the time of issue, provided the company has at least one other class of shares in issue, which is not redeemable.

7.2 Features of Preference Shares

Preference shares are the second most common form of shares issued by companies, and as with ordinary shares, they come in a variety of forms.

The usual form of preference share has the following characteristics:

- They pay a fixed rate of dividend unlike the variable/discretionary dividend paid for ordinary shares.
- Preference shareholders are preferred over ordinary shareholders in two respects:
    ○ a company must pay the preference share dividend in full before it can pay a dividend to ordinary shareholders
    ○ in the event that the company is wound up, the preference shareholders will be repaid the nominal value of their shares before the ordinary shareholders can be paid (assuming that there is sufficient to pay that is!).
- There is no security attached to preference shares.
- They do not usually have voting rights, although there is typically an exception which allows voting rights if the preference shareholders haven't received a dividend for five years or more.

When investors buy preference shares, the dividends are fixed, so they will not benefit from any significant increase in the company's profits, but they are however protected from some of the downside. Variations on the usual form include:

Cumulative Preference Shares

If a dividend is not paid to cumulative preference shareholders because the company makes insufficient profits, the next year a dividend cannot be paid to the ordinary shareholders until any arrears in the payment of dividends to the cumulative preference shareholders has been made up. The rights to be paid a preference share dividend are effectively carried forward. Most preference shares take this form.

Non-Cumulative Preference Shares

With this type of share, if a dividend is not paid, it is lost. The arrears do not have to be made up before a dividend can be paid to ordinary shareholders.

Participating Preference Shares

The owners of these shares have the right to receive additional dividend when the profits of the company exceed a certain level. The additional amount payable is usually expressed and paid as a proportion of the ordinary dividend. Holders of these shares participate more in the risks and rewards of share ownership than normal preference shares.

Redeemable Preference Shares

These are shares that will be bought back by the company at a pre-agreed price on a pre-agreed date. They are identifiable by the fact that they will have a date in their title.

Convertible Preference Shares

Holders of convertible preference shares will, at some point, have the option of converting them into ordinary shares.

Practically, if the company doesn't do well and the share price falls, they can be held as a fixed income investment, and if the share price rises, the investor can convert.

7.3   Shareholders' Rights and Their Responsibilities

Since the board of directors has responsibility for the day-to-day management of the company, a mechanism is needed to ensure shareholders can exercise some control over them. This is achieved by a series of shareholder rights as laid down in the Companies Act.

Basic rights

- to receive annual accounts
- to be notified of annual general and extraordinary general meetings
- the right to attend meetings and vote
- the right to share in the profits of the company
- the right to a share of the surplus on winding up after all liabilities have been paid.

Statutory rights

- companies must hold annual general meetings at least once a year
- shareholders with more than 10% of voting rights can call extraordinary general meetings
- shareholders with more than 5% of voting rights can propose resolutions
- any shareholder can petition the court on the grounds that the affairs of the company have been conducted in a manner unfairly prejudicial to the interests of some or all of its members

- pre-emptive rights (or rights of pre-emption) – any rights shareholders may have to be offered shares in a company before they are made available to anyone else. They can arise on the allotment, transfer or transmission of shares. Such rights may be important to ensure that a shareholder's proportion of the voting and other rights in the company are not diluted
- pre-emptive rights on allotment can arise under the Companies Act or the company's memorandum and articles.

As seen above, the holders of primarily ordinary shares have a right to vote at company meetings.

Voting at these meetings is generally by way of a show of hands where one shareholder has one vote. Larger shareholders can demand a poll, in which case votes are counted in proportion to the number of shares held.

If a shareholder is unable to attend a meeting in person, they can appoint a proxy to vote on their behalf.

When sending out proxy forms, companies usually suggest names of directors of the company who will act as proxies, voting as they see fit unless otherwise instructed.

A representative is sometimes appointed by corporate bodies as an alternative to a proxy. For the duration of the meeting, the representative has the same rights to speak and vote as a member.

The shareholders' responsibilities for the company's financial liabilities are limited to the value of shares that they own but haven't paid for. This is unlikely to happen in plcs – it is more a private company issue.

Private Companies

Unlike public limited companies (plcs), shareholdings in private limited companies are not readily available to the public. Just as a member of the general public cannot readily buy shares in a private limited company, any shareholder in a private limited company cannot readily sell those shares to a member of the general public.

The unfortunate effect of this is that shareholders are often locked in to a company and, although their shareholding may be very valuable on paper, they are unable to realise that value on sale. Even if a buyer can be found, shareholders often then face a number of further hurdles before the sale can proceed.

Pre-Emption Rights

The problems faced in trying to realise the value of a shareholding in a private limited company can be made all the more difficult by provisions in the Companies Articles or (if there is one) in a Shareholders Agreement. In particular, it is very common to find that these documents contain further restrictions on the disposal/transfer of shares. For example, they may provide that only a certain class of individuals can hold shares in the company (such as the relatives of the original shareholders). Most commonly, restrictions on the transfer of shares take the form of 'rights of pre-emption' whereby the shares which are to be sold/transferred must first be offered for sale to a prescribed class of individuals (normally the other remaining shareholders). This is, in effect, a right of first refusal before the shares can be sold elsewhere or to someone who may be a stranger to the remaining shareholders.

Share Value

A right of first refusal in itself does not present any great problem to a shareholder wanting to dispose of his holding, but the catch often comes in the price to be paid. In a typical right of pre-emption, the price to be paid by those exercising their right of first refusal is expressed to be a 'fair value' (to be independently determined in the absence of any agreement, often by the company auditors).

Unless the shareholding to be sold represents a majority shareholding in the company, a fair value will normally include a very substantial discount on what the owner will normally regard as the real value. This is known as a 'minority discount' and it seeks to reflect the fact that the shareholding is not a majority shareholding and does not therefore in itself carry the ability to control the company.

This can lead to seemingly harsh results and substantial undervaluations against what many would regard as the true value of the shareholding. For example, if a 49% shareholder in a £20 million company sells his entire shareholding to the 51% majority shareholder (who else would want to buy?) a crude example of the likely fair value might be:

> Company value – £20 million
>
> 49% of £20 million = £9.8 million
>
> minority discount, say 75%
>
> = valuation @ £2.450 million

While the true value to the 51% shareholder might well be seen as something in the order of £9.8 million (or more), he might well only have to pay £2.450 million by reason of the calculation of a fair value.

Non-Registration

A further difficulty sometimes faced in seeking to sell a minority shareholding is that the articles of association for many companies will also contain provisions enabling the board of directors to refuse to register (in broad terms to recognise or ratify) a transfer of shares on specific grounds or, in some circumstances, on whatever grounds they choose and without giving any particular reason.

7.4   Bonus/Scrip/Capitalisation Issues and Their Effects

A bonus, scrip or capitalisation issue is a free issue of shares to existing shareholders, pro-rata their existing holding. The shares are issued without cost, and the companies undertaking such an issue are not raising any additional finance.

The main reason for a company undertaking a bonus issue is to reduce the price of the shares in the market, increasing demand for the shares and therefore making them more liquid.

Convention in the UK is that the company announces the bonus issue in terms of the number of new (free) shares that a shareholder will receive for an existing number of shares. For example, a one for five bonus issue is an issue where shareholders will be allocated one new free share for every five existing shares that they own (the figures can be whatever the company wants). The US convention is to describe the total number of shares instead of just the new shares, so a UK one for five issue becomes a US six for five issue. Unless otherwise stated in this book, assume the UK convention. In the real world you will often have to clarify the convention being used to understand the terms of the issue.

Let's look at an example of how a bonus issue impacts on a company's share price:

> Terms of the bonus issue 2 for 5
> Current price of each share £7.30

For the purposes of the example, we will assume that the shareholder owns the minimum number of shares needed to participate in the issue, ie, five.

	No. of shares	Price	Value
Before the bonus issue	5	£7.30	£36.50
Bonus Issue	2	nil	nil
After the bonus issue	7	£5.21	£36.50

The total value of the shares is now distributed across a larger number of shares, reducing the market price of each share.

This process is also known as a capitalisation issue, because in accounting terms, it is achieved through the capitalisation of the company's reserves. The impact of a £100 million capitalisation issue of shares at £1 each on a company's balance sheet would be as follows:

Before		After	
Net assets	£550m	Net assets	£550m
Share capital 300m @ £1	£300m	Share capital 400m @ £1	£400m
Share premium account	£100m	Share premium account	-
Revenue Reserves account	£150m	Revenue Reserves account	£150m
Shareholders' funds	£550m	Shareholders' funds	£550m

7.5   Rights Issues and Their Effects

A rights issue is an issue of new shares to existing shareholders for cash, pro-rata their existing holding. The price of the shares is normally heavily discounted from the current market price. It is a way for companies to raise additional finance.

Pre-emption rights under UK law require that existing shareholders are all offered the same opportunity to buy shares and therefore maintain their proportion of shareholding in the company concerned.

Issues are typically underwritten by investment banks, who guarantee to buy any unsold shares if the issue is not fully subscribed.

Convention in the UK is that the company announces the rights issue in the same way as they do bonus issues, so in terms of the number of new shares that a shareholder will receive, based on the existing number of shares.

A four for seven rights issue enables all existing shareholders to buy four new shares in the company for every seven that they already own. As before, the figures can be whatever the company wants.

Let's look at an example of how a rights issue impacts on a company's share price:

> Terms of rights issue: four for seven
> Current price of each share: £4.10
> The subscription price of the new shares is £3.30 each

For the purposes of the example, we will assume that the shareholder owns the minimum number of shares needed to participate in the issue, ie, seven.

	No. of shares	Price	Value
Before the rights issue	7	£4.10	£28.70
Rights issue	4	£3.30	£13.20
After the rights issue	11	£3.81	£41.90

£41.90 ÷ 11 (known as the theoretical ex-rights price [TERP])

After the rights issue has gone through, the average price of all the shares will reduce, because of the number of discounted shares just issued.

With regard to the actions shareholders should take when faced with a rights issue, they have a number of options:

- exercise the rights and buy the shares at the discounted price
- let the rights lapse and do nothing – received lapsed rights proceeds
- sell the rights nil-paid in the market
- split the rights
- sell some of the rights nil-paid, and use the money generated to purchase the remainder of the discounted shares.

Selling the Rights Nil-Paid

If in the example above, our shareholder chose to let the rights lapse and do nothing, the shareholder would be out of pocket after the rights issue had gone through. This is because before the rights issue, the shareholder would have owned seven shares worth £4.10 each, with a value for the total holding of £28.70. After the rights issue, the share price will have fallen. The shareholder will own seven shares, theoretically worth £3.81 each, with a total value of £26.67. The shareholder would suffer a loss of £2.03.

To avoid this loss, the shareholder can sell the right to buy the shares at a discount in the market for a value. This value is known as the nil-paid price, and is calculated as the theoretical ex-rights price (TERP), less the subscription price. In our example:

TERP	=	£3.81
Less subscription price	=	£3.30
Each right	=	£0.51

4 rights x £0.51 = £2.04 (the difference is down to rounding)

Splitting the Rights/Maximum Subscription at Nil Cost

If a shareholder has insufficient money to take up the rights, but is still keen to increase their holding in the company, this might be a suitable option. It involves selling some of the rights nil-paid to generate some money, and using that money to purchase some of the discounted shares.

There is a formula that can be used to calculate the number of rights that need to be sold nil-paid:

$$\frac{\text{number of rights x subscription price}}{\text{theoretical ex-rights price}}$$

If we apply this formula to our example and assume that our shareholder has 7,000 shares, that gives us:

$$\frac{4,000 \times £3.30}{£3.81} = 3,465 \text{ (the number of rights to be sold nil-paid to fund taking up the remainder)}$$

The sale of 3,465 rights at the nil-paid price of £0.51 will generate proceeds of £1,766.

The shareholder is now free to exercise the remaining rights (4,000 – 3,465), and purchase 535 shares at the subscription price of £3.30 each, total cost £1,766.

As the shares are sold at the minimum of par value, there is no addition to the share premium account.

The impact of a £100 million rights issue of shares at £1 each on a company's balance sheet would be to increase the share capital and total value of the company by £100 million.

Before		After	
Net assets	£550m	Net assets	£650m
Share capital 300m @ £1.00	£300m	Share capital 400m @ £1.00	£400m
Share premium account	£100m	Share premium account	£100m
Revenue Reserves account	£150m	Revenue Reserves account	£150m
Shareholders' funds	£550m	Shareholders' funds	£650m

7.6 Share Buy Backs and Their Effects

If a company has surplus cash, it can retain the money within the business for future use or return it to its shareholders through either the payment of a dividend or by buying its shares back in the open market.

Shares that have been bought back can be cancelled or retained as Treasury shares. (Treasury shares are bought-back shares, which are not cancelled but held in case they need to be resold. They are sometimes used to fulfil share options as an alternative to a company having to issue more new shares.)

After a share buy back, the profits made by the company are distributed across less shareholders (described as 'earnings enhancing'), often leading to the payment of an increased dividend per share.

In addition, if the company believes that the shares are trading at a value below that of the net assets represented by each share, then the buy back exercise will also increase the value of the company.

Example

Company A has a net asset value (NAV) of £5 per share yet its shares trade at £4 in the market.

The company has 500 million shares in issue:

*   total NAV of £2.5 billion
*   market capitalisation of £2 billion.

It buys back 100 million shares in the market, for cancellation costing the company £400 million.

*   the company then has 400 million shares still in issue
*   total NAV of £2.5 billion – £0.4 billion = £2.1 billion.

So now the new net assets per share = £2.1 billion/400 million shares in issue = £5.25.

Although the total market capitalisation of the company is smaller, the company has increased NAV per share by 5% (ie, (£5.25–£5)/£5). One of the main jobs of the directors of a company is to give shareholder return. They have to consider how the cash they have is best invested and it may therefore be that they decide that the best way to give shareholder return is to buy back shares below NAV to boost the NAV of the remaining shares, and consequently the share price.

In addition, the laws of supply and demand suggest that if there are fewer shares available in the market, the price will rise. This rise in the share price gives shareholders the benefit of capital gains as opposed to the income they would have received if the company had paid a higher dividend. Shareholders have a choice as to when to realise this capital gain, and can minimise their tax liabilities in a way which they cannot do if there is a mandatory dividend payment.

Buy-backs can be viewed negatively as they imply that there is nothing more worthwhile that the management of the company could do with the cash in order to grow the company and can therefore be seen as a sign of lack of potential growth in the company in future.

From the company's perspective, if it increased its dividend because it had surplus cash, it would be difficult for it to reduce the dividend in the future as it would be seen as a sign of weakness by the market, and investors relying on a stream of dividends prefer to see stability in the pattern of dividends paid out by a company.

Buy-backs are often undertaken when the senior management of a company consider their shares to be undervalued in the market. There is a widespread suspicion that management engage in share buy backs to increase earnings, and thereby enhance share options and meet targets for bonuses.

7.7   Risks and Rewards of Investing in Equities

 Analyse

Think of as many advantages and disadvantages and risks and rewards of investing in equities as you can. When you have a list, compare it to the answers below.

Risks and Rewards of Share Ownership

Rewards

- Shareholders share in the equity and therefore profits of the company.
- Returns are not limited to a specific amount.
- In the longer term they can provide capital growth in a portfolio.
- Generally speaking, equity ownership gives inflation protection.
- Voting rights give an opportunity to influence the direction of the company.
- There is a liquid market in the shares of most major quoted companies, giving narrow spreads.
- The main stock exchanges are generally well regulated and well established.
- Most shares can be bought in tax shelters such as ISAs, eliminating income and CGT.
- Certain shares have other shareholder perks usually connected with the products of the company.

Risks

- Capital invested in shares is at risk.
- Ordinary shares rank below other creditors on winding up and may receive nothing if the company goes into liquidation.
- The dividend income is not guaranteed. It can fall, or may not be paid at all.
- Past performance is no guarantee of future performance.
- Shares are subject to CGT on gains and income tax on dividends.
- Some shares can be illiquid and difficult to sell at a fair value and the liquidity of all shares can change from day to day.
- There may be a significant difference between the buying and selling price, meaning if you want to buy and sell quickly, you may do so at a loss.
- Share prices can be volatile.
- Long-term investment.

7.8   Beta Values

To understand betas it is useful to understand a little bit about risk. Risk to an investor in the context of equities is mainly about volatility of returns and the potential for capital loss.

Risk can be split into two components:

- unsystematic risk/specific risk
- systematic risk/market risk.

Unsystematic Risk/Specific Risk

Specific risk factors are risks which are unique to the company that has issued the share. For example:

- strength of the management team
- range of products
- geographical location
- financial position.

Systematic Risk/Market Risk

Systematic risk factors include factors that affect all companies within a market, for example:

- inflation
- recession
- interest rates
- political instability
- exchange rates.

These types of risk affect all companies and industries.

Total Risk

Specific risk and systematic risk, added together, make up the total risk faced by an investor.

Diversification

One of the key concepts of investment management and portfolio planning is that of diversification. Diversification can reduce the volatility in a portfolio by reducing unsystematic risk. In a well-diversified portfolio, an investor will have investments that move up while others move down (negatively correlated) under certain different market events, with the overall effect being less volatility in the value of the total portfolio value. In theory, if you could find two stocks that were perfectly negatively correlated then you would only need to hold these two stocks in order to diversify away all systematic/ specific risk in the total value of the portfolio. In practice, stocks will tend to vary in their correlations to one another over time, depending on the changing influences. In practice, therefore, the more uncorrelated or negatively correlated holdings there are in a portfolio, the better the diversification and the bigger the reduction in specific risk: specific risk can be diversified away. This is, however, an exponentially reducing effect, ie, each holding added has a smaller effect on the reduction of specific risk (what is left is systematic risk).

At the same time, the cost of purchasing and managing a larger number of holdings increases.

Different studies have produced different results, but it is generally accepted that for practical purposes most of the specific risk can be diversified away using a portfolio of 15 to 25 holdings. (nb, the number has increased in recent years due to the increasing correlation between all stocks and other assets under some circumstances.)

Example

An investor who only had banking and financial sector equities in their portfolio from 2000 to 2010, would have seen the value of their shares drop hugely (about 45% excluding income). If the investor also owned shares in the mining sector, only part of their portfolio would have been affected by the large fall in value and would have been offset by the huge (although volatile) rise in value in the mining sector over the same period (about 350% excluding income). So, £100 invested in banks alone in 2000 would have resulted in 2010 in a portfolio worth about £55, while an equal combination of both sectors would have resulted in a portfolio worth about £203. This having been said, the portfolio with an equal combination of both would have had a value of about £92.5 in the height of the market crash at the end of 2008/beginning of 2009, thereby still making a loss after having been invested for eight years, as would having invested in a FTSE tracker fund over the same period. This period is a good demonstration of systematic risk as, at the end of 2008, most assets fell in value as institutions desperately sold large volumes of stock in a bid to raise cash.

Systematic risk cannot be diversified away and is measured by beta.

Beta, which you will see denoted as β, measures the sensitivity or volatility of a stock compared with the sensitivity or volatility of the market as a whole.

Understanding Beta Values

- **Beta of 1**
  The beta for the stock market as a whole is one. The price of an individual stock with a beta of 1 will move to the same extent as the market. If the market rises 20%, the value of the share will rise by 20%. These shares are described as 'neutral'.

- **Beta of less than 1**
  The price of the security will be less volatile than the market. If the market falls by, say, 10%, a price of the share with a beta of 0.8 will fall by 8%. Stocks with a beta of less than one are often referred to as 'defensive' stocks.

  Shares with a beta of less than one will be bought if stock markets are expected to fall, as the share price should fall less than the market as a whole.

- **Beta of more than 1**
  The price of the security will be more volatile than the market. Should markets go up by, say, 10%, a share with a beta of 1.2 should go up by 12%. These shares are described as 'aggressive' or 'cyclical'.

  If stock markets are expected to do well, say as the economy pulls out of recession, shares with a beta of more than one should increase in value more than the market.

There are other aspects to beta values of which you should be aware.

- Betas may be positive or negative. If the sign is positive, the investment moves the same way as the market. If it is negative, the investment moves the opposite way to the market.
- If a beta is zero, it means that there is no correlation between how the particular investment moves and the way the market moves. It may, for instance, for a given aspect of market risk, go up sometimes or down other times (ie, uncorrelated).

7.9 Analytical Measures of Equity Valuation, Their Merits and Uses

There is no one precise way for analysts to value equities. They have a number of techniques at their disposal. The two main approaches are, however:

- absolute methods, where discounted cash flow techniques are used to try and value the shares, and
- relative value methods, which provide a multiple which can be used to compare the performance of one company with its peers (eg, those of a similar size, sector and risk).

In terms of absolute methods, analysts may use fundamental analysis rather than technical analysis to estimate the intrinsic value of a company. The intrinsic characteristic is the expected future net cash flows to the company calculated by a discounted cash flow valuation.

An alternative, though related approach, is to view intrinsic value as the value of a business' ongoing operations, as opposed to its accounting based book value, or break-up value. Warren Buffett is known for his ability to calculate the intrinsic value of a business, and then buy that business when its price is at a discount to its intrinsic value.

Another absolute method of valuing a share is to use Gordon's Growth Model. This is a simple method of deriving a share valuation or price from the current dividend, expected dividend growth, and return required.

The formula for calculating the share valuation using this approach is as follows:

$$\text{Share price} = \frac{\text{dividend}}{(\text{return required} - \text{dividend growth})}$$

For example, if the dividend is 20p, the required rate of return is 10% and the expected dividend growth is 5% the valuation is:

$$400p = \frac{20p}{0.10 - 0.05}$$

The next section contains the ratios specifically listed in the syllabus that you need to know. But to be able to evaluate equities, there are a number of other ratios of which you should be aware.

Profitability Ratios

These measure the effectiveness of the company at generating profits using the company's assets/resources.

Return on Equity (ROE); Return on Shareholders' Funds

ROE measures the percentage return the company is achieving on the amount of funds provided by shareholders, which come from two main sources:

- the share capital and share premium, being the funds paid by investors for new shares in the company
- retained earnings, ie, accumulated from profits not paid out as dividends over the years.

$$\text{ROE} = \frac{\text{profit after tax and preference dividends}}{\text{capital and reserves (shareholders' funds)}} \times 100$$

An ability to earn consistently above average rates of return on equity is the most fundamental characteristic of a good company.

Return on Capital Employed (ROCE)

ROCE is a better comparison between companies than ROE since ROE is heavily affected by differences in the capital structure of companies, some of which have a much higher degree of debt funding than others.

$$\text{ROE} = \frac{\text{profit before interest and tax}}{\text{capital employed}} \times 100$$

Interest and tax are excluded from the calculation because we are trying to identify how much profit a company has generated from its assets, and different companies have different financial commitments and may be subject to different tax rates.

Capital employed is calculated as:

$$\text{Capital employed} = \text{share capital} + \text{reserves} + \text{loans} + \text{overdrafts}$$

Gearing Ratios

These are useful to those providing finance to the company in assessing the level of risk involved.

Debt to Equity Ratio

$$\text{Debt to equity} = \frac{\text{interest bearing loans} + \text{preference share capital}}{\text{ordinary shareholders' funds}}$$

Note that preference share capital is usually, as here, included on the top line of the calculation, as it closely resembles interest bearing debt. It also ranks above ordinary shareholders in the priority list for repayment in the event that the company is liquidated.

Interest Cover

The interest cover looks at the same problem from a different angle. How many times over could the interest bill be paid out of current profits?

$$\text{Interest cover} = \frac{\text{profit before interest and tax}}{\text{(net) interest paid}} \times 100$$

Net interest is interest paid less interest received. Capital and income cover, and priority percentages, provide a more specific breakdown.

Liquidity Ratios

Liquidity is crucial to a company's fortunes. Even with an impressive order book and plenty of assets, companies sometimes fall into liquidation because they do not have enough cash to pay the bills.

Liquidity ratios are therefore watched very carefully by analysts and investors.

Working Capital (Current) Ratio

$$\text{Current ratio} = \frac{\text{current assets}}{\text{current liabilities}}$$

As a general rule, the current ratio should be between 1.5 and 2 although this will depend on the type of business and the economic conditions. Clearly the higher the number, the better. A low number may indicate a higher chance of the company falling into liquidation.

Liquidity Ratio

The difficulty with the working capital ratio is that current assets include stock which, as we have seen, do not, in practice, always sell easily in times of financial crisis.

The liquidity ratio is also known as the quick assets ratio or the acid test since it measures only those assets which can be quickly and definitely turned into cash.

$$\text{Liquidity ratio} = \frac{\text{current assets} - \text{stock}}{\text{current liabilities}} = \frac{\text{cash} + \text{accounts receivable} + \text{short-term investments}}{\text{accounts payable} + \text{bank overdraft}}$$

Cash Flow

Most companies will include a cash flow statement in their company accounts which provide a more dynamic view of the money flow within a company. This gives the investor a far greater insight into the operations of a company than just relying on the bottom line profit figure.

When considering cash flow, the following need to be taken into consideration:

- **increases in assets = a use of funds** – for example, buying machinery (this will be shown in brackets since it is a negative cash flow)
- **decreases in assets = a source of funds** – for example, selling an asset
- **increases in liabilities = a source of funds** – for example, a new loan or an increase in creditors
- **decreases in liabilities = a use of funds** – for example, repayment of a loan (this will also be shown in brackets).

Key considerations when analysing cash flow statements will include the following:

- **Cash flow at operating level – is this positive?** If not, the position cannot continue for long. Borrowing may provide a short-term solution but this cannot continue indefinitely. This is therefore of crucial significance.
- **How much cash is being generated from non-operating sources?** This is the money which is being squeezed from working capital, for example by reducing stock or debtors or from the sale of fixed assets. This is a sound practice but cannot be repeated indefinitely, so cannot be relied upon to cover for cash shortages from operations.
- **What changes to loans have occurred?** The detailed notes within the accounts will provide useful information on relevant aspects of the company's debts, for example the dates of repayment and whether the rate of interest is fixed or variable.

Investors' Ratios

Earnings per Share

$$\text{Earnings per share} = \frac{\text{profits after interest, tax and preference share dividend}}{\text{number of ordinary shares in issue}}$$

This ratio takes the profits attributable to ordinary shareholders that a company makes, and divides it by the number of ordinary shares it has in issue. It therefore provides investors with a 'profits made per share figure'.

The profit figure used is the profit after all deductions, except the ordinary dividend, ie, the maximum amount that could be distributed to ordinary shareholders.

Looked at on a year-on-year basis, it is particularly useful for identifying trends in profitability, and it can also be used to compare one company's performance against another.

Diluted Earnings per Share

As you can see, the above figure is calculated by dividing the profits by the number of ordinary shares in issue. There are a number of reasons why a company may have to increase the number of shares it has in issue, which would reduce the earnings per share figure. For example:

*   convertible loan stocks in issue
*   warrants in issue
*   share options issued but not yet exercised.

The diluted earnings per share figure looks at a worst case scenario by increasing the number of shares on the bottom line of the calculation to a maximum.

7.10 Ratios and Yields-Equities

Dividend Cover

This ratio looks at the ability of the company to maintain the current level of dividend that it is paying out. The higher the level of dividend cover the better, as this would indicate that the company can continue to maintain its current level of dividend, even if profits drop.

It is calculated as follows:

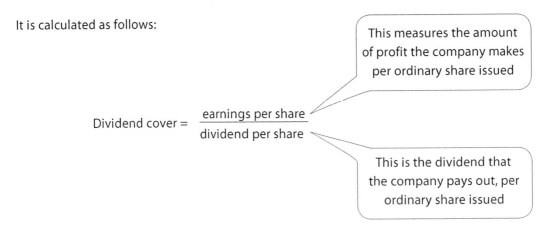

$$\text{Dividend cover} = \frac{\text{earnings per share}}{\text{dividend per share}}$$

This measures the amount of profit the company makes per ordinary share issued

This is the dividend that the company pays out, per ordinary share issued

A high dividend cover may also imply that the company is retaining the majority of its profits for future investment in the company. The ratio needs to be considered in the context of the stability of the company's earnings. It may be acceptable for a company with a stable profit stream to have a lower level of dividend cover than a company with a more volatile profit stream.

One point of note – it is not necessarily the case that because a company is profitable it has sufficient cash to be able to pay a dividend!

The ratio is of particular use to income seeking investors.

Investors tend to feel more at ease when a dividend is comfortably covered by earnings, although there are occasions when an uncovered dividend is considered acceptable – if a business is about to win a large contract, for instance, and the stock market knows this to be the case.

Dividend Yield

This ratio compares the year's dividend paid out on a share against its current market price, and expresses it as a percentage return. It therefore provides investors with an indication of how much they are earning on their shares.

It is calculated as follows:

$$\text{Dividend yield} = \frac{\text{dividend per share}}{\text{share price}} \times 100$$

Points of note:

- as companies tend to have different policies on how much of the profit they pay out by way of dividend and how much they retain by way of reserves for future use, the dividend yield is not directly comparable between companies
- growth stocks tend to have low (or zero) dividend yields as they reinvest a large proportion of their profits if they make a profit, but having a low yield does not necessarily mean a company will grow
- high dividend yields may indicate a more mature company with lower growth prospects or as the result of a particularly low share price, perhaps because investors perceive that the dividend may be cut. It may also be an indication that the share is undervalued
- demand for a particular share will drive the price up, therefore lowering the yield
- from an investor's perspective, a high historical dividend yield is no guarantee that the company will continue to pay those levels of dividend in the future.

Price/Earnings (P/E) Ratio

This ratio is a multiple, which looks at how many times the price of a company's share exceeds the level of profits per share.

The higher the P/E ratio, the more the share will cost in terms of a multiple of profits.

It is calculated as follows:

$$\text{Price/earnings ratio} = \frac{\text{current market price per share}}{\text{earnings per share}}$$

It provides an indication as to the level of confidence that the stock market has in the company.

As a rule of thumb, a high P/E ratio relative to the market or industry average indicates that the company is expected to do well and grow, whereas a low P/E ratio may indicate a lower growth, more established company. An extremely low P/E ratio is likely to indicate that investors fear that future earnings will be substantially lower or may be because the company is undervalued.

It is useful for comparing companies in the same sector, and you will find P/E ratios in the financial pages of newspapers. As with the majority of these ratios, you should note that the P/E ratios that you will see listed in the financial press and on investment websites are usually based on historic figures; the same also being true of dividend yields.

As investors are typically more interested in future dividends and growth prospects, the prospective P/E ratio may be of more use to them. This is calculated in the same way as the historical P/E ratio, but uses forecast earnings for the current year. This, in itself, will have limitations, in that it uses estimated earnings figures.

As the P/E ratio uses earnings in the way it is calculated, it cannot be used for companies that don't make profits.

 Analyse

Have a look at the *Financial Times*, and view the P/E ratios for different sectors. Why do some have a dash? In the financial pages, it tells you the average P/E ratio for the FTSE 100. Can you find it and will you know it for the exam?

Earnings Yield

The earnings yield is the reciprocal of the P/E ratio expressed as a percentage.

It is calculated as:

$$\text{Earnings yield} = \frac{\text{earnings per share}}{\text{current market price of the share}} \times 100$$

It calculates the profits the company makes per share as a percentage of the current share price. For instance, a company that has a share price of £3.00 and has earnings per share of 15p would have a P/E ratio of 20 and earnings yield of 5%.

It shows the return that an investor would make, if the company paid out all its profit by way of dividend.

The earnings yield is more easily used in comparisons against dividend yields, bond yields and interest rates, but the P/E ratio above is the most commonly used form of the formulae.

The more risk an investor is taking, the higher a return they would expect.

Price/Book Ratio

The last of the ratios that we need to consider is the price-to-book ratio.

It is calculated as follows:

$$\text{Price/book ratio} = \frac{\text{current market price of the share}}{\text{book value (ie, net tangible assets per share)}}$$

This is the NAV of the company, divided by the number of ordinary shares that the company has in issue

This ratio provides us with an alternative to the P/E ratio, to use if the company is making losses.

The book value is calculated taking the company's assets, less intangible assets, less the value of all of its liabilities, and dividing it by the number of ordinary shares in issue. This gives us the value of the company per ordinary share issued.

The current market price of the share is then divided by the price/book ratio giving the book value per share.

If the price-to-book value is less than one, the market is valuing the shares at less than the value of the company's assets. This may indicate that the share is undervalued, that investors consider the assets to be overvalued, or that they perceive some other problem with the company which is depressing the share price.

The ratio is a widely used measure, but care should be taken in its application. It is a better indicator with companies with large tangible assets (eg, building firms with large land banks and property companies), and is of less use if the company has more intangible assets such as copyrights, patents or goodwill, which are more difficult to value, or if the company has large amounts of debt which negate the value of the tangible assets in the calculation.

A high price-to-book value would suggest that investors are prepared to pay more for the shares because they expect the management team to generate significant profits from the assets the company owns (and they would therefore be using other investor ratios), that investors consider the assets to be undervalued or that a company is in difficulties.

The ratio can also be useful in telling an investor if they are paying too much for a share.

7.11   The Reverse Yield Gap

The yield gap is the difference between the dividend yield on ordinary shares (usually index such as FTSE100) and the redemption yield on gilts (a benchmark gilt, or gilt index).

You would normally expect there to be a higher dividend yield received from shares than the gross redemption yield on gilts to reflect the much higher level of risk taken by equity investors. However, from the late 1950s this positive yield gap was reversed for the majority of the time, with gilts yielding more than shares. The reason for this was that investors began to invest for future growth in dividends and capital growth which could be achieved through equity investment, not just the short-term income stream.

History and Current Position

Until about 1959, equities yielded more than bonds, explained by the risk premium argument.

After that time, we saw a reverse yield gap, whereby gilts have returned more than equities.

Arguments justifying the change from the pre-1959 position time, centred on the effect of inflation, which undermines the returns on gilts as the real value of the coupon and capital reduces over time. At the same time, inflation increases company's profits, allowing dividends to be increased. It was argued successfully that gilts needed to pay a higher yield to compensate for the erosion in the spending power of the cash flows, and that buying shares with an initial yield that was lower than gilts, was acceptable because the potential for dividend growth would outweigh the risk.

As more investors bought into this argument, the demand for equities increased, pushing prices up and yields on equities even lower, widening the gap.

After 2008 this trend reversed itself mainly due to quantitative easing and lower inflation expectations which have taken gilt yields to unprecedentedly low levels.

One way of looking at investments is considering whether equities are cheap, relative to bonds. The yield gap gives us a useful insight into this.

 Analyse

Have a look at the *Financial Times* and compare the yield on equities with the average yields on gilts. What is the current position? Has the gap been closing or widening recently?

8. Financial Derivatives

8.1 Introduction

For your examination, you need to know and understand derivatives. You should ensure that you are familiar with how derivatives can be used, as well as how they work.

They are called derivatives because they derive their value from the value of something else, for instance, the price of an option over Barclays shares is derived, in part, from the price of the underlying share itself.

For the purposes of the exam we will be looking at four main categories:

*   futures
*   options
*   warrants
*   contracts for differences.

As an introduction to this chapter, we will cover the basics of how each of these work, and then go through the syllabus requirements.

8.2 Futures

Definition

> A future is an agreement to buy or sell a *standard quantity* of a *specified asset* on a *fixed future date* at a *price agreed today*.

It is, in essence, an agreement where the buyer and seller of an asset agree the terms upon which they will buy/sell the asset concerned, but the actual purchase/sale transaction doesn't happen until an agreed future date. Once the agreement is made, each side then has an obligation to the other.

Terminology

*   **Buyer** – the party agreeing to buy the asset under the future is described as the 'long'.
*   **Seller** – the party agreeing to sell the asset under the future is described as the 'short'.

Futures are traded on exchanges, and to maintain liquidity in the markets, the terms on which futures are agreed are standardised. The standard terms for each specific type of future are described as the 'contract specifications' and the contract specifications for each future include the following:

Standard Quantity

By way of example, wheat futures traded on ICE (Intercontinental Exchange) Futures Europe are all for 100 tonnes of wheat. If a buyer wants to buy 500 tonnes of wheat, they buy five wheat contracts. If they want to buy an odd amount of wheat, say, 531 tonnes, they can't do it exactly; they have to round up or down to the nearest whole future.

Specified Asset

It is logical that if you are agreeing to buy something in the future, you want to know exactly what you are buying. If, for instance, a buyer agrees to buy oil, are they agreeing to buy crude oil or refined oil, and of what grade? For this reason, the asset is also clearly defined in the contract specifications.

Fixed Future Date

The actual purchase and sale under the future, which is known as 'delivery', can only take place on specific dates set by the exchange, known as 'delivery days'. The exchange sets the available delivery days and as one date expires, another is added.

Price Agreed Today

The price that the buyers and sellers under futures contracts agree to pay or receive for the specified asset, is agreed in advance on the date that the future is bought or sold. As with share prices, these are published by the exchanges.

The Obligation

There are two ways that the parties to a futures contract can fulfil their obligation:

- see the contract through to delivery, or
- close out the contract. This is achieved by entering into an equal and opposite contract.

Example

Let's say a farmer sells five wheat futures for November delivery at a price of £100 per tonne, and his crop fails.

This has committed him to deliver 500 tonnes of wheat on a date in November at £100 per tonne. To cancel out this obligation, he can enter into an equal and opposite futures contract, which commits him to buy 500 tonnes of wheat for the same November date delivery. In this way, he is agreeing to sell 500 tonnes of wheat and buy 500 tonnes of wheat on the same date. The buy and sell cancel each other out and the farmer doesn't have to deliver or take delivery of any wheat.

When a futures contract is closed out in this way, the closing contract is entered into at the market price for the day, which means that the farmer may suffer or gain from the price differential.

Our farmer has agreed to sell 500 tonnes of wheat at £100 per tonne. If the closing contract to buy wheat is priced at over £100, say £120 per tonne, the farmer will have effectively bought wheat at £120 per tonne and sold it at £100 per tonne, causing him a financial loss of £10,000 (500 tonnes at £20 per tonne).

The reverse is also true, if the price falls say to £85 per tonne, the farmer is effectively buying the wheat at £85 per tonne and selling it at £100 per tonne, making a £15 per tonne profit!

Uses of Equity Index Futures

The main uses of all futures are:

- **Hedging** – the origins of futures are in the world of commodities, where traders such as farmers were looking for certainty (ie, to reduce risk). A farmer could work for most of the year on a field producing wheat, which represents a significant investment on the part of the farmer, but, without futures, they face the risk that the price of wheat in the market at the time they come to harvest may not cover their costs of producing it in the first place. Having sold the future, the risk to the farmer would then be that they have to actually be able to produce that much wheat or they will have unwanted exposure to the commodity price. A large bread manufacturer may take the opposite side of the wheat contract from the farmer so that they can predict the costs of their ingredients months ahead to help manage their risk. Such players in the futures market would be described as hedgers as they are seeking to hedge (reduce/limit) their risk.
- **Speculation** – the practice of being able to close out a future means that futures can also be used for speculating on price changes, as in practice you don't have to deliver the underlying commodity to trade the futures in that commodity. Unlike the hedger, the speculator seeks risk as they perceive the potential for reward in taking a directional bet.
- **Arbitrage** – arbitrageurs seek low risk profits by exploiting pricing anomalies, for example, simultaneously selling the underlying asset and buying the future. Although private investors do not usually have the ability to carry out such trades at low enough cost to make it viable, the fact that such trades are carried out by professionals helps to keep markets fairly efficiently priced: the act of trading against the pricing anomaly helps to remove that anomaly.

A long futures position has the potential to make a limited (although geared) loss (ie, a price can only fall to zero), but an unlimited gain. A short futures position has the potential to make a limited gain (the maximum would be if the price fell to zero), but an unlimited loss (ie, a price could in theory continue to rise without limit).

Futures are now available on numerous products including financial indices and interest rates. For the purposes of your exam, you need to be particularly familiar with the features of financial futures on equity indices.

8.3 Operation and Relevance of Margin in the Clearing and Settlement Process

Clearing and settlement include the following stages:

- Matching of the trade details.
- During the life of the future, managing margin payments.
- Arranging for either delivery or cash settlement of the contract on expiry/closing out.

For the purposes of your exam, you need to understand how the concept of 'margin' in this process works. To understand the purpose of margin, you need to understand the role and liabilities of the clearing house.

In the way that we have looked at futures so far, the implication is that the buyer and seller deal with one another directly. In practice, this is not the case.

After the trade details have been matched, the clearing house becomes the legal counterparty to each side of a futures trade, through a process known as 'novation'. This means that they become the buyer to every seller and the seller to every buyer. From this point forward, they also guarantee that both sides of the contract are fulfilled.

Novation

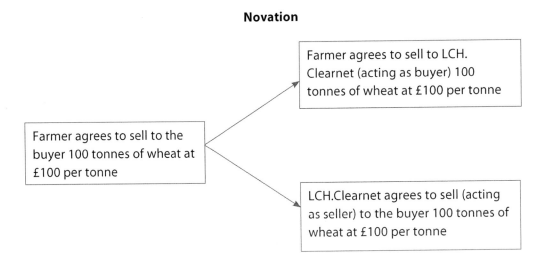

The guarantee:

- LCH.Clearnet guarantees that even if the farmer does not sell the wheat to them, that LCH.Clearnet will sell the wheat to the buyer at £100 per tonne. This could mean that LCH.Clearnet have to go out into the market, buy the wheat at the current market price (which could be more than £100 per tonne) to sell to the buyer at £100 per tonne, potentially making a loss.

- LCH.Clearnet also guarantees that they will buy the wheat from the farmer for £100 per tonne, even if the buyer will not buy it from them for £100 per tonne. This potentially leaves LCH.Clearnet in the position of buying wheat from the seller at £100 per tonne and having to sell it in the market at the current market price (which could be less than £100 per tonne), potentially making a loss.

To cover themselves against these eventualities, LCH.Clearnet use a system of margin payments.

Initial Margin

Initial margin is payable when a futures contract is taken out. It is effectively a returnable good faith deposit and is paid by both buyers and sellers of futures, and can be paid in the form of cash or acceptable forms of collateral.

It is described as a returnable good faith deposit because if a party taking out a future honours their obligations under the contract, the initial margin will be returned to them.

A risk-modelling program called SPAN (Standard Portfolio ANalysis and risk) is used to calculate the amount of initial margin to be paid, and it equates to the worst probable one-day loss that the buyer or seller of the futures may incur. The more volatile the markets, the higher the initial margin.

Initial margins are usually payable by 9:00am on the business day following the trade.

Variation Margin

In addition to the initial margin, variation margin is payable if the futures contract that has been bought or sold loses money. It is paid by the loser (through the clearing house) to the winner. The amount of the variation margin payable/receivable equates to the profit/loss on the futures contract each day.

The amount of variation margin payable is calculated at the close of business each day and is payable by the futures trader, usually by 9:00am on the next business day. If it is not paid by the required time, the amount due is taken from the initial margin paid, and the contract will be closed out, with any surplus being returned to the exchange member.

Example

1 August – bought 1 FTSE 100 Index
December future at 6709

At the end of the trading day, the daily settlement price is calculated and is 6699. The buyer has bought a future, which needs to go up in value for the buyer to be in profit. It has fallen in value, so the buyer is initially making a loss. Variation margin will be payable by the buyer to cover this daily loss.

In this particular case, the variation margin payable will be £10 per index point, per futures contract bought. The index has fallen by 10 points x £10. £100 is therefore payable.

This daily margining process ensures that any profits or losses are calculated each evening and realised (paid or collected) first thing the next morning, not just at the expiry or closing out of the future. If the futures price moves in your favour, payment is received. If the futures contract moves against you, payment must be made.

The process of comparing the daily price to the futures price, and working out the margin payable, is often described as 'marking the contract to market'.

In practice, to avoid the need for cash to be constantly moving between brokers and their customers, an amount of cash is usually left on deposit with the broker, and payments are credited to, or debited from, the margin account.

You may need to be aware that although these are the two main types of margin used by ICE Futures Europe in London, there are other types of margin used both in London and on other foreign exchanges:

Spot Month Margin

This is extra margin charged to cover additional risk for contracts in certain months (often delivery months).

Intra-Day Margin

Intra-day margin is called in times of high volatility in the price of a contract during a trading day. In such circumstances, if the amount of initial margin originally called for is considered inadequate by the clearing house to cover the additional risk, extra margin is called.

Maintenance Margin

Certain exchanges (particularly some of the American exchanges) operate a different system for calculating initial margin, which results in a higher initial payment needing to be made. No variation margin is then payable unless the balance on the margin account falls below what is described as the maintenance margin level, which is usually two-thirds of the initial margin level. At this point, investors are required to pay sufficient margin to bring it back up to the initial margin level.

8.4   The Relevance of Cost of Carry and Fair Values

The next step is to understand how futures are priced.

Contango

The futures market is described as being in 'contango' if the price of the asset in the future is higher than the spot price.

To explain, let's consider the position of a farmer who has some wheat to sell. The farmer can sell it today or at an agreed date in the future.

If the farmer agrees to a future sale, he will incur additional financial costs (the farmer may not be able to repay an overdraft for instance until the wheat is sold, thereby incurring extra interest costs). The farmer may also have to pay to store and insure the wheat. These additional costs are described as the 'costs of carry'.

$$\text{Fair value} = \text{spot price} + \text{costs of carry}$$

Put simply, if the farmer is going to agree to sell wheat in the future, he is going to work out how much it is going to cost him and the price will be calculated accordingly!

Backwardation

In practice, the futures price is a result of the spot price, the costs of carry and the interplay of a number of other factors such as supply and demand, market sentiment, practical issues, interest rates and more. Given these additional factors, the futures price is sometimes lower than the spot price. You will find it is also the case for a number of metals.

When the futures price is lower than the spot price, the market is described as being in 'backwardation'.

8.5 Features of Financial Futures on Equity Indices

The wheat future we saw above is capable of being physically settled, ie, the wheat can actually change hands. Some futures trade the prices of investments, which you cannot physically deliver. One such example is that of an equity index. You can buy and sell futures based on the value of the index, but it is not physically possible to deliver an index, so they are settled by paying the cash equivalent of the difference between the buying and selling price, ie, they are 'cash settled'.

Let's consider the example of the FTSE 100 index. If you think the value of the FTSE 100 index is going to go up (you're bullish about the market), you should buy FTSE 100 futures contracts. Buying at a low value and selling (closing out) when the price has risen will generate a profit. Conversely, if you think the value of the FTSE 100 is going to fall (you're bearish about the market), you should sell futures while the value is high and buy (close out) the contract when the price has fallen. You will still have bought low and sold high generating a profit; you just did it by selling first.

The contract specifications for the FTSE 100 index are:

- tick size 0.5 point
- tick value £5.00.

The 'tick' is the smallest permitted price movement by an exchange. The 'tick value' is the amount that the exchange will pay out on a futures contract, for a one tick price change.

Profit/Loss Calculation

The formula for calculating the profit or loss on a future is:

$$\text{Number of ticks} \times \text{tick value} \times \text{number of futures contracts}$$

Example

Let's imagine, you could buy a FTSE 100 December future at 6729. In December, the FTSE 100 index has risen to 6859 and calculate the profit.

The FTSE 100 has moved 130 points. Each half a point is a tick, therefore 260 ticks.

We bought and the index rose, so we bought low and sold high, generating a profit.

Each tick is worth £5.

$$260 \times £5 \times 1 = £1,300 \text{ (profit)}$$

Hedging is the process of protecting an underlying investment. Take the example of an investor who has a portfolio of shares worth £100,000 and is expecting the equity market to fall by 20%. If they continue to hold their shares and the market falls, the shares will fall in value to £80,000. If they went short futures (sold futures – sell high – buy [close out] while low), and calculated correctly, they could make enough profit on the short futures position to make a £20,000 profit, compensating them for the £20,000 loss on the equity portfolio. If the market moves the other way, our investor would make a profit on his shares but a corresponding loss on the short futures position.

With a perfect hedge, the status quo is maintained.

Market falls	
Portfolio	−£20,000
Profit on future	+£20,000
Equity portfolio	+£80,000
Profit on future	+ £20,000
Overall position	+ £100,000

Market rises	
Portfolio	+£20,000
Loss on future	−£20,000
Equity portfolio	+£120,000
Loss on future	−£20,000
Overall position	+£100,000

Futures are available on a number of leading indices. ICE Futures Europe for instance, has futures available on:

- FTSE 100
- FTSE 250
- FTSE Eurotop 100 (pan-European selection of 100 stocks)

and many more, including a selection of more country specific indices. Futures on American indices are available through the CME Group (Chicago Mercantile Exchange) and Chicago Board of Trade (CBOT).

When using equity index futures for hedging purposes, to achieve a perfect hedge, the contents of the index must exactly match the contents of the portfolio being hedged. It is important to select the index with care. If the investments are UK blue chip shares, it wouldn't be appropriate to select an index of European mid-caps!

Exam Tip! For the exam, be aware of any limitations. A recent question required students to note that there weren't any futures available on AIM stocks and therefore their use as a hedge wasn't perfect.

8.6 Features of Contracts for Differences

A contract for difference (CFD) is similar to a future which has no expiry date. They are not capable of being physically delivered for settlement and are therefore cash settled.

They are, in effect, agreements to pay out the cash difference between the starting price of an index, share, interest rate etc, and the closing price. If you buy low and sell high you make a profit and receive money. If the price moves against you and you buy high and sell low, you make a loss and have to pay out the difference.

Features

- Unlike financial futures, CFDs can be taken on individual major companies in the UK, not just indices.
- They allow investors to make money (and lose money) on movements in prices, without them having to buy the underlying asset. It's very difficult to buy an index, but you can buy a CFD on an equity index, which will make you a profit if the price moves the right way!
- They can be used when prices are rising or falling. They allow investors to go short and potentially make money in a falling market.
- A long CFD position has the potential to make a limited (although geared) loss (ie, a price can only fall to zero), but an unlimited gain. A short CFD position has the potential to make a limited gain (the maximum would be if the price fell to zero), but an unlimited loss (ie, a price could in theory continue to rise without limit).
- Due to the system of margining, you don't have to pay out the full value of the contract/shares etc up front, and the outlay is much smaller.
- CFDs are geared products and will magnify an investor's profits and losses. Investors can control a much larger number of shares for a smaller outlay, compared with actually buying the shares for instance, giving them more profits if the price rises and higher losses if the price falls.
- No stamp duty is payable on CFDs.

- For long CFDs over shares, the buyer is also entitled to any dividend paid by the underlying company on which the CFD is based, during the life of the contract. (CFD brokers cover their side of the contract by trading in the underlying shares, to match their CFD obligations.)
- CGT is payable on gains, in the same way as investors would be liable if they made profits trading the shares outright.
- Stop losses are available, and guaranteed stop losses mean that the investor cannot lose more than a predetermined amount, even in a rapidly changing market.

Spread Betting

Spread bets and CFDs are very similar. The key difference is that spread bets constitute gambling, so:

- no stamp duty is payable, and
- winnings are free from CGT.

They are available over a much more diverse and varied subject matter, but are generally less flexible than their CFD counterparts. For example, they have set expiry dates, whereas a CFD can be closed at any time.

8.7 Introduction to Options

Definition

> An option is a contract that gives the right, **but not the obligation**, to buy or sell an asset at a given price on or before a given date.

In the same way as a future, an option allows an investor to purchase or sell an asset at a future time for a price agreed today. The main distinction between the two types of derivative is that with a future, the parties have an obligation under the contract, but with an option, the buyer has a choice about whether to use it.

The investor's choice will be determined by how the price of the asset in the current market compares with the price they are able to buy or sell under the option. If the price is favourable, the investor will exercise the option. If the price is not favourable, the investor has the right to let it lapse.

Terminology

- **Buyer** – the party purchasing the option is described as the 'long', the 'buyer' or the 'holder'.
- **Seller** – the party selling the option is described as the 'short', the 'seller' or the 'writer'.
- **Intrinsic value**:
  - for a call option, the intrinsic value is the current market price of the underlying asset minus the exercise price. It is zero if the result is negative
  - for a put option, the intrinsic value is the exercise price minus the current market price of the underlying asset. It is zero if the result is negative.

- **Time value** – the premium is the sum of intrinsic value and time value. So time value is premium minus intrinsic value.
- **In-the-money** – intrinsic value greater than zero.
- **At-the-money** – current market price of the underlying asset equals the exercise price.
- **Out-of-the-money** – intrinsic is zero, premium is all time value.

Options

Options may be traded on exchanges, or over-the-counter (OTC), and they come in two types:

Call Options

A call option gives the buyer (the long position) the right to buy the underlying asset if they choose to do so. If the long decides to do so, the seller of the option must sell (deliver) to the buyer the underlying asset at the agreed price.

Put Options

A put option gives the buyer (the long position) the right to sell the underlying asset if they choose to do so. If the long decides to do so, the seller of the option must buy (take delivery) of the underlying asset at the agreed price.

Candidates should be careful not to confuse the buyer of an option, with an option that gives the right to buy an asset!

To add a little clarity, you may find it helpful to think of options in terms of the following structure. There are four basic positions.

These are:

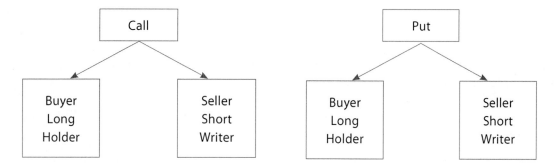

Underlying Asset

The underlying asset, often referred to as merely 'the underlying' is the subject matter of the option, the particular share, commodity or other asset.

Exercise Price/Strike Price

This is the price at which the underlying asset will be bought or sold, should the holder of the option choose to exercise it.

Premium

This is the cost of the option. It is the amount that the holder pays for the opportunity to be able to choose whether to buy or sell the asset at the agreed price in the future. The premium is paid, whether the holder of the option exercises it or not.

Expiry Date

All options have expiry dates, and expiry dates come in a number of styles, the two most common being:

- **American style** – these options can be exercised at any time after the option is purchased, through to, and including, the expiry date
- **European style** – these options can be exercised only on their expiry date.

Option Strategies

Buying a Call Option

In this case the holder of the option is 'long a call' of the underlying asset, and they are hoping that the price of the underlying asset in the market will rise above the strike price.

Let's look at an example.

```
Strike – 560p
Premium – 55p
Expiry – March 2019
```

Each option is for 1,000 shares (set by the exchange), so an investor buying this option has the right to buy 1,000 shares @ 560p. If the price rises to more than 560p, the investor should exercise the option. If they do so, they can buy the shares at 560p and sell them at a profit. If the price falls below 560p, the investor will not exercise the option (it's cheaper to buy them in the market at this point!) and will therefore forfeit the premium.

Buying call options is a bullish strategy. The investor hopes that the price will rise. The writer of the option is hoping precisely the opposite! If the price stays the same or falls, the writer of the option has to do nothing and can keep the premium.

Selling a Call Option

Selling a call option is therefore a bearish strategy.

Risk and Returns

Call Options		
	Maximum Profit	**Maximum Loss**
Writer	Premium	Unlimited
Holder	Unlimited	Premium

The buyer of an option can make an unlimited profit. They have an arrangement whereby they can buy shares at 560p. The price, in theory, could rise infinitely. The maximum they can lose is the premium, if they choose not to exercise the option and therefore forfeit it. In this respect, options are sometimes compared with insurance policies. With an insurance policy, you pay a premium for the right to be able to claim if you need to. You don't get the premium back if you don't make a claim!

Buying a Put Option

In this case, the holder of the option is 'long a put' of the underlying asset, and they are hoping that the price of the underlying asset in the market will fall below the strike price.

Let's take another look.

Strike – 560p

Premium – 39.5p

Expiry – March 2019

This time, the investor has the right to sell 1,000 shares @ 560p. If the price falls to less than 560p, the investor should exercise the option. If they do so, they can sell the shares at 560p and buy them back at a lower price in the market, and make a profit. If the price rises above 560p, the investor will not exercise the option (it's more beneficial to sell the shares at the higher market price than it is to sell them at 560p under the option agreement) and will therefore forfeit the premium.

Buying put options is a bearish strategy. The investor hopes that the price will fall. The writer of the option is still hoping the opposite. If the price rises, the writer of the option has to do nothing and can keep the premium, because as we have seen above, the investor will choose to sell the shares in the market because he can get a higher price for them there.

Selling a Put Option

Selling a put option is therefore a neutral or bullish strategy.

Risks and Returns

	Put Options	
	Maximum Profit	**Maximum Loss**
Writer	Premium	Strike price less premium
Holder	Strike price less premium	Premium

The buyer of a put option can only make a limited profit. The price can, at worst, only fall to zero. If, in our example, this happened, the investor could sell the shares to the writer of the option, for 560p. They will have paid 39.5p per share premium.

The maximum profit they can make is 560p – 39.5p = 520.50p. As before, the maximum that the holder can lose is the premium.

The maximum that the writer can lose is the flip side of the holder's position. The writer may have to purchase the shares for a maximum price of 560p, against which they can offset the premium that they have received. The maximum profit that the writer can make is, once again, the premium.

8.8 Features of UK-Traded Options on Individual Securities and Indices

Only traded options are being discussed in this section – traded options are those which are traded on an exchange. Exchange-traded options are similar to futures in that to ensure maximum liquidity in the market, the terms are standardised. For example, with the shares traded option that we have already looked at, each option is for 1,000 shares.

The table below compares and contrasts the differences between equity and index-based traded options:

Equities	Indices
Each stock has a predetermined expiry date based on quarterly cycles. Stock options, for example, expire in March, June, September and December. A number of expiry dates are available at any one time, allowing the investor some choice with regard to maturity.	Index options are available for monthly expiry dates for the first three months, and then continue in quarterly cycles to 24 months.
Equity options are physically settled.	There is no physical underlying asset that can be delivered.
Available on 'ICE Futures Europe on just under 100 leading stocks.	Available on 'ICE Futures Europe, FTSE 100 Index options and FTSE Index Flex Options.
The expiry date of equity options is American style.	FTSE index options are European style expiry dates.
Pricing (the premium) is quoted in pence per share. If the premium is quoted as 15p, it will need to be multiplied by 1,000 to work out the total premium cost of the option.	The amount paid under an index option is £10 per index point (tick size 0.5 points; tick value £5).
A range of exercise prices are available for each option, with different prices quoted for each.	A range of exercise prices are available for each option, with different prices quoted for each.
Holders of call options over an individual company's shares are not entitled to any dividend on that company's shares unless the option is exercised prior to the share going ex-dividend.	Index options do not pay dividends.

8.9 The Effect and Treatment of Scrip Issues, Rights Issues and Dividends in the Underlying Security

Scrip (Bonus Issues)

As we have already seen, an investor with a traded option has the right to be able to buy or sell 1,000 shares per single option contract. If a company announces a bonus issue, the terms of any pre-existing traded options will be adjusted to reflect the increased number of shares per issue.

Let's say that a company announces a one-for-one bonus issue. For existing shareholders, this will have the effect of doubling the number of shares that each shareholder owns and in theory, halving the price. Any pre-existing traded option is adjusted in the same way, pro-rata the issue. The terms of the original call option that we looked at will therefore change from:

> Number of shares – 1,000
> Strike – 560p
> Premium – 55p
> Expiry – March 2019

to:

> Number of shares – 2,000
> Strike – 280p
> Premium – 27.5p
> Expiry – March 2019

Rights Issues

If a company announces a rights issue, the terms of an existing option contract will be adjusted to reflect the rights issue. As above, this will result in changes to the number of shares, the exercise price and the premium.

Dividends

If the buyer under a call option exercises an option during the 'cum-div' trading period, they will be entitled to the dividend payment on those shares. If they exercise the option during the 'ex-div' period, they will not be entitled to the dividend payment on those shares.

8.10 The Features of UK Company Warrants

Definition

A warrant is a security issued by a company that gives the holder the right (but not the obligation) to buy new shares in that company, at a fixed price, on a fixed future date.

They can be issued on a stand-alone basis, but tend to be issued together with other instruments, such as bonds, as a sweetener to the deal, to tempt investors to buy the bonds.

In reading their description, you might think that they are very like call options. They are, but there are a number of important differences:

- warrants are issued by the company itself and if exercised, the company issues new shares. The exercise of a call option results in the purchase of existing shares in the market
- warrants tend to be much longer dated than call options. When issued, the expiry date is likely to be many years in the future, whereas call options are available for expiry dates of the next three quarters, ie, maximum nine months
- warrants are traded on the LSE in much the same way as shares, whereas call options are traded on ICE Futures Europe.

8.11   The Features of Covered Warrants on Individual Securities and Indices

Although a covered warrant market had been around in many other countries across the world since 1985, they were introduced in the UK in 2002, when the LSE launched a service allowing them to be bought and sold on the exchange in a similar way to equities.

Definition

Like an option, a covered warrant will give an investor the right (but not the obligation) to buy or sell an underlying asset at a specified price on or before a pre-specified date.

Covered warrants can be issued, not only over shares and a range of indices, but also over popular shares in other markets, commodities, exchange rates, baskets of investments and many other types of underlying asset. For the purposes of your exam however, you will need to concentrate on covered warrants for shares and indices.

Much of the jargon around the use of covered warrants is the same as options, and they too are issued in the form of call (investor can buy the asset) and put (investor can sell the asset) warrants.

They are, in effect, securitised derivatives issued by highly regarded financial institutions. In plain English, this means that financial institutions (there are five in the UK) issue call or put options and cover themselves against exercise by purchasing or selling the underlying asset at the same time.

Example

A company issues a covered call warrant allowing the purchaser the right to buy 1,000 Barclays Bank ordinary shares at £2.85. (Warrants are always issued with a strike price set [well] above the current market price at the time of issue.)

The issuer wants to make sure that it doesn't lose a fortune on the Barclays warrant, so at the same time, it goes out into the market and purchases an equivalent number of Barclays shares at £2.50 to hedge their position (they 'cover' their position).

In a year's time, the price of Barclays shares has risen to £3.00.

The investor will benefit from the price rise, as the shares are trading above the strike price of £2.85, so they are in profit. The issuer will also benefit from the price rising from £2.50 (cost of hedge) to £3.00. Although it will have to pass 15p per share profit on to the investor, it is still well up on the trade.

Cover Ratio

Traditional company warrants tend to (but don't have to) be issued with a ratio of one for one, ie, one warrant entitles the holder to one share in the company.

In the covered warrant market, this is not the case. It may require many warrants to give entitlement to one share. This is expressed in terms of the 'cover ratio'. If 25 covered warrants are exercisable into one share, then the cover ratio is 25:1.

If the share is particularly expensive, it can make the covered warrants look expensive. Using a cover ratio brings the price of each individual warrant down to an easily tradable and marketable level.

The cover ratio is of particular note when trading index covered warrants. The value of a whole index will be very expensive, resulting in expensive covered warrants. No issuer has issued a covered warrant on a one-for-one basis. The ratio may be as low as ten or could be as high as 500.

Features/Contrast with Options:

- As with the company issued version, covered warrants are securities traded on the LSE. The market is transparent and liquid. There are currently (May 2016) 326 different covered warrants listed and traded on the LSE.
- The covered warrant market can be accessed through a stockbroker.
- Covered warrants have a typical lifespan of between one and eighteen months, which is much longer than a typical traded option.
- Dealing commissions are payable in the same way as they are with shares.
- The spread (the difference between the buying and selling price) is usually tighter than it is for a similar option.
- They are targeted at retail investors.
- They provide a way for retail investors to benefit when stock markets are falling.
- Covered warrants can only be cash settled.
- A purchaser of covered warrants never actually owns the shares, so stamp duty is not payable, dividends are never payable and the purchaser will never acquire any voting rights.

- They are high-risk, leveraged products, but the maximum the investor can lose is the amount of money originally invested.
- There are different types of covered warrant available, eg, basket, barrier, capped, corridor covered warrants.
- Covered warrants are issued on shares that are already in existence, not new shares.
- Prices can be volatile with a small change in share price causing a substantial decline in the value of a covered warrant.
- They are available in American and European style.

Valuation and Quotation of Warrants

If you know what goes into a warrant's price, you will be better positioned to work out whether it represents good value. A 50p warrant, for example, can be expensive compared to a £2.00 warrant.

This is because there are a number of factors that influence the price of a covered warrant including:

- the price differential between the strike (exercise) price and the current market price
- supply and demand
- the time until expiry.

To analyse the price, the first thing to do is to consider the differential between the strike price and the current market price. This is called the 'intrinsic value' (also known as the 'formula value' in the context of warrants) and measures the immediate profit that an investor would make, if they exercised the warrant (ignoring costs).

The cost (premium) of a warrant is split into two parts:

Warrant premium = intrinsic value + time value

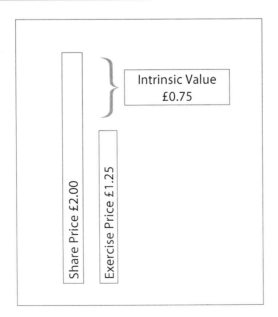

Any premium over and above the intrinsic value is time value and accounts for the other factors.

Company Issued Warrants	Covered Warrants
Issued by companies.	Issued by financial institutions.
Exercise results in the issue of new shares.	Exercise results in cash settlement.
Stamp duty is payable.	No stamp duty is payable.
Market can be illiquid.	More liquid market.

9. Unit Trusts and Open-Ended Investment Companies (OEICs)

9.1 Introduction

In this chapter, we examine the two most commonly used collective investment schemes (CISs), unit trusts and Unit Trusts and open-ended investment companies (OEICs). Please also bear in mind that the Financial Conduct Authority (FCA) and often many of the providers will refer to OEICs as ICVCs (investment companies with variable capital), as this is a direct translation of the European equivalent SICAV (Sociétés d'Investissement à Capital Variable), in order to make them recognisable to a European client.

While both types allow investors to pool investments in the same way, there are differences that reflect the development of the CIS industry over the last 20 years. Being able to recognise and articulate these differences is important in the context of private client advice.

Classification of Collective Investment Schemes

The FCA rules on the operation of CIS are covered in the specialist sourcebook Collective Investment Schemes (COLL). Here, the FCA does not make a distinction between unit trusts and OEICs. Instead it classifies funds into one of three categories:

UCITS Retail Schemes – those funds that comply with the EU directive undertaking for collective investments in transferable securities (UCITS) rules, and are designed for retail investors. From the product provider's perspective, the principal advantage of being a UCITS fund is that they are able to market the fund within the European Economic Area (EEA) without the need for further approval – a process known as 'passporting'.

Basic features of a UCITS IV fund:

- Can be sold anywhere in the EEA.
- Investors have access to a simplified prospectus.
- Can be sophisticated or non-sophisticated:
  - **non-sophisticated** – can continue to operate using the same portfolio structure as traditional long only funds, consisting primarily of physical assets such as equities and bonds

◦ **sophisticated** – have access to a range of other collectives, eg, index funds and exchange-traded funds (ETFs), and fund managers can adopt new strategies to enhance their portfolios. This includes long/short strategies, hedging and derivative strategies. While physical short selling is not permitted within a UCITS III fund, shorting is achieved through the use of derivatives, creating a synthetic short position. An example of this is a 130/30 fund where the fund can go short up to 30% of the value of the portfolio to go long with. This means that 130% is available to go long with. Another example of a UCITS III fund is Absolute Return Funds which use a variety of hedging strategies in an attempt to produce a positive return in any market condition.

Non-UCITS Retail Schemes (NURS) – with wider powers which exclude it from UCITS qualification but still aimed at retail investors, ie, a property fund.

Qualified Investor Schemes (QIS) – not designed for retail investors, but the more sophisticated investor. This does not, however, mean that it will only have professional clients investing in them. In reality, these schemes are often created for substantial private clients, charities or family trusts.

Unit trust and OEIC structures could be used to create any of these categories.

9.2   Unit Trusts

Unit Trusts arrived in the UK in the early 1930s, with the effect of the great stock market crash still being felt, and investors reluctant to return to the markets with the same risk remaining. The schemes were considered to be a way to tempt them back by showing them the reduced risks.

They are defined as trusts, and have trustees who are ultimately responsible for safeguarding both the assets and cash of the investors (known as beneficial owners). As Chapter 4 on trusts and trustees points out, there is a lot of historical baggage that comes with the formation of trusts, and it is difficult to make direct comparisons with similar structures in Europe. This can prove problematic if you are trying to translate documentation in other European languages.

For this reason, unit trusts have been historically more difficult to sell into the European markets and particularly to European institutional clients. Whereas in the UK, institutional investors are substantial supporters of the CIS industry. Another reason for European investors to shy away from unit trusts is their normal pricing method and we will cover this shortly.

In the 1990s, we began to see a significant shift away from the unit trust structure, and a move toward the OEIC structure. Probably the largest migration of funds from unit trust to OEIC was Invesco Perpetual in 2003, when over one weekend, they converted 48 unit trusts to ICVCs. Invesco Perpetual, along with other large providers, would argue that this allows them to position their funds in such a way that the UK range is saleable across the EU.

9.2.1   Unit Trust Structure

Section 237 of the Financial Services and Markets Act 2000 (FSMA 2000) recognises unit trusts as CISs created by a trust deed entered into by the fund manager and the trustee who must be independent of one another. Unit trust holders have a direct beneficial interest in the unit trust's portfolio of investments. The unit trust itself does not have a separate legal personality so cannot be sued in its own name. The trustee undertakes all its actions on its behalf.

Most unit trusts have two unit classes – income or accumulation. However, under the FCA *COLL* sourcebook, they can create others, very similar to OEICs – see below.

9.2.2   Dual Pricing

The most common form of unit trust pricing is dual pricing or bid/offer. The FSA (the regulator at that time) had planned to move all open-ended CIS to a single price methodology, but a number of high-profile providers, including Schroders, successfully lobbied to keep dual pricing as a legitimate method of pricing. Some would argue that it actually represents a more transparent form of pricing, as investors can easily see the basis of the valuation. It is equally true to say that some investors in unit trusts have always found the spread between the bid and the offer, and how it is arrived at, difficult to understand.

Price – Cancellation of Units

Bid value of all shares within the portfolio	−	Stockbroker fees for selling those shares on the stock market	+	Any cash being held within the portfolio (inc. dividends received)	÷	Number of units in issue

= True Bid Price or Cancellation – the price paid to the trustees to cancel the units.

Price – Creation of units

Offer value of all shares within the portfolio	+	Stockbroker fees for purchasing those shares on the stock market + stamp duty	+	Any cash being held within the portfolio (inc. dividends received)	÷	Number of units in issue

= Creation Price – the price paid to the trustee to create units.

Creation Price + Initial Charge (norm 5 – 6%) = Full Offer Price

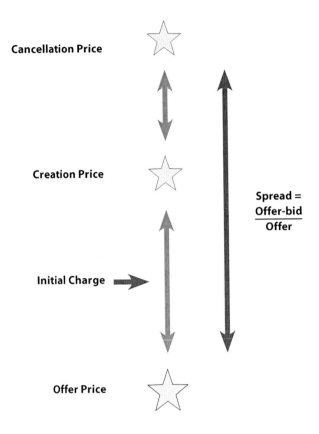

9.3   Open-Ended Investment Companies (OEICs)

We have already established that the OEIC structure is relatively new to the UK. However, they have been available in Europe for many years as the CIS of choice, the SICAV.

9.3.1   The OEIC Structure

It is empowered by Section 262 of FSMA 2000, and is a corporate body; hence it issues shares and not units. This company must have at least one director referred to as the ACD (authorised corporate director). The OEIC then appoints a depository to hold the scheme's assets and provide oversight. Unlike unit trusts, it has no direct beneficiaries, but shareholders (ie, investors). As a legal entity, it can be sued.

The real flexibility with an OEIC structure comes from its ability to create a holding with a number of sub -funds beneath it. Each sub-fund can then create as many share classes as it wishes, and this is normally done to suit the investor profile and needs.

```
                    ┌─────────────────┐
                    │     The UK      │
                    │   series OEIC   │
                    └─────────────────┘
          ┌──────────────────┼──────────────────┐
   ┌─────────────┐    ┌─────────────┐    ┌─────────────┐
   │  UK growth  │    │  UK equity  │    │  UK small   │
   │             │    │   income    │    │  companies  │
   └─────────────┘    └─────────────┘    └─────────────┘
   ┌──────────┬───────────────┬──────────────┐
```

Group 1 shares – 5% initial charge 2% AMC	Group 2 shares – 0% initial charge 0.5% AMC (min £1 million)	Group 3 shares – euro denominated

It is cheaper and quicker to set up a new sub fund and/or share class under this structure compared to the establishment of a new unit trust with its own trust deed. However, as mentioned before, unit trusts are now able to establish new unit classes in a similar way to OEIC share classes.

9.3.2 Single Pricing

Under FCA rules, OEICs can choose to be dual priced. However, this would remove the significant European selling point. So they mainly opt for single pricing to be comparable with the SICAVs. Single pricing, by nature, is quite straightforward, until like dual pricing, you have more sellers than buyers or vice versa and need to reflect your pricing basis, ie, bid or offer valuation.

Put simply:

- Single pricing – mid-market value of the underlying investments.
- Charges to clients are not quoted in this price.
- The price for buying or selling a share at any point in time will be the same:
  - 100 shares x £10.00 = £1,000
  - Initial charge of 5% = £50
  - Total = £1,050

However, by allowing all buyers and sellers to use this price, problems could arise. If you are net buyers or sellers of shares you may disadvantage the fund. The following example shows the problem, and the resolution used by most OEIC managers:

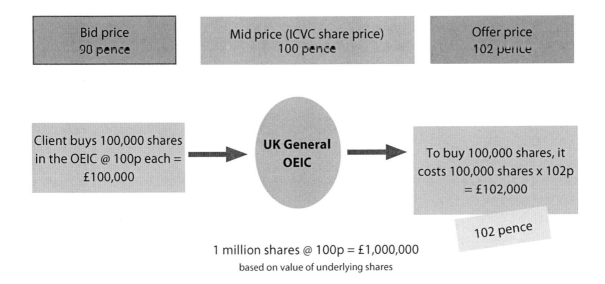

This is an example of dilution adjustment or single swinging price. Obviously the fund has been moved on to an offer valuation and everyone will be using this price. The manager does not have to make this public but must inform investors if they ask. In reality, most managers will be swinging the price of smaller funds on a frequent basis. The alternative is a dilution levy applied only to larger investors, and this can prove very unpopular.

In the case of both dual and single pricing, there is the capacity to include the initial charge for buying new units or shares. The annual management charge or fee (AMC or AMF) is taken daily from the funds, as a figure calculated on the NAV.

9.4 Dealing and Settlement

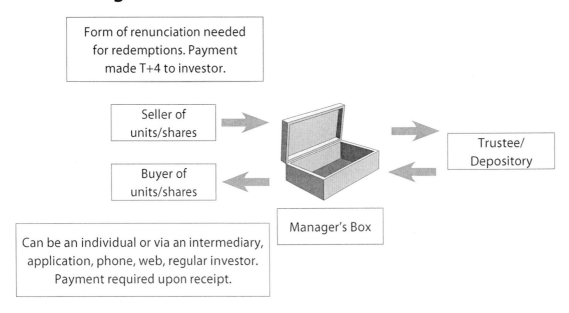

9.5 Types of Funds

To help all advisers and clients measure how their fund is performing, the Investment Association (IA – formerly known as the Investment Management Association [IMA]) produce and maintain sector classifications to enable us to review a fund's performance against others in its sector. These are shown below. Investment funds used exclusively for the provision of life and pensions products will use sector classification created by the Association of British Insurers (ABI), so while there are over 2,000 CISs available in the UK, this does not include the life and pensions funds.

Funds Principally Targeting Capital Protection

Money Market

These are funds which invest at least 95% of their assets in money market instruments (ie, cash and near cash, such as bank deposits, certificates of deposit, very short-term fixed-interest securities or floating rate notes).

Protected/Guaranteed Funds

These are funds, other than money market funds, which principally aim to provide a return of a set amount of capital to the investor (either explicitly guaranteed or via an investment strategy highly likely to achieve this objective) plus some market upside.

Funds Principally Targeting Income (by Asset Category)

Fixed Income Sectors

UK Gilts

These are funds which invest at least 95% of their assets in sterling denominated (or hedged back to sterling), AAA-rated, government-backed securities, with at least 80% invested in UK government securities (gilts).

UK Index Linked Gilts

These are funds which invest at least 95% of their assets in sterling denominated (or hedged back to sterling), AAA-rated, government-backed, index-linked securities, with at least 80% invested in UK index-linked gilts.

Sterling Corporate Bond

These are funds which invest at least 80% of their assets in sterling denominated (or hedged back to sterling), BBB-minus or above corporate bond securities (as measured by Standard & Poor's or an equivalent external rating agency). This excludes convertibles, preference shares and PIBs.

Sterling Strategic Bond

These are funds which invest at least 80% of their assets in sterling denominated (or hedged back to sterling) fixed-interest securities. This includes convertibles, preference shares and PIBs. At any point in time, the asset allocation of these funds could theoretically place the fund in one of the other fixed-interest sectors. The funds will remain in this sector on these occasions, since it is the manager's stated intention to retain the right to invest across the sterling fixed-interest credit risk spectrum.

Sterling High Yield

These are funds which invest at least 80% of their assets in sterling denominated (or hedged back to sterling) fixed-interest securities and at least 50% of their assets in BBB-minus fixed-interest securities (as measured by Standard & Poor's or an equivalent external rating agency), including convertibles, preference shares and PIBs.

Global Bonds

These are funds which invest at least 80% of their assets in fixed-interest securities. All funds which contain more than 80% fixed-interest investments are to be classified under this heading regardless of the fact that they may have more than 80% in a particular geographic sector, unless that geographic area is the UK, when the fund should be classified under the relevant UK (sterling) heading.

Note:

1. *Across all fixed income sectors, there is no prescription within the non-core parameters. Firms are expected to know. While the sectors provide freedom in respect of investment in the non-core element of the definitions, the investment strategy adopted must be transparent to the end customer, appropriate to deliver on the fund objective and take account of the firm's TCF (treating customers fairly) obligations.*
2. *Convertibles, preference shares and PIBs are excluded from the investment grade and government percentage in the fixed income sector classifications. This will allow a small holding in these instruments in the higher quality funds, and not inhibit investment in them for the higher risk/higher return funds.*
3. *Where ratings of a bond differ between the rating agencies, it is for the firm to decide which rating is relevant, taking account of their own assessment of the security of the bond. Consideration should be given to what would result from the most cautious interpretation, or if an average of the ratings were adopted.*
4. *Derivative usage should be within the spirit of the sector restrictions, and not lead to the actual exposure of the fund being outside the set limits of its sector. This will be self-policed (for now). The IA does not wish to inhibit funds from using their full UCITS IV powers, while recognising the limitations on monitoring at the present time.*
5. *In the gilt/bond sectors, a security with nil to three months to maturity will be treated as cash. Securities maturing within three to twelve months will be treated as bonds.*

Mixed Asset Sectors

UK Equity & Bond Income

Funds which invest at least 80% of their assets in the UK, between 20% and 80% in UK fixed-interest securities and between 20% and 80% in UK equities. These funds aim to have a yield in excess of 120% of the FTSE All Share Index.

Note:

1. *Please refer to any relevant fixed income notes.*
2. *In the managed (mixed asset) sectors (cautious managed, balanced managed, active managed and UK equity and bond income), cash and fixed income will be treated as interchangeable.*
3. *Hybrid instruments, such as convertibles, preference shares or PIBs, should not contribute to the minimum 20% required, in UK fixed income or UK equity.*

4. *Instruments that require clarification as to their treatment within the asset categories should not be used to contribute to the core parameters. Clarification of treatment can be sought from the monitoring company.*

Equity Sectors

UK Equity Income

Funds which invest at least 80% in UK equities and which aim to achieve a historic yield on the distributable income in excess of 110% of the FTSE All Share yield at the fund's year end.

General notes (applying to UK equity income and UK equity income and growth sectors):

1. *To ensure compliance with the sector criteria, funds should supply data for monitoring, to enable the calculation of historic yield, based on the IA guidelines set out in 'Yield Calculation and Disclosure by UK Authorised Funds – Guidelines for Managers Sept 2012'.*
2. *IA reserves the right to amend the yield parameters of the UK equity income and the sector(s) up or down to account for market factors.*
3. *IA reserves the right to adjust the relative yield parameter tests for the UK equity income sector should market conditions indicate that this is necessary to ensure the integrity of both sectors.*
4. *The term 'aim' is retained and will have discretionary application to be decided on a case by case basis by IA/the Performance Category Review Committee (PCRC). It is not retained to suggest that the yield test is aspirational.*

As a broad indicator, it could be used for a fund that has to deal with very large cash flows into the fund over a short period, which may impact on the fund's ability in the short term to meet the yield parameter test.

Candidates may want to visit www.trustnet.com for a full list of sectors and constituents.

Funds Principally Targeting Growth (by Asset Category)

Fixed Income Sectors

UK Zeros

Funds investing at least 80% of their assets in sterling denominated (or hedged back to sterling), and at least 80% of their assets in zero dividend preference shares or equivalent instruments (ie, not income producing). This excludes preference shares which produce an income.

Equity Sectors

UK Equities

UK All Companies

Funds that invest at least 80% of their assets in UK equities that have a primary objective of achieving capital growth.

Note:

1. *Instruments that require clarification as to their treatment within the asset categories should not typically be used to contribute to the core parameters. Clarification of treatment can be checked with the monitoring company.*
2. *The 'look-through' principle will apply when considering securities that are structured with the legal form of an equity (such as a listed investment trust and some listed ETFs), but manage or invest in different underlying assets such as property or commodities. If such entities themselves invest in equities, the holdings are classified as equities. Further details may be obtained from the monitoring company.*

UK Smaller Companies

Funds that invest at least 80% of their assets in UK equities of companies that form the bottom 10% by market capitalisation.

Note:

1. *The universe of eligible UK equities is constructed by the monitoring company and comprises all relevant securities available from the Reuters database from which a market capitalisation cut-off is derived.*
2. *Instruments that require clarification as to their treatment within the asset categories should not typically be used to contribute to the core parameters. Clarification of treatment can be sought from the monitoring company.*
3. *The 'look-through' principle will apply when considering securities that are structured with the legal form of an equity (such as a listed investment trust and some listed ETFs), but manage or invest in different underlying assets such as property or commodities. If such entities themselves invest in equities, the holdings are classified as equities. Further details may be obtained from the monitoring company.*

Overseas Equities

Japan

Funds that invest at least 80% of their assets in Japanese equities.

Japanese Smaller Companies

Funds that invest at least 80% of their assets in Japanese equities of companies that form the bottom 30% by market capitalisation.

Asia Pacific including Japan

Funds that invest at least 80% of their assets in Asia Pacific equities including a Japanese content. The Japanese content must make up less than 80% of assets.

Asia Pacific excluding Japan

Funds that invest at least 80% of their assets in Asia Pacific equities and exclude Japanese securities.

North America

Funds that invest at least 80% of their assets in North American equities.

North American Smaller Companies

Funds that invest at least 80% of their assets in North American equities of companies that form the bottom 20% by market capitalisation.

Europe including UK

Funds that invest at least 80% of their assets in European equities. They may include UK equities, but these must not exceed 80% of the fund's assets.

Europe excluding UK

Funds that invest at least 80% of their assets in European equities and exclude UK securities.

European Smaller Companies

Funds that invest at least 80% of their assets in European equities of companies that form the bottom 20% by market capitalisation in the European market. They may include UK equities, but these must not exceed 80% or the fund's assets. ('Europe' includes all countries in the Morgan Stanley Capital International indices (MSCI) and FTSE pan-European indices.)

Global Sector (Formerly Known as Global Growth)

Funds that invest at least 80% of their assets in equities (but not more than 80% in UK assets) and that have the prime objective of achieving capital growth.

Global Emerging Markets

Funds that invest 80% or more of their assets directly or indirectly in emerging markets as defined by the World Bank, without geographical restriction. Indirect investment, eg, China shares listed in Hong Kong, should not exceed 50% of the portfolio.

Note:

1. *If uncertainty arises about which countries are included in a specific regional equity sector, please make reference to the relevant FTSE or MSCI index for guidance. If there is a difference, the broader index should be used.*
2. *The above sectors also require funds to be broadly diversified within the relevant country/region/asset class. Funds that concentrate solely on a specialist theme, sector or single market size (or a single country in a multi-currency region) would be incorporated in the specialist sector (see below), or in the case of tech funds, in the technology and telecommunications sector.*
3. *In the smaller companies sectors, the universe of eligible equities is constructed by the monitoring company and comprises all relevant securities available from the Reuters database from which a market capitalisation cut-off is derived.*

4. *The 'look-through' principle will apply when considering securities that are structured with the legal form of an equity (such as a listed investment trust and some listed ETFs), but manage or invest in different underlying assets such as property or commodities. If such entities themselves invest in equities, the holdings are classified as equities. Further details may be obtained from the monitoring company.*

5. *Instruments that require clarification as to their treatment within the asset categories should not typically be used to contribute to the core parameters. Clarification of treatment can be sought from the monitoring company.*

Mixed Asset Sectors

Cautious Managed

Funds investing in a range of assets with the maximum equity exposure restricted to 60% of the fund and with at least 30% invested in fixed interest and cash. There is no specific requirement to hold a minimum per cent of non-UK equity within the equity limits. Assets must be at least 50% in sterling/ euro, and equities are deemed to include convertibles.

Balanced Managed

Funds would offer investment in a range of assets, with the maximum equity exposure restricted to 85% of the fund. At least 10% of the total fund must be held in non-UK equities. Assets must be at least 50% in sterling/euro and equities are deemed to include convertibles.

Active Managed

Funds would offer investment in a range of assets, with the manager being able to invest up to 100% in equities at their discretion. At least 10% of the total fund must be held in non-UK equities. There is no minimum sterling/euro balance, and equities are deemed to include convertibles. At any one time, the asset allocation of these funds may hold a high proportion of non-equity assets, such that the asset allocation would, by default, place the fund in either the balanced or cautious sector. These funds would remain in this sector on these occasions since it is the manager's stated intention to retain the right to invest up to 100% in equities.

Note:

1. *The 'look-through' principle will apply when considering securities that are structured with the legal form of an equity (such as a listed investment trust and some listed ETFs), but manage or invest in different underlying assets such as property or commodities. If such entities themselves invest in equities, the holdings are classified as equities. Further details may be obtained from the monitoring company.*

2. *In the managed (mixed asset) sectors (cautious managed, balanced managed, active managed and UK equity and bond), cash and fixed income will be treated as interchangeable.*

Specialist Sectors

Absolute Return

Funds managed with the aim of delivering absolute (ie, more than zero) returns in any market conditions. Typically, funds in this sector would normally expect to deliver absolute (more than zero) returns on a 12-month basis.

Note:

1. *Funds are classified to remain in this sector on the basis of self-election by firms with qualitative oversight by the PCRC.*
2. *There is no asset-based monitoring for this sector. Consideration should be given by those listing in this sector to the obligation for TCF.*
3. *Performance comparisons are inappropriate, due to the diverse nature of the objectives of the funds populating this sector, including differing benchmarks, risk characteristics and timeframes for delivering performance.*
4. *Absolute returns are made in the base currency of the fund. Investors may be subject to currency losses, should the base currency be different to their domiciled/invested currency. Currently, only funds that are trying to achieve an absolute return in sterling are classified to the sector.*
5. *Funds listed in this sector do not guarantee returns.*

Personal Pensions

Funds which are only available for use in a personal pension plan (PPP) or free standing additional voluntary contribution (FSAVC) scheme.

Present arrangements for unit trust personal pension schemes require providers to set up separate personal pension unit trusts under an overall tax-sheltered umbrella. These funds then, in turn, invest in the group's equivalent mainstream trusts. Pension funds are not to be confused with exempt funds which are flagged separately.

Property

Funds which predominantly invest in property. In order to invest predominantly in property, funds should either:

- invest at least 60% of their assets directly in property, or
- invest at least 80% of their assets in property securities, or
- when their direct property holdings fall below the 60% threshold for a period of more than six months, invest enough of the balance of their assets in property securities to ensure that at least 80% of the fund is invested in property, whereupon it becomes a hybrid fund.

Notes:

1. *Funds falling into the first two categories will be flagged as 'direct property funds' and 'property securities funds' respectively.*
2. *If a fund has a minimum of 80% in property (direct and securities), but does not exceed the 60% direct property threshold, then it is a 'hybrid property fund'.*
3. *Property securities are admissible assets within the investment limits indicated, if included in an appropriate, independently constructed index.*
4. *Property securities held within the 80% limit are intended to be equities.*

5. *IA expects that member firms will follow good practice guidelines when using techniques to value property assets.*

6. *Newly launched property funds that are intending to invest directly in physical property will be permitted a period of 12 months to come into compliance with the sector definition. The funds will be asked to make an appropriate commitment at the outset to the IA.*

Specialist

Funds that have an investment universe that is not accommodated by the mainstream sectors. Performance ranking of funds within the sector as a whole is inappropriate, given the diverse nature of its constituents.

Technology and Telecommunications

Funds that invest at least 80% of their assets in technology and telecommunications sectors, as defined by major index providers.

Candidates are encouraged to review the IA website (www.investmentuk.org) for sector updates.

Unclassified

Funds which do not want to be classified into other IA sectors such as private funds or funds which have been removed from other IA sectors due to non-compliance.

 How would you expect to use the sector categories when discussing performance with a private client? By looking at the sector, you will be able to see how many similar funds there are. Depending on where the fund manager and provider ranked, you will need to decide if this is satisfactory and meeting client expectations as you know them. Questions that you often ask might be:

• How does this compare to others?
• How does this compare to the fund's own benchmarks?
• What is the fund manager's comment on this performance, and are there specific reasons for underperformance or overperformance?

9.6   Tax Treatment

An advantage of investing in CIS is that they do not pay any CGT from within the fund. They are subject to corporation tax in respect of income arising in the fund.

However, as with other investments, personal taxation will apply to the individual.

Authorised Unit Trusts
Income & Corporation taxes Act 1988
Capital Gains Act 1992

OEICs
Open-Ended Investment Companies
(TAX) Regulations 1997

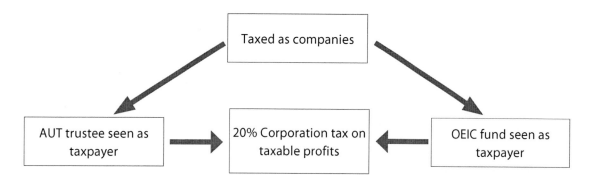

For the calculation of tax due, the following is used:

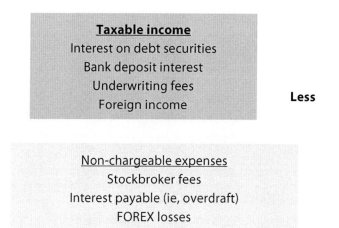

Taxable income		**Chargeable expenses**
Interest on debt securities		Alternative Fund Manager (AFM) fees
Bank deposit interest		Depositary fees
Underwriting fees	**Less**	Safe custody fees
Foreign income		FCA fees
		Auditor's fees
		Interest expenses
Non-chargeable expenses		Registration fees
Stockbroker fees		Interest distributions
Interest payable (ie, overdraft)		
FOREX losses		

10. Exchange-Traded Funds (ETFs)

10.1 Introduction

These funds are commonly referred to as ETFs, and were established in 2000 to rival the index tracker funds, which were first launched in the UK in 1988. This newer competitor to index trackers can similarly mirror market indices, but via a share rather than a fund. They have several advantages over index tracker funds but have been relatively slow to take off in the UK retail investment market, although their popularity and the variety of funds available has accelerated dramatically in the last few years.

10.1.1 Structure and Objectives

ETFs are funds that are traded on a stock exchange. These CIS assets mirror the price movements of the underlying share portfolio of an index, sector or commodity. Examples might be the FTSE 100, water sector shares or gold. By trading a single share, users can effectively gain access to an entire index without the burden of investing in each of the constituent stocks, making ETFs a highly efficient and cost-effective investment tool.

ETFs are open-ended CIS and they replicate a very wide range of indices, investing in everything from shares and property to more exotic asset classes such as private equity, energy, commodities, infrastructure, property and water.

One of the largest providers of ETFs is iShares. There is, for example, the Water iShare, which tracks the S&P Global Water index, and provides exposure to 50 companies around the world involved in water-related businesses. Similarly, the Private Equity iShare tracks the S&P Listed Private Equity index, which consists of 25 leading private equity companies. The iShare FTSE UK Dividend Plus tracks the higher dividend paying companies of the FTSE 100 and the iShare property mirrors the FTSE UK property sector.

10.1.2 Types of ETFs

Index ETFs

Hold securities and attempt to replicate the performance of a stock market index. An index fund seeks to track the performance of an index by holding in its portfolio either the contents of the index or a representative sample of the securities in the index.

Commodity ETFs or ETCs (Exchange-Traded Commodities)

Invest in commodities, such as precious metals and futures. ETCs track the performance of an underlying commodity index, including total return indices based on a single commodity. They are similar to ETFs and traded and settled exactly like normal shares on their own dedicated segment. ETCs have market maker support with guaranteed liquidity, enabling investors to gain exposure to commodities, on-exchange, during market hours.

Bond ETFs

Invest in various fixed income sectors and durations.

Currency ETFs

The first ever currency ETF was launched in 2005 and was called the Euro Currency Trust New York. Since then, several have been issued, tracking all major currencies, both long and short different currency crosses.

Actively Managed ETFs

Publishing their current securities portfolios on their web sites daily, these funds are at risk from arbitrage activities by market participants who might choose to front-run their trades.

Hedge Fund ETFs

A hedge fund ETF tracks a hedge fund and follows a group of hedge funds' activity.

Leveraged ETFs

A leveraged ETF is a special type of ETF that attempts to achieve returns that are more sensitive to market movements than a non-leveraged ETF.

10.1.3 Comparisons with Other Collective Investment Schemes

Both ETF and traditional index tracker funds are similar, in that they aim to mirror an underlying index. The difference is that an ETF can be traded at any time of the trading day, whereas an index tracker fund is normally either a unit trust or OEIC fund which can only be traded at one point in the trading day (a valuation point dictated by the fund manager).

Their charging structure is also different. With an ETF, you only have to pay a stockbroker's commission and, significantly, no stamp duty. However, as we have learnt with unit trusts or OEICs, there are both initial, and annual, management charges. Additionally, with a traditional CIS, there is stamp duty reserve tax (SDRT) which is levied against the new shares or units that the fund may need to create. Although this is not charged separately to investors, it is a charge against the fund.

The charges on an ETF can be slightly lower than those associated with index tracker funds. The annual total expense ratio (TER) for an equity-based ETF is typically around 0.4% per annum, which can be slightly lower than the annual charges on some unit trust tracker funds, but careful comparison is required as it is not the case for all ETFs.

ETFs are open-ended funds. This means that the share price of the ETF is close to the value of the underlying assets.

10.1.4 Dealing and Settlement

In the UK, ETFs are traded on the London Stock Exchange (SETS). In the European markets there are a number of markets that trade ETFs, namely Euronext Paris, Euronext Amsterdam, SWX Swiss Exchange, Frankfurt and Borsa Italiana. Settlement therefore replicates normal equity trading.

10.1.5 Tax Treatment

There is no tax difference between holding, say, a FTSE 100 index tracker and an ETF tracking the FTSE 100. Capital gains are subject to CGT and income to income tax even if it is not physically received by the investor. Within an ISA or self-invested pension plan (SIPP), both will be free of CGT and income tax. But, many ETFs are based outside the UK and they may be subject to withholding tax in the country concerned.

10.1.6 Criticism

It has been argued that ETFs represent short-term speculation, that their trading expenses decrease returns to investors, and that most ETFs provide insufficient diversification.

In a survey of investment professionals, the most frequently cited disadvantage of ETFs was the unknown, untested indices used by many ETFs. Many of the indices have actually been created specifically for ETF to mirror and track. This obviously calls into question the issue of the relationship between the ETF issuer and the index provider. This dilemma is wedded to the overwhelming number of choices.

Some critics claim that ETFs can be, and have been, used to manipulate market prices, including having been used for short-selling, which many believe contributed to the market collapse of 2008.

There are also concerns that, while liquidity is not an issue when markets are rising, there will be some that might be tested in the event of a stock market collapse.

Despite these reservations, ETFs are the fastest growing type of fund, because they are generally the cheapest form of passive investment and they often have good marketability throughout the trading day.

11. Investment Trusts

11.1 Introduction

Investment trusts are probably the oldest structured form of collective investments, with the first trust created in the 1860s. They are public limited companies and their 'product' is to invest in other companies, quoted or unquoted.

As public companies, investment trusts are run by a board of directors. The directors can choose to self-manage, which means they undertake the investment management themselves. Alternatively, and more commonly, they can outsource the investment management, along with other tasks such as administration, registration and accountancy.

Unlike unit trusts and OEICs, investment trusts are closed-end funds, meaning they have a fixed number of shares in issue at any time. The shares of investment trusts are traded as normal on the stock market, with the price fluctuating according to supply and demand.

Another major difference to unit trusts and OEICs is the option for investment trust managers to borrow money freely to buy shares and other assets when they see good investment opportunities. This 'gearing' (or 'leveraging') adds to the possibilities of greater rewards, but at greater risk.

Categories of Investment Trusts

There are a vast number of different investment trusts offering a variety of investment objectives and risk levels, ranging from security of capital with no income, to very high income with low capital security.

The Association of Investment Companies (AIC) classifies investment trusts into several main sectors, five property sectors, 15 specialist sectors and nine covering different categories of venture capital trusts (VCTs). These are based on the combination of regional and sectoral focus of a particular portfolio. For example:

*   **UK smaller companies** sector includes investment trusts with a policy to invest at least 80% of their assets in smaller, UK based company securities.
*   **European emerging markets** sector includes investment trusts with at least 80% of their assets in European emerging market securities.

The combination of region and sector focus creates the very diverse levels of risk possible.

11.2 Closed-End Funds and Net Asset Values

As already mentioned, unlike unit trusts and OEICs, investment trusts are closed-end funds. This means that the amount of money that the investment trust raises to invest is fixed at the start by issuing a set number of shares to investing shareholders. Having a stable pool of money to invest enables the fund manager to plan ahead. Every investor looking to purchase or sell shares must be matched to a potential seller or buyer, via the stock market, before a transaction can take place. The company's own investments are not affected.

11.2.1 Net Asset Values (NAV)

The share price of an investment trust obviously depends, to some extent, on the value of the underlying investments, but not as directly as is the case for a unit trust or OEIC. It can depend on a number of other factors that affect supply and demand. In many cases, the share price of an investment trust is less (at a discount) than the net asset values (NAV) per share. The NAV is the value of an investment trust's investments per ordinary share, after taking liabilities into account. The NAV is calculated by taking:

- the total value of a trust's listed investments at mid-market prices
- plus its unlisted investments as valued by the directors
- plus cash and other assets
- minus the nominal value of loans and preference shares
- the resulting figure is known as the 'shareholders' funds' and is divided by the number of ordinary shares in issue to arrive at the NAV.

 As a simple example, what would be the NAV per share of an investment trust, if shareholders' funds are worth £80 million and there are 20 million ordinary shares in issue?

The NAV would be 400p (80 million/20 million).

11.2.2 Discount and Premium

As the share price of an investment trust is determined primarily by supply and demand, it is highly likely that the share price will not match the NAV.

In many cases, the share price is less than the NAV. In this situation, the investment trust is said to be trading at a discount.

If the share price is more than the NAV, the investment trust is said to be trading at a premium. This is less common, and few trusts trade at a premium for long.

The existence of discounts and premiums for investors in investment trusts is crucial, as they can exaggerate returns either way.

For example, a trust with a narrowing discount can enhance an investor's return, as we will see from the following example:

- XYZ IT plc is trading at 80p and has a NAV of £1.00. This is a discount of 20%.
- Six months later, XYZ IT plc is trading at 135p and has a NAV of £1.50. This is a discount of 10%.
- While the NAV has increased by 50% (£1.00 to £1.50), the share price has increased by 69% (80p to £1.35).
- This is excellent news for the investor!

Alternatively, a trust may have a widening discount:

- XYZ IT plc is trading at 90p and has a NAV of £1.00. This is a discount of 10%.
- Six months later, XYZ IT plc is trading at 120p and has a NAV of £1.50. This is a discount of 20%.
- Whereas the NAV has increased by 50% (£1.00 to £1.50) the share price has only increased by 33% (90p to £1.20).

In these two examples, the investment trust managers performed identically, increasing the NAV from £1.00 to £1.50. However, the movement of the share price, which they cannot control, meant very different returns for individual investors. During the 1990s, a major appeal of investment trusts was due to the generally narrowing discounts.

So, in capital terms, an investor is not affected by the discount or premium, if it does not widen or narrow.

 What factors do you think affect the discount?

The factors include:

- Investor sentiment towards a particular market (for example, emerging market investment trusts tend to have a higher discount than general investment trusts).
- The reputation of the investment managers.
- The existence of a savings plan and an ISA, as these have tended to provide a steady demand for certain investment trust shares.
- Share buy-backs, which reduce the supply of stock.
- The provision of warrants.
- The structure and cost of any debt funding (gearing).

Discounts can also generate a significant income advantage for investors. In effect, a discount boosts the net yield of an investment trust. This is due to the fact that the yield on the underlying investments is based on the NAV, but the yield is expressed as a percentage of the market price.

Example

XYZ IP plc has a NAV of 100p on which UK dividend income received is 3p. The share price is 80p (a 20% discount), giving a yield of 3p/80p x 100 = 3.75%. Even taking typical management charges into account of, say, 0.5%, this is still a good return.

11.2.3 Share Buy-backs

If the discount to NAV becomes very wide, investment trust managers sometimes choose to buy back some of the shares, thereby reducing the excess supply and possibly (hopefully!) narrowing the discount.

As for other public limited companies, a buy-back by an investment trust of its own shares requires the permission of shareholders. There are also FCA rules that the investment trust will need to adhere to.

Investment trusts are allowed to hold a limited level of shares bought back 'in treasury' (known as 'treasury shares'). This means the shares aren't cancelled and can be sold again at a later date. This mechanism offers a trust an effective way of balancing supply and demand for its shares at different times.

11.3 Gearing

As already mentioned, investment trusts can borrow to purchase additional investments. This is called financial gearing. This facility allows investment trusts to take advantage of a long-term view on a sector, or to take advantage of a favourable situation or a particularly attractive stock, without having to sell existing investments.

The ability of investment trusts to gear can work to the advantage of shareholders, if the investment returns achieved with the borrowed money exceed the cost of the loan. However, if returns do not exceed costs, the trust's performance will clearly suffer.

So gearing adds to the risk element of an investment trust, but it also adds to the potential returns. Financial gearing magnifies a trust's performance. If a trust 'gears up' and then markets rise and the returns on the investments outstrip the costs of borrowing, the overall returns to investors will be even greater. On the flip side, if markets fall and the performance of the assets in the portfolio is poor, then losses suffered by the investor will be also be magnified.

This is probably best seen via an example.

Example

XYZ IT plc has 20 million shares issued and assets of £25 million. It borrows £5 million for a specific investment, at an interest rate of 6%. The trust has 20% gearing and annual interest payments of £300,000.

Prior to the borrowing, the NAV of the trust is £25 million/20 million = £1.25 per share. The assets bought with the loan increase the overall assets to £30 million, with debts of £5 million. This gives a NAV of £30 million less £300,000 interest = £29.7 million. The NAV is £30.0 million less £5 million loan = £25 million/20 million shares = £1.25 per share.

If the trust assets grow by 10%, the asset value would be £33 million. Less the interest payment of £300,000 = £32.7 million. The NAV would be £32.7 million less £5 million = £27.7 million/20 million shares = £1.385 per share. This represents a growth in NAV of 10.8%.

If the trust had not borrowed, the 10% asset increase would have led to a NAV of £27.5 million/20 million shares = £1.375 (a straight 10% increase in the NAV).

If the trust assets fall by 10%, the asset value would be £27 million. Less the interest payment of £300,000 = £26.7 million. The NAV would be £26.7 million less £5 million = £21.7 million/20 million shares = £1.085 per share. This represents a fall of 13.2%.

If the company had not borrowed, the 10% asset decrease would have led to a NAV of £22.5 million/20 million shares = £1.125 per share.

If the assets had grown or fallen by 20%, the NAV would have risen by 22.8% and fallen by 25.2% respectively.

So gearing increases the volatility of an investment, as the effect of a fall in the value of assets bought via borrowing will be made worse by the effect of the interest payments on the overall picture.

11.4   Capital Structure of Investment Trusts

Investment trusts are generally divided into two types:

- conventional, and
- split-level.

These reflect significant differences in their capital structures.

11.4.1 Conventional Trusts

Conventional trusts will issue just one main class of equity share: an ordinary share. These entitle investors to all of the income and capital gains produced by the trust investments (subject to any borrowing).

Conventional trusts are usually set up for an indefinite term.

11.4.2 Split Capital Trusts

A split capital investment trust is still a single portfolio of investments, but it issues different classes of share to meet different investors' needs. A single trust may issue two, three or even four different classes of share, and each will be entitled to different returns.

A split capital trust is also different to conventional trusts, in that at least one of the share classes will be likely to have a limited life with a fixed wind-up date. Therefore, each different class of share mentioned above is ranked in a particular order of priority for repayment when the trust is wound up. A typical trust may be set up for an initial life of five to ten years, often with the provision to extend it by, say, three years at a time.

 What different classes of share can you think of that may be incorporated into a split capital trust?

We will come on to these in a minute. The basic structure of the first split capital trusts that were introduced in 1965 comprised two classes of share:

- income shares, the shareholders of which were entitled to all the income generated from the investments held by the trust during its life, and
- capital shares, the shareholders of which received, at wind-up, the capital value of the trust including any capital growth achieved over its lifespan.

Since then, the market has expanded, along with the different classes of shares on offer. We will now look at some of the key aspects of the main share classes on offer, the investor needs they are designed to fulfil, and their priority order on wind-up.

Zero Dividend Preference Shares (Zeros)

These are a class of share with a limited life, offering a capital return from the assets of the trust in the form of a predetermined (but un-guaranteed) redemption value at wind-up. They have no right to receive dividend income (hence their name!).

Investor need
These meet the requirement for a predetermined capital return at a specific date. The investor should have no requirement for income.
This class of share can be useful for tax planning, especially by using the CGT annual allowance to shelter profits.
Order of priority
As a preference share, these are usually ranked first in the winding-up order. This is, of course, still after prior charges such as bank debts or loan stock.

Income Shares

There are different types of income share and investors should be clear about the terms of each. In essence, all income shares aim to provide dividend income generated from the trust's underlying assets. The different types vary in their income entitlements, and in their capital entitlements on wind-up.

Some income shares have a predetermined (but un-guaranteed) maturity value. This is known as the redemption price and it might be as high as the original price of the shares. Other, more recent alternatives may offer a high income level but only a nominal redemption amount.

Investor need
These meet the requirement to provide an income stream, with entitlement to capital at wind-up.
The shares that offer high income with a nominal redemption value may be attractive to investors who have capital gains on other investments that can be set off against the capital loss generated by this sort of investment.
Order of priority
This depends on the structure of the trust. Even the distributable income will depend on the entitlements of any prior ranking charges. Any predetermined capital entitlement also ranks after the payment of any prior ranking charges.

Income and Residual Capital Shares

These are also known as ordinary income shares or highly geared ordinary income shares. They offer a high and rising income plus all the surplus assets of the trust at wind-up (after other prior-ranking classes of shares have been repaid). They have no predetermined redemption value.

These may be issued by a trust with a stepped preference share, where the holder receives all excess revenue after the predetermined dividend payment to the other class of share has been made.

Investor need
They offer the investor high dividends and capital returns. The high gearing involved with this type of trust does make them a relatively high-risk investment.
Order of priority
Low priority, although if issued with a stepped preference share, this will be higher in the priority list.

Capital Shares

These shares do not pay dividends. Shareholders have no predetermined capital value, but are entitled, to all of the surplus assets on wind-up of the company, after prior ranking charges.

The absence of guarantees means that capital shares are inherently risky, along with the low priority order held by the shares. They do have the potential for impressive growth (or significant losses) through the use of gearing, as explained earlier.

Investor need
Potential for capital growth, at a higher risk relative to other classes of share.
Order of priority
Low priority

Comparing Returns from Split Capital Trusts

There are a number of methods used to analyse the attractiveness of spilt capital investment trusts, including:

* **Gross redemption yield (GRY)** – which measures the capital and income return on a particular share until wind-up. It is expressed as an annual percentage, allowing it to be compared easily with other investments such as bank deposits and fixed-interest investments. A GRY of 5% on a zero, for example, means that if an investor bought the share at the quoted price, a lump sum at wind-up would be paid, equal to the investment, plus 5% a year for the whole of the term.
* **Hurdle rates** – which show how much the assets of a trust have to grow (compounded annually) to repay the redemption price. A negative hurdle rate is therefore good news in this respect as it indicates that there are already surplus assets and that the total assets can decline by a certain percentage each year and there would still be enough to pay the redemption price at wind-up.
* **Asset cover** – which is a different way of measuring a trust's ability to meet or cover the liability to a zero from its assets. A cover of one indicates that the assets exactly cover the zero redemption price. A cover of 0.5 indicates that half of the redemption price is covered.

Advice Issues

You will undoubtedly be aware that, at the start of the millennium, split capital investment trusts were involved in reviews by both a Treasury Select Committee and the FSA (the regulator at that time). The issues arose as a result of many trusts, sold originally as 'low risk' investments, having trading in their shares suspended as the value of their assets fell to below (or very close to) the level of their borrowing. This was due to a number of factors, including high initial gearing and also the poor performance of global stock markets (particularly after the September 11th terrorist attacks). Also blamed was the surprising pattern of investments, where trusts purchased each other's shares for their portfolios (known as the 'magic circle').

New rules, effective from November 2003, limit the cross-holdings between trusts to 10% of the gross assets of the investing trust company. Additional risk warnings also had to be included in an investment trust prospectus and promotional literature.

11.5   Other Types of Shares

Despite us covering a number of shares associated with split capital trusts, there are still a few more to cover including B, C and S shares, as well as warrants.

Before we briefly look at each of these, what is your understanding?

11.5.1 B Shares

B shares have equal rights with ordinary shares of the investment trust, except that the shareholder receives no rights to dividends. Instead, the shareholder receives additional shares equivalent in value to the dividend distribution.

When these shares were first introduced in 1967, there was a tax advantage to this approach. That tax advantage no longer exists, as the shareholder is taxed on the scrip issue of the additional shares in the same way as they would have been had they received the cash dividend.

11.5.2 C Shares

C shares are initially allocated on a new issue of shares by an investment trust. When a new issue takes place, the cash received may not be invested immediately, and so could distort the overall situation for existing shareholders, with an increased holding in cash rather than equities.

C shares are therefore only converted into ordinary shares when the bulk of the new cash has been invested, being converted on a NAV basis.

11.5.3 S Shares

S shares are also known as 'perpetual C shares'. They are used to issue new shares on the market without incurring the costs generally associated with launching a new investment trust. The investment strategy will be close, but not identical to, the existing investment trust.

S shares form a distinct and different portfolio, which will remain separate throughout, with separate price quotes and NAVs.

11.5.4 Warrants

Warrants are a form of share derivative, designed to provide an incentive for investors to buy the shares of a new investment trust. When the new investment trust shares are issued, there will be no discount to NAV which, as we have seen, is a way of exaggerating returns for an investor. To encourage investors to invest, warrants may well be issued, giving the holder a right to buy shares in the investment trusts at a later date at a specified strike price.

The warrant should have some kind of value, even if the trusts are trading below the strike price, as the trust price should be expected to rise. This is of interest to speculative investors in particular, so warrants are relatively high-risk investments used for potential capital growth (as there are no dividends).

The issuing of warrants can distort the NAV, which we have already established is 'the value of an investment trust's investments per ordinary share'. This inclusion of just ordinary shares in the NAV calculation ignores warrants, and is known as the undiluted NAV. There is also a NAV calculation that makes the assumption that all warrants are exercised, thereby increasing the overall shareholding. The NAV will therefore be lower, as the trust's assets are being divided by a greater number of shares. This is known as the diluted NAV.

11.6   Tax Treatment of Investment Trusts

Investment trusts that have been approved by Her Majesty's Revenue & Customs (HMRC) are not subject to CGT on gains made from the sale of assets. They are also not subject to additional tax on the dividend income they receive from their shareholdings in UK companies (franked income). They do pay corporation tax of 21% on income from sources such as foreign share dividends and interest from gilts and bank deposits (unfranked income). Trusts can reduce their liability by offsetting their expenses against unfranked income.

11.7   Real Estate Investment Trusts (REITs)

REITs were launched in the UK at the start of 2007, having been available in many other parts of the world (including the US and Australia) for many years. They are designed to provide a widely accessible vehicle for investors, providing a liquid market in property investment with tax treatment similar to a direct investment in property.

REITs must be closed-end, as explained earlier. To qualify for REIT status, they must also be listed on a recognised stock exchange (thereby excluding AIM companies). They must be UK resident and can only have one class of ordinary share.

A REIT has two separate elements for tax purposes:

- a ring-fenced property letting business
- a non-ring-fenced business.

A minimum of 75% of a REIT's total profits from both elements must originate from the ring-fenced element. The tax situation for each element is as follows:

Ring-fenced property letting business	Non-ring-fenced business
• Exempt from corporation tax.	• Subject to corporation tax at 20%.
• At least **90%** of each accounting period's rental profits must be paid as a dividend to investors within 12 months from the end of the accounting period.	
• Payments are classed as property income and paid net of 20%. • Non-taxpayers may reclaim the excess tax deducted.	• This is taxed as any other UK dividend and the dividend allowance applies.

Gains on REITs are subject to CGT in the normal way for investors.

Existing listed property companies may convert to a REIT for a one-off corporation tax charge which is equivalent to 2% of the gross value of properties entering the ring-fenced element.

For investors, they are a relatively liquid investment, which are marginally less tax-effective than property unit trusts and OEICs for basic rate taxpayers, but are more tax efficient for non-taxpayers.

12. Individual Savings Accounts (ISAs)

12.1 Introduction

ISAs were introduced in the UK on 6 April 1999, as a replacement for tax exempt special savings accounts (TESSAs) and personal equity plans (PEPs).

There are three types of ISA:

- stocks and shares ISAs
- cash ISAs, and
- innovative finance ISAs.

An ISA is not a product as such, but a 'wrapper' that makes an existing investment more tax-efficient. The extent of effectiveness of this tax efficiency depends largely on the tax status of the individual investor.

12.2 Types of ISA

As already mentioned, there are now three types of ISA. Let's look at some of the investment rules that determine whether an investment is regarded as a stocks and shares, cash or innovative finance ISA.

12.2.1 Stocks and Shares ISA

Eligible investments include:

- shares that are officially listed on a recognised stock exchange anywhere in the world (this means that unquoted or unlisted shares do not qualify although, from 5 August 2013, AIM shares were eligible)
- officially listed corporate bonds
- gilts and similar securities issued by EEA governments
- UK-authorised unit trusts and UCITS, qualifying non-UCITS retail schemes
- UK-listed investment trusts, including REITs
- shares acquired within the previous 90 days from an all-employee save as you earn (SAYE) scheme or share incentive plan. These qualify, even if the shares wouldn't normally, for example they are not listed on a recognised stock exchange
- life assurance policies, as long as they are single life
- stakeholder medium term investment products
- cash and deposits.

12.2.2 Cash ISA

Eligible investments include:

- cash deposits or share accounts with a building society
- a deposit account with a UK or EU-authorised bank
- some NS&I products
- stakeholder cash deposit products.

12.2.3 Innovative Finance ISA

Qualifying investments are:

- peer-to-peer loans, and
- cash.

For a peer-to-peer loan to be eligible it must be facilitated by an operator authorised under FSMA. All loans must be made using cash held by the ISA manager and must be on genuine commercial terms.

12.2.4 Help to Buy ISA

Help to buy ISAs are designed to help first-time buyers, boosting savings by 25% towards the cost of their first home. The maximum bonus is £3,000 per person and for every £200 saved they will receive the bonus of £50. The minimum saving to qualify for the bonus is £1,600.

12.2.5 Stakeholder Standards

Stakeholder standards are those laid down by the government, so products that are marketed as stakeholder have to meet certain conditions. These stakeholder standards replaced the original CAT standards (charges/access/terms) in 2005.

To meet the cash ISA stakeholder requirements:

- there must be no charges to pay
- the minimum deposit cannot be higher than £10
- unlimited withdrawals must be allowed, and these should be paid within a maximum of seven days.
- the interest rate that is paid must be no less than 1% below the Bank of England base rate (not too attractive at the moment!)
- if and when the base rate increases, the minimum interest rate must also increase within one month.

To meet the stocks and shares ISA stakeholder requirements:

- the annual charge is limited to 1.5% per annum of the fund during the first ten years, and 1% thereafter, with no other charges
- the minimum investment cannot be higher than £20
- no more than 60% of the fund can be invested in riskier assets such as shares and property (known as 'risk controlled').

12.2.6 Subscription Limits

The overall annual subscription limit for ISAs is **£15,240** in 2016–17. Subject to this overall limit, an investor can subscribe any amount split in any proportion between a stocks & shares ISA and a cash ISA. But an investor can only subscribe to one ISA of each type in any tax year.

If you are aged between 16 and 18, you can hold a cash ISA but cannot open a stocks and shares ISA. You can pay up to £15,240 into your cash ISA for the tax year 2016–17. This is in addition to any amounts that you pay into a Junior ISA that you hold.

12.2.7 Transfers between ISA Managers

It is possible for investors to transfer their ISA investments. The regulations stipulate that ISA managers have to allow transfers (but receiving managers do not have to accept transfers).

If an investor wants to transfer the **current year's** ISA subscription, the current year's subscription must be transferred in its entirety.

If an investor has made subscriptions in **previous years**, all or part of the previous year's subscription can be transferred to another ISA manager at any time. The transfer does not impact on the current year's subscription.

Since 1 July 2014, you have been allowed to transfer from a cash ISA to a stocks and shares ISA or from a stocks and shares ISA to a cash ISA.

If you transfer savings from a cash ISA to another cash ISA, your transfer must usually be completed within 15 business days of you requesting it. Any other type of account transfer must usually be completed within 30 days of you requesting it.

It is important, when making a transfer, that the cash or investments do not pass directly to the investor, because the subscription rules would prevent them being reinvested in an ISA.

12.3 Eligibility

An ISA investor must be an individual who is:

- resident in the UK, or
- a Crown employee working overseas and paid by the government (and their spouse or civil partner).

There are different age restrictions depending on the type of ISA:

- 16 or over to be able to invest in a cash ISA
- 18 or over to be able to invest in a stocks and shares ISA.

12.4 Tax Treatment

ISA investments are free of UK income tax and CGT for an eligible investor. Indeed, part of their attraction is that they do not even have to be declared on a Self-Assessment tax return.

Cash ISAs and stocks and shares ISAs are free of income tax, with interest credited gross.

For stocks and shares ISAs:

- interest, dividends and property income distributions are exempt from any additional income tax
- the ISA manager receives interest distributions from corporate bond and interest-bearing funds (if at least 60% of the fund is invested in interest-bearing securities) without any deduction of income tax
- property income distributions from REITs are paid gross to ISA managers
- capital gains on ISA investments are exempt from CGT (although losses from ISAs cannot be allowed against other gains).

The market value of a plan at the date of death forms part of the deceased's estate for inheritance tax (IHT) purposes. As ISAs cannot be written under trust, there is no way to avoid this.

For deaths since 3 December 2014, a surviving spouse or civil partner can, in effect, inherit the tax wrapper of the deceased with the probate value of any ISA assets being available as an additional subscription for the survivor. This extra allowance is available for the surviving spouse or civil partner even if, under the deceased's will, the ISA was left to someone else.

12.5 Flexible ISAs

Since 6 April 2016, ISA managers have been allowed to offer flexible ISAs, which allow investors to replace cash they have withdrawn without the replacement counting towards the annual subscription.

13.   Child Trust Funds and Junior ISAs

13.1   Child Trust Funds (CTFs)

CTFs were long-term savings and investment accounts specifically for children, born on or after 1 September 2002 and before 3 January 2011. After starting to claim child benefit, the parent or guardian automatically received an information pack and a voucher for £250 for their child. They could then use this voucher to open a CTF account. Children in families that were eligible for the full Child Tax Credit were sent an additional voucher of £250.

From August 2010, the government paid only £50 (£100 for a low-income family) when starting the CTF; and there are no further government contributions.

From January 2011, all government contributions ceased.

Child Trust Funds can be transferred into a Junior ISA.

13.2   Junior Individual Savings Account (Junior ISA)

Child trust funds were phased out at the end of 2010, although parents who already have them can continue paying in. Junior ISAs are the new scheme for saving and investing for children that started in November 2011.

A child can have a Junior ISA if they:

*   are under 18
*   live in the UK
*   weren't entitled to a CTF account (changes from April 2015).

Only parents or guardians with parental responsibility can open a Junior ISA for under-16s. Children aged 16 and 17 can open their own Junior ISAs.

Money in a Junior ISA belongs to the child and cannot usually be taken out until they are 18. At 18, the child can encash the investment or it automatically becomes an 'adult' ISA.

There are two types of Junior ISA:

*   a **cash Junior ISA**, no tax on interest on the cash saved
*   a **stocks and shares Junior ISA**, no tax on any capital growth or dividends received.

A child can have one or both types of Junior ISA.

The maximum total contribution was £4,080 (2016–17).

14. Private Equity Schemes

14.1 Introduction

In this section, we will concentrate on the characteristics of AIM, enterprise investment schemes (EIS) and Venture Capital Trust (VCT) investments. All of these sit under the separate asset class of 'private equity', which involves taking a stake in, or acquiring, companies that are not publicly traded on a stock exchange.

The essence of private equity investment is to provide medium-term to long-term finance to unquoted companies, in return for an equity stake in that company. The hope is that the company will provide high growth, as companies backed by private equity have been shown to grow faster than other types of companies. This is often as a result of the capital and personal input provided by specialist private equity firms, such as Permira and the 3i Group. However, the key word here is 'hope', as private equity investments sit at the higher end of the risk and reward scale. They enjoy certain tax concessions to make them more attractive to potential investors.

14.2 Alternative Investment Market (AIM)

The AIM was launched in June 1995, to provide trading facilities for companies either too small or too new for a listing on the official list of the stock exchange. It bills itself as the *most successful growth market in the world*, with over 1,200 companies traded on the exchange today, with a total market capitalisation of over £71 billion. Although AIM share prices are quoted, the companies are not officially listed, and HMRC regards the shares as being unquoted for tax purposes, which can be particularly useful.

There is generally a lot less trading in AIM stocks and so shares may be less easy to buy and sell, occasionally leading to delays in being able to realise investments. The market in unlisted shares is particularly illiquid, but being quoted on AIM certainly helps the liquidity issue. The majority of investors in AIM are mainly experienced, professional investors, who balance the additional risk with the possible additional return (or at least seek advice that helps them understand the additional risks involved).

14.2.1 Tax Relief on Investments in AIM Shares

As we mentioned in the introduction, there are certain tax concessions that may help attract investors to these investments.

Firstly, there is income tax relief on certain capital losses:

*   this is available when an investor acquires AIM shares by subscription, and realises a capital loss. The loss can be offset against any other income in the tax year of the loss, or the previous tax year, rather than against gains made from other assets
*   this relief now only applies to shares in trading companies that meet the EIS regulations (see later) from 6 April 1998, and to all qualifying shares issued before 6 April 1998.

The next example is interest relief:

- this is another income tax relief, where tax relief is allowed on the interest paid on loans raised to buy shares in a trading company controlled by its directors, or by five or fewer people. These companies are known collectively as 'close companies'
- to be able to claim the relief, the borrower has to meet certain conditions at the time the interest is paid. They should either own more than 5% of the shares or, if they own less than 5%, work for the greater part of their time in the management of the company's business.

A third example is a relief against IHT:

- this is because shareholdings of any size in unlisted trading companies qualify for 100% business property relief (BPR), and so benefit from 100% relief from IHT once they have been owned for two complete years.
- this is also exempt from stamp duty and stamp duty reserve tax.

14.3   Enterprise Investment Scheme (EIS)

The EIS replaced the Business Expansion Scheme (BES) at the start of 1994. It had the same intention as the BES in encouraging private investors or 'business angels' (Dragon's Den type investors) to invest in certain types of smaller unquoted UK companies. The way the government provides this encouragement is by providing tax incentives on investments, provided the receiving company meets set criteria.

 We briefly looked at the tax concessions in Chapter 2: Investment Taxation. What details can you remember?

See Section 14.3.1 to see how well you did.

The set criteria for companies to provide shares that qualify as EIS shares include:

- it must be unlisted when the shares are issued, with no arrangements for it to become listed. Companies whose shares are quoted on AIM meet this requirement
- it must be carrying out a 'qualifying trade' wholly or mainly in the UK. Most trades qualify, but those that are specifically excluded include property development, hotels, nursing homes, farming and companies providing financial, legal & accountancy services
- the gross assets of the company must not exceed £15 million immediately before issuing eligible shares, and £16 million immediately afterwards
- the company must have fewer than 250 full-time employees at the date on which EIS eligible shares are issued.

14.3.1 Tax Relief on Investments in EIS Shares

To be able to benefit from the tax concessions associated with investments into EIS shares, the investor must be a 'qualifying individual'. This is basically someone who is not connected with the company when subscribing, although they can subsequently become a paid director of the company. Mostly investors are UK residents, although non-UK residents are eligible, but they can only claim tax relief against any liability to UK income tax.

Along with 'qualifying individuals', the shares purchased need to be 'eligible shares'. These are basically new ordinary shares that are not redeemable for at least three years.

The main tax reliefs are given below:

Income Tax Relief on Contributions

- This is currently given at a rate of 30% up to a maximum contribution of £1,000,000 per tax year (the maximum limit amount has changed frequently over the years, and may well change again in the future). The relief is given as a tax reducer (see Chapter 2 for details).
- A contribution to an EIS can be carried back to the previous tax year, provided there is scope to invest (ie, the investor hasn't used up the full £1 million in that previous tax year).
- This income tax relief is withdrawn if the shares purchased are disposed of within three years (except to a spouse, and the death of the investor also does not count).

Capital Gains Tax Relief

- On EIS investments after 5 April 2000 where income tax relief has been given, gains made are free of CGT if the shares have been held for three or more years.
- For EIS investments on or before 5 April 2000, the period was five years.

Capital Gains Tax Deferral Relief

- This is a special concession when investing capital gains into EIS eligible shares.
- Any capital gain can be deferred by reinvesting that gain into an EIS company with no upper limit (although the gross asset rules for the company listed earlier effectively provide a limit).
- The reinvestment must take place in the period beginning one year before, and ending three years after, the disposal that gave rise to the gain.
- The deferred gain is then charged when the EIS shares are disposed of (unless a further qualifying reinvestment is made).

Capital Gains Tax Loss Relief

- Losses made on EIS investments (and there are likely to be some!) are allowable where either income tax relief or CGT deferral relief has been obtained. In this case, a deduction is made for any initial income tax relief that has been given.
- The loss can be set against either chargeable gains or against income (as seen earlier for unlisted shares purchased before 6 April 1998).

Inheritance Tax Business Property Relief (BPR)

- As seen earlier for unlisted shares, EIS shares qualify for 100% BPR once they have been owned for two complete years.

14.4   Venture Capital Trusts (VCTs)

Earlier we looked at investment trusts, which are listed companies, run by fund managers that invest in other companies. VCTs are very similar, except that they must invest predominantly in the shares and securities of unlisted companies. As with EIS shares, the government encourage investment in VCTs, by providing tax concessions to investors.

 Now the EIS has jogged your memory, what details can you remember of the tax concessions that apply to VCTs?

See Section 14.4.1 to see how well you did.

Again, for VCTs to be approved by HMRC (and therefore for an investor to benefit from the tax concessions), a number of conditions must be satisfied, including:

- the VCT itself must be listed on the Stock Exchange
- its income must be wholly or mainly derived from shares or securities
- at least 70% of its investments (by value) must be in 'qualifying holdings', which are newly issued shares in qualifying unlisted trading companies:
  - the 'qualifying unlisted trading companies' are basically ones that meet similar criteria to that we have seen apply to EIS companies.
- not more than 15% of a VCT's total investment can be invested in a single company or group of companies
- at least 30% of the VCT's qualifying holdings (by value) must be in new ordinary shares, and
- at least 10% of the total investment in any one company must be in ordinary shares
- a VCT cannot invest more than £1 million in total each tax year, in any single qualifying unlisted trading company.

14.4.1 Tax Relief on Investments in VCT Shares

The main tax reliefs are given below:

Income Tax Relief on Contributions

- This is currently given at a rate of 30%, up to a maximum contribution of £200,000 per tax year (the maximum limit amount and percentage relief have changed frequently over the years, and may well change again in the future). The relief is given as a tax reducer (see Chapter 2: Investment Taxation for details).
- Unlike EIS investments, VCT investments cannot be carried back to a previous tax year.
- This income tax relief is withdrawn if the shares purchased are disposed of within five years (except to a spouse, and the death of the investor also does not count).

Income Tax Dividend Relief

- VCTs themselves are exempt from corporation tax on gains arising on the disposal of its investments.
- These gains can be distributed to investors as dividends, and are exempt from any additional income tax for the investor (although the 10% tax credit cannot be reclaimed).

Capital Gains Tax Relief

- VCT investments are exempt from CGT on disposal, with no minimum holding period.
- It should be noted that, due to this concession, losses incurred on VCT investments are not allowable losses for CGT purposes.

CGT Deferral Relief (No Longer Available)

- Up until 5 April 2004, individuals could defer a chargeable gain on disposal of any asset by reinvesting the gain in VCT shares in the same way previously described for EIS shares. This is no longer possible.

14.5   Suitability of Private Equity Investments

As highlighted in the introduction, these investments provide opportunities for high returns, but with high risk. It is a truism that companies generally grow at their fastest when they are young, but it is also a truism that the majority of young companies fail. That could be because of cash-flow difficulties, reliance on the success of a single product, or being more vulnerable to domestic downturns and recessions. Indeed, in the recent recession, many private equity investments had been adversely impacted, as they have had to reduce debts, and this 'de-leveraging' had an effect on returns.

Prior to the recent recession, private equity investments had enjoyed a run of exceptional returns, when the economy was booming. 2005 and 2006 were particularly good years. However, the downturn in the market mirrored that of the last recession in the early 1990s when debt-to-equity ratios were also high, and private equity investments were hit by economic downturn and, at that time, rising interest rates.

Liquidity is a key factor, or rather the lack of it. Private equity securities are less liquid than other listed securities, are sold less readily in large amounts, and the transaction costs are often higher. With the majority of shares in private hands, the trading volumes can be very low.

Of the areas we have covered, VCT investments are the least risky for two reasons. Firstly, they are a form of collective investment and therefore benefit from a degree of diversification within the trust. Secondly, as a minimum of 70% of the investment has to be in 'qualifying shares', in theory, that leaves 30% of the investment to be invested elsewhere. That includes listed shares, so a VCT could include investments in large FTSE 100 shares. It is still a high risk approach, however – 70% minimum in small companies is a significant amount!

Private equity investments are therefore not deemed appropriate for inexperienced, small-scale investors. They are more suited to wealthy 'sophisticated' investors who can weigh up the risk against the rewards and who, importantly, have the overall resources to put a relatively small amount of their investments into these riskier assets.

15.   Life Assurance and Protection Policies

Introduction

In this chapter, we will concentrate on the purpose and key features of life assurance and other protection products, along with the tax implications of investing in life assurance products.

15.1   Life Assurance Products – Terminology

To begin, we will concentrate on the three main types of life assurance policies:

* term assurance
* whole life assurance
* endowment assurance.

Throughout these areas there will be elements of recurring terminology that we might as well cover right at the start.

- **the proposer** is the person applying to the insurer for a policy
- **the life assured** is the person on whose death the payment is triggered
- **the assured** is the person who effects the policy and is the original owner
- frequently, the life assured and the assured are the same person, in which case the policy is known as an own life policy
- however, this is not always the situation and life assured and assured could be different. These policies are then known as **life of another policies**
- most life assurance policies are **single life**, so the death of the life assured will result in the policy payout and the end of the agreement
- policies can also be written for **two lives assured** (which is the most common, although it is possible to write policies for more). Joint life policies are either joint life first death, paying out (unsurprisingly!) on the death of the first life assured to die. These are commonly used for family protection needs. Joint life second death policies pay out on the death of the second life assured. They are commonly used on whole-of-life assurance policies to meet IHT liabilities.

15.2 Term Assurance

Term assurance is the most basic and cheapest form of life assurance. The sum assured will be paid out only if the life assured dies during the agreed term. If they don't, no payment is made, as generally there are no surrender or cash-in values. The policy then expires.

There are seven types of term assurance policies that we will briefly cover in this chapter, looking at how they are structured and their uses and merits.

 Before we look at what these are, see how many of the seven you can list.

15.2.1 Level Term Assurance

We start with the most basic form. The sum assured on a level term assurance policy does not vary during the policy term and, once the term expires, the policy expires with (normally) no value. It is a cheap form of basic cover.

Uses:
- This type of policy is often used to provide protection for the 'breadwinner' in a family scenario. This may not be ideal as most would expect their income to increase, and the sum assured remains static on a level term policy.
- Level term policies have also been used to provide cover alongside an interest-only mortgage. As no capital is being paid out, the liability remains the same, which is ideally covered by a level term policy.
- As mentioned in Chapter 2, level term assurance can also be used for IHT planning when a previous gift may mean all or part of an estate falls above the nil-rate band (NRB) for a set period (seven years). Although the NRB generally increases each year, possibly reducing the IHT liability, it can also be expected that the estate value will grow, and therefore level term assurance remains appropriate.

15.2.2 Increasing Term Assurance

Similar to level term, except the sum assured increases. Generally this increase will be at the annual renewal, but there are some policies where the increase takes place after a longer set period, say five years.

The rate of the increase differs. Many life offices offer set percentage increases, say by 3% or 5%. Probably the most appropriate are policies that increase the sum assured in line with the increase in the RPI. There is no guarantee that the RPI will increase, despite the fact that other costs may be increasing.

Some offices offer 'guaranteed insurability options', which allow the sum assured to be increased by much more substantial amounts (say, 50% of the original sum assured). These increases are offered alongside key events in an assured's life, such as marriage, the birth of a child or a remortgage.

The initial premium for this type of policy is slightly higher than that for level term policies, but this premium increases each time the sum assured increases throughout the term.

> **Uses:**
> - This type of policy is also used for family protection, with the added bonus of being able to keep up with inflation.

15.2.3 Renewable Term Assurance

The renewable option provides the opportunity for the life assured to take out a further term assurance at ordinary rates, without requiring further evidence of health (known as guaranteed insurability). The length of the renewed term is normally restricted by the original term, and also possibly by a maximum age. Each subsequent policy will have the same renewability option, incorporating the restrictions noted.

The initial premium will be higher than for a level term policy. When the policy comes up for renewal, the premium will increase further as it will be based on the increased age of the life assured.

> **Uses:**
> - This type of policy is used when there is a definite need for cover, but it is not known how long that need will last.
> - Often this may be the case with business insurance scenarios, such as key person protection, where an employee may be deemed a key person now, but may not be expected to remain so indefinitely.

15.2.4 Convertible Term Assurance

This is a term assurance which allows the assured to convert it to a whole-of-life or endowment assurance contract. This conversion can take place at any time during the policy term, and there will not need to be any further evidence of health.

The original premium will be higher than that for a level term assurance, as it carries this greater flexibility. Significantly, on conversion the premium will be based on the nature of the new type of life policy, both of which are very much more expensive than term assurance.

> **Uses:**
> • This type of policy is used when there is a current need for term assurance (some kind of cover) but the likelihood of a more substantial policy requirement in the future. Ideally, the whole-of-life or endowment policy option would be chosen immediately, but there may be an impediment, primarily cost, that is stopping an assured from being able to pursue that route initially.

15.2.5 Decreasing Term Assurance (DTA)

DTA policies have a sum assured which reduces each year by a given amount, decreasing to zero at the end of the term.

Although the cover is decreasing, the premium remains level. The initial premium would be lower than for level term assurance, as the overall liability for the insurer is less. Occasionally, the premiums are actually payable for less than the full term, to try to remove the temptation for individuals to lapse the policies in the last few years when the cover is relatively low.

> **Uses:**
> • Primarily to cover reducing debts, such as on a repayment mortgage.
> • A special form of seven-year DTA, a 'gift inter vivos' policy, can be used by recipients of gifts that exceed the IHT NRB, but have a decreasing liability due to taper relief.

15.2.6 Family Income Benefit (FIB)

This is a form of DTA, designed to provide the beneficiaries of the policy with regular income payments as opposed to a lump sum. A policy will pay a selected level of (tax-free) income each year, from the death of the life assured until the expiry of the term of the policy. The later the death during the term, the fewer income payments are made, so the total benefit decreases. At the end of the term there is no remaining value in the policy.

The income payments themselves can usually be paid monthly, quarterly or annually. Alternatively, there is often an option for the income payments to be commuted to a lump sum payment.

The policies are, again, very cheap due to the decreasing nature of the cover. A slightly more expensive version would be an increasing FIB, where the income benefit increases automatically at a prearranged rate during the term of the policy.

> **Uses:**
> • As cheap family protection. Many individuals like the thought that the replacement cover will be in a form they are comfortable with, income, as opposed to a lump sum that will require investing to produce the level of income required.

15.2.7 Unit-Linked Term Assurance

These are still term assurance policies that only pay the sum assured on the death of the life assured during the term. However, in the background, the structure of the policy is such that the performance of the invested premiums may be more important.

Each month, the premiums paid buy units, and each month enough units are cancelled to pay for that month's life risk. The remaining units remain invested in a chosen fund. For term assurance, this may be a default fund set up by the life office, or possibly a very small selection of standard life office funds.

Assumptions are made by the actuaries at the start of the policy for the performance they expect the units in the fund to achieve. If these assumptions are matched, the cover continues as normal. If the units outperform, it is possible the sum assured may be increased at no extra cost or that a cash value will build up and become available to the assured at the end of the policy term.

If the units underperform, a policy review may lead to the premium having to be increased to sustain the existing sum assured, or the premiums remaining the same with the sum assured being decreased.

> **Uses:**
> - As we are just talking about a change in policy structure, the uses are the same as those covered (ie, you can have level, convertible, renewable, increasable etc unit-linked term assurance policies).
> - Potentially, they may be more attractive to individuals with a higher risk appetite, due to the link to fund performance, but fund performance is normally towards the bottom of the priority list when looking at life assurance protection.

15.3   Whole-of-Life Assurance

The clue as to what these policies are all about is in the title really! Whole-of-life policies will result in the payout of the sum assured on the death of a life assured, whenever that is.

Due to the permanent nature of the cover, and the certainty of a claim as long as premiums are maintained, the premiums are more expensive than for term assurance policies. Whole-of-life policies also build up cash-in values, although these can be very low (particularly in the early years). Certain whole-of-life policies have been established more as investment than protection vehicles, and we will look at them later in this section. For the time being, we will put the emphasis on protection.

There are four types of whole-of-life assurance policies that we will briefly cover in this chapter, looking at how they are structured and their uses and merits.

 Before we look at what these are, see how many of the four you can list.

15.3.1 Non-Profit Whole-of-Life Policies

Non-profit whole-of-life policies have level premiums, payable throughout life. They pay out a fixed sum assured, whenever death occurs.

It is possible to obtain products of this nature that cease collecting premiums at a specified age, such as 80 or 85. The initial premiums will be slightly higher as a result.

Uses:
- These types of contracts are rarely sold, but have become more popular in the Inheritance Tax (IHT) market recently.
- They are also the type of policy promoted by direct advertising to the over 50s (the adverts that pop up during *Countdown* with, generally, some respected celebrity doing the gardening and talking about the need to plan for the future). The proposal forms for these tend to be very short, with few medical questions. However, it is common for the sum assured to only be paid out if death occurs more than two years after the policy's commencement, and there is unlikely to be a surrender value.

15.3.2 With-Profit Whole-of-Life Policies

With-profit policies offer the opportunity for the sum assured to be increased by the addition of bonus payments. These bonuses aren't guaranteed but, once allocated, can't be removed. The level of the bonus depends on the performance of the life office and its funds, its assets and liabilities.

Bonuses that are added regularly are known as 'reversionary'. They are usually expressed as a percentage of the sum assured, and may be simple (based purely on the original sum assured) or compound (based on the original sum assured plus previous allocated bonuses).

It is possible that another bonus may be added when a policy comes to the claim stage (rather than surrender). This is known as the 'terminal bonus' and is usually expressed as a percentage of the total reversionary bonuses.

As mentioned, once a bonus has been allocated it cannot be removed. However, most offices reserve the right to apply a market value reduction (MVR) factor if an assured surrenders the policy or wants to switch out of the with-profit fund. The MVR enables the life office to reduce the surrender or switch value in an attempt to apply fairness across all with-profit members (including those who are remaining in the fund). Bonuses are allocated from surpluses, but during times of market downturns these surpluses are reduced. If an assured is allowed to keep their full allocated bonus, it could impact negatively on those who are remaining in the fund. Therefore MVRs are generally only applied in periods of poor market performance if a policy is switched or surrendered early.

The amount payable on death on a with-profits whole-of-life policy is the sum assured plus whatever profits have been allocated up to the date of death. The premiums are likely to be higher than for a non-profit policy, due to the potentially higher payout.

> **Uses:**
> - As a standard form of whole-life cover, for example family protection or IHT planning.
> - The with-profit format should, in theory, be less risky than a unit-linked approach, as allocation of bonuses should provide a smoother increase in benefits.
> - Risk depends on the relative importance of reversionary and terminal bonuses; the greater the former, the lower the risk to the investor.

15.3.3 Low-Cost Whole-of-Life Policies

These are products sold as one policy, but in effect are a combination of two policies we have already considered:

- a with-profit whole-of-life policy element
- a DTA element.

The policy will pay out a full sum assured on early death, based on the combined value of these two elements. In the longer term, the bonuses added to the with-profit element will increase payout from that element, while the DTA sum assured is progressively reducing.

Example

A low-cost whole-of-life policy provides a sum assured of £100,000. This might be made up of £60,000 with-profit whole-of-life cover and £40,000 DTA. So, if the life assured dies immediately, there is a combined payout of the required £100,000. Over the years, bonuses should be added to the with-profit element, taking it up to, say £70,000, over ten years. In the same time period, the DTA sum assured will have fallen by the equivalent amount to, say, £30,000. The sum assured payout on death would therefore be the same amount of £100,000.

The attraction of these policies is hinted at in the name – they are significantly cheaper than full with-profit policies. That is because, as we have already seen, DTAs are a very cheap form of life assurance.

The surrender values of these policies, as they are based on just the with-profit element, are even less than those available on a full with-profits policy.

> **Uses:**
> - They are used for much the same purposes as full with-profit contracts, but at a much reduced cost.

15.3.4 Unit-Linked Whole-of-Life Policies

We touched on unit-linked policies when looking at term assurance and the same basics apply: premium buy units, and each month enough units are cancelled to pay for that month's life risk. The remaining units remain invested in a chosen fund.

The key benefit of unit-linked whole-of-life policies is their flexibility (indeed, they are often referred to as 'flexible whole-of-life policies'). At the outset, the assured has a choice for a given premium between:

- A standard sum assured (the sum assured the life office have calculated they should be able to maintain for that premium based on an assumed fund rate growth).
- A maximum sum assured, where the initial sum assured is higher than the standard one. That will result in more units having to be cancelled each month to pay for the cover, and so fewer units remain invested. It is likely, therefore, that at a policy review (usually after ten years and every five years thereafter) the premium will have to be increased to be able to maintain that level of cover.
- A minimum sum assured, where the initial sum assured is lower than the standard one. That will result in fewer units having to be cancelled each month to pay for the cover, with more units remaining invested. The hope is to build up the surrender value or a bit of 'fat' into the cover at a time when a higher sum assured isn't required.

Uses:
- The attraction is the flexible level of cover, enabling a high degree of protection in the early years (for example when children are still dependent) and less protection with more investment in later life (when the children should be long gone).
- In essence, the maximum cover option is fairly similar to a ten-year convertible term assurance, with only a small amount of units actively being invested.
- It is unlikely that anyone would opt for the minimum cover option at outset, as there are probably better ways to invest money if that is the intention.

15.4 Endowment Assurance

Endowments combine life cover over a specific term (like term assurance), with the guarantee that there will be some kind of payout (like whole-of-life assurance). They provide a steady mix of protection and investment, and are the most expensive form of assurance.

Endowments have a very bad name in the marketplace due to many policies being sold, particularly in the 1980s and early 1990s, to repay interest-only mortgage debts. Despite the fact that ultimate cash-in values are very rarely guaranteed on any form of endowment, there were many clients who were not informed of this fact. You can imagine their surprise (putting it mildly) when many received a letter from their life office informing them there was likely to be a shortfall in their endowment funding and therefore they would not be able to fully repay their mortgage if they kept premiums at the existing level. The 'endowment misselling scandal' then followed.

Endowments are still sold because they have some advantages. However, the word 'endowment' is so tarnished it is rarely used in the product name, with alternatives such as 'regular savings plans' proving more acceptable.

We will look at five types of endowment assurance policies in this chapter, looking at how they are structured and their uses and merits.

 To continue the familiar pattern, before we look at what these are, see how many of the five you can list.

15.4.1 Non-Profit Endowment Policies

The most basic form, with level premiums and a payout of only a fixed guaranteed sum assured on maturity or early death.

> **Uses:**
> * These are now very rarely sold.

15.4.2 With-Profit Endowment Policies

These guarantee the sum assured will be paid out on death or on maturity at the end of the term. In addition, there are likely to have been reversionary bonuses added during the term, and the possibility of a terminal bonus added at maturity. In theory, therefore, the eventual payout should meet a mortgage requirement (if there is one) and provide an excess payment.

> **Uses:**
> * Due to the guaranteed nature of the payouts, these are comparatively expensive and therefore rarely purchased.

15.4.3 Low-Cost Endowment Policies

These operate much in the same way as low-cost whole-of-life plans with two different policies operating under the structure of one:

* a with-profit endowment element
* a DTA element.

They guarantee to pay out the full sum assured on death. However, there is no such guarantee on the maturity of the plan, as that will depend on the bonuses added to the with-profit endowment element throughout the term. They often rely substantially on the terminal bonus payout to determine whether the amount required will be met.

For example, a low-cost endowment might be set up with an overall sum assured of £100,000, made up initially of, say, a £60,000 with-profit endowment and a £40,000 DTA. After 24 years and 364 days of a 25-year term, the bonuses added to the with-profit element might only have taken the value up to, say, £90,000; a bit short on the amount required! However, on maturity the next day a terminal bonus of, say, £20,000 might be added, providing sufficient funds to repay the debt and benefit from a reasonable surplus.

The attraction of these policies is that the initial cost is a lot less than that for a full with-profit endowment.

> **Uses:**
> - Sold a lot in the 1980s and 1990s to repay interest-only mortgages at a (seemingly) reasonable monthly cost.
> - Often surrendered early, for example when people moved houses and changed their mortgage deal and term. This provided extremely poor value for money, with very low surrender values in the early years (often a lot less than the premiums paid).
> - It has become popular to sell these policies on the traded endowment policy market, as the original life assured is likely to receive a higher benefit than by simply surrendering the policy to the life office.

15.4.4 Low-Start Endowment Policies

Low-start endowments are a development of low-cost endowments, but have a lower initial premium. That is because the premium rises, typically for the first five years of the policy, and then settles at a higher figure than would have been the case under a low-cost endowment for the remainder of the term.

> **Uses:**
> - These policies were originally aimed at professional people who could realistically expect their income to increase at a reasonable rate across a short period of time, for example solicitors, doctors or accountants.
> - Unfortunately, due to lower initial premiums, they were often sold to individuals whose income was not likely to rise, or certainly not by as much as was required to keep up with the payments.
> - Again, a lot of these policies were therefore surrendered early, providing a minimal return to the assured.

15.4.5 Unit-Linked Endowment Policies

These operate in the same way as the unit-linked policies we have already covered. The fund choice selection is often wider than for whole-of-life policies, as it is more of a pure investment product.

The maturity value of the policy will always be the bid price of the units, so they are very transparent (particularly in comparison with an alternative such as a low-cost endowment). As a result, if the maturity value reaches the amount required to, for example, repay a debt the policy could be stopped immediately – saving premiums having to be paid in the future. However, this assumes that the fund performance is such that it reaches the required amount, which has certainly not always been the case.

> **Uses:**
> - Unit-linked policies in general offer greater transparency and so could appeal for that reason.
> - The possibility of early repayment of a debt is also attractive.
> - Along with other forms of endowment, the surrender values in the early years were very low, due to the high level of initial charges. Despite this, many unit-linked endowments were surrendered early.

15.5   Qualifying Policies

Given what we have just covered, you might be wondering what the appeal of endowment policies is. That appeal lies in its tax treatment, and the fact that they are sold as 'qualifying policies'.

The qualifying rules can be complicated, but broadly, a life assurance plan will be qualifying if the:

- policy term is ten years or more
- premiums are payable annually or more frequently
- sum assured is not less than 75% of the premiums payable over the term
- premiums paid in any one year are not more than twice that paid in any other year
- premiums paid in any one year are not more than 1/8th paid over the term.

Life assurance policies all have tax to pay within the fund, which can restrict growth. The actual nature of this tax, taken as corporation tax, again can be very complex, but the net result is that funds are assumed to have paid tax at 20%. The advantage of a policy meeting the qualifying rules is that there will not be any more tax to pay, **regardless** of the tax status of the assured on policy maturity or earlier death.

This was, and is, the appeal of endowments. They are always sold as qualifying policies and benefit from the 'no additional tax' treatment after ten years, or three-quarters of the term if that is sooner (ie, a 15-year policy would be qualifying after ten years, a 12-year policy qualifying after nine years).

This 'no additional tax' status covers income tax and CGT (as for ISAs). Unlike ISAs, however, these policies can be written in trust. This is less of an attraction for endowments, where the life assured is generally intended to be the beneficiary and therefore we are into the realms of a 'gift with reservation' (see Chapter 2). However, whole-of-life plans, when used for protection purposes, are also qualifying policies and it often makes sense to write these in trust.

For joint life second death whole-of-life plans, taken out to cover an IHT liability, it doesn't just make sense, it is absolutely crucial!

15.6   Non-Qualifying Policies

In the last chapter, we saw some of the rules for a life assurance plan to be qualifying. One of these is that premiums are paid regularly (annually or more frequently). As a result, any single premium life assurance plan will be non-qualifying, which impacts on its tax treatment. Despite this, single premium life assurance bonds (SPLAB) play an important part in the UK investment environment, as they offer something different to other collective investments already covered.

Unlike qualifying policies, non-qualifying policies are liable to additional tax. This additional tax liability is an income tax liability NOT a CGT liability. The possible reason why people often get confused about this is that gains are measured to confirm the additional income tax liability.

As with qualifying policies, SPLABs pay tax within the fund, equivalent to 20% (see Sections 5.1.16 and 5.2.2). Non-taxpayers cannot reclaim this tax as it is part of the product structure. Basic rate taxpayers have no further liability. Higher rate taxpayers, however, will have an additional liability of 20% of the chargeable gain (see below); or 25% if they are additional rate taxpayers.

Significantly, this liability will only be measured when specific events occur and not on an ongoing annual basis. These events are known as 'chargeable events'. The main chargeable events are:

- **D**eath
- **A**ssignment for money or money's worth
- **M**aturity
- **P**artial surrender (over a specified limit)
- **S**urrender.

We deliberately put them in this order, as a way to remember the chargeable events is to recall the acronym **DAMPS**.

When a chargeable event occurs, a chargeable gain is calculated. It is this that we will explore next.

As considered in Chapter 2 (Investment Taxation), an investor in a SPLAB is entitled to withdraw 5% of the original investment per annum, with no immediate tax liability. In the chargeable events list above, this is therefore the specified limit on partial surrender. The reason why it is termed a partial surrender is that these withdrawals are not officially classed as income, although they may be used by an investor as such.

The 5% available withdrawals are cumulative and so if they are not used for a number of years an investor may be able to take out a large withdrawal and not have an immediate tax liability.

Example

Harry invested £50,000 in a SPLAB just over nine years ago. He has never taken any withdrawals. As he is now in the tenth policy year, he is allowed ten 5% withdrawals for there to not be an immediate tax liability. He is therefore able to withdraw £25,000 on this basis.

As we can see from the list of chargeable events, a partial surrender over the permitted limit would result in an immediate tax liability. So, if Harry withdrew £35,000 rather than the £25,000 he is entitled to, it would be a chargeable event and a chargeable gain would have to be calculated. Whether Harry has any additional tax to pay would depend largely on his tax status at the time of the chargeable event. He is also able to utilise the top-slicing facility we saw in action in Chapter 2.

Example

Harry has withdrawn £35,000, which is £10,000 above the amount allowed. He has made this gain over nine years, so he is into his tenth policy year. When top-slicing a partial surrender, we are able to use **part** years. So:

- £10,000 ÷ 10 = £1,000 slice

This is then added to Harry's taxable income (ie, after allowances) for that tax year.

If we firstly assume he has taxable income of £29,000:

- £29,000 + £1,000 = £30,000
- This is below the basic rate band 2016–17 of £32,000
- Therefore Harry has no additional tax to pay

If we then assume he has taxable income of £31,500:

- £31,500 + £1,000 = £32,500
- This is £500 over the basic rate band for 2016-17 of £32,000
- This £500 is taxed at 20% = £100
- We then need to multiply by the number of part years the plan has been running
- £100 x 10 = £1,000
- Harry would have an additional tax liability of £1,000

The same basic concept applies to a full surrender, although the calculation is slightly different.

Example

Let's assume that Harry has never taken any withdrawals, but instead chooses to totally surrender the SPLAB in the tenth policy year. The surrender value is £62,000 (based on his investment of £50,000). When top-slicing a full surrender, we use full policy years in the top slicing calculation. So:

- (£62,000 – £50,000) ÷ 9 = £1333.33.

This is then, again, added to Harry's taxable income for that tax year

If we firstly assume he has taxable income of £29,000:

- £29,000 + £1,333.33 = £30,333.33
- This is still below the basic rate band for for 2016-17 of £32,000
- Therefore Harry has no additional tax to pay

If we then assume he has taxable income of £31,500:

- £31,500 + £1,333.33 = £32,833.33
- This is £833.33 over the basic rate band for 2016-17 of £32,000
- This £803.33 is taxed at 20% = £160.66
- We then need to multiply by the number of full years the plan has been running
- £106.66 x 9 = £1,445.99, which is Harry's tax liability on the surrender

---

A similar calculation on full surrender can take place if the assured has previously taken partial surrenders within the 5% limit.

Example

Let's assume that Harry took a £25,000 withdrawal, as he was entitled to, in the tenth policy year. He then took no further withdrawals, but chose to surrender the plan fully after 15 years, with the policy value sitting at £55,000.

His chargeable gain is:

- (£55,000 [policy value]+ £25,000 [untaxed withdrawals]) – £50,000 (original investment)= £30,000

Remember, when top-slicing a full surrender, we use full policy years in the top-slicing calculation. So:

- £30,000/15 = £2,000.

This is then, again, added to Harry's taxable income for that tax year.

If we firstly assume he has taxable income of £29,000:

- £29,000 + £2,000 = £31,000
- This is below the basic rate band for 2015–16 of £31,785
- Therefore, Harry has no additional tax to pay

If we then assume he has taxable income of £32,000:

- The £32,000 already sits above the basic rate band for 2015–16 of £31,785
- The full £2,000 is taxed at 20% = £400
- We then need to multiply by the number of full years the plan has been running
- £400 x 15 = £6,000, which is Harry's tax liability on the surrender

In this last example there was absolutely no point in top-slicing. When an investor is already a higher rate taxpayer, on a chargeable event, all you need to do is multiply the chargeable gain by 20%:

- £30,000 x 20% = £6,000. Saves a bit of time!

That's probably enough examples for now. Just one last point to make is that, when a chargeable gain is assessed following a chargeable event, that particular gain will not be part of any future calculations. For example, when Harry took a partial surrender of £35,000, £10,000 was assessed because that was over his entitlement of £25,000. That £10,000 amount will not form part of any future chargeable gain calculation, although the £25,000 will. For onshore bonds, if the chargeable event is a second or subsequent part or full surrender the gain is top sliced by the number of complete years since the previous chargeable event (however, for offshore bonds the gain is always divided by the number of full years the bond has been in force, irrespective of previous chargeable events).

15.6.1 Using Non-Qualifying Policies as Investments

There is a continuous debate in the financial services industry about the use of SPLABs as investments as opposed to, say, unit trusts and OEICs. Despite the fact they may be invested in roughly the same types of assets, their tax treatment is very different.

- SPLABs pay more tax in the fund, and in isolation that would appear a good reason for using the more tax efficient unit trusts and OEICs, as the fund should grow more quickly.
- Non-taxpayers can never reclaim the tax paid in SPLABs, whereas they can do so if invested in interest-bearing unit trusts/OEICs.
- Withdrawals from SPLABs do not count as income, and therefore can be very tax efficient for higher rate taxpayers and investors who are over 65, as the withdrawals do not count against their age allowance.
- Due to the ability to defer a tax liability, a canny investor can wait for an appropriate time to create a chargeable event. The most obvious example is to invest in a SPLAB when earning well and falling into the higher-rate tax bracket. Then, once income has decreased into the basic-rate tax bracket following retirement, create a chargeable event by surrendering the policy (or part surrendering above the 5% cumulative amounts) and have no further tax liability due to top-slicing.
- Generally very high and opaque charges compared with unit trusts, OEICs, and investment trusts.
- The proponents of unit trusts and OEICs argue that the ability to limit tax from these types of products is more under the investor's control, ie, through the use of CGT allowances and ISA

wrappers, and therefore the above arguments carry little weight. Even if they pay CGT, it is a lower rate than income tax.

These types of policies are exempt from individual CGT in the hands of the original investor. Some policies, mainly qualifying, are sold on (assigned to a new owner) and it is possible these will be liable to CGT in the future.

As with qualifying policies, non-qualifying policies can be written in trust to help avoid an IHT liability. Indeed, many SPLABs written under trust have helped reduce IHT liabilities.

15.6.2 Guaranteed Income Bonds

These are single premium non-qualifying life assurance policies. The concept is simple. In return for the single premium investment, the bond will provide a guaranteed income each year for a specified period. The income is usually payable annually in arrears, with terms normally up to five years. On maturity, the capital is returned.

They follow the same tax rules as we have already covered for non-qualifying policies.

15.6.3 Guaranteed Growth Bonds

Guaranteed growth bonds are similar to guaranteed income bonds except that they pay no income. Instead, an investor invests a single premium and is guaranteed a capital sum in three, four or five years' time.

While the bond is invested, it generates no income for the investor.

They follow the same tax rules as we have already covered for non-qualifying policies, with the investor benefiting from guaranteed capital appreciation that is free of CGT and basic-rate income tax because it is levied on the fund, not the individual investor.

15.7 Annuities

An annuity is a contract to pay a given amount on a regular basis (generally annually or more frequently) during the life of the annuitant (the person on whose life the contract depends). The size of the annuity depends on a number of factors, including the age (and therefore the life expectancy) of the annuitant, the prevailing interest rates, the number of options ('bells and whistles') built into the annuity, the health of the annuitant, even sometimes the annuitant's postcode.

The tax situation of annuities differs depending on the nature of the annuity. We will take a quick look at the most common types of annuity.

15.7.1 Purchased Life Annuities

These are annuities that can be purchased from any source of money at any age.

The annuity payment is treated partly as a return of capital and partly as interest. The return of capital amount each year is based on the life expectancy of the individual – the older they are, the shorter the life expectancy, the higher the proportion of the annuity is deemed to be simply the annuitant getting their capital back. This return of capital element is tax-free.

The interest element is taxed as savings income, with tax deducted at the basic rate of 20%.

It is possible for non-taxpayers to receive the whole annuity gross, even the interest element, by completing an R89 form.

15.7.2 Pension Annuities

Pension annuities must come from accumulated pension funds.

Pension annuity payments are taxable in full and are generally operated under the pay as you earn (PAYE) system, with the provider deducting the appropriate amount of income tax by reference to the annuitant's tax code.

15.7.3 Immediate Needs Annuities

Immediate needs annuities are impaired life annuities used for long-term care. An impaired life annuity is one where the annuitant has specific health issues that adversely affect their life expectancy. They are underwritten on an individual basis.

There is no income tax liability on this type of annuity when it is used for long-term care and payments are paid directly to the care provider.

15.8   Protection Products

Having looked at life assurance products, we will now study the insurance solutions for when the situation isn't quite so extreme – policies that provide benefits based on the health of the life assured.

15.8.1 Critical Illness Cover (CIC)

The history of CIC is relatively short, having first been developed in South Africa in the 1980s. The concept is to pay out a lump sum on the diagnosis of one of a number of specified critical illnesses (also occasionally referred to as 'dread diseases').

The list of illnesses covered by life offices differs, but the majority of claims are made from the assured contracting cancer or suffering a heart attack or stroke.

Following poor publicity about claims being rejected due to the small print in the definition of illnesses, an industry working party has produced a set of standard definitions. Most insurers have adopted these definitions.

There has also been an issue over recent years about non-disclosure, where claims have been rejected due to information not being disclosed by applicants on proposal forms. The ABI published guidance on this issue, and in 2008 their guidance was credited with helping produce a record level of CIC claim pay-outs.

When CIC started to be marketed in the UK in the late 1980s and early 1990s, most policies were whole-of-life based and attached to life assurance cover. The market soon changed to offer term-based solutions, with CIC operating as a stand-alone benefit. This stand-alone nature introduced the concept of the survival period, with the life assured having to survive after diagnosis by, say, 14, 28 or 30 days before the claim is paid. This supports the notion that CIC is survival insurance.

Most CIC policies are now reviewable policies. This means that premiums are only guaranteed for a fixed period of the overall term, say for the first five years. Due to the ever-changing advancements in the medical profession, this is an important safety net for life offices. With diagnosis techniques becoming progressively more advanced, the likelihood that an illness covered under the policy will be diagnosed earlier than anticipated is growing, leading to earlier pay-outs for insurers. It is important to note that policy reviews do not look at the health of the individual life assured, but at general medical advancements.

A CIC payment is not a chargeable event and so there is no possibility of an income tax liability. No transfer of value is involved either and so there will be no IHT liability either.

Uses:
- CIC is commonly used to protect a debt, particularly a mortgage. This could either be on a level or decreasing basis.
- It is particularly attractive to single people who have no real need for life assurance. A CIC payout can help them retain their independence.
- The payout of an additional lump sum in addition to that required to cover a debt, is also advised. This additional amount can be used to help pay for alterations to a home, or to a car, that may be required following the illness.
- At least one life office is also marketing CIC as retirement protection, based on the concept that suffering a critical illness could seriously impair an individual's chances of building up a sufficient retirement fund.
- CIC is also commonly used in business protection insurance.

15.8.2 Income Protection Insurance (IPI)

Whereas CIC provides a lump sum benefit, IPI provides a regular income following an illness or accident leading to an insured person being unable to work. This income continues until the insured recovers and is able to return to work, reaches a specified age, retires or dies. If the insured does recover, the insurer cannot cancel the cover based on the fact they know their risk has been increased, as long as the insured continues to pay premiums. This is why this form of cover was previously known as permanent health insurance (PHI) and is preferable to general insurance such as accident and sickness cover where the insurer can cancel cover at renewal.

There are many factors that impact on the premium for IPI in addition to the standard ones of age, gender and amount of cover.

What other key pricing factors can you think of for IPI?

Examples include:

- The choice of **deferred period**. Standard deferred periods (the period before any income is paid out) are four, 13, 26 and 52 weeks. The longer the deferred period, the cheaper the cover. The choice should be tied in with any possible sickness benefits paid by an employer, or the degree of cash funds built up for an emergency situation such as this.
- The **occupation** of the insured. Occupations are commonly split into classes, typically one – four, with Class 1 being the least risky, admin-based jobs and Class 4 being skilled workers in hazardous jobs. Some occupations are simply too risky and are excluded altogether.
- The **type of incapacity cover**. Some insurers offer 'own occupation' cover where the insured will be paid if they are unable to undertake their own occupation. Others offer the less attractive 'suited occupation' or even 'any occupation' options where the insured will only be paid the benefit if they are unable to perform a suited occupation, or any occupation whatsoever.
- The **term** of the cover. Often this will be up to an individual's retirement age, to provide income protection throughout a working life, but shorter terms (say of five or ten years) are available.

The underwriting for IPI is a lot stricter than for life assurance, and frequently certain pre-existing conditions (such as knee or back problems) are excluded.

The tax situation of IPI policies is interesting, because the benefits are totally free of income tax. For this reason, and to provide an incentive for individuals to stop watching daytime television and return to work, the maximum level of cover is restricted to between 50% and 75% of the insured's pre-incapacity earnings. Again, different insurers have different rules, some incorporating state benefits and some not – this is not an FCA requirement but a standard industry approach.

Uses:
- An IPI policy can benefit almost anyone who is working.
- For an employed person, the benefit can be tied in with any sick pay they receive from their employer.
- For a self-employed individual, the deferred period might have to be shorter, but the need might be greater, as it is possible that an illness could lead to all income ceasing.
- Some firms also offer IPI cover for homemakers, conscious that an illness could lead to greatly increased costs for the family as a whole.

15.8.3 Private Medical Insurance (PMI)

Living in the UK, we have the benefit of the National Health Service (NHS) and therefore, in theory, free medical cover. However, it is probably fair to say that while the NHS provide a fantastic service for chronic conditions (conditions that are long lasting and usually incurable), the service for acute conditions (those that are rapid in their onset and usually curable) is less impressive. Anyone who has had a relative on a waiting list for a hip replacement, for example, will know what we mean. The market for PMI has therefore grown, by trying to meet this requirement for treatment of acute conditions.

There are many different types of PMI, from budget plans with low costs, high excesses and limits on cover, to comprehensive plans which are the most costly, but provide the fullest cover. There are also hospital cash plans, which pay a fixed cash sum for each day spent in an NHS hospital, plus fixed cash sums for specified treatments, including optical and dental treatment.

To try to keep costs down, the initial underwriting process is often fairly cursory. However, this is on the condition that pre-existing medicals won't be covered. Sometimes this is based on a minimum time period, such as two years.

PMI is a general insurance contract, so premiums are subject to insurance premium tax (5%).

> **Uses:**
> - For anyone who would like more control over the timing of medical procedures for acute illnesses.
> - Also for those who don't want to be treated in an NHS hospital but would prefer a private room with treatment in keeping with the surroundings.
> - Dental plans are fairly common due to their affordability.

16. Pension Provision and Eligibility

16.1 Introduction

In this chapter, we will concentrate on all forms of pension provision, from the state, to employers, to personal provision.

16.2 State Pensions

Despite many attempts to try to get individuals to take more personal responsibility for their pension income, the state remains a major provider.

 List as many state pension benefits as you can.

We are going to look at five state pensions, some in more depth than others, to establish an understanding of this important form of pension provision.

16.2.1 Basic State Pension (BSP)

A BSP was the pension paid by the state if a person reached state pension age before the 6 April 2016 (a man born before 6 April 1951 or a woman born before 6 April 1953).

- How much they received depended on how many years of National Insurance contributions (NIC) the individual made over their working lifetime.

- The maximum pension paid for 2016–17 is £119.30 per week. This increases every year by whichever is the highest of the average percentage growth in earnings, the percentage growth in prices as measured by the Consumer Price Index, or 2.5%.

The actual BSP amounts are increased each new tax year, currently in line with the RPI announced the previous September. This benefited pensioners in 2009–10, as the RPI in 2008 was at an unusually high level of 5%. The coalition government announced that from April 2011 the BSP would be linked to the higher of average earnings, prices (CPI), or 2.5% (known as the 'triple lock'). The single person's maximum BSP in 2016–17 is set at £119.30 pw.

From April 2016, a new 'single-tier' state pension will be paid, currently calculated at £155.65 pw but could be more or less for those who worked prior to 6 April 2016.

16.2.2 State Graduated Pension Scheme

This is a relatively little known scheme that ran from 1961 to 1975. It was the government's first attempt to compensate employees for the additional NICs they pay in comparison to the self-employed, by providing them with an additional state pension.

Many occupational pension schemes (OPS) contracted out of the graduated pension scheme and provided their members with an equivalent pension benefit.

16.2.3 State Earnings Related Pension Scheme (SERPS)

The graduated pension scheme was stopped in readiness for a new employee-only state pension scheme introduced in 1978 – SERPS. This was to run until 2002.

Employees who were eligible for SERPS were those who earned over the lower earnings limit. The benefit itself was then on an individual's earnings between the lower earnings limit and the higher earnings limit, sometimes referred to as 'middle band earnings'.

The original SERPS benefit was set at 25% of revalued middle band earnings, with an individual's best 20 year's earnings counting. It was soon clear that this was too generous, and so in 1988 it was announced that those eligible employees retiring after April 2000 would have their SERPS benefits reduced to 20% of revalued middle band earnings, with lifetime average middle band earnings counted. The percentage benefit has been reduced on a sliding scale from the 25% figure before April 2000, to 20% for those retiring after April 2000.

16.2.4 State Second Pension (S2P)

S2P replaced SERPS in 2002, and extended the eligibility a bit. Employees who earn over the lower earnings limit (LEL) are still eligible, but they are joined by carers (who meet certain requirements) and disabled individuals entitled to state benefits as a result of their disability.

S2P is earnings-related (similar to SERPS). To ensure that the principal aim of government was met, that is that low and non-earners received a greater benefit from S2P, there were originally three bands of accrual. To accommodate three bands a low earnings threshold (LET) and a secondary earnings threshold (SET) were introduced in addition to the LEL and UEL that were used for SERPS. Since 6 April 2010 there have been two bands.

Since 6 April 2012, it has been no longer possible to contract out of S2P using a money purchase or appropriate personal pension/stakeholder plan, meaning it is currently only possible to contract out of S2P using a final salary scheme.

16.2.5 State Pension Credit

The state pension credit is made up of two elements: guarantee credit and savings credit. They work in combination to give each individual in the UK a guaranteed minimum level of weekly income with, possibly, a little extra based on previous savings.

16.2.6 The New State Pension (BSP)

In 2016, the old state pension system was replaced in total by the new state pension. It applies to all eligible claimants who reach state pension age on or after 6 April 2016. To be able to claim the new state pension, a man must be born on or after 6 April 1951 and a woman born after 6 April 1953.

How much they receive depends on how many years NI they have made over their working lifetime. To qualify, they need to have made at least ten qualifying years – either by working, being credited while caring for a family, or voluntarily paying to make up missed years. To get the new full state pension, individuals will need 35 qualifying years (for those without a pre-April 2016 NI record).

To pay NICs, individuals must earn over the primary threshold (£155pw for 2016–17). However, qualifying years can be established if a person earns more than £112 per week from one employer.

Some individuals are credited with NICs even if they do not earn this amount.

 When do you think NICs will be credited?

The most common examples of NIC credit are:

- Receiving certain state benefits, such as Statutory Sick Pay (SSP), Statutory Maternity Pay (SMP), Jobseekers Allowance.
- Carers (on carers allowance) and some parents and foster carers.
- Being in full-time education between the age of 16 and 18 (university years aren't credited).
- Unemployed men who have reached women's state pension age (without the need to sign on to receive Jobseekers).

For those who have qualifying years before April 2016, there will be a reduction in the state pension for any period that they contracted out of the additional state pension schemes. Qualifying years can be added after 5 April 2016, but not if the pension is already above the full new state pension.

16.2.7 State Pension Forecast

Anyone wanting an idea of their overall state pension entitlement can go online and access www.gov.uk/check-state-pension. Alternatively, they can write to the Future Pension Centre in Newcastle and ask for a forecast application form (BR19). The individual can ask for the completed form to be sent to their nominated financial adviser if they choose.

People born between 6 April 1960 and 5 March 1961 will reach state pension age between 66 and 67. People born on or after 6 March 1961 will reach state pension age when they're 67 or older. In March 2016, the government announced a further review of the state pension age.

An eligible claimant can defer their state pension. For those reaching state pension age before 6 April 2016, the state pension will increase by 1% for every five weeks the claim is delayed. This is equivalent of 10.4% for every full year. For those reaching state pension age on or after 6 April 2016 the minimum deferral period is nine weeks and the pension will increase by 1% for every nine weeks (just under 5.8% per year)

Source: www.gov.uk/state-pension-age

16.3 Occupational Pension Schemes

OPS have been in the news recently, as pension liabilities begin to feature greatly in the financial health of a company. The statement, for example, that British Airways is a large pension provider with a small airline business on the side, is a slight exaggeration, but you get the idea.

OPS have long been seen by employers as key employee benefits, helping build loyalty in a firm and rewarding that loyalty with, in effect, deferred pay. The cost associated with certain types of OPS, however, is beginning to be seen by many as extortionate, and with a more mobile workforce in general, the golden age of OPS may well be behind us.

There are two key structures of OPS:

- **defined benefit** (also referred to occasionally as 'final salary')
- **defined contribution** (also referred to occasionally as 'money purchase').

 Before we go on to look at these in more detail, what do you think are the advantages and disadvantages of both structures?

16.3.1 Defined Benefit Schemes

The benefits from defined benefit schemes are based on three factors:

- the years' service, in the pension scheme, of a member
- the member's final pensionable salary (or some derivation on this), and
- the scheme's accrual rate.

Example

Gareth joined XYZ ltd when he was 44 and, having served a one-year probationary period, was allowed to join the company's OPS. He is soon to retire at age 65, and has a salary of £40,000pa, £7,000 of which is made up from bonuses for sales. The rest is his basic salary. The OPS is a '60th' scheme that pensions basic salary only. His estimated pension benefit is:

£33,000 x 20/60 = **£11,000pa.**

Some schemes, generally in the public sector such as the NHS scheme, provide a tax-free cash payment in addition to the pension entitlement. Other schemes allow tax-free cash to be taken, but only via commutation, ie, forsaking some annual pension for a lump sum amount.

The funding of defined benefit schemes is complicated because the scheme is promising the member a level of benefits that has to be met in the future. This is a hard objective to achieve, as the vagaries of long-term investments play a big role in the success or failure of the scheme funding, but the promise remains. The risk is therefore predominantly carried by the employer, as they are committing themselves to a promise to pay for an unknown period of time, because they do not know how long the member will live, post-retirement. Some schemes are contributory where, for an employee to be a member, they have to contribute a fixed per cent of salary, say 5% pa. Some, more generous schemes, are non-contributory.

There are now strict rules that govern the safekeeping of pension funds, so that they are not used to prop up an ailing company (as was the case with the Mirror Group in the 1990s), and to try to ensure, as far as possible, that the scheme funding is sufficient to meet the liabilities. The ownership of the scheme assets lie with the trustees, who must safeguard the assets on behalf of the members. Most of these rules were laid out in the Pensions Acts of 1995 and 2004, which we will look at later.

OPS are also committed to statutory increases in pension entitlements. This impacts individuals who leave an OPS, but have built up 'preserved benefits'. They do not lose these benefits. Indeed, there is a statutory requirement on the OPS to revalue the final salary to retirement, at least trying to ensure the salary keeps pace with inflation. In addition, at retirement, there are statutory requirements on OPS to increase the actual benefit amounts being made, again in an attempt to try to ensure they at least match inflation. All of these statutory requirements add to an OPS's liabilities, and therefore its costs.

The advantages and disadvantages of a defined benefit scheme can briefly be summarised as follows:

Advantages	Disadvantages
• Member knows roughly what they will receive	• Scheme carries all the investment risk
• Member benefits from statutory revaluing to keep pace with inflation	• Scheme must appoint trustees, actuaries & auditors and formulise costing structure
• Helps retention of staff for an employer, particularly as such schemes are becoming rarer	• Scheme must contribute to compensation schemes, adding to costs

You can see from this very short comparison, that the advantages of a defined benefit OPS lie mainly with the member and not the employer. As a result, in the recent past we have seen many trustees of OPS reacting by trying to reduce costs. Examples are:

- Closing the scheme to new members, and therefore just maintaining their liability to members who joined before a certain date.
- Closing the scheme to all members, which is a more drastic approach to the one above.
- Reducing the accrual rate, say from a 60th scheme to an 80th scheme.
- Increasing the normal retirement age, so the pension will be paid for a shorter period.
- Altering the definition of 'final salary'. There has been a growing trend for 'career average' schemes, which use the average of the revalued earnings for an individual over the whole of their period in the scheme, rather than just the final, probably highest, salary.
- Insisting on an increase in employee contributions.
- Reducing pension increases to the statutory minimum, if the scheme was used to pay higher discretionary benefits in the past.

16.3.2 Defined Contribution Schemes

With a defined contribution OPS, the only known factor is the initial amount that is invested on behalf of the member. From then on there are many uncertainties, from the performance of the fund the money is invested in to the level of charges applied by the provider, to the annuity rate that will be available at retirement if the fund is converted into income, to the value available for drawdown under new pensions legislation.

Because defined contribution OPS come under occupational scheme rules, trustees must still be appointed, but their role is less significant as far as the funding of the scheme goes. They have no liabilities to meet – in a defined contribution scheme that has been done simply by paying the contribution. The **risk** associated with the ultimate scheme benefits is therefore transferred almost entirely to the member.

The statutory revaluation requirements that apply to defined benefit schemes do not apply to defined contribution schemes. If a member leaves the scheme, the possibility of the benefits increasing will rely greatly on the performance of the fund that the member is invested in. If the member wants to ensure their pension benefits increase in retirement, they will have to incorporate an escalation option in their annuity. They can do this, but the initial annuity will be greatly reduced (by some calculations, by so much that it will take roughly 12 years for the income level to match the amount that could have been taken immediately as a level pension, and a further eight years to have actually received more money overall from the annuity provider).

The advantages and disadvantages of a defined contribution scheme can briefly be summarised as follows:

Advantages	Disadvantages
• Employer knows exactly where their commitment ends	• Member carries all the risks, investment and annuity
• Good fund performance could lead to higher benefits	• Poor fund performance could lead to lower benefits
• Helps retention of staff for an employer	• Unknown benefits – so hard to plan ahead
• Lower costs for an employer to run	
• Funds can be transferred to a new employer or personal pension	

Don't be fooled by the discrepancy in the number of advantages and disadvantages. The really important ones for the member are in the 'disadvantages' column, which is why the growing spate of defined benefit schemes being closed is filling so many column inches in the press.

16.3.3 Pensions Acts

As we've already mentioned, the key Pensions Acts that are relevant to the protection of current members of OPS are those that were passed in 1995 and 2004. The Acts were clearly very thorough and detailed when looking at them in their entirety, but we will concentrate on the key aspects of each.

Pensions Act 1995

- It established a new regulator, the Occupational Pensions Regulatory Authority (OPRA).
- It requires trustees to draw up a statement of investment principles (SIP).
- It introduced the concept of a minimum funding requirement (MFR), which had the objective of maintaining a defined benefit scheme's assets at least to the point where they covered 100% of the scheme's liabilities.
- It established a Pensions Compensation Board (PCB) to cover losses up to 90% in case of company fraud and misappropriation of scheme assets. This was a particular reaction to the Mirror Group situation.
- Trustees must appoint a fund manager authorised under the Financial Services Act.
- Members of large OPS (100 members or more) have a right to appoint at least one-third of the trustees. These are designated member nominated trustees (MNT).
- Equal treatment of all persons in occupational schemes is required.
- When contracting–out of SERPS, the fund had to satisfy a 'reference scheme test'.
- It introduced the concept of limited price indexation (LPI), which initially was indexation up to the lower of RPI or 5%. In this Act, LPI was designed to apply to both defined benefit and defined contribution benefits in payment.
- It introduced internal dispute resolution procedures which, under this Act, was a two-stage process starting with a nominated person examining the grievance, and trustees subsequently getting involved if required.

Pensions Act 2004

- This Act established the **Pension Protection Fund** (PPF) which provides compensation if an employer becomes insolvent, and they run a defined benefit pension scheme which is under-funded. The details of the PPF are listed below.
- A new **pensions regulator** (TPR – The Pensions Regulator) took over from OPRA, extending the previous powers. TPR has specific objectives to protect the benefits under occupational schemes and reduce situations that may lead to compensation being paid from the PPF. It has proven to be a more proactive regulator than OPRA.
- Employers have to consult members before making significant changes to schemes, giving 60 days for consultation.
- It replaced the MFR with the concept of **scheme specific funding**. By the turn of the century, the actuarial methodology involved in the MFR was proven to be questionable and so it was abolished in 2001. Scheme specific funding was designed to provide a long-term funding standard of a scheme that had to be agreed by the trustees and employer. The funding should reflect the specific circumstances of the scheme.
- LPI was reduced to 2.5% for defined benefit schemes and scrapped for defined contribution schemes.
- Increased state pensions for individuals who defer state pensions beyond normal state retirement age.

Pension Protection Fund (PPF)

The PPF is a compensation scheme for members of defined benefit schemes, excluding public sector schemes. To be eligible to fall under the PPF remit, the employer must have become insolvent **after** 5 April 2005, and there must be no possibility of rescuing the scheme. For employers that became insolvent **before** this date, they may be entitled to join the financial assistance schemes (FAS).

The PPF levels of compensation include:

- 100% of pension entitlement for members over the scheme's normal retirement date
- 90% of pension entitlement for members who have not yet reached the scheme's normal retirement date, subject to an overall monetary cap. For 2016–17 this cap is £37,420.42; 90% of that is a maximum payment of £33,678.38
- a spouse's pension of 50% of the member's PPF compensation amount
- statutory increases in pension, but only for pensions earned since April 1997 and only then at LPI with a maximum limit of 2.5%.

The pensions freedoms that were introduced in 2015 do not affect payments from the PPF (or the Financial Assistance Schemes).

Financial Assistance Schemes (FAS)

The FAS covers 'qualifying defined benefit schemes' (an insolvency event must have occurred in respect of the employer) which began to wind up from 1 January 1997 to 5 April 2005.

The FAS levels of compensation include:

- 90% of accrued pension entitlement at the date of commencement of the winding up is guaranteed. This amount will be revalued up to an individual's retirement date, but is subject to a cap of £26,000 per annum
- the benefit will be paid from the scheme's normal retirement date, subject to an earliest payment date of age 60
- payment of benefits based on service after 5 April 1997 will be increased in line with inflation, subject to a maximum increase of 2.5%
- there is also provision for a 50% spouse's or civil partner's pension.

16.4   Personal Pensions

Occupational pension schemes form another important part of the pension world in the UK, but there are many individuals who are not eligible to join them. This may be because they are not employed or because their employer does not offer an OPS.

There are alternatives, which we will look at now. They are all money purchase arrangements, so the benefits are unknown and the risks include investment risk, inflation risk and annuity risk.

16.4.1 Retirement Annuity Contracts (RACs)

RACs were the first form of personal pension planning, and some individuals still fund them, despite the fact that no new RACs have been sold since June 1988. They did have unique rules about the tax-free cash entitlement but, since A-Day (see later), they now closely resemble the other types of personal pension provision. Probably the main differentiator is that it is unlikely that contributions can be paid net, with tax relief given at source. This is not a legislative restriction, more a technology restriction as many providers' old platforms that contain RAC details cannot be modified to collect contributions net rather than gross. Tax relief is still available, so the individual often has to claim it via Self-Assessment.

16.4.2 Personal Pension Plans (PPPs)

PPPs replaced RACs in a wave of publicity in July 1988. They were the brainchild of the Conservative government and were designed to revolutionise the pension world, with individuals encouraged to 'take personal control' of their pension planning. Unfortunately, this led to a large number of individuals being advised to transfer their benefits out of their defined benefit occupational scheme into the money purchase world of PPPs. As we have seen, this involved a transfer of risk from the employer to the individual and it wasn't long (the early to mid-1990s) that it became clear that in the vast number of situations the individual would have been better off staying in the OPS. The subsequent pension misselling scandal did nothing for the reputation of the industry and cost a lot of money to put right – around £12 billion in compensation was paid out between 1994 and 2002.

Despite this, PPPs remain an integral part of the UK pension scene, creating the basis for what followed with stakeholder pension plans and, indeed, the basis for pension simplification. A couple of its main innovations were the concept of pension relief at source on contributions (given at the prevailing basic rate of income tax), and a tax-free lump sum entitlement of 25% of the pension fund.

Group PPPs also became popular, offered by employers who did not want to set up an OPS (with all of the resulting paperwork and trustee requirements) but wanted to allow their employees to contribute to a pension plan via their work. Sometimes the employer would contribute themselves to these plans, and sometimes they just allowed a source for employees to pay.

A derivation of the PPP format (the 'appropriate personal pension', or APP) also allowed an individual to contract-out of, at the time, SERPS. This had been allowed previously via occupational schemes, but many thousands of people welcomed the chance to try to see if they could beat the guaranteed nature of the state benefit by investing in stock market funds. As with many money purchase arrangements, some individuals did better than others!

16.4.3 Stakeholder Pension Plans

These were another new government innovation, launched in 2001 when Tony Blair's Labour government was in its first term of office. The idea was to make pension planning accessible for the masses by limiting charges and setting very low minimum premiums.

At heart, stakeholder pensions are very similar to PPPs, with basic rate tax relief given on the contribution and a tax-free lump sum of 25% of the fund. Stakeholder pensions introduced the idea that people who were not even working could contribute, up a maximum of £3,600 gross per annum, and still receive tax relief. The minimum age requirement that previously applied to PPPs was also removed, which introduced a new market of third party stakeholder pensions, where individuals could fund on behalf of another. Often this has turned out to be relatives, like parents or grandparents, funding pension plans on behalf of children/grandchildren.

The government was particularly keen to keep the charges for stakeholder pensions as low as possible. Initial charges were banned, with only ongoing annual management charges allowed. Even these were restricted, initially to 1% pa of the value of the fund. Mainly due to pressure from the pension industry, in 2005 the allowable charges were increased to 1.5% pa for the first ten years of a plan, and 1% pa thereafter. Most PPPs now follow this structure as well.

The minimum contribution to a stakeholder pension remains an incredibly low £20 per annum. This has stopped a number of pension providers offering a stakeholder pension option, as it is not commercially viable, preferring instead to brand their PPPs as 'stakeholder friendly'. In other words, they are remarkably similar to stakeholder pensions, but have a minimum contribution of, say, £50 a month or £500 per annum.

From April 2005, stakeholder pensions must offer a **lifestyling** option. This is an investment strategy whereby the member's fund is automatically moved away from riskier investments, such as equities, into more secure investments, such as gilts and cash, as retirement approaches.

Stakeholder pensions also introduced a form of compulsory pension entitlement availability to employees. Any employer with five or more employees has to offer their employees access to a stakeholder plan, unless they are exempt. Note that the employer does not have to contribute to the plan, they just have to provide access. Many employers are exempt as they offer either an OPS or a Group PPP that meets set minimum requirements. This requirement is set to become irrelevant when Personal Accounts are introduced.

16.4.4 Auto-Enrolment and National Employment Savings Trust (NEST)

The Pensions Act 2008 introduced a requirement for employers to automatically enrol their eligible jobholders into a qualifying pension scheme. A new workplace pension scheme called the National Employment Savings Trust (NEST) has been established to provide a low-cost form of pension savings. This time the compulsion is to enrol and contribute, not just provide access, as was the case with stakeholder pension plans. Individuals are still allowed to opt-out of the scheme, but must not be encouraged to do so.

- Jobholders (employees but also other contracted staff) will be required to pay 4% of their middle band earnings.
- Employers will be required to pay 3%.
- Tax relief at basic rate, equivalent to 1% of qualifying earnings, will also be credited to the member's account by the state.

The duties will apply to all employers on a staging date over a four year period from 1 October 2012. This will be done largely by PAYE scheme size, such that the largest employers will become subject to the duties before smaller employers.

16.5   Pension Simplification – A-Day

The 6 April 2006 was a momentous date in the history of pension regulation in the UK. Better known as A-Day, it marked the date when the many disparate rules that governed pensions were consolidated under one regime. Effectively there were eight different pension regimes operating at the time of A-Day. The idea was to start afresh from 6 April 2006. The rules apply to 'registered pension schemes'. All old schemes which had previously been approved before A-Day were included automatically.

16.5.1 Annual Allowance

There is no legislative limit on the amount of contributions that can be paid into a registered pension scheme, either by the member or their employer. Rather, there is a limit on the amount of contributions paid by or on behalf of an individual that qualify for **tax relief**.

The Annual Allowance includes pension savings that individuals or someone else such as their employer makes on their behalf. The Annual Allowance is not a restriction on the amount of tax relief given, but works by applying a tax charge when the Annual Allowance is exceeded.

The annual allowance limit started at £215,000 for 2006–07, and rose, but has since fallen and is currently £40,000. There is a tapered Annual Allowance for individuals with income for a tax year greater than £150,000. Depending on their earnings, this will reduce their annual allowance to £10,000.

For individuals who have flexibly accessed a money purchase pension arrangement (see section 16.5.2), and the tapered annual allowance does not apply, where contributions exceed £10,000, they will be subject to the Annual Allowance charge. This is known as the Money Purchase Annual Allowance (MPAA).

The individual is responsible for paying the Annual Allowance charge although they can ask the administrator of a scheme to pay it out of their benefits in the scheme. In some circumstances the administrator is required to pay.

16.5.2 Valuing Different Pension Plans against the Annual Allowance

We have already established that the current annual allowance is £40,000 for all registered pension schemes. When dealing with a money purchase arrangement, it is very straightforward to see how much of this allowance has been used up. With defined benefit schemes it is not so obvious as there is no defined 'contribution' as such.

In order to be able to include contributions to defined benefit schemes in the whole picture, we need to look at the increase in an individual's pension entitlement over the course of the year, and then apply a multiplier to the increase.

16.5.3 Lifetime Allowance

There is no limit on the total amount of benefits a pension scheme can provide. However, if a scheme provides benefits that amount to more value than the lifetime allowance, then excess over and above their allowance is subject to a tax charge. From the 6 April 2016, the lifetime allowance is £1 million. Where this is exceeded, the lifetime allowance charge will be applied.

This will only be tested following a 'benefit crystallisation event' (BCE). Simplistically, a BCE occurs when an individual:

*   takes a pension or a lump sum
*   reaches age 75
*   dies
*   transfers to a qualifying recognised overseas pension scheme (QROP).

It is quite conceivable for one individual to have a number of BCEs throughout their lifetime.

The tax charge applicable following a BCE if the lifetime allowance is exceeded depends on the way the excess benefits are taken:

*   if they are all taken as income, the excess is taxed at **25%**
*   if they are all taken as a lump sum, the excess is taxed at **55%**.

Although this appears to be a 'no-brainer', it should be considered that the income (after the charge is taken) is likely to be taxed at 40% or 50%. The net result is therefore about the same.

16.5.4 Valuing Different Pension Plans against the Lifetime Allowance

A similar issue of valuing pension funds to that we looked at above applies when dealing with defined benefit schemes and the lifetime allowance. To value how much of the allowance has been used for money purchase arrangements is, again, very easy – just get a fund valuation! For defined benefit schemes there is no fund as such and therefore there are two more factors we need to be aware of to calculate a deemed fund:

- If the pension is not yet in payment, it is the accrued pension amount x 20.
- If the pension was in payment before A-day (2006), it is the pension amount x 25.

Example

Returning to the situation of Julia, a member of the AUK ltd pension scheme, she is in a 1/60th scheme, earning £39,000 pa with 26 years' service. Her deemed fund to set against the lifetime allowance will be:

26 ÷ 60 x £39,000 = £16,900

£16,900 x 20 = £338,000

Example

Keith is 63 years old. He retired from his job as a company director in 2005, and enjoys a pension of £60,000 pa from this employment. He started to do some consultancy work a couple of years ago and is considering starting a new pension plan based on the earnings he receives. He would like to know what scope he has for pension planning.

£60,000 x 25 = £1,500,000 (ignore the lump sum as the pension was in payment before A-Day).

Based on the current lifetime allowance of £1.25 million, he has no scope.

16.5.5 Transitional Protection

It was not impossible for an individual to fund close to, or even exceed, the lifetime allowance when it was introduced in April 2006, since then the value of the lifetime allowance has increased and decreased over time. The post A-Day limits were therefore perceived as unfair to those who had always stayed within the old limits under the previous regime(s), but were subsequently exceeding the new limits. As a result, higher allowances were and are available via a number of protections and enhancements:

- primary protection
- enhanced protection
- fixed protection
- fixed protection (2014)
- individual protection (2014)
- fixed protection (2016)
- individual protection (2016)
- pension credits and debits on divorce
- non-UK residents or international transfers.

Each individual had three years from A-Day (ie, until 5 April 2009) in which to register for primary and enhanced protection.

Primary protection is only available if the individual's pension rights were valued at more than £1.5 million on 5 April 2006. A 'primary protection factor' is then calculated using the following formula:

$$\frac{\text{total value of benefits at 5 April 2006} - £1.5m}{£1.5m}$$

The result is rounded to two decimal places and can then be added to 1 to be applied to any existing lifetime allowance amount. This will increase the lifetime allowance for that particular individual.

Example

Karen had combined pension funds totalling £1.8 million on 5 April 2006. Her primary protection factor is:

$$\frac{£1.8m - £1.5m}{£1.5m}$$

The result is 0.2, and then adds to make 1.2. This can now be applied against any lifetime allowance.

For example, in 2016–17 Karen's lifetime allowance would be £1.25 million x 1.2 = £1.5 million.

Although primary protection increases the lifetime allowance, it does not guarantee that the total pension planning an individual has made is protected (ie, a fund might grow beyond the increased lifetime allowance figure, particularly as the lifetime allowance figure has been reduced from £1.8 million to £1.25 million in recent years).

Enhanced protection, as its name suggests, does provide **full** protection for the value of the whole of an individual's pension rights. There are a couple of key points to clarify about enhanced protection:

- The combined value of pension funds at 5 April 2006 did not necessarily have to have been an amount in excess of £1.5 million. An individual could safeguard all future growth by using enhanced protection.
- However, in return for this additional protection, no further relevant **benefit accrual** can be made to registered pension schemes. Benefit accrual basically means further contributions to defined contribution schemes or increases in defined benefit schemes greater than 5% or RPI.

Fixed protection relates to the reduction of lifetime allowance from £1.8 million. This could be retained at £1.8 million if the individual applied before 6 April 2012 and requires that no further benefit accruals are made in future. An individual can't have fixed protection if they have either primary or enhanced protection.

Fixed protection 2014 relates to the reduction of lifetime allowance from £1.5 million. This could be retained at £1.5 million if the individual applied before 6 April 2014 and requires that no further benefit accruals are made in future. An individual can't have fixed protection 2014 if they already have primary, enhanced or fixed protection.

Individual protection 2014 relates to the reduction in lifetime allowance to £1.25 from April 2014. It can fix a personal lifetime allowance equal to the fund value at 5 April 2014, up to £1.5 million. It does not require benefit accruals to cease.

Fixed protection 2016 relates to the reduction of lifetime allowance to £1million on the 6 April 2016. The allowance could be retained at £1.25 million, but no further benefit accruals can be made in the future except in limited circumstances.

Individual protection 2016 relates to the reduction in lifetime allowance to £1 million from April 2016. An individual's personal lifetime allowance can be fixed to the value of the fund at 5 April 2016 or £1.25 million, whichever is lower. It does not require benefit accruals to cease, but any value above the protected lifetime allowance will be subject to the lifetime allowance charge.

Applications for 2016 protection started in July 2016. Applications for Individual Protection 2014 close on the 5 April 2017.

16.5.6 Eligibility to Tax Relief on Contributions

For an individual to be eligible for tax relief on their contributions they must be:

- an active member of a registered pension scheme
- a relevant UK individual
- in the tax year in which the contribution is paid. Tax relief can only be claimed for the tax year that the contribution is actually made. Unused tax relief can no longer be carried backwards or forwards to other tax years.

An individual is a relevant UK individual if they:

- have the relevant UK earnings chargeable to income tax for that tax year
- are resident in the UK at some time during that tax year
- was resident in the UK at some time in the five years immediately before the contribution in question and were also resident in the UK when they joined the scheme
- be an individual (or spouse or civil partner of that individual) with earnings from overseas Crown employment that is subject to UK tax.

Although a member can pay contributions once they have reached the age of 75, they do not qualify for tax relief.

16.5.7 Tax Relief on Contributions

Contributions from both individuals and employers qualify for tax relief.

The maximum amount which a member of a scheme can have relieved is potentially the greater of:

- the 'basic amount', currently £3,600, and
- the amount of the individuals relevant UK earnings that are chargeable to income tax for the tax year.

There are three methods for tax relief to be received by individuals and the main two are explained in more detail below. The first is tax relief at source. This is the method used for most personal plans, such as PPPs and stakeholder pension plans. The relief at source mentioned in the name is **immediate** tax relief at the basic rate applied in that tax year. This is currently at a rate of 20%.

Very simply, this means that an individual only needs to contribute £800 to have £1,000 invested on their behalf – not a bad increase! The method of calculation is similar to the grossing-up calculation for interest payments that we looked at in Chapter 2 (Investment Taxation) where it is divided by 0.8.

Tax relief at source is always given at basic-rate, despite the fact the individual paying the contribution could be a non-taxpayer, a basic rate taxpayer or a higher rate taxpayer.

- A non-taxpayer can pay up to £3,600 (gross), £2,880 net, and still receive relief at source on the contribution.
- Basic rate taxpayers receive their correct amount of tax relief immediately.
- Higher rate taxpayers are eligible to claim back an additional 20% of tax relief. They will have to do this via their Self-Assessment tax return (see Chapter 2 for details).

The second method is the 'net pay' method of providing tax relief. This is the method used by OPS. Here, the pension contribution is paid gross and deducted from earnings **before** being liable for income tax. As a result, an individual will receive full tax relief at the relevant rate, immediately.

The third method is to make gross contributions and claim the tax relief through Self-Assessment.

16.6 Retirement Benefits

The main purpose of pension planning, particularly from the view of HMRC, is to provide an income in later life. Now, depending on the type of pension, an investor can withdraw as much as they wish, irrespective of other income, subject only to income tax at their marginal rate on the amount withdrawn in any tax year in excess of the initial tax-free sum. This flexibility does not apply to defined benefit pension schemes.

The normal minimum age is 55 (previously 50 up until 2010) and some action should be taken before 75. The starting age is due to increase in the future if benefits are taken before 55. They will then be treated as an unauthorised payment unless it is due to ill health or where they have a protected pension age.

There are a number of options for taking benefits, which we will cover now.

16.6.1 Lump Sums

When a member becomes entitled to authorised pension benefits, providing certain conditions are met, current tax rules allow the scheme to provide a tax-free lump sum. Generally, this will be a 'pension commencement lump sum' (PCLS). The maximum amount payable is the lower of 25% of the members lifetime allowance available at the time and 25% of the capital value the pension. In certain circumstances, a person may have a higher percentage where the lump sum was protected.

Alternatively, where the fund is uncrystallised, the 25% tax-free lump sum can be taken as part of each withdrawal, which might be more tax efficient. The remaining 75% is taken as taxable income. This is known as uncrystallised funds pension lump sum (UFPLS), and technically it is not drawdown. The individual must have sufficient lifetime allowance available to use UFPLS.

Other authorised lump sum payments include serious ill health, trivial commutation, winding up and small pension payments. To avoid an authorised payment charge, the rest of the pension should be taken as income. But there are various different methods of doing this.

16.6.2 Secured Pension

A pension paid through the purchase of a lifetime annuity or paid as a scheme pension directly from the scheme is known as a secured pension.

Lifetime Annuity

This is the term applied to income taken from a money purchase arrangement (whether personal or occupational).

Basically, the individual is using their fund to buy an income (the annuity). The rate used for this conversion will depend on their age, sex, health and the number of options they want included (ie, single/joint life, level/increasing, paid in advance/in arrears).

One of the choices available to an individual is that of **capital protection**. As suggested in its name, this is where the amount used to purchase the initial annuity is protected, less instalments paid up to the individual's death.

Another possibility is to select a **guarantee period** – the period of time the annuity provider guarantees to pay the income for, regardless of whether the annuitant is alive or not! The maximum guarantee period is ten years, and has to be paid as an income (before A-Day it was possible to commute the remaining income into a lump sum).

Individuals are allowed to shop around to try and find the best annuity rate – you will have come across the term **open market option** (OMO) which is related to this. Each pension fund provider of money purchase arrangements must offer the individual a choice of taking an annuity with it or with a different annuity provider. Often it is better for an individual to use the OMO – just because a company is good at providing fund growth does not mean they will necessarily have the best annuity rates.

It is useful to note that some old pension schemes (particularly RACs) offer **guaranteed annuity rates** which are often more competitive than the best available annuity now on the open market. The availability of these should be explored before transferring the money away via the OMO.

Scheme Pensions

This is the term applied to income that must be taken from a defined benefit scheme, as the scheme itself may administer the pension or arrange for a specialist company to do so. A defined contribution scheme can offer a scheme pension as well, but only if they offer an OMO to a lifetime annuity as well.

Don't forget, with a defined benefit scheme, the employer has 'promised' an income level based on the three key factors of years of service, final/career average salary and the scheme accrual rate. It is therefore their responsibility to meet this promise!

16.6.3 Unsecured Pensions

The previous two examples are known as secured pensions – the amount of income is secure until death (or the end of a guarantee period if longer). The problem with secured pensions, particularly the lifetime annuity option, is that once committed, that is it – the money is handed over and there is no flexibility. This can appear unattractive, particularly for someone relatively young with a long period in retirement.

The alternative to purchasing an annuity is 'drawdown' where the fund remains invested but an income is drawn from the income and capital.

16.6.4 Income Drawdown

Income drawdown (**drawdown pension**) is where the pension fund is left invested rather than being converted into an annuity. It is possible to take 25% of the pension fund as tax-free cash, leaving the remainder of the fund invested.

From 6 April 2016, drawdown consists of two methods:

- flexi-access drawdown
- short term annuity.

Prior to 6 April 2016, there were three types of drawdown: flexible drawdown, capped drawdown and short term annuity. On 6 April 2016, these ceased when **flexi-access drawdown** was introduced. On 6 April, all those in a flexible drawdown were automatically converted to the new flexi-access drawdown. However, those in capped drawdown can continue which means that their level of benefits are restricted.

The maximum that can be withdrawn under capped drawdown each year is set by tables produced by the GAD, which show the relevant annuity rate at each age. The maximum payable is 150% of the GAD annuity rate. The additional conditions are:

- no income has to be taken at all
- there is no upper age limit
- the upper income limit is reassessed every three years for those under 75, based on age and fund size
- the upper income limit is reassessed every year for those over 75, also based on age and fund size
- in the event of death, the remaining fund can be used by a dependent to continue to draw income, or buy an annuity
- the fund can also be paid to a charity in the event of death and is not then taxed
- the advantage of remaining in capped drawdown is that the money purchase annual allowance rule will not apply.

There are, of course, disadvantages to drawdown plans:

- annuity rates could go down, if an individual later decides they want to buy an annuity with their remaining funds
- the drawdown fund could fall in value
- the ongoing income is not guaranteed and could go down
- for capped drawdown it also requires ongoing monitoring of the plan
- charges are higher for drawdown than annuity purchase.

Flexi-access drawdown does what it says. Any amount can be drawn by crystallising the pension fund and making it a drawdown pension. A PCLS can be taken up to a maximum of one third of the value of the fund put into flexi-access drawdown. When the member accesses the remaining fund whether in the form of drawdown, or a short–term annuity, then the money purchase annual allowance will apply on any future money purchase contributions.

Any money drawn will be taxed as income in the year it is taken. This means that by drawing a large amount, a person could become a higher or additional rate taxpayer. There are complicated rules for calculating the actual amount of tax deducted from the payment and although tax will be deducted under pay as you earn (PAYE), a further tax payment or a refund may be payable depending on when the recipients total income for the tax year has been assessed.

If an individual draws an income from a flexi-access drawdown pension then they will trigger the Money Purchase Annual Allowance (MPAA) and can therefore only contribute a maximum of £10,000 per year before becoming subject to the annual allowance charge.

16.7   Self-Invested Options

The self-invested market has grown rapidly since pensions simplification, as some of the key eligibility rules, particularly for the employed, have been relaxed. There is now a massive market in SIPPs, in addition to the self-invested option favoured for years by small family companies – small self-administered schemes (SSASs). We will take a brief look at these two options, which are primarily aimed at high earners.

16.7.1 Self-Invested Personal Plans (SIPPs)

A SIPP is basically a PPP with wider investment opportunities. The contribution limits, tax rules and retirement options are the same as we have already covered. There are broadly three types of SIPP available in the market, with different emphasis on these wider investment opportunities.

Full SIPP

These offer the widest range of investment opportunities, including direct investment in commercial property and individual listed securities, in the UK and overseas. For a long time, in the run-up to A-Day, the indication was that residential property was also going to be allowed to be part of a SIPP investment. This created great excitement in the pension industry! However, about six months before A-Day, the Chancellor announced that residential property was to remain a 'prohibited asset' along with other investments, such as investments in art or fine wine. The full SIPP is therefore not quite as full as many industry experts would have liked, although the general consensus is that the decision was correct.

Hybrid SIPP

These are insurance company products typically offering a choice of the provider's insured funds and non-insured investments, with many providers stipulating a minimum investment to the insured element.

Deferred SIPP

This is a personal pension written under a SIPP trust. It therefore allows the opportunity to use SIPP investments on request.

A further difference between SIPPs and PPPs is the charging structure. As already mentioned, most PPPs are now stakeholder friendly, operating with a charging structure similar to that specified for stakeholder pensions. SIPP providers have usually charged fixed annual fees, whereas personal pensions have a percentage fee. This means that SIPPs are more expensive for funds up to about £50,000, but cheaper for much larger sums. A much wider range of SIPP products have been offered in recent years and fees can be competitive with insured personal pensions at most levels.

As mentioned, SIPPs are able to invest in commercial property, and another feature that facilitates this is that they are able to borrow funds. In fact, a SIPP can borrow 50% of the net scheme assets. So a SIPP with assets of £200,000 would be able to borrow a further £100,000 to potentially buy a commercial property and make it an asset of the SIPP. This property is frequently the property the business operates out of, and so future rental payments are paid to the SIPP. The SIPP itself would have to pay a commercial rate of interest on the borrowing.

SIPPs can also be used to help finance an individual's business by using SIPP assets to purchase private company shares.

16.7.2 Small Self-Administered Schemes (SSASs)

Just as SIPPs are a derivation of PPPs, SSASs originally started as a derivation of executive pension plans (EPPs). These were popular with company directors of small and medium-sized businesses. SSASs were marketed at the same type of companies, but with the added extras of the self-investment options and borrowing facility.

The 'small' nature of SSASs is defined by having a maximum of 11 members. All members have to be trustees with an equal say in the running of the SSAS and so, in reality, most SSASs have a maximum of three to four people. They are generally family run businesses that may offer a separate type of pension plan for the employees and keep the SSAS element for the directors.

Just as with SIPPs, SSASs are able to borrow up to 50% of the net scheme assets. Often this may be used for the same purpose of bringing a company's commercial property under the ownership of a pension scheme, with the tax benefits (ie, no CGT) that attracts.

Unlike SIPPs, SSASs are also able to loan money from the scheme to the sponsoring employer, and not face unattractive tax penalties. There are certain conditions for these loans to meet such as:

*   Not more than 50% of the scheme assets can be lent.
*   The SSAS must charge interest at a minimum rate of 1% over the average base rate.
*   The maximum term of the loan is five years, which may be rolled-over once.

If any conditions aren't met, the loan will be an unauthorised payment, which could, ultimately, result in the SSAS being deregistered.

SSASs can invest in the sponsoring employer, although the extent of this investment has been limited since A-Day. Now, a SSAS can only invest up to 5% of scheme assets in any one sponsoring employer, and under 20% of scheme assets if the shareholdings relate to more than one sponsoring employer.

16.7.3 Uses of Self-Invested Options

Sophisticated investors who use the self-invested options to invest in diverse and risk-appropriate assets can benefit greatly from self-investment. The possibility of getting the business premises that you operate out of, under pension funding rules, is certainly attractive and makes sense for many. Also, if an individual has a portfolio of shares and bonds, a SIPP provides a good tax-efficient wrapper for them.

However, there are dangers of self-investment. It is a high risk approach, for example, for an individual to invest heavily in the shares of their own company, as they are then relying on that company for income in retirement as well as their working-life. It should also be remembered that unlisted shares are particularly illiquid.

The FCA is keeping a keen eye on the burgeoning SIPP market (mainly funded by transfers from PPPs), and has issued guidance to advisers. This focuses on costs and cost comparisons, and on the need of advisory firms to be able to demonstrate that a particular consumer genuinely requires investment flexibility and control.

16.7.4 Pension Death Benefits

You should note that this section does not cover the death benefits relating to the state pension scheme.

Death benefits can now be paid to any nominated person except in the form of a pension from a defined benefit scheme which can only be paid to a dependent of the person who died. A dependent will normally be the spouse or civil partner, a child under age 23 or a financial dependent. If it is paid to another person, it will be taxed at 55% as an unauthorised payment. Apart from that, death benefits can be paid to a beneficiary either as a lump sum death benefit or pension death benefit. In addition, the recipient of a pension death benefit can nominate a successor to receive that benefit providing the pension is in flexi-access drawdown.

The tax deducted will depend on the type of scheme, age of the pension holder at death and the type of benefit paid.

Scheme Pension

When a pension is paid by the scheme (whether from a defined benefit or defined contribution scheme) income tax will generally be deducted by the administrator.

Other Pensions

Type of Pension Scheme	Benefit Type	Age its owner died	Income Tax payable?
Defined contribution or defined benefit	Most lump sums	Under 75	No
Defined contribution	Annuity or money from a new drawdown fund (set up or converted and first accessed from 6 April 2015)	Under 75	No
Defined contribution	Money from an old drawdown fund (a 'capped' fund or a fund first accessed before 6 April 2015)	Under 75	Yes
Defined contribution or defined benefit	Trivial commutation lump sums	Any age	Yes
Defined contribution or defined benefit	Most lump sums	75 or over	Yes
Defined contribution	Annuity or money from drawdown fund	75 or over	Yes

However, it is important to note that there is an important time frame in the case of most lump sums and untouched drawdown if the pension owner was under 75 when they died. Tax will be payable if the money is paid to the beneficiary more than two years after the provider has been told or ought reasonably to have known of the death of the holder.

Tax may also be payable if the pension holder who died had pension savings worth more than £1 million, the benefit was paid over within the two-year window and the pension holder's total pension savings exceeded their lifetime allowance.

If the death benefit is taxable, the money paid is added to the beneficiary's income in the year of payment and will be subject to income tax accordingly. Depending on the amount the beneficiary receives this could increase their rate of tax.

Unless the provider has the recipients tax coding, the provider will deduct tax on a month one basis which means that more or less tax will be deducted than is actually due and the recipient may receive a tax refund or have to pay more tax later.

Chapter Six
Principles of Financial Advice

An exam specification breakdown is provided at the back of this workbook

1.   Introduction

In this chapter we will be building on your existing understanding of how to establish a client's investment objectives alongside any constraints associated with their own circumstances, before designing an appropriate investment strategy.

Much of this will be familiar to you already, not just from your work but from your own personal dealings as a client. Your existing knowledge will form a good base to build on certain aspects from a more theoretical basis that will ultimately help in your examination.

This chapter is also closely linked with Chapter 7, which considers portfolio performance and review.

You must continue reading and extending your understanding of the topics covered, through additional study. This chapter does not represent everything you may be expected to know for the examination.

You will see icons or symbols alongside the text. These indicate activities or questions that have been designed to check your understanding and help you validate your understanding.

Here is a guide to what each of the symbols mean:

 Question

This identifies a question that will enable you to check your knowledge and understanding.

 Analyse

This gives you an opportunity to consider a question posed and compare your answers to the feedback given.

1.1   Objectives

Establish Client Objectives and Constraints

1. Understand risk and return objectives and how to construct a risk-return profile.
2. Identify the major types of investment risk, and where and how they typically arise.
3. Explain the impact of inflation, deflation, taxation and charges on investment returns.
4. Understand the importance of timescale in relation to risk and the time value of money.
5. Understand the essential features and purpose of a customer profile, particularly the customer's personal details, income, assets, liabilities, expectations, risk tolerance and existing investment provision.
6. Understand the importance of knowing the customer's knowledge and experience of investing.
7. Understand the regulatory requirements regarding the need for, and content of, client agreement documentation and related communications.
8. Understand and be able to address customer concerns about confidentiality and security, data protection, fees, periodic reporting and customer communications.

Design an Investment Strategy

9. Understand the key features and risk-reward profile of the main investment approaches, including passive/active, buy/hold, momentum, core/satellite, value, growth, direct, indirect, ethical/SRI, lifestyle, hedge and structured fund approaches.
10. Determine a suitable investment strategy with regard to the preferred investment approach, time horizon, income, growth, balance, tax position, costs, market and sector diversification and expected risk and return.
11. Analyse the means to implementing that policy, including short-term liquidity, available investments, choice between UK and overseas markets and direct and indirect routes.
12. Specify or recommend appropriate portfolio components, taking into account overall suitability, cost and ease of implementation and maintenance.

2. Investment Objectives and Risk

2.1 Introduction

In this section we will discuss the relationship between an individual's investment objectives and how they correlate with the level of risk they wish to undertake.

We shall then go on to introduce, and briefly explain, various types of risk that could be encountered by an investor.

 Before we move on, consider how an individual's own circumstances and needs could have an impact on the level or type of returns they require from investment funds.

2.2 Investment Objectives

Individuals have many different savings and investment needs. The investment objective expressed by individuals can vary further, depending upon their attitudes and circumstances. It is vital to identify a basic framework of information that will be required from an investor, so that their position can objectively be assessed and suitable recommendations can be made:

- What are the investor's aims and objectives for this investment?
- What are their timescales?
- What percentage of the total investable assets is the amount being considered for investment?
- Do they require income and/or capital growth?
- Do they have more than one need?
- What are their priorities?
- Do they want investments to be based on ethical considerations?
- What are they expecting in performance and returns, compared with the level of risk they are prepared to take?

This last point is very important. We must ensure that an investor fully understands the various risks that may attach to his investment choices, and knows the impact that these may have on the required return from his savings or investment portfolio.

The higher the sum that is available to invest, the greater the amount of flexibility and choice that will be available. Larger investment funds could also impact on other factors, such as the level of risk that the individual is willing to take.

As mentioned above, the timescale is an important factor. Before any recommendations can be made, the savings or investment term needs to be established. Again this can have an impact on the level of risk that the investor may be prepared to take. In addition, if certain investments are encashed early, the individual could possibly incur early surrender charges, which can make a severe dent in the overall investment returns.

The economic, legal and political environment may impact on an individual's savings and investment needs and how they are tackled.

Relevant questions could be:

- Should individuals consider saving more for their retirement if the government of the day has a policy of continually reducing pension benefits provided via the state system?
- Should an individual invest over the short to medium term in property, if it appears that over that period, economic factors will force the property market into a slump?

Other external factors certainly could impact on the choice of product recommended. For example, will the product be most suitable, bearing in mind its and the individual's tax status? What will be the type and level of charges imposed on the prospective product? The higher the tax levied for a particular investor and the greater the charges, the lower the ultimate returns.

2.2.1 Variance in Income Needs

Individuals may have a variety of income needs from their investment portfolios. Some will want a high level of income, to supplement income from other sources. Realistically high levels of income have been difficult to achieve in recent years, and on many occasions this is at the price of zero or negative growth. The investor may accept a gradual erosion of capital over time so that the required level of income can be provided.

To others, the requirement for income may be low because the investor's aim is to achieve capital growth.

Some investors will want the income from their investments to grow over time. If this is the case, the choice reduces, but there are still products available in the market that can and do achieve reasonable increases (often at the price of increased risk, less flexibility or perhaps a lower initial income).

2.2.2 Variance in Growth Needs

There are numerous reasons why capital growth is required. The type and level of growth will vary depending upon the specific requirements and risk profile of the investor. Capital growth could be in the form of real value being added to an asset, or the reinvestment of income to purchase a further quantity of the particular investment.

2.2.3   Variance in Combined Income and Growth Needs

If an investor wants a combination of income and capital growth, he should understand that a variety of product types may need to be used. And if an individual wants high levels of income, the effect of inflation on the underlying capital should be considered. Often a combination of income and growth can be provided within the same product, and this may satisfy an investor's objectives. However, it may have drawbacks – not least the generally held belief that savers and investors should diversify their portfolios to a reasonable level to reduce risk.

We shall now discuss risk in greater detail.

2.3   Risk

Finding out an individual's true attitude to risk is essential in assessing product suitability and making an appropriate investment recommendation. Risk should always be explained in a way that a customer understands. It is necessary to establish a client's investment experience.

People's attitude to risk can vary at different times in their life, and as we have said previously, it is relative to their circumstances and their investment objectives. It is important that a customer's investment portfolio is reviewed regularly so that a change in their risk appetite can be taken into account.

When explaining to a customer why a recommendation is suitable, reference should be made to how the recommendation reflects the customer's risk profile.

Firms use a variety of questions and tools to ascertain a customer's risk profile before making a recommendation. These might come as a paper document or point of sale, as part of the standard fact-find or as a risk profiling/asset allocation tool supplied by a third party. The FCA do not approve or endorse the use of these tools, but as the conduct of business rules require firms to ensure customers understand risk, the use of these tools could be a useful aid and help in assessing the client's profile. If firms do use risk profiling/asset allocation tools, it should be recorded on the customer's file. These tools do not take away the responsibility of the firm to ensure that the customer has the necessary level of understanding.

Irrespective of the method used to establish a customer's risk profile, questions need to be asked and explanations made in relation to:

- capital security
- shortfall risk
- interest rate risk
- inflation risk
- regular income withdrawals
- charges
- penalty fees
- age
- family commitments
- the need for income and/or growth
- whether there is an investment target
- the investment time horizon.

This is certainly not an exhaustive list. For example, account should also be taken of the customer's existing portfolio, so if the customer's risk profile suggests that 10% of their investment portfolio should be in higher risk assets, and they already hold 10% in the higher risk category, no additional investments in that category should be made.

A typical 'attitude to risk' questionnaire may look like the following:

Risk Attitude Profiling Questionnaire

Complete the questionnaire to confirm how closely your clients agree with each statement about their current situation, feelings and attitude to risk.

How it works

- confirm how closely your clients agree with 12 statements about their current situation, feelings and attitude to risk
- the answers are converted into a score between 1 and 100
- the score is mapped to one of our seven risk attitude categories. These cover the full range of risk profiles, from very cautious to very adventurous.

You can then generate a report which confirms your client's answers and defines their attitude to risk.

- 'Your name' is a required field
- 'Your company name' is a required field
- 'Forename' is a required field
- 'Surname' is a required field
- 'Retirement age' is a required field
- please ensure all 12 risk questions have been answered
- 'DOB' should be in the dd/mm/yyyy format.

Your Details

Your name [   ]   Your company name [   ]

Client Details

Title [   ] Forename [   ] Surname [   ]

Date of birth [dd/mm/yyyy]   Retirement age [   ]

Risk Statements

For each of the 12 statements, select which of the answers most closely matches your client's current situation, attitudes and feelings.

1. People who know me would describe me as a cautious person.
    - strongly agree   - agree   - no strong opinion   - disagree   - strongly disagree

2. I feel comfortable about investing in the stock market.
    - strongly agree   - agree   - no strong opinion   - disagree   - strongly disagree

3. I generally look for the safest type of investment, even if that means lower returns.
    - strongly agree   - agree   - no strong opinion   - disagree   - strongly disagree

4. Usually it takes me a long time to make up my mind on financial matters.
    - strongly agree   - agree   - no strong opinion   - disagree   - strongly disagree

5. I associate the word 'risk' with the idea of opportunity.
    - strongly agree   - agree   - no strong opinion   - disagree   - strongly disagree

6. I prefer the safety of keeping my money in the bank.
    - strongly agree   - agree   - no strong opinion   - disagree   - strongly disagree

7. I find investment and other financial matters easy to understand.
    - strongly agree   - agree   - no strong opinion   - disagree   - strongly disagree

8. I am willing to take substantial financial risk to earn substantial returns.
    - strongly agree   - agree   - no strong opinion   - disagree   - strongly disagree

9. I have little experience of investing in stocks and shares.
    - strongly agree   - agree   - no strong opinion   - disagree   - strongly disagree

10. When it comes to investing, I'd rather be safe than sorry.
    - strongly agree   - agree   - no strong opinion   - disagree   - strongly disagree

11. I'd rather take my chances with high-risk/high-return investments than have to increase the amount I am saving.
    - strongly agree   - agree   - no strong opinion   - disagree   - strongly disagree

12. I am not willing to take any financial risk.
    - strongly agree   - agree   - no strong opinion   - disagree   - strongly disagree

An individual's ability to withstand risk (both psychologically and physically) will have an impact on the investments selected.

The risk categories are broadly divided as below. However you may see low risk described as cautious and high risk as adventurous or speculative, but with similar descriptions. As these are broad descriptions, an adviser must be certain that they understand what the client understands by such illustrations and quantify what they mean to the client. This is because low, medium and high risk have different meanings to different people.

Risk Category			
Risk averse	**Low risk**	**Medium risk**	**High Risk (speculative)**
People who do not wish to take any risk with their capital and therefore favour cash on deposit. They understand that while their capital is safe, returns may be low and often barely keeping pace with inflation.	People who accept the need to invest in areas other than cash, but wish to minimise the risk. These investors might consider gilts and bonds as part of their portfolio, as the risk is low and there is an element of capital guarantee. However, some capital could be lost.	People who understand that to retain the capital value and achieve capital growth, they will need to balance risk against the potential reward.	People whose priority objective is capital growth, and who understand and accept that in order to achieve it, there is a significant risk to their capital. These investors might choose individual shares or international funds as part of their portfolio.

Suitability Report

The purpose of a suitability report (which is often in the form of a letter) is to explain why and how a particular product or products have been recommended as suitable to meet the customer's needs and objectives. How a firm uses it may depend on their business model and the services that are provided. They have to be used in the following cases:

- a regulated collective investment
- a life policy
- an investment trust
- a personal or stakeholder pension policy
- a pension transfer, conversion or opt-out.

The suitability report must be written in plain English, be fair, clear and not misleading, and written by a person who is authorised to advise on the recommended products. It must at least specify the client's demands and needs, explain why the recommendation is suitable having regard to the information provided by the client and explain any possible disadvantages of the transaction for the client.

Consideration should be given to the following additional points when compiling a suitability report/letter:

- tailored to the customer
- highlights the risks associated with the recommendations
- explains costs, charges and potential penalties attached to the products
- provides a balanced view
- highlights if any objectives have been omitted
- emphasises how the customer will be advantaged or disadvantages by the advice.

 Some customers do not wish to disclose all their financial information. This can make it difficult to understand whether the recommendation is truly suitable. What do you need to do in these cases?

If an adviser does not obtain the necessary information to assess suitability, they should not make a personal recommendation to a trade customer. However, a customer can always ask the adviser to undertake the transaction based on the limited information. The customer must give instructions to the adviser in writing. In these circumstances, they will need to make it clear that any advice they provide will be based on the information that has been provided. In addition the adviser will need to advise the customer that their recommendation will not take into account any information not disclosed. For example, if the client who has 10% already invested in a high-risk category does not disclose this, they may be overexposed in their overall risk profile. The FCA does not accept blanket disclosure as acceptable across all customers. They should also bear in mind the client's best interests rule and if relevant (for non-advised transactions) the appropriateness test.

2.3.1 The Relative Risk of Different Types of Financial Investment

The risk associated with different types of investments is often captured graphically with investments such as cash and government backed securities at the safer end, with unlisted shares and derivatives at the opposite end. This is illustrated below.

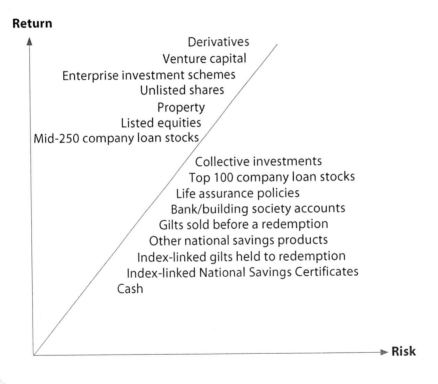

Derivatives are anomalous. While specific investment into them can be perceived in certain instances as very high risk, they are often used as a hedging mechanism within portfolios or investment products to reduce the overall effects of volatility, for example by taking an opposite position to the rest of the assets held.

2.3.2 Types of Investment Risk

The following is a summary of some of the types of risk that could affect investment returns:

Default Risk

This is the risk of a loan not being repaid. With gilts there is negligible risk. However, an unsecured loan made to a company which is in financial difficulty will involve far greater risk. Default risk in relation to companies is often termed credit risk, covering both missed interest payments as well as capital defaults.

Liquidity Risk

There is always a risk when you need to find a buyer for the asset you are holding before you can turn it in to cash. Some assets are very liquid, like no-notice deposit accounts; whereas some are illiquid, for example, direct investment into property.

Inflation Risk

This is the risk that the rate of inflation will erode the purchasing power of the investment by more than the increase in value of the investment. An investor locked into a low rate of interest may be susceptible to an increase in the rate of inflation.

Interest Rate Risk

We discussed how the prices of fixed-interest assets are affected by changes in interest rates. An increase in interest rates will normally have a negative effect on bond prices. This represents a risk to investors in bonds, especially if there is the possibility that they may need to sell them prior to redemption.

Systematic (or Market Risk)

This is the risk that will affect all assets in that class, for example a recession or market crash.

Unsystematic Risk (or Specific/Diversifiable Risk)

This is a risk that affects just one company irrespective of the overall market. For example, company A may have trading difficulties due to the inefficiency of its manufacturing plant when compared to its competitors that have invested in new technology. If competing companies are able to reduce their prices, Company A may have to follow suit to remain competitive. This will reduce its margins and if it cannot reduce costs, profits will be affected. The impact of this reduction in financial stability could be a downgrading in its credit rating, which could have a negative effect on its corporate bonds.

Foreign Currency Risk

This is the risk of the effects of exchange rate variances to your returns. For example, you could invest in a security based in Germany and make 10% in a year. However, if the value of the pound against the euro were to go up by 7% in that year, your real return should you want to realise your investment and convert back into sterling would, in effect, only be 3%.

3. The Impact of Inflation, Deflation, Taxation and Charges

3.1 Introduction

There are several factors that have an impact to a greater or lesser extent on investment returns. In this section we shall discuss some key areas, namely inflation, deflation, taxation and charges.

3.2 Inflation

Inflation can be defined as a persistent tendency for the general level of prices to rise.

Inflation will have an impact on all investments to a larger or smaller extent. At low levels it doesn't cause great difficulties to an economy, but if rises are persistently high, they can have a damaging impact on investment returns as their real values erode.

Unabated, inflation will cause an economy to 'overheat' as demand outstrips supply and prices spiral. In addition, a country with high inflation can have any advantage of a competitive nominal exchange rate erased if the rate of inflation is high and prices continue to increase.

Equities have traditionally been seen as a good hedge against inflation because income and capital values can be anticipated to increase in line with the economy in the long term.

Fixed interest stocks, such as gilts, are not a good hedge against inflation because the fixed returns are eroded by the fall in value of money. That is why some government stocks are index-linked, meaning the interest and capital payments are adjusted for inflation. Index-linked stocks are by their nature very useful, but this means they are priced at a level where the real return is very low or even negative.

In recent years, monetary policy has been aimed at increasing economic growth, with low interest rates and quantitative easing. The reduction in interest rates has boosted the prices of government stocks, which have outperformed equities.

The opposite of inflation is deflation, where prices actually decrease. This would usually be accompanied by declines in output and demand as falling prices can give the incentive of delaying investments or business purchases. Deflation should not be confused with disinflation, which is the term used for the drop in the rate of inflation.

3.3 Tax

The taxation of savings and investments will frequently take two forms. Often, any taxation will be payable on income and/or capital gains enjoyed by the investor.

Additionally, many investment vehicles will pay tax from within their own funds on the income and capital gains that they make. Some investments will have a competitive advantage where some or all returns from them are tax-free.

In many instances, the asset type and the investor can be protected from paying income tax or capital gains tax (CGT) by, for example, investing within a tax-free wrapper such as an individual savings account (ISA), pension, or in a tax-free product such as National Savings Certificates (NSCs).

Saving via tax-advantaged products should be an important (but not the only) consideration when assessing an individual's overall investment requirements. As a general rule, higher rate taxpayers should look to minimise income and accumulate growth during the term of their investment. They should, however, understand the tax consequences of an investment on encashment. For instance, the disposal of shares would give rise to CGT on any net chargeable gains at 10% or 20% (except gains on CGT taxable residential property where the rates are 18% and 28%). Where possible, consideration could be given to reinvestment of proceeds into other investments whereby some form of CGT relief (eg, reinvestment relief) is available.

Some portfolios are specifically geared up to take advantage of specific tax reliefs, such as investments into securities that are, subject to a sufficient holding period, eligible to inheritance tax (IHT) business property relief.

Other factors must also be taken into account, for example the investor's residence and domicile status for tax purposes. If an individual is not a UK resident or is non-UK domiciled, offshore investment may be a far more tax-efficient solution, subject of course to their other circumstances being taken into account.

3.4 Charges

The types of charges that apply to investment products vary considerably.

In certain instances, they may be 'hidden'. For example, the charges arising from a deposit account will be reflected by the rate of interest payable. The cost to an investor of saving into a with-profits fund can only be indicated by the levels of bonus applied.

Charges applying to other investment vehicles are more transparent. For instance, buying (higher) and selling (lower) prices applicable to securities, and administration fees for packaged products such as initial charges, annual management charges and lower allocation periods for the early years.

Costs can be higher if funds are actively managed. If that active management does not beat, for example, a comparative benchmark index, then that product becomes very expensive for the returns that it is delivering. Conversely, if the fund is passively managed, following the performance of a benchmark index, then charges are likely to be much lower. The disadvantage of these funds is that after charges, they can never really outperform the index that they follow.

3.5 Balancing a Portfolio

By diversifying across a range of different asset classes and sectors, individuals can provide a balance to their portfolios to reduce risk. The following list of asset classes demonstrates the potential returns and pitfalls that could be experienced when allocating funds towards them.

Variable rate cash deposits	These provide protection against rising interest rates. Poor long-term performers in providing real returns, especially after accounting for tax.
Fixed interest securities	Perform well in times of falling interest rates, providing secure income and known capital returns at redemption. Lose value in times of rising inflation and interest rates. More volatile the longer the term to redemption.
Index linked securities	Provide protection against inflation if held to redemption. Long-term performance likely to be less than that derived from equities.
Equities	Over the longer term, can provide rising income and capital returns. In the shorter term, equity values are volatile. In times of economic slowdown, equities tend to perform badly. Overseas equity markets do not necessarily move in line with each other, so diversification by selecting international investments could be viewed as a way of reducing risk.
Property	Normally a good hedge against inflation over the longer term. Not directly correlated with other asset classes such as equities, so can be used to reduce volatility in a portfolio.
Commodities	Can also reduce risk in a portfolio in terms of volatility, through diversification. Again, little correlation with other asset classes.

4. Timescale

4.1 Introduction

There is a strong connection between required returns on investments and their accessibility.

If capital needs to be preserved and accessed immediately in order to cover, for example, short-term emergency costs, then choices are restricted to products such as current or short-notice deposit accounts.

It is clear that as a result of the need to access funds without penalty, the investor is going to have to compromise and accept potentially much lower real returns than, say, an equity backed investment over the medium to longer term.

Likewise, an investor in equities would have to understand that while it will be possible to access his funds virtually at any time, he faces a greater risk of sudden falls in capital values, loss of dividend income etc, which could significantly reduce returns.

 How much would you recommend that a client retains in cash within their investment portfolio?

4.2 Cash Liquidity

Every personal investment portfolio should retain an element of cash liquidity.

There is no set amount that should be on deposit. Recommended cash levels will be entirely down to the individual's circumstances. Each case needs to be judged on its own merits. Some factors are worth considering, which will help to determine the required amount.

- Most investors need funds that are instantly accessible for emergencies and to cover known expenditure in the short term. That being the case, a fair proportion of cash could be held on deposit with longer notice periods in return for higher rates of interest. The key point here is to ensure that the client is not penalised for accessing funds.
- Someone with high income needs from their portfolio may require much higher sums in cash-based investments than someone who works in highly paid and secure employment.
- Funds held on deposit could enable an investor to take advantage of investment opportunities at short notice, such as a new share offering or rights issue.

It should be remembered that an excess of funds held in cash could eventually be an inefficient way to invest, particularly in the case of higher rate taxpayers.

4.3 Time Value of Money

The time value of money is a way of appraising the valuation of investments based on expected future returns. The theory looks at the anticipated value of money at a future point in time, and discounts it back to the present day to assess its current worth.

The formula for the time value of money is:

Present value (PV) = Future value/$(1 + r)^n$

Where r is the rate of interest and n is the period

A simple example is shown below:

Example

John wants to know what amount needs to be invested today to achieve a figure of £100 in one year's time, assuming an interest rate of 5%.

PV x 1.05 = £100

PV = £100/1.05

= £95.24 (rounded to two decimal places)

In terms of its importance to the timescale of an investment, a number of issues need to be taken into consideration when deciding upon an appropriate rate of interest:

- In reality, the rate of interest may change over the period in question.
- The rate of return chosen needs to take into account any taxation that may be applied, thereby reducing it.
- If the interest is to be reinvested, the rates earned will fluctuate over time.

5. Customer Profiles

5.1 Introduction

We touched on this area in Section 2 of this chapter. This section provides more specific detail on all areas of customer profiles.

Before providing clients with investment advice, it is important to accurately record sufficient information concerning individuals' personal and financial situations and their prioritised objectives. It may be that a standard fact-find form used by an adviser is not sufficient to cover the breadth of detail required to provide recommendations to a more sophisticated investor. Where possible therefore, enough information should be documented on interview records and the adviser's own reports to verify the suitability of the advice given.

The following notes will provide you with a summary of the type of information that is likely to be needed, and the extent to which it can be used with portfolio management.

5.2 Personal Information

This will include the client's name and address, date and place of birth, residence and domicile status for tax purposes, marital status, health, hobbies and pastimes, and details of any children or other members of the family who are dependent on the client in some way, especially financially.

These points are important in that they can open up questions for later on in the interview process. For instance, a client's marital status over his or her lifetime may vary from single to married to partner, to divorcee to being widowed. An adviser can find out a great deal about future plans and expected settlements (lump sum and income). This could then lead on to potential needs/uses of any sums received or about to be received. It could also be that the adviser is restricted in the advice that he gives, eg, only to UK residents and domiciled customers. As such, this information can be gleaned early on.

 What different sources of income could a client have?

5.3 Financial Information

5.3.1 Income and Expenditure

Employment Income

An adviser needs to ascertain details of all sources of income. The logical place to start is to find out the client's employment status. Is he an employee, company director, self-employed, business partner, home maker, unemployed or retired?

When dealing with an employee, their entire income, ie, pay, bonus, overtime, commission and fringe benefits such as car allowance, private medical insurance, share option schemes and other benefits in

330

kind should be ascertained. The adviser will need to be able to understand which of these benefits are taxable and which are tax-free.

If the employee is a director with a controlling shareholding in a limited company, it is likely that the individual will be able to achieve corporate and personal tax efficiencies. It is worth obtaining a copy of the company's Memorandum and Articles of Association, audited accounts for the past three years and projections for the current year.

In addition, asking the director questions about the business generally will give you useful information:

- Who owns the company?
- What has been planned to happen to the company in the event of death, retirement and ill health of directors/shareholders?
- Have any plans been made for continued succession?
- Who are the key people in the company?
- Is any more capital needed to fund the business?
- What are the client's plans for the future?
- What provision is being made for income in retirement?

If the client is self-employed or in a business partnership, then there is no distinction between the business entity and the individual. Income will, more or less, be the individual's net profit (or share of the profits if a partner). However, many of the questions above could also be equally relevant.

If a client is leaving or has left his employer, full details will be needed of any preserved pensions provided, redundancy benefits or any benefits in kind that have been provided with a continuation option, eg, life assurance.

Details of any previous employment are important, especially in terms of providing the adviser with information about any preserved pension benefits. The adviser/client should, of course, obtain full information from the former employer.

Pension Income

Clients may have built up pension income from several sources of work over the years. The adviser needs to identify all sources from both the state and privately. This will help to ascertaining the tax position of the individual. In cases where income is very low, it could assist in establishing whether any extra state benefits are due to the individual.

State Benefits

The adviser should establish full details of any state benefits payable or due to the client. These could include: Child Benefit, Working Tax Credit, state pension benefits, Jobseekers Allowance, Income Support, Employment and Support Allowance, Housing Benefit and Disabled Allowances. The adviser should have a reasonable working knowledge of these benefits to assist the client in obtaining what is rightfully due to them.

Investment Income

The adviser should identify all sources of client income and draw up a schedule of income. This will assist with the assessment of net disposable income. It is important to question whether any of this income is being received from trusts, covenants or similar.

Outgoings

These can be divided between ongoing regular expenditure, for example mortgage, maintenance of property, provision for school fees, travel to and from work, and irregular commitments such as holidays and home improvements.

Calculating the individual's net income will assist in establishing whether there is any scope for further savings and investment provision.

5.3.2   Assets and Liabilities

Assets

Individual client assets can be placed into different categories. Personal assets will include residential and holiday homes, personally owned car(s) and antiques.

Business assets will include those that are specifically earmarked for the client's business, for example, shares or ownership of business property. It should be noted that these assets are likely to be highly illiquid. In any event, considerable reliefs are provided to them, such as IHT business property relief and CGT entrepreneur's relief, so care should be taken as to when to dispose of these assets.

The client is likely to have some investments. Every attempt should be made to obtain full details, including current values, contribution levels, projected values, income taken, tax status and allowances.

The adviser should also ensure that the true ownership of assets has been established. If owned jointly, are the assets held on a joint tenants or tenants in common basis? In addition, the client may also beneficially own assets within a trust. The terms of the trust and details of the individual's current and/or future entitlements should always be ascertained.

Liabilities

These will be in the form of debts owed to individuals or to lending institutions. Again, full details need to be obtained, for example the type of loan and the amount of debt outstanding, any early repayment penalties, loan term, repayment levels, redemption charges, whether held solely or jointly, secured or unsecured, and any associated insurances that the client holds, eg, endowment policy.

The adviser should also establish details of all other forms of debt, such as overdrafts and credit card balances. The FCA regard a recommendation to repay debt as the first course of action, as good practice.

5.3.3 Existing Insurances

Life Assurance

Full details of all existing life assurance policies should be obtained, including start dates, lives assured, policy owners, length of term, any trusts in place, underwriting terms offered, qualifying status, fund type, eg, with profits or unit linked, policy options, whether assigned and on what basis. Current surrender and fund values, and projected maturity values where relevant, should also be requested.

Health Insurance Policies

Again, all health insurance policies need to be ascertained to a similar level of detail as mentioned for life assurance. Likely products that will need to be investigated under this broad category include income protection, private medical insurance, critical illness cover (CIC), accident and sickness policies and long term care.

Existing Savings, Investment Products and Pensions

It is important to obtain full details of all savings and investment products currently held. This includes product type, amount invested, current value, savings/investment purpose, when started, whether held solely or jointly and how funded.

The adviser will also need to discuss the subject of pensions with the client. If the individual is a member of an occupational pension scheme, full details of benefits provided and accrued to date will need to be gathered, as well as projections at retirement. The individual may also have the opportunity to top up pension benefits. This can be achieved through a number of registered pension arrangements such as additional voluntary contributions (AVCs) or concurrent personal pension plans (PPPs), as well as non-pension associated products such as ISAs.

If the client contributes to his own personal pension arrangements, full details of the type of plan and projections will be needed, as well as other information that might be useful in establishing the amount of retirement benefit available and the type of benefit taken. For example, is it segmented to allow phasing of benefits? Is it able to accommodate pension fund withdrawals? Are they in receipt of a state pension?

5.3.4 Knowledge and Experience

Before a personal recommendation can be made, an adviser must establish the knowledge and the experience of the customer in the investment field relevant to the service that is being offered. This could include knowing about the types of investments the client has held in the past and present, the nature, volume and frequency of the client's transactions, and their level of education, profession or former profession. The adviser will then have to take all this into account when explaining the risks and assessing whether a particular type of investment will be suitable.

5.3.5   Inheritance

Wills

If a client has made a will, full details need to be obtained to establish what effects the terms of the will have on survivors and beneficiaries of the estate. For example, what guardianship arrangements have been made for children? What trusts will be settled as a result of the will? Who are the executors? It is also important to find out when the will was written, in order to assess whether any major changes have occurred that make the will no longer valid, eg, marriage.

Power of Attorney/Enduring Power of Attorney/Lasting Power of Attorney

It needs to be established whether these arrangements have been made, with whom and for what reason. If any power of attorney has been written, it is essential that the attorney proves their authority by providing the original or authorised copy of the power of attorney. When dealing with the attorney, you must be able to confirm that the power was duly executed, is still valid and gives authority for the intended transactions. In some instances, it may only be the attorney that the adviser will speak to, as the client may be incapable of acting on his own behalf.

 Potentially, how many lasting power of attorney documents could be held in respect of one individual?

Two. One would specifically deal with the individual's financial affairs, and the other would deal with personal health and welfare issues.

5.3.6   Attitude to Risk

It is vital that this information is obtained as soon as possible (as explained in more depth in Section 2 of this chapter), not just from the perspective of recommending any future investments but also to establish whether existing needs are being met with products that fall within the investor's own risk parameters.

5.4   Client Plans and Objectives

5.4.1   Shorter-Term Objectives

Emergency Funds

The adviser should establish with the client the extent of the emergency fund that will be required. There is no right or wrong answer to this, and discussions would have to be conducted with clients to ascertain an amount that they would consider suitable.

Trading Up

Any intention to move to a more expensive property or to purchase a holiday home would need to be considered before contemplating any longer-term investment.

334

Trading Down

People often decide that they are going to move to a smaller/less expensive property for economic reasons. Such a move could have been prompted by a change in marital status, eg, divorce. It might be that a client is about to retire and feels that he no longer needs the space that is being enjoyed with the current property. Some people, of course, trade down simply to pay off debts.

Other Future Changes

There are a number of other future short-term changes that could affect the investment advice being given. These could include future change in marital status, occupation or anticipated future assets or liabilities, eg, gifts and loans.

There is a need to question customers about any anticipated expenditure, and how it is to be funded. Furthermore, disposal of assets may lead to funds available for investment.

5.4.2 Longer-Term Objectives

It is advisable to explore likely future costs by taking a view of the current cost and adjusting for inflation to the point where the cost is likely to be incurred.

 Identify some potential longer-term financial aims and objectives that a client may have.

Some examples are listed below:

- **Family** – clients may wish to help to finance relatives in respect of their marriage, education, business or even new homes.
- **Private/further education costs** – this is a common long-term (and expensive) objective. It is very much the case that estimates will need to be made of likely future costs but it is worth bearing in mind that in recent years, average private fees have risen at rates well above inflation.
- **Family home** – any potential home move will need to be factored into investment recommendations.
- **Career** – how long a client will want to stay in their existing role can give an idea of the plans that he or she has for the future in terms of career development. This can give an indication of likely rises in employment income. There may even be a desire expressed by the customer that they wish to start their own business at a later date.
- **Financial** – certain aims may be expressed purely in financial terms. For instance: 'At age 65, I wish to receive pension and investment income of £40,000 per annum.' Or: 'In ten years' time, I hope to have repaid my £50,000 mortgage, five years ahead of schedule.'

5.5 Client Priorities

Clients will have varying priorities in respect of their financial needs and objectives. As a guideline however, the following order is usually recommended:

1. ensure sufficient funds to meet immediate living expenses
2. ensure short-term savings and investment needs are addressed
3. ensure that sufficient protection needs are met, both in respect of early death and illness

4. ensure pension needs are addressed
5. address longer term savings and investment needs
6. address any estate planning issues.

5.5.1 Determining Investment Needs

Prior to considering the different investment asset types (available in Chapter 5), we should address how needs are determined.

In the first instance, timescale is important, not just from the perspective of how long it gives the individual to generate sufficient funds, but also their ability to access the investment without penalty.

As already discussed, the client will need to generate sufficient liquidity to pay for everyday costs and also to fulfil short-term objectives.

The client may need income to be generated from the investment portfolio. It will be a matter for discussion as to what constitutes a reasonable amount. In some instances, the client's expectations as to the level of income they can draw will need to be managed.

The client may need their investment or savings to generate capital growth. An adviser would need to discuss the level at which the investment should grow over the required timescale, taking into account the client's attitude to risk.

The client will need to understand the various risks that can be incurred through savings and investment. Suffice to say that if the client is advised to enter into a savings or investment contract above or below the level of acceptable risk, the adviser may be accused of making inappropriate recommendations.

6. Client Agreements

6.1 Introduction

As we have already mentioned in Chapter 1, the new Conduct of Business Sourcebook (COBS) is far less prescriptive than previously, and the rules on the issuance of client agreements are no different.

The rules state that a firm, before entering into an agreement or providing any services relating to designated investment business for a retail client, must provide that client with:

- the terms of any such agreement
- information about the firm and its services, including information on communications, conflicts of interest and authorised status.

The information can be provided after the client is bound by the agreement, if the agreement was concluded using a means of distance communication. The agreement can be issued in 'any durable medium', therefore encouraging firms to introduce more contemporary methods of communication.

Similarly, a durable method can be used to communicate material changes to the agreement. Any changes should be notified to clients in *'good time'*, which is not, however, defined.

Details of the rules around other communications, such as periodic and occasional statements, can be found in Chapter 1, Section 5.7.

Record-Keeping

In order to be able to demonstrate suitability, firms must keep copies of client records. There have been a number of fines because of inadequate record-keeping. Consequently, regulated firms must, more than ever, look beyond specific record-keeping requirements and ensure that they are able, at all times and in all respects, to produce the records necessary to demonstrate 'know your customer' (KYC) and suitability compliance. Remember the old adage **'if it isn't written down, it hasn't happened'**!

A firm must keep a record of client agreements for whichever is the longer of:

- five years
- the duration of the relationship with the client
- indefinitely, in the case of pension transfers, conversions pension opt-outs or free standing additional voluntary contributions (FSAVCs).

Also, remember that complaints can be forthcoming after a number of years and certainly later than five years after a relationship has finished.

 Find a client agreement and examine the headings.

7. Confidentiality, Data Protection, Reporting and Communication

7.1 Introduction

Clients will naturally expect to be advised to the highest professional standards, in accordance with current regulatory requirements. This section briefly covers some of the concerns that are likely to be raised by clients during the advice process.

7.2 Customer Confidentiality

From a professional perspective, maintaining confidentiality with a client over their financial affairs is a standard that clients should expect as a prerequisite for doing business with an adviser and his firm.

Much regulation affecting client confidentiality stems from laws on data protection (see Section 7.3 below) and the FCA's rules and principles concerning conflicts of interest (covered in Chapter 1), which are contained in SYSC, the FCA's Senior Management Arrangements, Systems and Controls sourcebook.

7.3 Data Protection

7.3.1 Overview

The Data Protection Act 1998 applies to manual data as well as electronic data, and imposes a series of obligations on those affected by the legislation.

Data is widely defined. It can even include telephone and CCTV recordings and photographs.

Firms need to appoint a Data Protection Compliance Officer with sufficient authority to ensure that the Act is adhered to.

 Which independent public body oversees enforcement of the Data Protection Act 1998?

The Information Commissioner's Office.

7.3.2 Data Protection Act Terminology

There are several terms defined in the Act that you need to be aware of:

- **Personal data** – information in respect of a living individual who can be identified from the information held by the data controller, eg, the person's name and address.
- **Sensitive personal data** – this term is used in respect of a person's racial or ethnic origin, religious, political or other beliefs, mental or physical health, sex life or criminal record.
- **Processing** – deals with the day-to-day activities that affect personal data, including disclosure to a third party.
- **A data subject** – the individual whose personal data is held.
- **A data controller** - decides the circumstances in which personal data should be processed.
- **A data processor** – a body (usually an organisation) that actually processes the data on behalf of the data controller.

 Before moving on, jot down what you believe to be the main principles of the Data Protection Act 1998 and consider how this legislation affects the way you do business.

7.3.3 Data Protection Principles

All businesses that handle data must abide by the principles applicable to personal data.

Personal data must be:

- handled fairly and lawfully. The individual data subject should have explicitly consented to the data processing, and there should be evidence in writing of this, in the terms of business letter or a separate form
- obtained only for a specified and lawful purpose and processed in line with those purposes. Data obtained for one purpose should not be used for another without obtaining the data subject's consent. If the firm plans to send out marketing material to data subjects, this should be made clear to them

- adequate, relevant and not excessive in relation to the purposes for which it is processed
- kept accurate and up to date
- retained for no longer than is necessary
- processed in accordance with data subjects' rights, eg, to have access to the data and veto the use of the data for marketing
- kept secure – specifically by the use of appropriate technical and organisational measures against misuse, damage or destruction
- only transferred outside the EEA if there are comparable protections.

7.3.4 Penalties

There are a number of criminal offences under the Act, including:

- failure to make a proper notification of processing to the Information Commissioner
- failure to comply with an information notice or an enforcement notice
- processing data without the data controller's authorisation – an offence that could be committed by a firm's data processors or other individual employees.

The penalties for non-compliance with the Act could result in unlimited fines and penal/informative notices issued by the Commissioner.

7.4 Fees

Disclosure regulation ensures that clients are clearly and accurately advised of the level of fees they are likely to be charged for the services provided. The following sections provide some indication of the fees charged for a variety of typical products and services on offer in the marketplace today.

7.4.1 Direct Investment

Charges levied by investment managers and stockbrokers could include:

- stamp duty and stamp duty reserve tax at 0.5% on the purchase of shares
- private client stockbroker fees, which vary depending upon the value of securities. The percentage charged will usually decrease as the sums involved increase, subject to minimum fees.

 John wishes to invest £50,000 in ordinary shares of BDF plc. What would your firm typically charge for a private client stockbroking service on this level of transaction?

A typical answer may be:

First £12,500 charged at 1.95%
Next £12,500 charged at 0.7%
Balance charged at 0.5%.

Fees will also vary depending on the type of security, eg, UK government and corporate stock transactions would incur a lower fee. In the above example, John would also pay stamp duty or SDRT on the purchase.

7.4.2   Collective Investment

Charges levied with collective schemes such as unit trusts and OEICs include:

- initial charges of 3–6%
- annual management fees of about 0.5–1.5%.

7.4.3   Discretionary Fees

In addition to the stockbroker fees for direct investment or initial and annual management charges for collective investment, discretionary portfolio managers are likely to charge a further fee to cover the overall strategic planning of the portfolio.

 How would you describe a 'wrap account'?

7.4.4   Wrap Accounts

A wrap account is a platform that can provide access to any underlying fund or other type of investment and can administer any of the product wrappers an investor may want to use. A wide range of assets can be included such as unit trusts, OEICs, investment trusts, equities and bonds.

The wrappers can include ISAs, self-invested pension plans (SIPPs), pension plans, investment bonds and child trust funds (CTFs).

Most wrap accounts levy a single annual management fee that covers all fees for buying and holding underlying investments, and for administration within the wrap account. These fees can be between 0.5% to 2% of the portfolio's value per year, depending on size. Some wrap accounts may charge a small percentage of the portfolio, but it is then up to the investor to incur dealing costs.

7.4.5   Adviser Charging

These are the charges made by advisers in relation to personal recommendations on retail investment products. They can consist of an initial adviser charge and an ongoing adviser charge. An initial adviser charge is generally between 1% and 5%. An ongoing adviser charge will be in the region of 0.5% to 2.0%. To charge an ongoing adviser charge, the adviser must provide a service and both the charge and the service must be cancellable unconditionally. The client can either pay the adviser charge directly or can request that it is deducted from their investment. VAT may be payable on adviser charges depending on the service provided.

7.5 Role of Portfolio Managers

7.5.1 Summary of the Role of Portfolio Managers

The role and responsibility of the portfolio manager is to:

- assist clients to determine and prioritise their needs
- determine an appropriate investment strategy in terms of liquidity, risk, tax, income and growth
- identify and record in writing the client's overall objectives and risk tolerance
- act in the client's best interests in line with the agreed objectives
- exercise professional judgement and care in carrying out the management of the investment portfolio
- keep the agreed strategy under review and make changes in line with developments in the investment, economic and tax environments
- carry out the required administration and accounting in order to maintain the portfolio.

7.5.2 Advisory and Discretionary Management

Under an advisory service, the investment manager suggests a strategy or particular course of action such as buy, sell or hold an investment, but it is up to the client to either accept the advice or reject it. Advisory services are usually provided by stockbrokers.

With discretionary investment management, the investment manager has the right under the terms of business to purchase, sell and hold investments in accordance with the client's objectives, without giving prior warning to, or seeking approval of, the client.

7.5.3 Requirements for Client Reporting

The way in which client reporting takes place, and its frequency, will usually be contained within the client agreement. Otherwise it should be agreed in writing between the client and investment manager.

The main items of reporting will often be:

- purchases and sales
- summary portfolio valuation and statements showing income, interest received, dividends and cash outflows
- general market commentary and calculated investment returns compared with the agreed benchmarks
- recommended changes to the investment strategy.

A firm is required to send periodic statements when it acts as an investment manager for a retail client or as a discretionary investment manager for a non-retail client.

- Statements must be sent at least half-yearly in respect of securities or securities-related cash balances held at the valuation date.
- Statements must be sent on a monthly basis for uncovered open positions on derivatives.
- Periodic statements must be sent promptly, following the end of each valuation period.

A firm does not have to send periodic statements if customers:

- have told the firm in writing that they wish to receive less frequent statements. However, the client must be sent periodic statements at least annually, or
- are not resident in the UK and have given prior consent.

Periodic statements have specific content requirements laid down in the rules.

7.6   Customer Communications

In accordance with the Financial Conduct Authority's Principle 7 for businesses and approved persons, all communications with clients should be made in such a way that they are clear, fair and not misleading.

8.   Main Investment Management Approaches

8.1   Introduction

Many different investment management strategies exist. We shall discuss these before moving on to investment styles and types of funds.

8.2   Investment Strategies

8.2.1   Passive Management

It is always a topic of some debate, particularly with investors, that relatively few active portfolio managers consistently outperform their benchmark indices.

To many investors, passive management offers an attractive proposition, with the advantage of generally lower dealing costs. The disadvantage is that the manager is unlikely to employ any risk management strategies, for example short-selling or increasing cash weighting.

There are two main types of passive management involving equities – buy and hold and index tracking.

While using a buy and hold technique will generally incur lower dealing costs, the possible disadvantage may be a lack of dynamism and the loss of opportunity of investing elsewhere, particularly with smaller portfolios.

Passive management is more commonly found in tracker funds, which aim to track the performance of a particular investment market or index. Clearly there is a need for a credible and liquid index to track – in the UK this is usually the Financial Times Stock Exchange (FTSE) All Share, but some index funds track the FTSE 100.

Tracker funds normally incur lower charges, and the returns should be close to the index with a low tracking error. These investments are suitable for clients requiring a vanilla product with a broad exposure to a market/index. They are usually fully invested to track the index, ie, there is normally no cash position.

Some large pension funds/insurance companies split funds into a passive core and actively managed satellites. We shall discuss this strategy in more depth in Section 8.2.5.

With a typical market capitalisation index, there are three ways in which an investment manager may employ a tracking technique.

1. Full Replication

This involves the manager tracking each constituent holding in an index, in the same weighting as it appears in the index, eg, if 2% of the index was comprised of a holding in Z plc, the fund manager would ensure 2% of his portfolio was held in Z plc shares.

This is more expensive to achieve, since frequent adjustment to the portfolio would be necessary to keep it in line with the index weightings. For that reason, this technique is really only suitable for the larger portfolios.

2. Stratified Sampling

In this technique, the investment manager selects representative stocks from each sector contained within the index. This is cheaper than full replication, but can lead to the fund manager subjectively picking those stocks he considers will outperform others within the sector, which can get away from the original objective of tracking an index.

3. Optimisation

Using sophisticated computer modelling, the investment manager will build a portfolio by finding holdings that broadly represent the characteristics of the index. This is cheaper than full replication.

Which of the above three strategies is likely to track its benchmark index the closest?

Full replication produces the lowest tracking error in terms of either overperforming or underperforming the benchmark index.

A passive fund incurs dealing costs when a company enters or leaves the index or when weightings change due to takeovers, mergers or rights issues. These costs are not reflected in the calculation of the index itself. Although an index fund is by its nature diversified, in terms of portfolio construction, the index will not lie at the efficient frontier, since the constitution of the portfolio usually depends on market capitalisation (ie, size) and does not take into account risk covariance. An example of this was the technology boom in the late 1990s, which resulted in all telecoms and technology sectors becoming a high proportion of the FTSE 100.

8.2.2 Active Management

Actively managed funds are managed by a fund manager with the objective of producing a return above the index for an appropriate level of risk. Returns can vary substantially depending on market conditions and the manager's skill. In choosing active funds, close attention should be paid to the investment house offering them, its track record, the fund manager's experience, investment philosophy and process. Active funds provide access to specific areas of the market (small cap) or specific styles (eg, income, special situations), which would not be achieved by the passive route.

There are two methods of constructing portfolios using an active management technique.

Top-Down Active Management

This method is usually employed for internationally diversified portfolios.

An assessment is made of the overall economic environment, rather than individual stocks, when constructing the portfolio.

This may take the form of considering the outlook for relative growth rates in different countries or regions. Will emerging markets represent a better option than Europe? Will China have better profit growth than the US? This could lead to a particular asset allocation.

In larger organisations, asset allocation is often decided on by an investment committee or asset allocation committee that will meet monthly and often use sophisticated and computerised quantitative models to assist them.

For pension funds, these decisions are often made with reference to a peer group median asset allocation like the Combined Actuarial Performance Service (CAPS) median or WM median. The use of tracking error parameters to these peer groups can be set up in order to help minimise the possibility of the fund underperforming.

Once the asset allocation has been decided, top-down active managers will consider how the funds should be allocated by sector within the chosen equity markets.

In practice, many fund managers will start by looking at their benchmark and try to mirror the sector weighting in that index or peer group average in order to avoid underperformance. The decision to go underweight or overweight in certain sectors will be taken with reference to their view on the economic outlook for the sector and other factors, eg, political, sociological, technological, environmental or legal.

Finally, once the sector split has been decided, the fund manager will select the stocks within those sectors, usually with reference to fundamental and technical analysis.

Bottom-Up Active Management

This form of investment management is more common in funds investing in a particular country or those following a particular theme.

With this technique, the investment manager concentrates their attention on individual stock selection (stock picking) in order to achieve positive returns. While other external events may be considered in the investment managers decision making process, their primary concern is the attractiveness or otherwise of the individual companies operating within the market or country in which they are investing.

They will hope to time their purchases and sales to take advantage of future events, for example, a new discovery of gold for a mining company or a possible takeover bid being launched.

As a result of this approach, there are often large tracking errors against the benchmark, which may lead to underperformance. Alternatively, fund managers can become too defensive, trying to track the benchmark index to avoid underperformance and getting away from their chosen investment style. This, in itself, can become self-defeating, since it can result in higher costs and a resulting underperformance against peers.

Some managers are wholly bottom-up, but most also take into account top-down factors (eg, macroeconomic and market background) in choosing stocks. For example, the 2008-09 credit crisis might influence attitudes to banks.

There are many things to look for when selecting funds adopting a bottom-up active management approach:

- track record of effective stock selection (generation of good ideas and research)
- investment process-stock evaluation (which methods they use, resources available)
- fund limitations (numbers of stocks to be held, limits on overweight or underweight positions in individual stocks and sectors, permitted level of cash holding).

8.2.3   Absolute Return Management

Most traditional investment funds aim to produce relative returns by which they mean to perform better than the index or sector average return. This means that if the index loses 10% in a particular year, they will aim to lose less than 10%.

An absolute return strategy should mean that, regardless of market performance, the fund will aim to produce a positive investment return each year.

In order to achieve this, the fund manager will usually employ a variety of strategies, including the following:

Long/short equity – many hedge fund managers use this strategy, which involves buying shares in companies which they believe have the best prospect for growth and go short (sell shares they do not own, hoping to buy them back at a later date) on companies they believe will perform less well.

Example

There may be two building materials companies, X & Y, which trade on similar profit multiples, despite company X benefiting positively from regulatory change in the construction market requiring greater use of insulation products. In a weakening construction market, this is likely to have important implications for future profitability. The fund manager could go long on company X and go short on company Y.

Use of derivatives – many absolute return managers will make use of derivatives to hedge against potential risk and create synthetic long or short positions. Using the example given above, they could use contracts for differences (CFDs) in order to make money on the shares in company Y performing less well than company X (pairs trading). The advantage of this strategy is the ability to trade at margin, increasing potential return for a given investment.

The investment strategies used by long/short funds are substantially different from long only funds, and returns are likely to vary considerably. In particular, a fund with both long and short positions is unlikely to achieve the same capital growth as a long only fund in a rising stock market and, conversely, should not experience the same level of decline in a falling stock market. However, neither of these outcomes is guaranteed, and the value of the investment can go down as well as up!

8.2.4   Liability Driven Investment (LDI)

A liability driven investment strategy (LDI) is where, rather than working to a benchmark set by reference to an external index, the target of the fund is the liability of the fund, as calculated by actuaries.

In pension funds, clearly the promises made to pensioners in terms of benefits will represent the liabilities of the fund. Two of the biggest risks faced by pension funds are the effects of interest rate changes and inflation. In the past, these risks have been partially hedged by the extensive use of bonds. In LDI, the focus has been on hedging these risks by the use of swaps and other derivatives. This provides greater flexibility and capital efficiency than the use of bonds.

8.2.5   Core and Satellite Strategy

This is an investment strategy incorporating traditional fixed income and equity based securities held in passively managed funds known as the core portion of the portfolio, with a percentage of individually selected securities known as the satellite portion.

Core Portfolio

The core is made up of passively managed securities (index funds, exchange-traded funds [ETFs], passive mutual funds) and uses a traditional benchmark, eg, the FTSE 100 or the Standard & Poor's (S&P) 500 index to compare performance.

The core funds may have a particular style investment bias (eg, more small cap stocks over mid/large cap companies, more value positions over growth positions, higher or lower concentration in developed international markets).

Because of the holding's passive nature and the belief that this structure allows for longer-term planning and growth, core holdings are generally not replaced by another type in this class or style, and are rarely sold unless the client either needs cash for personal use, the allocation is out of bounds within the constraints of the portfolio's plan, or the client's mix of fixed income/equities ratio is modified, based on premeditated or unforeseen client events.

Satellite Portfolio

The satellite part of the portfolio will comprise holdings that the adviser expects will outperform the market. Holdings may include actively managed stocks, mutual funds, and separate account managers with a particular sector, region of positions, or passively managed assets with a certain style that is counter to, or even enhances, the style bias of the core.

 Identify as many actively managed investment styles that you can think of.

8.3 Investment Styles

Active management, top-down or bottom-up, can employ a variety of investment styles in order to achieve its aims.

8.3.1 Growth Investing

There are different forms of growth investing. At its most aggressive, growth investing may focus on companies which are on a rising trend, with their price gathering greater momentum as more and more investors jump onto the bandwagon. This is also known as momentum investing.

Day trading is an example of momentum investing. Day traders will look for two things in a share: liquidity and volatility. Liquidity will ensure that the stock can be bought and sold at a good price (ie, with a small spread) and a higher volatility will mean that more profit can be made within the day.

Relative strength is a very important measure for momentum investors.

The change in a share's price in percentage terms relative to that of other shares in the index (eg, FTSE 100 is calculated and ranked on a scale of 1–100 against all other shares in that index. For example, a share with a relative strength of 80 has seen a greater increase in its share price over the past year than the price increases seen on 80% of the other shares within that index.

While momentum investors take great interest in relative strength, clearly this is a historic measure and, as we all know, past performance is not necessarily a guide to future performance.

A less aggressive growth investment style is buying **growth at a reasonable price (GARP)**. The focus will be on finding shares in companies which will produce above-average earnings growth in the future, but with share prices that do not currently reflect this.

Typical growth stocks will be those that have a product with a real competitive advantage and can charge a premium for their product and/or have an unusually low cost base. Innovative products will clearly fall into this category and the next successful technology company, or a pharmaceutical company inventing the next wonder drug, would be a prime target for the growth investor.

Since earnings growth is the prime driver to a growth investor, close scrutiny of the earnings potential of a company will be the key to success. A company with a high **price/earnings ratio (PER)**, will be expected to deliver on the earnings growth in the future, and a profit warning is likely to have a disastrous effect on the share price.

Example

Company A trades on a PE ratio of 60 and is priced at £10 per share.

The average P/E for the sector is 15.

The implication of this is that on current earnings, it will take 60 years for company A to earn the price at which investors are prepared to pay for the shares, compared to, on average, 15 years for other companies in the sector. Clearly, investors in company A are expecting future earnings to grow ahead of the rest of the sector; otherwise it would appear that they are paying too much for the shares, based on current earnings.

If company A were to issue a profits warning stating that earnings will be the same as the previous year, investors could be concerned that the expected growth will not materialise in the future, and rate them less highly. This may cause investors to switch into other companies in that sector offering better growth potential.

At a share price of £2.50 per share, the PER of Company A would be in line with the average for the sector. This would be quite a fall for any investor to bear.

During the dotcom boom, P/E's of certain companies were pushed up to 100 and more – many were very new companies with little in the way of historic earnings, but a highly perceived growth potential. As we saw in the fallout that followed, prices can go down as well as up and the key to success has been to sort out the wheat from the chaff. Wouldn't it have been good to buy Microsoft or Apple shares when they first came to market?

8.3.2 Value Investing

A generally more cautious approach to investing is value investing. Here, the investment manager will be looking for established companies who appear to have been ignored in the market, and are set for recovery.

Unlike the growth investor, the value investor will not concentrate on earnings growth but will look for the potential to recover from temporarily depressed conditions in the market. The value investor will look at the fundamental or intrinsic value of the company. As they will generally look for companies with stable earnings and usually a high dividend yield, low PE ratio, and low price/book ratio, there will be greater security against the share price falling even further.

8.3.3 Thematic Investing

This type of investing was introduced in the UK in the mid-1980s. It will typically focus on specific sectors linked by a common investment opportunity, no matter where in the world the sectors are located.

For example, the price of energy is a concern to most of the world at the present time. This may lead to an investor concentrating on either the theme of oil, or more likely, alternative renewable energy suppliers, which may be best placed to offer better potential for future growth. A number of successful funds in recent years focused on the theme of consumer non-durable companies (eg, food , drink, washing and cleaning) as largely recession-proof.

The key to the thinking behind thematic investing is that investment is a worldwide phenomenon these days, with more and more companies operating globally. To restrict your investment potential by looking at companies domiciled in one particular country is perceived as far too limiting.

Some investment managers will adopt more than one investment theme at any one time, thereby achieving an element of diversification. Others recognise that some opportunities will be cross-sectorial and will not limit themselves to one sector. The key to successful thematic investing is to identify global opportunities for above average performance.

Socially responsible investment (SRI) is an example of thematic investing. More and more people are taking an interest in ethical issues, covering subjects as diverse as environmental improvement, climate change, genetically modified foods, gambling and the destruction of rain forests. SRI has become a very popular investment theme as awareness of these issues increases.

SRI gives an emphasis to 'progressive', smaller growth companies and screens out companies with possible contingent liabilities (eg, tobacco). But it can produce a restrictive choice of investments; yields tend to be below average; it is not suitable for income seekers; and results in a less diversified portfolio.

The difficulties of defining SRI are both theoretical and practical. What ethical stance should be adopted? Should it be based on religious or other moral principles? If religious, there will be differences between, say, Christian and Muslim. Both would be against alcohol, tobacco and gambling, but Muslims are generally also opposed to insurance, banking, pork production and borrowing. Should the criteria encompass both positive and negative criteria?

 Describe what is meant by 'fashion led' investing.

8.3.4 Fashion-Led Investing

This is similar to a growth momentum style of investing in that it is assumed that a trend or fashion will continue to outperform the market. However, the problem with fashion is that, one day, the current fashion will go out of style. Today's latest designer wear will no doubt appear in a charity shop near you soon. Rarely do the exceptional performing companies of one year, repeat that performance consistently in the following year. We have seen many boom and bust cycles in the past – technology, media and telecom (TMT) stocks were a classic example at the end of the last millennium. The key to success will be to stay ahead of fashion, ie, get in early and get out before the rest of the herd. If only investing were that simple!

8.3.5 Contrarian Investing

Ever met someone who did the opposite to what everyone else was doing?

Depending on the results, that person can be classified as a fool or an absolute genius!

Contrarian investing is similar to value investing, in that it is all about taking a position against the general market consensus. The contrarian investor may take a view that the market has overreacted to a particular situation and believes that a company offers better prospects in the future as a result.

It is of some debate whether contrarian investing is actually a style – more of an approach taken by a value/recovery manager who fishes for undervalued or unloved stocks.

The difficulty is that consistent success will depend upon last year's losers always being this year's winners. As a result, this approach is usually too inflexible and mechanised to achieve long-term success.

8.4 Other Ways of Investing

Some investment managers will use a combination of the above styles (known as multi-style) or not adopt a particular style at all, believing that being limited to a rigid style will inhibit future performance of the fund. Hence fund managers may describe their investment style in various other ways (such as 'pragmatic' or 'research/stockpickers') or clearly state their intention not to adopt any particular style.

8.4.1 Lifestyle Investing

One of the uses of lifestyle investing is within pension funds.

As the investor approaches retirement, assets are moved in this way for two reasons. One is to prevent people who are about to retire from losing large amounts of their pension savings in a stock market crash. The other is to try to match the value of the assets to annuity rates. Annuity rates are usually calculated using the yields on gilts, so if the price of gilts falls in the pension, this will be compensated for by higher rates on an annuity – in theory offering more protection against value losses.

As the investor grows older the proportion in bonds and cash increases relative to equity. A common rule of thumb is to set the weighting in bonds and cash equal to age; eg, a 60 year old might have 10% in cash, 50% in bonds, and 40% in equities. This is intended to reduce risk and increase yield. However this strategy night be questionable with record low bond and cash yields.

8.5 Investment Funds

As you are aware, there are thousands of different funds competing for business, and these adopt a number of different approaches/styles to attract new investors. A small selection of funds follows as examples of the variety available.

8.5.1 Enhanced Index Funds

Enhanced index strategies offer a good alternative to traditional passive index management, adding the potential to outperform the index while only marginally varying the characteristics of the index. Enhanced index funds offer many of the benefits of traditional passive index management, such as low fees and diversification. However, the difference is that these funds usually combine an index fund with a quant methodology to provide a bit of a kick.

Quants are quantitative models performed by computers, which select stocks based on several different criteria (quantitative analysis looks at actual data and statistics as opposed to qualitative analysis which looks at intangible factors such as the quality of management). Proponents of quantitative funds argue that their management style takes human emotions out of the investment decision-making process, and leads to more objective stock selection.

8.5.2 130/30 Investing

This strategy takes advantage of the third directive in the UCITS III and, in particular, the ability to short a percentage of the portfolio in order to improve performance.

The reason for the name is that the fund manager will rank shares in order of their expected future return, and invest 100% of the funds in securities which the fund manager thinks will perform better in the future. He will then short-sell those securities at the bottom of his ranking, to raise up to 30% of the value of the fund. The money raised by the short-selling will then be invested in the top ranking securities, allowing for further diversification.

There are clearly more risks involved in this type of fund. It requires experience to manage short positions. Price rises in short positions not only lose money, but the relative size of the position also magnifies. Leverage also means that returns can also be more volatile. So, if the manager gets both the short and the long selections wrong, this will have far greater impact than a traditional long-only fund that picks the wrong stocks.

8.5.3 Focus Funds

Focus funds are concentrated funds. Some have a fixed number of stocks which must be held in equal proportions, while others have holdings which can be weighted.

For example, instead of picking the usual 80 to 100 or so securities, in a focus fund the manager could be forced to select the best 20 to 35 stocks which will offer the best prospects for growth in the next 12 months. While mainstream funds tend to pick securities which broadly mirror the asset allocation and securities which make up an index, the focus fund manager is given the freedom to select a small number of stocks from the sector, which they feel offers the most potential. The idea is that with a mainstream fund that follows the broad asset allocation of the index, it is often difficult to outperform that index. The focus fund aims to outperform the index by really testing the stock picking ability of the fund manager.

If a stock is not performing, since there are so few other stocks in the portfolio, the fund manager will have to make a hard decision about whether to keep faith in that stock or not. As mentioned above, some funds set a rebalancing limit which forces them to sell if the stock becomes too large or small a percentage of the overall fund. This instils a strict selling policy and ensures the fund is kept fresh. The fund manager will generally be looking for value. The downside of these funds is that with fewer stocks comes increased risk (less diversification). However, you will be getting very active management and a real focus on outperforming the market.

8.5.4 Equity Income

Equity Income funds focus on high-yielding stocks. These tend to be cheap by dividend yield and often other measures, and so fall into the 'value' style of investing. Potential investment opportunities are often found in the mid cap and smaller company areas of the market, which have performed well over the past ten years. Active managers have also benefited from reduced analytical coverage by major brokers in this area of the market.

Under Investment Association (IA) classification, qualifying funds must yield 10% or more above the index. Fund managers usually seek to offer both an above index yield together with a growing income stream, although the weight given to the two can vary. Some investors will rely on these funds for income and hold income units, while others will use them for growth, rolling up the income via accumulation units.

Many of the star fund managers are to be found working in this sphere of investment, and the returns over recent years have been very impressive indeed.

8.5.5   Multi-Manager Funds

This is an extension of the traditional active manager approach. In the UK, it has a small, but growing, market share, although it has been more established in a number of other markets, for example North America and South Africa, for some time.

Multi-manager funds are designed to make an investor's life easier by packaging together teams of specialist investment managers into a single fund. The main multi-manager fund categories are fund of funds and manager of managers.

There are quite obvious differences between the two categories, most notably that the first invests in funds, whereas the second invests in stocks and shares through appointed investment managers.

The primary advantage of fund of funds over manager of managers is that underlying assets and fund records offer greater visibility and speed of management. They have also generally outperformed manager of manager funds in the past. However, this approach can add an extra layer of charges.

An advantage of this approach to independent financial advisors (IFAs) is that some may feel that they do not have the resources to select funds or decide asset allocation. Equally, they may segment their client base and may feel that different levels of investment require a different approach in order to improve their own profitability.

Manager of manager funds may fit smaller investors who cannot afford the full service, and therefore effectively outsource the investment management.

9.   Choosing a Suitable Investment Approach

9.1   Introduction

In Chapter 7 we shall discuss the mechanisms that an investment manager has available in order to measure (and hopefully improve upon) the performance of a portfolio. These include how to assess the likely returns of the portfolio relative to the rest of the market, while also accounting for the level of risk being taken.

In this section, having considered the various methodologies used within investment management, we now start to look at the actual construction process of a suitable portfolio for an individual investor. So where do we begin?

'What do you want to achieve or avoid? The answers to this question are objectives. How will you go about achieving your desired results? The answer to this you can call strategy.' – William E. Rothschild

9.2   Setting the Strategy

One place to start is to determine exactly what the investor wants to achieve and by when. Of course, there may be a number of objectives requiring different sorts of returns at different times, all of which need to be considered, and a suitable approach should be adopted for each.

Given the client's desired returns, are they realistically achievable against his attitude to risk, the market or sector he wishes to invest in and the strategy he wishes to adopt?

How will the client's current tax status affect the returns received from the portfolio? Are the likely costs and charges associated with the considered investments an acceptable price to pay relative to likely returns?

By the time the client is ready to invest funds, he should generally have agreed the outline investment strategy. The agenda would often follow something along the lines of the following:

- agreed asset allocation
- approach to thematic investment such as SRI
- fund selection strategy and criteria
- choice of tax wrapper if investment is not being made directly into assets.

 How would you agree a suitable asset allocation strategy with a client?

9.3   Asset Allocation

Any asset allocation structure should set out the asset classes in which the client should invest, given their investment objectives and attitude to risk. The following table provides a simple range of asset allocation models using three key asset classes. Of course, classes could be split even further, eg, between UK and international assets, and between different industrial and commercial sectors. In addition, other asset allocation models will include other classes such as cash and commodities.

A client who primarily requires income will often skew the asset allocation decision towards the more cautious end of the scale.

Asset allocation							
	More cautious			More adventurous			
	1	2	3	4	5	6	7
% Equities	20	30	40	45	55	70	90
% Alternative investments including property	10	10	15	15	15	10	5
% Fixed interest	70	60	45	40	30	20	5

9.4   Ethical Issues

Ethical issues are important to many investors and in some cases could be the overriding issue for the client.

There are two key aspects of ethical or SRI, and the criteria used in selecting the appropriate investment:

- **The underlying themes** – is the client concerned about environmental, animal rights, other issues?
- **The approach adopted by fund managers** – for instance, some funds will have a policy of avoiding certain activities, while others take an interventionist approach. There are other strategies adopted or variations on a theme.

9.5   Fund Selection

Even if an investment manager agrees with the client on a suitable asset allocation strategy taking into account any ethical issues, will the actual investment funds from the wide range available be chosen competently? Much will depend on the resources and expertise of the investment managers and those working for their organisations.

 What criteria, as an investment manager specialising in fund selection, would you use in order to choose suitable funds for your client?

Such an organisation would commonly pick funds on the basis of a number of criteria:

- Strength of investment process and length of time it has been in place.
- Continuity of investment managers.
- An investment style that has been proven over a period of time.
- Clear investment objectives.
- Charges and expenses.
- Consistently strong past performance record.

We have already considered, in the previous section, the different investment strategies and fund styles that can be adopted. Fundamentally however, the aim of asset allocation and fund selection is to design a portfolio that matches the client's risk profile and investment objectives. This is always likely to be an imprecise art!

The basis for the selection of both asset classes and funds is largely down to past performance, which is a relatively accurate guide to future returns in some conditions, but in others, can be hugely disappointing.

9.6   Wrapper Selection

If the client is not going to invest directly into different asset classes, it is important that the investment vehicles or tax wrappers being used are appropriate for their own tax situation.

The main tax wrappers include:

- collectives
- ISAs
- UK life assurance policies
- offshore life assurance policies
- registered pension schemes.

A summary of the tax position of each is shown below for easy reference:

Tax wrappers			
Wrapper	**Initial contribution**	**Growth**	**Encashment**
ISA	No relief	Tax-free	Tax-free
Collectives	No relief	Income fully taxable, CGT free	Gains chargeable to capital gains tax
UK life assurance policies	No relief	Income basic-rate equivalent, CGT taxable	Higher-rate income tax on gains or tax free on qualifying policies
Offshore life assurance policies	No relief	Tax-free	Full income tax on gains
Registered pension schemes	Full relief (restricted by annual allowance charge, and for high income individuals)	Tax-free	25% of fund tax-free Balance taxable as income

9.7   Conclusion

With clear investment objectives and adequate understanding of the client's own circumstances and risk profile, it is perfectly possible to select suitable assets and/or packaged funds within an investment portfolio. With many computer software systems available in the modern investment world, the process has become more straightforward and certainly less time consuming. It is, though, important to always remember the fundamentals of building a solid investment portfolio for a client.

In the next section, we shall discuss further the implementation of an investment strategy, considering the advantages and disadvantages of the different routes which can be taken.

10. Implementing the Investment Strategy

10.1 Introduction

In this final section we discuss some final decisions that need to be made in building a private client's portfolio. We revisit the need for liquidity, consider what to do with any existing investments a client holds, analyse the advantages and disadvantages of making direct investments into assets against purchasing packaged products, before finally discussing the merits and pitfalls of UK and overseas investment.

10.2 Advisory or Discretionary Service

When it comes to selection of other asset classes, the client needs to decide the type of service required. In Section 7 of this chapter, we introduced advisory and discretionary management services.

With an advisory service, the portfolio manager still needs to fully understand the client's circumstances, objectives and attitude to risk before making recommendations, although the client will have the final say on accepting or rejecting any recommendations made. In recent years, the number of portfolio managers offering an advisory service to private clients has dropped considerably as the regulatory burden involved with making recommendations has increased.

A discretionary service gives the manager the ability to act quickly to sell or purchase individual stocks that may be common to a number of portfolios, if it would just not be practical to consult with the client on each and every transaction. It is possible to limit the discretionary service so that, for example, certain stocks are not sold without prior consultation with the client.

10.3 Liquidity

In Section 4 of this chapter, we mentioned the need for liquidity and the reasons why funds should be held on deposit for short-term access. It is worth reiterating that clients must feel comfortable with the amounts they hold on deposit so as to avoid the need for early encashment of other investments which could, due to market volatility, cause severe losses in value or even incur penalties for early withdrawal.

 You have been asked to meet a client to provide investment advice following a recent inheritance she has received. She has a number of existing investments in place. Would you advise the client to retain or liquidate these investments?

10.4 Existing Investments

If your answer to the above question was to liquidate the existing investments, beware!

A switch of investments takes place when a new investment is effected as a result of a full or partial encashment of an existing investment.

Churning takes place when investments are switched with the primary intention of generating commission/fees rather than acting in the client's best interests. This would break the FCA's Conduct of Business Rules.

Switches therefore can be justified if:

- there has been a clear alteration in the client's investment objectives or circumstances, requiring investments to be moved in accordance with a different risk strategy or to produce different returns
- market conditions adversely affect the current investment or are balanced in favour to an alternative
- the client gives clear instructions to go ahead with a switch
- there has been consistent underperformance of an investment over a medium to longer-term period
- the value of an investment is returned as part of a takeover or restructuring of capital.

There could also be tax penalties imposed as a result of an investment being disposed of, such as CGT. Advisers and portfolio managers should try to mitigate these penalties with careful planning, eg, passing assets over to a spouse prior to disposal to use up their allowances, or offsetting gains against other losses.

10.5 Direct Investments vs Collective Investments

Once the investment adviser has established the client's objectives and agreed an appropriate asset allocation in accordance with their risk profile, the format of the portfolio should be discussed. A key consideration will be whether to invest directly into different asset classes or indirectly via collective investment products. We will now have a look at the advantages and disadvantages of each route.

10.5.1 Direct Investment

Investment is usually only suitable if portfolios are large enough in order to be able to accommodate charges and provide sufficient diversification among investments.

Advantages

- Many clients are interested in having direct holdings in particular companies because they enjoy following the fortunes of those companies.
- Direct investment is likely to interest investors prepared to accept risk to a certain degree.
- Low costs on switching investment managers due to the transferability of stocks without the need to encash them.
- The portfolio can be tailored to accommodate the investor's requirements.
- It is easier to exclude holdings in specific stocks.
- Greater transparency of costs.
- Exemptions and reliefs can be used to offset capital gains made that are subject to CGT.
- Larger portfolios can enjoy an economy of scale and lower expense ratios than can be achieved via collective investments.

Disadvantages

- Potentially higher volatility of performance because fewer investments are likely to be held compared to a collective investment scheme (CIS).
- Costs are higher for smaller portfolios.
- Usually need greater involvement by an investment manager.
- Results may be more volatile as they depend on individual managers, and the performance of one or two stocks can provide a disproportionate effect on returns.

- It may be necessary to switch investments more within a large portfolio, thus potentially incurring gains subject to CGT (after exemptions and allowances).
- Potentially more administrative costs than with collective investments.
- Value added tax (VAT) will be charged on management fees, which are not tax relieved in any way.

10.5.2 Collective Investments

Collective investment holds several attractions, not least the ability to pool relatively small resources with others in order to manage a large portfolio of diversified investments. Outlined below are some further advantages and disadvantages of CISs.

Advantages of unit trust/OEIC investment management services

- A wide variety of funds available, allowing most needs to be catered for.
- A spread of risk can be achieved, even for small investors.
- Specialised unit trusts and OEICs can give exposure to specific markets or sectors, which might otherwise be inaccessible.
- No CGT on gains realised within a unit trust/OEIC.
- VAT not payable on the annual charges levied within the funds.

Disadvantages of unit trust/OEIC investment management services

- Further management fees are payable on top of the initial and annual management charges levied by fund management groups. Some low charging unit trusts and OEICs, however, exist.
- Changes to the portfolio could be expensive due to bid offer spreads that most funds operate.
- Little direct involvement from investors.
- Higher costs could be incurred upon changing investment managers.

ETFs generally have the lowest charges, with many specialist funds, particularly sectoral and single country, and provide a hybrid, with some advantages of both direct and collective investments. Investment trusts generally charge lower initial fees compared to unit trusts or OEICs. Annual management charges for older investment trusts are often lower than unit trusts/OEICs.

 Assuming that investment is made into the same type of fund, how does the risk and potential reward of an investment trust compare with unit trusts and OEICs?

The risk and reward of investment trusts is often considered greater, mainly due to the fact that price movements follow supply and demand and may operate at a discount or premium to net asset value (NAV). In addition, investment trusts have unlimited borrowing capability and as a consequence may 'gear up' to extend returns. However losses will be equally exaggerated.

The discount to NAV that could apply to investment trusts could also provide higher levels of income to investors than would otherwise be received by unit trusts/OEIC investment.

10.5.3 Pound Cost Averaging

The basic idea behind pound cost averaging is to invest the same amount on a regular basis as opposed to investing a lump sum.

This way, more units are purchased when the price is lower and less units are bought when the units are more expensive. As a result, the average price paid for each unit held is less than the average of the price of the units over the period of investment.

An example may help explain how this principle works in practice:

£100 per month invested over 12 months:

Month	Price of units	Units purchased
January	1.00	100.0
February	1.10	90.9
March	1.20	83.3
April	1.25	80.0
May	1.50	66.7
June	1.55	64.5
July	1.60	62.5
August	1.40	71.4
September	1.25	80.0
October	1.30	76.9
November	1.35	74.1
December	1.65	60.6

Number of units bought	910.9
Investment amount	£1,200
Average price paid for units	1.317
Average price of units	1.346

Calculation for average price paid – £1200 ÷ 910.9

Calculation of average price per unit – (1.00+1.10+1.20+1.25+1.50...)/12

10.6 UK versus Overseas Investment

When building the client's investment portfolio, serious consideration should be made as to whether funds are allocated towards UK or overseas securities, or a combination of both. Many asset allocation models will accommodate investment into foreign stocks and shares as part of the recommended allocations splits, depending upon the client's risk profile and circumstances.

Investing overseas holds the obvious advantage of further diversification into international markets and specialist sectors that would not otherwise be available from UK securities. However, the downside of such investment is the additional foreign currency risk presented. Any gains made could be wiped out by a worsening exchange rate between the UK and the country in question. In addition, financial and trading information on foreign companies may be difficult to understand or even obtain!

Investing solely in UK securities removes the immediate exchange rate risk, but most of the largest UK companies have substantial operations overseas, so there could still be a foreign currency exposure through imports/exports and profits generated from overseas activities.

Chapter Seven

Portfolio Performance and Review

An exam specification breakdown is provided at the back of this workbook

1.   Introduction

In this chapter we will be building on your knowledge, looking in greater detail at risk and return, the role of the investment manager, investment styles, performance measures and portfolio construction.

Some of the terminology and concepts will already be familiar to you in your present day-to-day work. We will build upon this knowledge and introduce different concepts with which you may be less familiar. We hope that this will give you confidence for your examination.

You must continue reading and extending your understanding of the topics covered through additional study. This workbook does not represent everything you may be expected to know for the examination.

You will see icons or symbols alongside the text. These indicate activities or questions that have been designed to check your understanding and help you validate your understanding.

Here is a guide to what each of the symbols mean:

 Question

This identifies a question that will enable you to check your knowledge and understanding.

 Analyse

This gives you an opportunity to consider a question posed and compare your answers to the feedback given.

1.1   Objectives

1. Understand the principles of time weighted and money weighted rates of return.
2. Understand the principles of risk including volatility, standard deviation, alpha and portfolio risk.
3. Know the main stock market indices and how they operate.
4. Understand the key features of indices published by FTSE and Wealth Management Association (WMA).
5. Apply appropriate indices and benchmarks to the comparative analysis of investment performance.
6. Evaluate and periodically review portfolio composition in order to continually maintain adherence to client objectives.

2. Risk and Return

Much research has been done into this subject over the years and important theories have been developed in an attempt to improve the construction of portfolios and manage risk more effectively. We will consider these in turn, after we have looked at a key risk evaluation measure.

2.1 Modern Portfolio Theory (MPT)

MPT was developed by Harry Markowitz in 1952.

The theory states that it is not enough to look at the expected risk and return of one particular stock. By investing in more than one stock, an investor can reap the benefits of diversification, primarily reducing risk (not putting all your eggs in one basket).

For most investors, the risk they take when they buy a security is that the return will be lower than expected. In other words, it is the deviation from the average return. Each stock has its own standard deviation from the mean, which MPT calls 'risk'.

The risk in a portfolio of diverse individual stocks will be less than the risk inherent in holding any single one of the individual stocks (provided the risks of the various stocks are not directly related). Let's consider a portfolio that holds two risky stocks: one that pays off when it rains and another that pays off when it doesn't rain. A portfolio that contains both assets will always pay off, regardless of whether it rains or shines. Adding one risky asset to another can, therefore, reduce the overall risk of an all-weather portfolio.

In other words, Markowitz showed that investment is not just about picking stocks, but about choosing the right combination of stocks among which to distribute one's nest eggs – hence the term intelligent diversification.

2.1.1 Diversification

The risk of holding two holdings, A & B, in isolation is given by their respective standard deviation of returns.

However, by combining the two stocks, it is possible to lower the weighted average sum of standard deviations in these two securities.

We use two concepts to quantify the diversification potential of combining securities when constructing a portfolio: correlation and covariance.

2.1.2 Correlation

In statistics and probability theory, correlation indicates the strength and direction of a linear relationship between two variables. If two variables tend to vary together (that is, when one of them is above its expected value, then the other variable tends to be above its expected value too), then the covariance between the two variables will be positive. On the other hand, if one of them is above its expected value and the other variable tends to be below its expected value, then the covariance between the two variables will be negative

In portfolio construction, diversification is achieved by combining securities that have returns which ideally move in the opposite direction to one another, or if in the same direction, at least not to the same extent.

Perfectly positive correlation, ie, when the returns of two securities move in exactly the same direction, to the same extent, is represented as +1. Perfectly negative correlation is represented as –1.

While securities A & B may individually have very high risk as measured by their standard deviations, the most important factor when deciding whether to include them in a diversified portfolio would be the correlation of the returns. If one moved in the opposite way to the other, then the risk would be reduced by including them both. It can be seen from this that the lower the correlation of the returns of A & B, the more that risk is reduced.

When there is no predictable common movement between the returns of two securities there is said to be zero or imperfect correlation. There may still be benefits of diversification since their returns will not react in the same way; in fact the only scenario when diversification will not reduce risk is when there is a perfectly positive correlation (+1).

As you may be aware, you are able to obtain correlation charts from Lipper. Using a series of charts, it is possible to create a correlation matrix to establish the relationship between the funds which comprise the portfolio.

2.1.3 Covariance

Covariance is a measure of the combined variability of two investments. It depends on their individual risks (standard deviations) and the degree of correlation between them (correlation coefficient).

An example of this would be if share A produces high returns whenever share B produces high returns and vice versa. These outcomes would mean that they have high positive correlation. Clearly in a diversified portfolio, the inclusion of Company A shares and Company B shares would not reduce risk as much as choosing two stocks with prices that react differently to each other, ie, have low positive or negative correlation.

Covariance is calculated by multiplying the correlation of two securities by the standard deviation of A and then by the standard deviation of B.

A positive covariance between the returns of A & B would mean that they have moved in the same direction, whereas a negative covariance would mean that they have moved in the opposite direction.

The lower the correlation and standard deviations of the two securities, the lower the covariance. Low covariance is a good thing since it means the risk is lower.

If one of the securities had a higher standard deviation than the rest, when combined with another security, because of correlation between them, risk will be reduced.

The key message here is that in order to reduce risk, portfolios should ideally contain shares as negatively correlated to each other as possible and with low standard deviations in order to reduce the covariance (and risk).

2.1.4 The Efficient Frontier

Now that we have looked at how diversification reduces risk, we need to find out how we can identify the best level of diversification.

For every level of return, there is one portfolio that offers the lowest possible risk, and for every level of risk, there is a portfolio that offers the highest return. These combinations can be plotted on a graph, and the resulting line is the efficient frontier.

Firstly, let's look at the efficient frontier for just two securities – Company A, a high risk/high return technology security and Company B, a low risk/low return consumer products security.

The line plots the best possible combinations of the two stocks to produce the highest returns for the lowest risk.

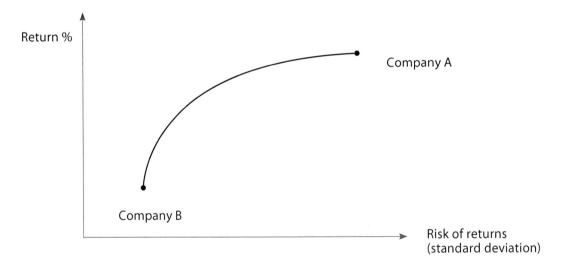

Any portfolio combining these two stocks that lies on the curve is efficient: it gives the maximum expected return for a given level of risk. A rational investor will only ever hold a portfolio that lies somewhere on the efficient frontier. The maximum level of risk that the investor will take on determines the position of the portfolio on the line.

If we now look at a portfolio of securities, we can plot all combinations of them held in different proportions on a chart that plots risk and expected returns to arrive at the efficient frontier for the portfolio.

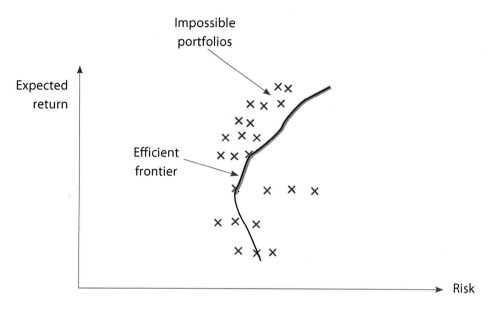

The efficient frontier will plot the combination of securities that will offer the maximum expected return for any given level of risk. Clearly, investors will have individual risk and return criteria and the point on the efficient frontier that they will choose will depend upon their appetite to risk, which is represented by an indifference curve.

The portfolio sitting on the efficient frontier will provide the best return for a given level of risk. It therefore follows that no portfolio will be above the efficient frontier, hence the term 'impossible portfolios'. However, this efficient frontier is based upon the risk and return of a given universe of stocks (for example, the constituents of S&P 500), and by investing in other markets (global diversification) or by using other asset classes (and using hedge fund techniques), it is possible to push out the efficient frontier. This is perhaps proof that, in investment terms at least, nothing is impossible!

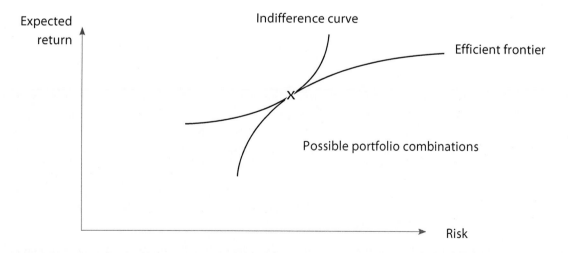

The portfolio to be selected for this client would be at X, where the two arcs are tangential.

2.2 Efficient Markets Hypothesis (EMH)

The Efficient Markets Hypothesis (EMH) states that in price efficient markets, securities respond immediately and rationally to publicly available price sensitive information and move independently of past trends.

There are certain assumptions made, for example that investors are rational and risk averse and that they have the ability to source and process accurately all publicly available information.

There are three common forms of market efficiency stated in EMH as follows.

2.2.1 Weak-Form Efficiency

In a weak-form price efficient market, no excess returns can be earned by using investment strategies based on historical share prices.

Weak-form efficiency implies that technical analysis techniques will not be able to consistently produce excess returns, though some forms of fundamental analysis may still provide excess returns.

In a weak-form efficient market, current share prices are the best, unbiased estimate of the value of the security. Because weak-form efficiency is theoretical in nature, its advocates assert that fundamental analysis can be used to identify stocks that are undervalued and overvalued. Therefore, keen investors looking for profitable companies can earn profits by researching financial statements.

2.2.2 Semi-Strong-Form Efficiency

Within a semi-strong-form price efficient market, share prices adjust within an arbitrarily small but finite amount of time and in an unbiased fashion to publicly available new information, so that no excess returns can be earned by trading on that information.

Semi-strong-form efficiency implies that fundamental analysis techniques will not be able to reliably produce excess returns.

To test for semi-strong-form efficiency, the adjustments to previously unknown news must be of a reasonable size and must be instantaneous. To test for this, consistent upward or downward adjustments after the initial change must be looked for. If there are any such adjustments it would suggest that investors had interpreted the information in a biased fashion and hence in an inefficient manner.

2.2.3 Strong-Form Efficiency

In a strong-form price efficient market, share prices reflect all information, public and private, and no one can earn excess returns.

If there are legal barriers to private information becoming public, as with insider dealing rules, strong-form efficiency is impossible, except in the case where the rules are universally broken.

To test for strong-form efficiency, a market needs to exist where investors cannot consistently earn excess returns over a long period of time. Even if some fund managers are consistently observed to beat the market, no refutation even of strong-form efficiency follows. With tens of thousands of fund managers worldwide, even a normal distribution of returns (as efficiency predicts) should be expected to produce a few dozen 'star' performers.

The key point here is that most well developed stock markets in the West are relatively price efficient and, on the basis that few fund managers consistently outperform the market, this would indicate at least some degree of strong-form market efficiency. However, less developed markets do not show strong-form price efficiency and therefore can provide opportunities for active fund managers to outperform.

2.3   Capital Asset Pricing Model (CAPM)

The CAPM says that the expected return of a security or a portfolio equals the rate on a risk-free security plus a risk premium. If this expected return does not meet or beat the required return, then you should not proceed with the investment.

The CAPM was introduced in the 1960s and developed MPT by stating that the risk for individual stock returns has two components:

Systematic Risk – these are market risks that cannot be diversified away, for example, recessions and wars.

Unsystematic Risk – also known as company specific risk, this risk is specific to individual stocks and can be diversified away as you increase the number of stocks in your portfolio. It represents the component of a stock's return that is not linked to general market moves.

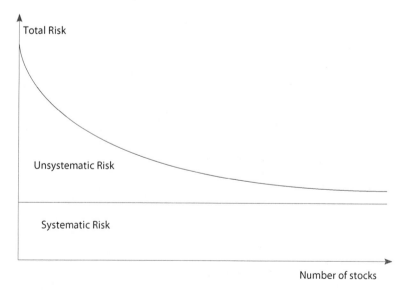

The general idea behind the CAPM is that investors need to be compensated in two ways: for the time value of money and for the risk that cannot be diversified away.

Beta is used to measure the non-diversifiable ('systematic') risk of a security relative to the overall market risk in this model. In fact, modern portfolio theory states that 95% of the unsystematic risk can be eliminated with 20 securities. The risk that would remain is the systematic risk, otherwise known as market risk.

2.3.1 Beta

Beta is the measure of the average historic volatility of a security's return to the broader market risk and is stated as a proportion of the market risk.

So the beta of security A is = systematic risk of A / market risk

The market itself is given an underlying beta of 1 and securities are ranked according to how much they deviate from the market. A security which is more volatile than the market has a beta above 1. If it moves less than the market it will have a beta of less than 1.

So if a security has a beta of 2, an increase in the market of 4% would result in an 8% increase in its value. However, a decrease of 4% would have the effect of an 8% decline in that security's value.

Betas can also be negative, so a security with a beta of –2 will move in the opposite direction to the market by a factor of 2; an increase in the market of 2% would result in a fall of the security of 4%.

An asset with a beta of 0 means there is no correlation with the market ie, that it is independent or it has no risk at all, ' ie, that it is has no systematic risk at all, although it is likely to have independent ('residual' or 'unsystematic') risk.

2.3.2   CAPM Equation

Getting back to CAPM, as we have just discussed, the amount of compensation the investor needs for taking on the additional risk is calculated by taking a risk measure (beta) and multiplying it by the market premium. The market premium is the expected market return minus the risk-free rate.

So the CAPM calculation looks like:

Expected return $= R_F + \beta(R_M - R_F)$

where R_F = average annual risk-free rate
R_M = average annual market return
β = beta of stock or fund

Try using the equation to work out the expected return for a fund with a beta of 1.4 in a market with an average return of 8%. There is a risk-free rate of 4%.

Expected return = [4% + 1.4(8% − 4%)]

Expected return = [4% + 5.6%] = **9.6%**

In other words, as the fund is more volatile than the market, the expectation would be for a higher return which, when taking into account average market returns and risk-free rate, would be 9.6%.

The equation can also be altered to calculate the beta required to, in theory, achieve an expected return:

$$\beta = \frac{\text{expected return} - R_F}{(R_M - R_F)}$$

Graphically, the following may be helpful:

The security market line (SML) plots the results of the CAPM for all different risks (betas). Any security that provides a return above the SML is providing an excess return ('alpha'), and is therefore undervalued. Conversely, any securities lying below the line have a shortfall in returns (negative 'alpha'), and are therefore overvalued.

2.3.3   Problems Associated with CAPM

CAPM as an investment theory has come in for its fair amount of criticism, no more so than in the aftermath of the credit crunch. Some common criticisms levelled at CAPM are:

- betas are based on historical data and are therefore not a reliable guide to future returns (you only have to look at the performance of banking shares since 2007 to see this is the case!)
- market risk can be difficult to establish
- some studies suggest unsystematic risk is being valued in the market which distorts predictability
- some hindsight studies have shown actual returns bore no relation to that expected under CAPM.

3. The Role of The Portfolio Manager

3.1 Role and Responsibilities of the Portfolio Manager

The main responsibilities of a portfolio manager can be summarised as follows:

- helping to determine the client's requirements
- formulating a strategy
- agreeing the performance benchmark
- monitoring the performance against the benchmark and keeping the client up to date with performance.

3.1.1 Implementing the Investment Strategy by the use of Suitable Asset Classes and/or Funds

As we have discussed, portfolios can be put together using a variety of different investment vehicles. These will include cash, bonds, direct equity investment, collectives, derivatives and hedge funds.

The features and benefits of various asset classes and financial products are covered in other sections. Meeting the client's needs and objectives as well as ensuring suitability is covered in Chapter 6.

3.1.2 Measuring/Evaluating Performance

Portfolio managers are usually measured in relative terms compared to a particular index and peer group. Most groups have their own internal measure to ensure consistency and alert managers to significant deviations from benchmarks. Of course when we decide to use the collective investments or investment vehicles of other providers it will be necessary for us to monitor their performance and evaluate them accurately for our clients.

3.1.3 Review

The portfolio manager must agree on the frequency of review with the client and bear in mind their regulatory responsibilities to ensure continued suitability.

This will not only include the necessity to review the portfolio to take into account changes in investment conditions. The client's objectives may change over time and it is important that the portfolio manager is still managing their investments suitably.

This will incorporate any changes to the client's personal circumstances and any external changes affecting them, for example, taxation.

At this time it may also highlight the need to change the benchmark against which he is being judged, for example, if the client has retired and asked for the portfolio manager to adopt a more cautious, income producing stance, it may be appropriate to review the index previously used when the portfolio was geared aggressively for growth.

4. Performance Benchmarks

Once a portfolio has been constructed, it is important that the portfolio manager and client agree a benchmark against which his performance will be judged.

The benchmark selected should reflect as closely as possible the asset split and the risk and return profile of the portfolio.

For private client portfolios it is more common for an index to be used, although sometimes the London inter-bank offered rate (LIBOR) or base rate may be deemed to be more appropriate. The key is that the benchmark used should represent a realistic alternative to the portfolio.

With collectives, often a sector type of benchmarks is used for example defensive, cautious and these are produced by the IA.

Thus tracking error is established.

4.1 Tracking Error

Tracking error is a risk measure as it measures the difference between the performance of a portfolio and the performance of a benchmark. This is a form of active risk as it is the risk that arises due to active management.

Tracking error can be demonstrated graphically as follows:

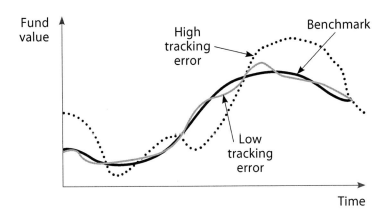

Tracking error indicates the level of risk the fund manager has taken against the benchmark. The higher the tracking error, the more risk taken.

A tracking error might be low, such as 0.5% or less, in which case the indication is that the manager is taking very little risk against the index. An index tracking fund would be expected to have this type of result. Actively managed equity funds would tend to have a tracking error between 2% and 6%, with bond funds generally running slightly lower at somewhere between 1% and 4%.

As with any risk measurement where a benchmark is used, it is important to use an appropriate benchmark! A very high tracking error, for example, might be no more than an indication that a portfolio is being measured against the wrong benchmark.

4.2 Equity Indices

Talking of benchmarks, these are often simply some of the well-known equity indices used in the UK and on a wider, global basis.

4.2.1 UK Indices

The UK stock market is one of the most international. Around 80% of revenues of companies in the FTSE 100 Index are derived from overseas, implying that global economic conditions are more important than what happens in the UK. Leading UK-domiciled companies, such as BP, HSBC, GlaxoSmithKline and Vodafone are multinationals with substantial interests all around the globe.

A UK investor can gain significant exposure to many sectors and to a range of countries without buying shares quoted on overseas exchanges.

Key Indices

FTSE All-Share
>   FTSE All-Share represents 98–99% of the UK market capitalisation. It is the aggregation of the FTSE 100, FTSE 250 and FTSE Small Cap Indices.

FTSE 100

This index comprises the 100 most highly capitalised blue chip companies, representing approximately 81% of the UK market. It is used extensively as a basis for investment products, such as derivatives and exchange-traded funds.

FTSE 250

This index comprises those 250 companies which, by market capitalisation, are positioned directly beneath the FTSE 100 and represent about 15% of the All-Share Index.

FTSE 350

This index comprises the combined constituents of the FTSE 100 and FTSE 250 indices.

FTSE SmallCap

This index comprises companies outside of the FTSE 350 Index and represents approximately 2% of the UK market capitalisation.

FTSE4Good

The FTSE4Good Index Series has been designed to measure the performance of companies that meet globally recognised corporate responsibility standards, and to facilitate investment in those companies. There is a number of indices available in this series, covering the UK, Europe, Australia, the US as well as global indices. The index constituents are screened by ERIS, the Ethical Investment Research Service and therefore veer towards the ethical end of the green investment spectrum. For inclusion, eligible companies must meet criteria requirements in five areas:

- working towards environmental sustainability
- developing positive relationships with stakeholders
- upholding and supporting universal human rights
- ensuring good supply chain labour standards, and
- countering bribery.

Companies that have been identified as having business interests in the following industries are excluded from the FTSE4Good Index Series:

- tobacco producers
- companies manufacturing either whole, strategic parts, or platforms for nuclear weapon systems
- companies manufacturing whole weapons systems
- owners or operators of nuclear power stations, and
- companies involved in the extraction or processing of uranium.

These indices form the basis of index-tracking funds as well as providing benchmarks against which fund managers measure the performance of UK equity portfolios.

4.2.2 Overseas Indices

Globalisation is a reality in the world of investors. In addition to UK investments, a well-diversified portfolio will include substantial exposure to overseas companies and markets. Many of these are quoted on the London Stock Exchange (LSE). A key issue is that investment in overseas markets will expose investors to currency risk. Currency changes can make a significant difference to sterling-adjusted returns from overseas investments.

FTSE Global Equity Index Series

The FTSE Global Equity Index series is the aggregate of over 7,700 stocks. The FTSE All-World Index series is a subset of over 3,000 large and mid-cap stocks. The series is divided into developed and emerging segments. The modular nature of the series provides the ability to structure portfolios with indices calculated at regional, national and sector level.

US

Key Indices

Dow Jones Industrial Average
S&P 500
NASDAQ (National Association of Securities Dealers Automatic Quote)

Continental Europe

Key Indices

FTSE Eurotop 100

A tradeable index, designed to represent the performance of the 100 most highly capitalised blue chip companies in Europe.

FTSE Euro 100

A tradeable index, designed to represent the performance of the 100 most highly capitalised blue chip companies based in European countries that form part of the European Monetary Union (EMU).

CAC 40 Index (France)
DAX 30 Index (Germany)

Since the launch of the euro in 1999, most investors focus on continental Europe as a whole rather than on specific countries.

Japan

Key Indices

FTSE Japan Index

The FTSE Japan Index forms part of the FTSE All-World Index Series. It contains over 470 large and mid cap stocks, capturing 90% of the Japanese market.

FTSE Japan Index is free float adjusted, liquidity tested and managed by an independent committee to provide the most transparent and predictable view of the market.

Nikkei 225
Topix

Emerging Markets

Fast-growing economies in Asia, Latin America and Eastern Europe.

Key Indices

FTSE Emerging Markets indices

FTSE Emerging Market indices are a segment of the overall FTSE Global Equity Index Series (GEIS). They cover over 2,000 companies in 22 emerging markets, ranging from Brazil to Turkey.

4.3 Bond Indices

There are many providers of indices relating to bonds.

4.3.1 UK Indices

Key Index

FTSE UK Gilt Indices

There are a number of indices that can be used for both conventional and index-linked gilts. These are subcategorised according to redemption date, ie, 0–5 years or 5–10 years. They are weighted according to the market value of each constituent stock and are calculated daily.

There is also a FTSE Sterling Corporate Bond Index.

4.3.2 Overseas Indices

Key Indices

FTSE Global Government Bond Indices

These provide indices and overall index for the government bonds issued by 22 countries. All are subdivided into maturity dates for a better comparison. There are similar Corporate Bond Indices for euro denominated bonds from developed and emerging markets.

Citi World Government Bond Index

An alternative index which can be used to monitor and evaluate portfolios of government bonds held in major government bond markets.

4.4 Peer Group Averages

Sometimes, instead of using an established index as a benchmark, a peer group average is used to evaluate the portfolio's performance.

The peer group used will, to a large extent, depend upon the type of portfolio in question (for example whether it is a pension portfolio or a retail portfolio.)

For pension fund portfolios, standardised benchmarks provided by the Combined Actuarial Performance Service (CAPS) are widely used. These are a range of standardised benchmarks, broken down by the size of the pension funds, which show the average returns of pension funds from surveys completed by pension fund managers on a quarterly basis.

In addition, WM Performance Services (part of State Street) perform a similar service, conducting surveys of investment houses, and are particularly useful for benchmarking charity portfolios.

For retail clients, in addition to the above, benchmarks provided by the Wealth Management Association (previously known as the Association of Private Client Investment Managers and Stockbrokers [APCIMS] are commonly used).

The FTSE WMA Private Investor Index Series provides investors with an objective measure of performance against which to measure their investment portfolios, based upon the assumption that they are domestic investors with sterling denominated accounts.

- **FTSE WMA Stock Market Growth Index** – measuring the growth/capital appreciation of a universe of predominantly equity-based constituents.
- **FTSE WMA Stock Market Global Growth Index** – measuring the growth/capital appreciation of a universe of predominantly international equity-based constituents.
- **FTSE WMA Stock Market Income Index** – measuring the income arising from a universe of predominantly equity- and fixed-interest-based constituents.
- **FTSE WMA Stock Market Balanced Index** – measuring the performance of a universe of equity- and fixed-income-based constituents as identified by their growth and income characteristics.
- **FTSE WMA Stock Market Conservative Index** – a diversified index comprising fixed income, cash, hedge funds and commercial property constituents.

The indices are designed to use as:

1. A measure for comparing the performance of income, growth, conservative, global and balanced funds.
2. A basis for reviewing the asset allocation and structure of a portfolio with fund managers or stockbrokers.
3. A benchmark for assessing and comparing the performance of discretionary fund managers.

Most fund managers measure themselves against both an appropriate index and their peer group. For retail CIS funds, those groups are the ones defined by the IA, for example, UK All Companies.

5. Risk Ratios

As part of the ongoing performance measurement process, it is important to consider returns against the risks taken. In this section we look at four generally acknowledged ways this measurement is undertaken.

5.1 Alpha

Alpha is a risk-adjusted measure of the active return on an investment. It is basically a measure of a fund manager's stock-picking skill, with alphas being used to measure individual securities, portfolios or funds.

A positive alpha is good news, and the higher the alpha the better!

The formula is

$$\alpha = \text{actual return} - [R_F + \beta(R_M - R_F)]$$

where R_F = average annual risk-free rate
R_M = average annual market return
β = beta of stock or fund

You may recognise the $[R_F + \beta(R_M - R_F)]$ formula as the CAPM. Alpha therefore is representing the return in excess of CAPM. Strictly, this is known as Jensen's Alpha (named after Michael Jensen who first used the measure in the 1970s), and it can also be known as the residual return.

 A fund has an average fund return of 9.5% against a market return of 7%. The risk-free rate is 4% and the fund's beta is 1.6. What is the fund's alpha?

$$\alpha = 9.5\% - [4\% + 1.6 (7\% - 4\%)]$$

$$\alpha = 0.7\%$$

Alpha can be used to compare funds and portfolios, and look beyond the 'headline' returns.

 For example, the above fund is compared with another that has a fund return of 8.2% and a beta of 1.1. The other factors stay the same – what is the alpha and what does that tell us about the two funds?

$$\alpha = 8.2\% - [4\% + 1.1 (7\% - 4\%)]$$

$$\alpha = 0.9\%$$

The alpha of the second fund is slightly higher than that of the first. This shows that the manager of the second fund, despite underperforming the first, added more value through 'better' stock picking.

We've put 'better' in inverted commas because, of course, the fund manager may have just got lucky – alphas measured over a number of different time periods would help determine the luck element.

5.1.1 The Information Ratio

This is a risk-adjusted return measure used to evaluate a fund manager's relative performance. It is a measure of active management rather than closet indexing. It looks at the return relative to the benchmark, divided by the risk taken by the manager against the benchmark.

As with alpha, the higher the positive information ratio, the better!

The formula for the information ratio is:

$$\text{Information ratio} = \frac{[R_P - R_B]}{\text{tracking error}}$$

where

RP = average annual portfolio return   RB = average annual benchmark return

The tracking error used for this equation is the standard deviation of relative returns. It measures the degree of uncertainty of the excess return (alpha). Thus the information ratio measures alpha divided by the amount of risk taken on in order to generate it.

 A portfolio has an annual return of 12.2% against a benchmark return of 9.8% The standard deviation is 6. What is the information ratio?

$$\frac{12.2\% - 9.8\%}{6\%} = 0.4$$

This would be regarded as not being a bad information ratio – anything above 0.5 is deemed good and would likely be in the top quarter (or decile even); anything above 1.0 is exceptionally good! Of course, information ratios could be negative and any result less than –0.5 would be deemed poor. A negative IR is effectively saying an investor would have achieved a better result by matching the index using an index fund or exchange-traded fund (ETF).

It should be noted that if a fund's returns are not normally distributed, then using the IR can be misleading since the tracking error may not be an appropriate measure of risk.

As an alternative to the information ratio, a number of fund management groups are now providing their active share for each fund. This is a measure of how much their holdings differ from the benchmark index. The figure can range from 0% to 100%. 0% indicates they have the same holdings as the index with identical weightings; perfect replication as a tracker. Whereas 100% means that there are no holdings in common with the index.

5.1.2 The Sharpe Ratio

The Sharpe ratio was originally called the 'reward-to-variability' ratio when it was devised by William Forsyth Sharpe, and this unambiguous original name effectively describes its use. The Sharpe ratio adjusts rates of return to incorporate the riskiness of an investment or fund. It measures the excess returns for every unit of risk (measured by standard deviation) which is taken in order to achieve the return.

The formula for the Sharpe ratio is:

$$\text{Sharpe ratio} = \frac{[\ R_P - R_F\ ]}{\sigma}$$

where

R_P = average annual portfolio return
R_F = average annual risk-free rate (often measured by the use of 90 Treasury Bills)
σ = standard deviation of returns

The excess return is measured on the top line and is the difference between the average performance of an investment and the rate of return from the risk-free investment. This is also known as the numerator, and if the numerator increases for the same level of risk the Sharpe ratio becomes greater. This is good news for an investor! Conversely, when the risk measure (the denominator) increases, the Sharpe ratio will decrease.

Sharpe ratios are most useful for comparing funds with the same benchmark and which provide performance data over the same time period.

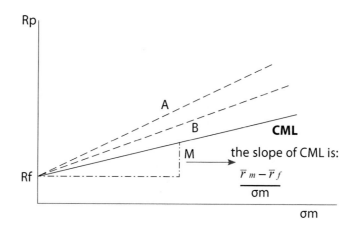

The Sharpe ratio is the slope of the excess return on a fund (Rp—Rf) relative to riskiness of the fund, measured by the standard deviation of the fund, σp. In the diagram fund A clearly outperforms fund B, and both outperform the index, represented by the market portfolio on the Capital Market Line (CML).

5.1.3   The Treynor Ratio

The Treynor ratio was developed by Jack Treynor and is a further risk-adjusted measure of return based on systematic risk. Again, it is similar to the Sharpe ratio, except that the Treynor ratio uses beta as the measurement of volatility.

The formula is:

Treynor ratio = $R_p - R_F / \beta$

where

RP = average annual portfolio return
RF = average annual risk-free rate
β = the beta

Like the Sharpe ratio, the Treynor ratio is a ranking criterion only as it does not quantify the value added by a fund manager. The Treynor index shows relative performance of funds to each other, and to the index. In the diagram fund A clearly outperforms fund B, but both outperform the index, represented by the market portfolio on the Security Market Line (SML).

The Treynor ratio is also sometimes called the 'reward-to-variability ratio'.

Graphically, the Treynor ratio of the securities market line and portfolios A + B will look like this:

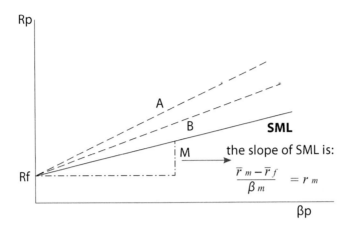

6. Statistical Data

6.1 Portfolio Return Calculations

The performance measurement process involves calculations of the investment return over stated periods. The portfolio return calculations can be measured in a number of ways, but we will look at the two most common in this section:

- money-weighted rate of return
- time-weighted rate of return.

6.1.1 Money-Weighted Rate of Return (MWR)

MWR measures the overall return on capital invested over a specific period. It looks at not just the difference between the value of the portfolio at the start and end of a certain period, but incorporates any income or capital distributions made from the portfolio during that period. It is also known as the **internal rate of return**.

The MWR calculation is a modification of the **'holding period return'** calculation, which looks at just the return made over the period of an investment, and is expressed as a percentage of the cost.

The formula for the holding period return is:

$$\text{Holding period return} = \frac{D + V_1 - V_0}{V_0}$$

where:

D = is the income received in the period
V_1 = the price on selling
V_0 = the price or value at acquisition

Example

An investment costs £2,000, pays a dividend of £100 and is sold for £2,050 after one year. The holding period return is:

$$\frac{(100 + 2050 - 2000)}{2000} = 0.075 \text{ or } (\times 100) = 7.5\%$$

When new funds are invested or withdrawn during the year, the calculation can be modified. This will allow for the differences in the timing of capital additions or withdrawals, with a weighting incorporating the number of months remaining at the time of the additions or withdrawals.

The formula for the MWR is therefore:

$$\text{Money-weighted rate of return} = \frac{D + V_1 - V_0 - C}{V_0 + (C \times n/12)}$$

where:

C = the new money introduced during the year (if added it is a positive figure, if withdrawn it is a negative figure)

n = the number of months remaining in the year at the time the addition/withdrawal took place.

Example

A portfolio was worth £30,000 at the start of the calendar year and £34,000 at the end of the calendar year. During that year an additional £4,000 had been invested at the end of April and £2,000 withdrawn at the end of October. There was an income payment of £150 during the year. The MWR would be:

$$\frac{D + V_1 - V_0 - C}{V_0 + (C_1 \times n/12) + (C_2 \times n/12)}$$

There has been a net cash inflow of £2,000 during the year (£4,000 – £2,000) =

$$\frac{150 + 34{,}000 - 30{,}000 - 2000}{30{,}000 + (4{,}000 \times 8/12) + (-2{,}000 \times 2/12)} = \frac{2150}{30{,}000 + 2666.67 - 333.33}$$

$= 0.0665$

Multiply by 100 to express as a percentage

$= 6.65\%$

One for you to have a go at! A portfolio was worth £25,000 at the start of the calendar year and £28,000 at the end of the calendar year. During the year no additional money had been invested, but £1,000 was withdrawn at the end of June. There were no income distributions. What is the MWR?

Money-weighted rate of return = $\dfrac{D + V_1 - V_0 - C}{V_0 + (C \times n/12)}$

D   =   0 no dividends
V1 =   28,000 value at end of year
V0 =   25,000 starting value
C   =   −1,000 <u>addition to the fund</u> in the year. NB: it is <u>negative</u> because money was <u>taken out</u>

$$\frac{0 + 28,000 - 25,000 + 1,000}{25,000 + (-1,000 \times 6/12)} \quad = \quad \frac{4,000}{25,000 - 500}$$

= 0.1633

= 16.33%

6.1.2   Time-Weighted Rate of Return (TWR)

Whereas the MWR measures the compound rate in the value of all funds invested over a specific period, the TWR measure the compound rate of return over a given period for one unit of money. The MWR is sensitive to the timing of external cash flows, whereas the TWR is not affected.

The TWR is therefore a more appropriate measure for evaluating managers who have no control over the size or timing of cash flows. Indeed, in order to comply with global investment performance standards (GIPS), returns must be presented on a time-weighted basis.

The formula for TWR can therefore appear extensive as a holding period return needs to be calculated for each sub-period, with a sub-period being the period of investment until the next cash inflow or outflow. The overall return is then established by compounding the returns of each sub-period.

For example, in the case of two investment periods:

Time-weighted rate of return = $\dfrac{V_1}{V_0} \times \dfrac{V_2}{(V_1 + C)} - 1$

where:

V0 = the initial value
V1 = the value at the end of the first investment sub-period
V2 = the value at the end of the second investment sub-period
C = the additional capital added at the start of the second investment sub-period

It may be best seen from an example.

Example

Assume that all investments are directed into a growth stock that is rising during the year. At the start of the year its value was 100p; after six months 105p; by the end of 12 months it was worth 125p.

Manager A receives £1,000 at the start of the period. Manager B, on the other hand, receives £500 at the start of the period and a further £500 after six months.

Manager A:
Value of initial fund: £1,000.00 (1,000 shares at 100p)

Value of final fund: £1,250,000 (1,000 shares at 125p)

$$\text{Holding period return} = \frac{D + V_1 - V_0}{V_0} = \frac{0 + 1,250 - 1,000}{1,000}$$

= 0.25, or 25.00%

Manager B:
Initial investment of £500 grows to be worth £525 after six months.

$$\text{Holding period return} = \frac{D + V_1 - V_0}{V_0} = \frac{0 + 525 - 500}{500}$$

= 0.05 or 5%

Second investment:
With the second investment of £500 the manager could only purchase 476 shares (500/1.05), so we start with 976 shares worth £1,024.80 (976 x £1.05). At the end of the period the 976 shares are worth £1,220 (976 x £1.25)

$$\text{Holding period return} = \frac{D + V_1 - V_0}{V_0} = \frac{0 + 1,220 - 1,024.80}{1,024.80}$$

= 0.1905, or 19.05%

This isn't the end of the equation though. We now need to link these returns, which we can do as they apply to exactly the same period:

The formula here is : $1 + \text{TWR} = (1 + r_1)(1 + r_2)$

where:

r_1 = the decimal return from the first investment period

r_2 = the decimal return from the second investment period

So:

$1 + \text{TWR} = (1.05)(1.1905)$

$1 + \text{TWR} = 1.25$

$\text{TWR} = 0.25$, or 25%

So both managers have achieved the same TWR, which makes sense as both were invested in the same stock, and the TWR hasn't been distorted by the additional cash flow Manager B received after six months.

If we had just used the MWR, the indication as to the manager's skill may have appeared different. Manager A's result would have been the same, at 25%. For manager B, however:

Money-weighted rate of return = $\dfrac{D + V_1 - V_0 - C}{V_0 + (C \times n/12)}$ = $\dfrac{0 + 1,220 - 500 - 500}{500 + (500 \times 6/12)}$

= $\dfrac{220}{500 + 250}$

= 0.2933 or 29.33%

Despite the fact both managers may have been instructed to invest in the same stock, by just using the MWR it may have appeared that manager B achieved a better outcome. However, that may have been just due to the fact his client was not able to provide the second half of the overall payment for six months.

For comparison purposes, therefore, TWR is the preferred measure as the result is not affected by cash flows and different new money flows. Based on what we have covered, an exact calculation of a TWR would require a full valuation of the portfolio whenever a cash flow occurs. In practice, approximations are made so that the TWR can be calculated using either monthly or quarterly valuations. For GIPS, portfolios must be valued for return calculations at least monthly, and also whenever large external cash flows occur. The definition of a large external cash flow can be formulated by the firm, but they must then use the definition consistently.

There are occasions when the MWR may be a more appropriate measure however. Considering the example we looked at, it may have been luck that the client was not able to provide additional funds for six months. Alternatively, it may have been the manager's recommendation to hold back half the payment for six months, in which case his decision was validated by the MWR. So, for situations where managers control the size and timing of cash flows, it may be more appropriate to judge them on the MWR.

6.2 Annual Equivalent Rate (AER)

The AER shows the rate of interest a saver will receive over a year, assuming the cash is left in the account for the full year.

The means of calculating AER is the same as that used for calculating the annual percentage rate (APR) for loans. AER is the term used for investments and savings, and APR is used for loans. They are both effective annual rates (EAR) and represent the higher rate of interest as a result of compounding. For example, it is apparent that an investment paying 4% per annum with interest paid quarterly in arrears will return more than an account paying 4% per annum with interest paid annually in arrears, but by how much more? That is where AER may prove helpful.

Formula: $AER = (1+r/n)^n - 1$

Where
r = annual rate of return
n = number of interest payments

So the account paying 4% per annum paid quarterly will return

$AER = (1+0.04/4)^4 - 1$

$AER = 4.06\%$

This is more than the 4% returned on the investment paying annually.

You can also work out the AER from the return over a longer period by using the following formula.

$AER = \sqrt[n]{(1+r)} - 1$

Where

n = number of years
r = return over period

So if a return is 40% over three years the annual equivalent rate is:

$AER = \sqrt[3]{(1+0.40)} - 1$

$AER = 11.87\%$ which is less than the simple annual rate of 13.33%, ie, 40%/3.

7. Performance Evaluation

In this section we will look at evaluating how a portfolio manager achieves their returns. Was it due to their skill in stock selection/their overall asset allocation or a combination of both?

7.1 Stages of Evaluation

There are five stages to the process.

7.1.1 Step 1: The Benchmark

We have already seen, in Section 4 of this chapter, examples of different benchmarks. As mentioned then, it is important the choice of benchmark is appropriate to the portfolio being reviewed or the review process will be next to useless.

7.1.2 Step 2: The Benchmark Asset Allocation

You then need to ascertain the asset allocation of the benchmark chosen. For example, the following asset allocation split is based on the FTSE WMA Stock Market Income index (May 2016):

Asset class	Asset distribution (%)
UK equities	35.0
International equities	17.5
Bonds	27.5
Commercial property	5.0
Cash	5.0
Hedge funds/Alternatives	10.0

7.1.3 Step 3: The Benchmark Returns

You then need to calculate the return that each asset class in the benchmark portfolio would have achieved if it had performed in line with the appropriate index for its sector (the percentage return figures shown are for illustration purposes only).

Asset class	Asset distribution (%)	Index performance for each class (%)	Contribution to the overall return (%)
UK equities	35.0	12	4.20
International equities	17.5	15	2.63
Bonds	27.5	10	2.75
Commercial property	5.0	6	0.30
Cash	5.0	4	0.20
Hedge funds/ Alternatives	10.0	10	1.0
Overall contribution to return			11.08%

So, if a portfolio manager had copied the asset distribution of the chosen benchmark and performed at exactly the index level for each asset class, they should have achieved an 11.08% return.

7.1.4   Step 4: Comparison of Asset Allocation

The next step is to compare the benchmark performance with the actual portfolio's performance, but in terms of asset allocation only. With comparisons of this sort, you need to maintain a control figure, and so at this point we ignore the actual performance achieved by the portfolio manager. We are just keen to concentrate on the returns they would have got had they achieved the index performance of each asset class.

The results show should how effective, or otherwise, the portfolio manager's choice of asset allocation was:

Asset class	Asset distribution (%)	Index performance for each class (%)	Contribution to the overall return (%)
UK equities	50.0	12	6.00
International equities	15.0	15	2.25
Bonds	30.0	10	3.00
Commercial property	0.0	6	0.00
Cash	5.0	4	0.20
Hedge funds/ Alternatives	0.0	10	0.00
Overall contribution to return			**11.45%**

The portfolio's over-weighting on the equities asset class and lack of hedge funds would appear to be effective, as the returns from both asset classes exceed that from the benchmark portfolio. These helped the overall return of the portfolio, just from the asset allocation scenario, exceed that from the benchmark.

7.1.5   Comparison of Stock Selection

The final step is to calculate the effect of the portfolio manager's stock selection. Again we need a control figure and so, in this case, we return to the benchmark allocation as seen in step 2 and ignore that chosen by the portfolio manager (as seen in step 4).

The aim of this stage is to see if the portfolio over or underperformed within each asset class relative to the appropriate index:

Asset class	Asset distribution (%)	Index performance (%)	Actual performance (%)	Contribution to return (%)
UK equities	35.0	12	9	−1.05
International equities	17.5	15	14	−0.18
Bonds	27.5	10	12	+0.55
Commercial property	5.0	6	N/A	−
Cash	5.0	4	3	−0.05
Hedge funds/ Alternatives	10.0	10	N/A	−
Overall contribution to return				**−0.73%**

The tables illustrate that overall asset allocation was good, but specific investment selection was poor.

So the manager underperformed the benchmark and index returns. The equity investment returns were particularly disappointing – maybe the manager stayed invested in a particular sector or stock for too long and that had the detrimental effect? This was worsened by being overweight in UK equities. On the other hand, this was compensated for in some way by the returns from fixed interest investments, where the positive relative performance was further improved by being overweight in bonds.

Glossary and Abbreviations

Investment Terms

This is your investment terms revision section. We expect most of these terms to be very familiar. However, it is designed to provide you with a short definition for revision purposes. For more expansive definitions, you should refer to the chapters and your own further reading and research.

Account

The individual account for a single client, or a group of clients whose assets are held in a single nominee account.

Accounting Reference Date

The closing date for a fund's annual accounting period. This date must be stated in the fund's prospectus (or scheme particulars).

Accrued Income

Interest that has been earned but not yet paid.

Accumulation Shares/Units

Shares or units in a portfolio that automatically have income reinvested.

Active Management

Active fund managers believe securities are mis-priced and can spot opportunities to outperform the market through asset allocation and/or stock selection. See also index tracking and passive management.

Active Risk

The risk arising from active management in excess of the risk that would be incurred if the portfolio was passively managed (ie, the weighting differential versus the benchmark/index).

Actuary

A professional skilled in evaluating and assessing the potential impact of risks. Actuaries monitor and advise on the solvency of life assurance companies and pension funds.

Added Value

Performance in excess of a stated benchmark or index (see **Alpha**).

Additional Voluntary Contributions (AVCs)

Employee contributions over and above any compulsory contributions to a tax-approved occupational pension scheme.

Agency Broker

A broker who is paid commission to secure the best possible trade for his clients.

Allotment Letter

Written confirmation from an issuing company to the subscriber of the allotment of new shares.

Alpha

The out-performance of a portfolio against the benchmark attributable to the manager's strategy.

Alternative Investments

Investments outside the mainstream areas of bonds, equities, cash and property. They normally form a small proportion of portfolios. Examples include hedge funds, venture capital, art and wine.

Alternative Investment Market (AIM)

The market for smaller company shares in the UK.

American Depositary Receipt (ADR)

An ADR represents a share, or a defined number of shares, of a non-US company. A depositary bank holds the shares and issues the Depositary Receipt. ADRs may be listed in the US, UK and Luxembourg. Unlisted Level I ADRs are traded OTC on NASDAQ.

Annual Management Charge

A charge imposed by the management firm on the portfolio. For unit trusts and OEICs this is usually 1–1.5% of the NAV of the fund. Other clients negotiate the fee with the fund manager.

Annuity

A fixed annual allowance. Normally paid in the form of a pension.

Approved Person

An individual who has been approved by FCA or PRA to perform one or more controlled functions on behalf of an authorised firm.

Arbitrage

A strategy used by market traders to exploit the price difference between similar assets.

Arbitrage Pricing Theory (APT)

Complex mathematical theory suggesting there are several factors that determine the rate of return on a security rather than just the movement of the overall market. The expected risk premium for each factor will be determined by the security's sensitivity to it.

Asset Allocation

The distribution of investments across categories of assets, such as equities, bonds and cash. Active managers will change asset allocation to improve fund's performance based on their forecast returns for each asset class.

Asset Class

Category of assets, eg, equities, bonds, property or cash.

Association of Investment Companies (AIC)

The trade association for closed-ended investment trusts.

At Best

An instruction to deal at the best price ruling in the market at the time, ie the highest price (selling) or lowest (buying).

At-the-Money

When the market price of the underlying instrument is the same as the exercise price of the option/warrant.

Auction

The normal process of selling government securities. The Central Bank accepts bids down to the lowest acceptable price (ie, highest yield).

Authorisation

Required by FSMA for any firm or individual that wants to conduct investment business in the EU. Regulated collective investment schemes are also authorised.

Authorised Funds

Funds authorised by the Financial Conduct Authority (FCA) restrict their investments to those laid out in the FCA Regulations. Can be freely marketed to the public in the EU.

Backwardation

This is when a future price is below the cash price. It is a negative contango (common in commodity markets but anomalous in financial futures). It is also used to refer to the anomalous situation when the best bid price for share is temporarily above the best offer price.

Balanced Funds

Funds invested in a range of asset classes (eg, bonds, equities, cash and property) under the discretion of the portfolio manager.

Bargain

Another name for a trade or transaction of the Stock Exchange.

Base Currency

The currency specified as the currency in which the accounts of a portfolio are prepared.

Base Rate

The minimum rate at which banks will lend money to individuals. In the UK, this is set each month by the Monetary Policy Committee (MPC) at the Bank of England.

Bear

Someone who believes prices will fall in the future (see **Bull**).

Bearer Securities

Although notionally no registration of ownership, these are usually held electronically in modern markets and physical paper does not transfer between buyer and seller.

Bed & Breakfast

Selling and buying back of shares to crystallise profits/losses for capital gains tax (CGT) purposes. Deals within 30 days are now treated as a continuous holding.

Benchmark

Target against which investment performance is measured. It may be an index or the average performance of similar portfolios (eg, CAPS/WM/Micropal/Lipper).

Beneficial Owner

The true owner of a security, regardless of the name in which it is registered.

Best Execution

Secure the best possible deal, taking into account all market conditions at the time of the transaction.

Beta

The relative move of a stock (or portfolio) against the market.

A security with a Beta of 1 would be expected to move in line with the index. Higher Beta stocks (or portfolios) are expected to outperform in rising markets and underperform falling markets. Lower Beta stocks (or portfolios) are defensive.

Bid Price

The price at which securities (or units in collective investment funds) are repurchased from the investor.

Bid-Offer Spread

Difference between the Bid (selling) and Offer (buying) price.

Bloomberg

Company that provides market and investment information including real-time share prices.

Blue Chip Company

Informal term for a large, well-known company with long-standing history of profit growth, strong branding and consistent dividend payouts.

Bond

Security issued by a corporate or government, to back borrowing. The issuer guarantees to repay the principal sum on redemption date plus interest (coupons) during the life of the bond. Bonds may be secured over assets of the firm, or unsecured.

Bonus Issue

Bonus, Scrip or free issues are equivalent terms. Free shares are issued to existing shareholders, out of company reserves.

Book

The stock (or line) of securities held by market makers.

Book Entry

Electronic settlement and record of ownership of a security.

Book Value

Value at which a security is recorded on a balance sheet. Usually the purchase cost, less any depreciation.

Bottom Up

Approach to investment management that gives priority to stock selection rather than asset classes. Bottom up managers rely on identifying and selecting securities to build an optimum portfolio.

Bourse/Bolsa

Stock exchange of European (or Latin American) markets.

Box

The stock of shares/units in a collective investment scheme that are held by the manager acting as principal.

Brady Bonds

Issued in 1994 to help a number of Latin American countries ease their excessive debt burdens. They are collateralised over 30 year US Treasury bonds.

Broker-Dealer Firm

Firm taking advantage of dual capacity to offer agency broking and market-making services.

Bull

Someone who believes prices will rise in the future (see **Bear**).

Call Option

The right to buy the underlying asset at the pre-determined strike/exercise price.

Cancellation

Units in open-ended funds are destroyed as cash is taken out of the fund (redemption).

Cancellation Rights

Private customers may have the right to cancel the purchase of an investment product and have their money returned by the firm.

Capital

The money injected into a business by the shareholders and bondholders.

Capital Account

An account relating to the capital property of a portfolio (ie, excluding income).

Capital Asset Pricing Model (CAPM)

An economic model for valuing securities. It is a mathematical model that enables investors to determine the expected return from a risky security. The model uses Beta as the main measure of risk

Capital Gains Tax (CGT)

Tax paid on profits realised from selling assets. In the UK there is an annual exemption limit. CGT is paid at different rates for higher- and additional rate taxpayers, adjusted for losses and the holding period. There are also different rates for taxable residential property.

Capitalisation

Total market value of share capital issued by a company. Calculated by multiplying the number of ordinary shares in free float by the price.

Capital Markets

The financial market for equity instruments and debt instruments with a maturity greater than one year.

Combined Actuarial Performance Services Ltd (CAPS)

Independent performance measurement service widely used by pooled funds to compare the performance of the portfolio manager.

Cash Call

A request for cash to be paid on partly paid securities.

Cash Flow

A measure of the cash generated by a company to allow a target share price to be set. Serves to exclude 'noise' from earnings (profits) figures.

Cash Memorandum Account

A record of a CREST member's running total of a day's payment obligations to or from its payment bank. CMAs are set to zero at the start of each day because at the end of each day net payments are settled between payment banks.

Chargable Accounting Period (CAP)

Usually the same period of time as a company's accounting year. A company calculates its profits for its CAP and then pays corporation tax on them. Large companies (those paying the full rate of corporation tax) pay tax in four quarterly instalments. Companies that are not large, make one corporation tax payment within nine months and one day following the end of the accounting period.

Chartist

Individual who studies charts of movements in financial and economic indicators to predict how security prices will move.

Chinese Wall

Separation of different activities in an investment bank, eg, investment management, corporate finance and broking. Aims to prevent confidential information passing from one area to another.

Chop Stocks

Stocks purchased for pennies and sold for pound or dollars values providing both brokers and stock promoters massive profits.

Class

Shares in a company/portfolio that have the same voting and dividend rights.

Clean Price

The price of a fixed income stock that excludes accrued interest.

Clearing

Confirmation of trade details with the counterparty or the exchange.

Collar (or Cylinder or Tunnel or Fence or Corridor)

The sale of a put (or call) option and purchase of a call (or put) at different strikes – typically both out-of-the-money and the purchase of a cap combined with a sale of a floor.

Collateral

A form of security, guarantee or indemnity provided by way of security for the discharge of any liability arising from a transaction.

Commercial Paper (CP)

Unsecured short-term debt issued by banks, corporates and other borrowers as part of a funding programme.

Commission

Fee paid to a broker for buying or selling a security. Usually a percentage of the cost. Investors also pay commission to IFAs.

Commodity

Any item that can be bought and sold. Usually a physical item, eg, gold, oil, meat, coffee, or sugar.

Concentration

The number of different shareholdings in a portfolio. The fewer the securities held, the more concentrated the portfolio is said to be.

Concert Party

Investors buying securities in agreement between themselves to suit some wider purpose (eg, to evade disclosure rules of the Takeover Panel).

Consideration

The monetary value of a deal excluding commissions, stamp duty, VAT etc. Total consideration will include the above.

Consultants

Actuarial and insurance firms that advise trustees eg choosing investment managers, meeting managers, asset allocation strategies.

Contango

Also known as 'forwardation' where the spot price is lower than longer-term prices (see also backwardation).

Contingent Liability

Future possible losses, which cannot yet be quantified.

Constraints

Limits or restrictions imposed on a portfolio manager in relation to stocks, sectors or markets.

Consumer Prices Index (CPI)

Measure of inflation used in the UK economy.

Contract for Difference (CFD)

A contract designed to make a profit or avoid a loss by reference to movements in the price of an item. The underlying item cannot change hands

Contract Note

A document sent to the investor on a purchase or sale being made, detailing the price at which the securities were bought or sold.

Convertible Loan Stock

Unsecured Loan Stock (ULS) that (usually) converts into equity of the issuing company. The UK government also issues convertible Gilts that convert into other government stock.

Corporate Actions

Actions involving issued securities other than trading. The decision may come from the issuer (eg, distribution, redemption etc) or the holder (eg, conversion or exercise of warrants). These are:

- **CAP** – Capitalisations
- **CPP** – Call payments/ Partly paid
- **CSL** – Consolidations
- **DRW** – Drawings
- **ESD** – Enhanced Scrip Dividends
- **OOE** – Open Offer Entitlements
- **PPU** – Pari Passu
- **SCD** – Scrip Dividends
- **SOA** – Schemes of arrangement
- **RDM** – Redemptions
- **CHD** – Cash Dividends
- **CRP** – Capital Repayments
- **CVN** – Conversions

- **ENF** – Enfranchisements
- **ITP** – Interest Payments
- **OOO** – Other types of Open Offer
- **RII** – Rights Issue
- **SDV** – Subdivisions
- **SUB** – Subscriptions
- **TKO** – Takeovers

Core/Satellite Portfolio

The partitioning of assets between a core portfolio (lower risk/tracking funds) and more actively managed satellite funds.

Corporate Bond

Securities issued by a company (as opposed to government). Investors accept credit risk in exchange for potentially greater returns.

Corporate Governance

The means by which shareholders govern the management of a company through the use of voting powers (see proxy).

Correlation

Correlation shows the strength of a linear relationship between two investments. A perfect correlation is when the investments behave in exactly the same manner.

Coupon

The regular payment made on fixed income securities.

Covered Warrants

A type of option issued by a third party, usually a major securities house. Those issued on single stocks and share indices can be traded on the London Stock Exchange trading service. Covered warrants may be issued on baskets of shares, debt securities, currencies, metals, and oil.

They are called covered, as the writer of the warrant (an investment bank) will often 'cover' or hedge their exposure under the covered warrant by buying the underlying stock or taking out futures or options on the derivatives exchange.

Creation

New units in open-ended funds are made to accommodate cash inflows.

Credit Rating

Rating given to a company or institution by a credit rating agency as an indication of the likelihood of default on its bonds or other debt. The highest (lowest risk) rating is AAA (triple A).

Credit Spread

Difference on the yield of a corporate bonds compared with a government bonds of a similar maturity. Credit spreads are higher for companies with lower credit ratings to compensate investors for the higher risk.

CREST

The UK settlement system for shares, gilts, money market securities, ADRs and mutual funds. Institutions may be sponsored members of CREST or settle using broker nominee accounts.

Currency Hedging/Currency Overlay

Reduction or elimination of exchange rate risk using futures, forwards or options.

Currency Swap

An agreement whereby two counterparties agree to swap interest and principal in two different currencies.

Custody

Safe keeping of client assets. Firms are required to be able to identify client assets separately from firm's assets. The firm may use nominee accounts (see below) to pool securities of different clients.

A global custodian is responsible for this operation on a worldwide basis. They may appoint local custodians (depots or sub-custodians) in certain countries.

Cyclical Stock

Security that is sensitive to fluctuations in the economic or business cycle (eg, capital goods, banks).

Dark Liquidity or Dark Pools of Liquidity

By definition cannot be seen by any potential market participant and its existence can only be imputed ex post facto. Dark liquidity is generally used to try to reduce market impact when trading large orders.

Debenture

Loan stock secured against the assets of the borrower (corporation). They are usually paid out first if the firm goes into liquidation.

Debt/Equity Ratio

The ratio of long-term debt to equity in a company. See also gearing.

Defensive Stock

Security that is less sensitive to movements in the economic or business cycle, eg, utilities, tobacco.

Denomination

The size in units of a currency of a security.

Depositary

Bank acting as custodian of the securities held by the sub funds of an OEIC.

Derivatives

Collective term given to forwards, futures, swaps and options. These are contracts that give the contract holder either the obligation or the choice to buy or sell a financial asset or commodity at some future time.

Designated Territories

Countries recognised by HM Treasury under the FSMA as being able to provide financial services in the UK since they provide equivalent investor protection to the UK. Include Jersey, Guernsey, Isle of Man and Bermuda.

Delivery versus Payment (DVP)

This is the ideal method of settlement whereby cash and securities are switched simultaneously between client accounts, reducing settlement risk.

Devaluation

Fall in value of a currency in the global markets.

Dilution

Effect on earnings per share and book value per share if all the convertible securities are converted and all warrants and stock options were exercised.

Also the impact on a pooled fund of transaction costs due to investors' buying/selling.

Dilution Levy

Charge imposed on a large purchase or sale of units in an open-ended collective investment fund (eg, OEIC, SICAV etc).

Dirty Price

The price paid for a fixed income stock, including accrued interest.

Discount Broker

Firm that charges low commission rates for execution-only business.

Discretionary

The client delegates decision making to a third party, eg, discretionary portfolio management or discretionary stock lending (undertaken by the global custodian).

Distribution Dates

The date when interest or dividends are distributed to investors. Also called Payment Date.

Distributor Status

Granted by HMRC to offshore funds that satisfy certain qualifying rules. A UK resident investor is liable to income tax on distributed income and CGT on realised capital gains.

Diversification

Risk reduction by spreading investments across a single of asset classes or across a single asset class.

Dividend

The distribution of profits by a company to its shareholders. The dividend may be passed or cut if profits fall. The technical term for the coupon on gilts is also dividend.

Dividend Cover

Company's total earnings (profits) divided by the total paid in dividends. Used as an indication of the company's ability to maintain its dividend payout.

Dividend Yield

The annual income (usually interim + final dividend) from a share divided by the market price of the share, as a percentage.

Domicile

A taxpayer only has one domicile. This is the country s/he regards as the natural home. This is not necessarily the same as residence or nationality.

Double Taxation Treaty

An agreement between two countries allowing tax paid in one country to be offset against that due in the other on the same income.

Dow Jones Industrial Average ('Dow')

Price-weighted arithmetic index of 30 industrial stocks.

Durable Medium

A paper or suitable permanent electronic file if the client is known to have access to the internet.

Duration

(Macaulay's) Duration is the weighted average term to maturity of the cash flows from a bond, including final repayment.

Duration to Worst

Approximate percentage change in the price of a bond given a 1% shift in the yield to maturity, or yield to call, whichever is the worse.

Dynamic Headroom

The difference during the day between a member's credit limit (cap) and its net payment obligations (It is dynamic because it expands as a result of a sold bargain settlement and decreases as a result of a bought bargain settlement).

Earnings

Net profits of a company after interest, tax, and any preference dividends, have been deducted.

Earnings Yield

Company's earnings per share divided by its current share price. The inverse of the P/E ratio.

Economic Indicator

Statistic that gives an indication of current point of the economic cycle eg price inflation, unemployment figures, wage rises etc.

Efficient Market Hypothesis (EMH)

The theory that the public availability of relevant information about the issuers of securities will lead to a correct pricing of those securities if they are freely traded in properly functioning markets.

Eligible Markets

Markets in which an authorised fund is permitted to invest without limits. There is a 10% cap on investments in non-eligible markets.

Emerging Market

A developing or newly industrialised country. Low gross domestic product per head.

Can deliver high returns due to rapid pace of industrialisation, but can be risky due to things such as poor legal protection, currency, custody & settlement risk and government corruption.

Endowment Policy

A life assurance policy that pays out a sum assured on the death of the life assured, or at the end of an agreed term, whichever is the earlier. The money is traditionally invested in a range of securities, including equities. A traditional with-profits policy may provide a higher payout by the addition of bonuses.

Equalisation

The amount of distribution from a collective investment scheme that represents the return of initial capital to new investors.

Equities

Ordinary shares, ie the risk-taking part of a company's capital. Equity holders rank last in the event of the winding-up of a company and for income distribution.

Equity Risk Premium

The extra return expected from investing in equities rather than a risk less asset.

Electronic Trade Confirmation (ETC)

Also known as I-shares.

Ethical Investment

Strategy to invest only in companies that make a positive contribution to an ethical issue (or avoid a negative contribution). Examples of usual exclusions include tobacco stocks, armaments manufacturers, alcohol producers and gaming companies.

Eurobond

International negotiable, bearer loan stock (bonds) issued outside the country of the issuer, traded OTC. Coupons are paid gross. Accrued income is calculated on a 30/360-day basis.

Euroclear

Euroclear is the alternative European settlement house with Clearstream. Euroclear settles international bonds, Gilts and shares. It is an International Securities Depository (ISD).

Exceptions Report

Daily report automatically generated showing queries in a fund/portfolio valuation.

Execution-Only

Instructions to buy or sell, given directly to a broker or fund manager without receiving any advice.

Exchange-Traded Funds (ETFs)

ETFs are exchange-traded open-ended funds that track an index. They are bought and sold on the LSE throughout the day on SETS and settle via CREST in dematerialised form.

Exempt Fund

A fund that is exempt from tax. Investment is restricted to non-taxpayers (eg, pension funds).

Exercise Price

The price at which the holder of an option or warrant can buy/sell the underlying asset.

Exit Charges

Managers can levy a charge on sale of shares/ units in a fund, rather than an initial charge.

Expiry

The date on which an option or warrant expires.

Fallen Angel

A bond that has migrated from investment to non-investment grade. It has increased credit (default) risk.

Financial Adviser

An authorised person who provides personal recommendations in relation to retail investment products to its retail client who is not independent. This is referred to as restricted.

Financial Adviser – Independent

An authorised person who provides personal recommendations in relation to retail investment products to its retail clients based on a comprehensive and fair analysis of the relevant market, and is unbiased and unrestricted.

Financial Conduct Authority (FCA)

The UK regulator responsible for conduct issues across the entire spectrum of financial services; it is also responsible for market supervision as well as prudential supervision of firms not supervised by the PRA.

Financial Policy Committee (FPC)

A committee established within the Bank of England with responsibility for macro-prudential regulation: regulation for stability and resilience of the financial system as a whole.

Financial Services Authority (FSA)

The former UK regulator responsible for fund management, product selling, broker-dealer firms, banks, market abuse and investor compensation.

Financial Services Compensation Scheme (FSCS)

Scheme established to compensate claimants where authorised persons are unable to satisfy claims against them in connection with regulated activities.

Financial Ombudsman Service (FOS)

Part of a statutory complaint procedure. The Ombudsman deals with complaints against investment firms, that neither the firm nor the regulator has been able to resolve.

Fixed Income Securities

Bonds and preference shares. Holder receives a regular fixed income. This may be waived in the case of preference shares.

Floor

A package of interest rate options whereby at each of a series of future fixing dates, if agreed reference such as LIBOR is lower than that of strike rate, the option buyer receives the difference between them, calculated on an agreed notional principal amount for the period until the next fixing date (see Collar).

Floor-Based Market

See **Open Outcry**.

Flotation

First issue of shares by a company of a stock exchange. An example of an IPO (initial public offering).

Forward Contract

A non-standardised contract calling for the future delivery of an asset at a specified price at the end of a designated period of time.

Franked Income

Income that has already had withholding tax deducted at source. Higher rate taxpayers may have a further liability. Non-taxpayers may be able to reclaim the deduction.

Front Office

The investment management area of an investment institution. Includes portfolio managers, analysts, economists, strategists and risk management.

FTSE 100 Index

The main UK index used to represent the price movements of (approximately) the largest 100 companies. The index is a market capitalisation weighted index of price relatives. It is a price index and excludes reinvestment of dividends.

FTSE All-Share Index

Summarises the state of the UK equity markets. It covers about 625 of the top UK industrial, commercial and financial companies.

Fully Paid

No further instalments are due on a new issue.

Fund

Usually single asset class over which several investors have pooled ownership.

Fundamental Analysis

Assessment of a company's share value and potential for future profit and dividends, based on accounting information and economic analysis.

Gaming

Ability to guess both the existence of large liquidity and the pricing mechanism being used. A very risky strategy often used in dark pools if another investor anticipates this and you miss your chance to deal at the favourable price.

Gearing

The amount of borrowing versus debt on a company's balance sheet (net debt/ordinary shareholders' funds).

Warrants and options also exhibit gearing; ie a small move in the price of the underlying asset can be magnified in the move in the price of the option.

Gilts

UK government securities. They may be for fixed terms or undated (eg, War Loan).

Global Depositary Receipt (GDR)

Negotiable OTC securities, usually priced in US dollars, issued by foreign companies. Listed on London, Frankfurt and Luxembourg stock exchanges.

Global Investment Performance Standards (GIPS)

New set of minimum performance presentation standards for investment managers. Sponsored by the Association of Investment Management & Research and intended for global comparison of Investment performance.

Global Custody

See **Custody**.

Grey Market

Period between the announcement of an issue and the time the issue takes place. Investors can buy and sell the shares during this period for settlement after the issue date.

Gross Redemption Yield (GRY)

The total return earned by holding a fixed income security to maturity (redemption). Includes coupon and the capital gain/loss on redemption. Calculated by using Discounted Cash Flow (DCF). Also known as Yield to Maturity (YTM).

Growth Stock

Company that is expected to achieve higher than average earnings growth. Growth stocks usually have a high P/E ratio relative to the market as a whole.

Guaranteed Bonds

Sold on a limited basis by life funds as single-premium products. Income is guaranteed over the selected term and the capital is returned on maturity.

Guaranteed Funds

Provide limited downside for the investor, usually by the purchase of derivatives. Capital may be guaranteed.

Hedge

Taking an opposite position to the main strategy of a portfolio. For example, the sale of futures contracts or purchase of put options, could limit or prevent a loss in the event of a market decline.

Hedge Fund

A limited partnership with few investment restrictions. Usually based offshore (eg, Cayman Islands) but shares in the fund are often quoted in Luxembourg or Dublin.

Hedge funds can use a number of strategies including sell short ie sell stock they do not own to profit from price falls.

Some hedge funds gear up to increase leverage (may result in large losses eg, LTCM).

High Yield Stocks

Shares that have a higher than average dividend yield or those where a high proportion of the total return is derived from dividend income. Examples include utilities.

Iceberg Orders

Generally specify an additional display quantity, smaller than the overall order quantity. The order is queued along with other orders but only the display quantity is printed to the market depth.

Income

Receipts from earnings or investments owned.

Income Account

Account relating to the income (actual and accrued) of a portfolio.

Income Tax

Tax paid on earned and unearned income by UK investors.

Index

A basket of shares/bonds to provide a benchmark for performance measurement. May be single sector/country, regional or global.

Index-linked Government Bonds

Some issuers increase the coupon and redemption value in line with an inflation indicator. In the UK, index-linked Gilts are linked to the RPI-X. US index-linked T-bonds are linked to the CPI.

Index-Tracking Fund

Fund that aims to match the returns on a particular index. Also called passive management.

Individual Savings Account (ISA)

Tax-efficient wrapper around investment products including cash.

Inflation

A measure of the rate of change in prices or earnings. In the UK, price inflation is measured using the RPI or CPI.

Information Ratio

The extra return from a portfolio versus the benchmark relative to the deviation from an index.

Initial Charge

Charge imposed on buyers of new shares/units in a Collective Investment Scheme.

Initial Public Offering (IPO)

The first issue of any class of security.

Insider Dealing

Knowingly trading in shares when in possession of price-sensitive information that is not widely known. This is illegal in several countries.

Institutional Funds

Assets managed by investment banks, life assurance and fund management companies. Includes pension schemes, insurance funds, unit trusts and investment trusts.

In-the-Money

When the exercise price of a call option or warrant is less than the underlying asset price or when the exercise price of a put option is more than the underlying asset price.

Intrinsic Value

The amount by which the exercise price of an option or warrant is in the money.

Inverted Yield Curve

When the redemption yields of short-dated gilts are higher than those of long-dated gilts.

Invest

To employ (money) in the purchase of anything from which interest or profit is expected.

Investment Company with Variable Capital (ICVC)

Same as an **OEIC**.

Investment Trust

A company whose shares are quoted on the London Stock Exchange, with a fixed number of shares. The company invests in shares of other companies. The value of the shares in the fund is set by supply and demand as well as the value of the fund (NAV). Closed-ended funds. Not regulated by the FCA. The FCA regulates investment managers and advisers who promote investment trusts.

Journal

Daily record of trades undertaken (debts and credits).

Junk Bond

Bond that has been given a low rating by the credit rating agencies.

Key Features

Factual information that must be sent out on request to inform new investors in an authorised fund, of the scheme objectives, charges and dealing procedures.

Kurtosis

Probability distribution of a real-valued random variable. Higher kurtosis means more of the variance is due to infrequent extreme deviations, as opposed to frequently modestly-sized deviations.

Issuing House

An investment bank that masterminds a new issue. It is responsible for launching and marketing the new securities in return for a fee from the issuer.

Ledger

Account showing assets and liabilities for a fund/portfolio.

Letter of Renunciation

Form attached to an allotment letter, which is completed, should the original holder wish to sell the entitlement (see Renounceable Documents).

Leverage

See **Gearing**.

Liabilities

Money owed.

Liquidity

The part of a portfolio that is held in cash or cash-like securities.

Or:

The ability to buy or sell an asset quickly or to convert to cash quickly.

Listed Investments

Investments that have an official listing on one of the world's recognised stock exchanges. Also known as quoted investments.

Loan Notes/Loan Stock

Unsecured corporate bonds. May be convertible or have a warrant attached.

London Inter-Bank Offered Rate (LIBOR)

The rate of interest charged by one bank to another from overnight loans. LIBOR is quoted daily. Corporate loans are quoted relative to LIBOR.

Long

Used to indicate a holding of a security or purchase of futures contracts.

Long-Dated Gilts

Gilts with remaining time to maturity > 15 years.

Managed Funds

See **Pooled Funds**.

Manager's Fee

Charge made from the value of a portfolio's assets payable to the investment management company.

Mandate

Contractual description of the service that a client will receive from the institution (eg, investment management or custody).

Market Capitalisation

Total market value of securities issued by a company, industry, sector or markets(s). Calculated by multiplying the number of securities in issue, by the current market price.

Market Maker

A market professional who buys and sells stock on behalf of the broker-dealer firm. In London, market makers are obliged to post firm two-way prices throughout the trading day. Market makers are exempt from stamp duty and are able to sell stock 'short', ie, sell more than they own.

Mark to Market

Valuing the price of a stock or portfolio on a daily basis, to record profits/losses.

Median

One form of the average. The middle item in a ranked order.

Medium-Dated Gilts

Medium-dated Gilts with 5-15 years remaining to maturity.

Mid Price

Halfway between the bid-offer spread (see above). OEICs and SICAVs operate on a mid-price basis.

MiFID

Markets in Financial Instruments Directive – European law that provides harmonised regulation for investment products and services.

Modified Duration

Modified duration is the percentage change in price resulting from a 1% point change in the gross redemption yield.

Momentum

Extent to which prices are influenced by strong investor buying/selling.

Money Laundering

Aiding drug traffickers, arms dealers and other criminals to invest their proceeds and take 'clean' money out of the system. An international criminal offence. It is an offence not to report the knowledge or suspicion of money laundering by a client.

Money markets

Short-dated securities, eg, Treasury Bills or CP. Compete with liquid funds (eg, cash deposits).

Morgan Stanley Capital International indices (MSCI)

Global, sector and regional indices, eg, EAFA (Europe, America and Far East). Compete with FTSE Global indices'.

Multilateral Trading Facility (MTF)

Regulated activity which allows you to trade shares or other securities by means other than on a Recognised Investment Exchange.

Naked Bear

A short seller (or the writer of a call option, or seller of financial future or CFD), ie, does not possess the underlying asset but believes the price will fall. The risk is unlimited if the price rises.

Net Asset Value (NAV)

This is the aggregate value of the securities in a fund, net of liabilities (eg, charges or tax manager's fee). This value is used as the basis for valuing the units (or shares) in a collective investment fund.

A company's break-up value. Used by value investors as a measure of the price to pay for a company's shares.

National Association of Securities Dealers Automatic Quote (NASDAQ)

The OTC market run in the US on a market-making basis specialising in high technology and biotechnology shares.

Neutral Position

The same investment in a stock/sector/region, as the relevant benchmark weighting.

Nil Paid

A new issue of shares on which no payment to the company has yet been made.

Normal Market Size (NMS)

The average size of bargains transacted in a particular share. A market maker's prices are firm for NMS. Prices are negotiable for deals outside NMS. NMS is 2.5% of the average daily volume, calculated on an annual basis.

Nominal Return

Return on an investment not adjusted for inflation (ie, headline return).

Nominal Value

Par value of a security (eg, redemption value on a bond).

Nominee

Legal owner of securities that are held by a third party on behalf of the underlying beneficial owner. Nominee accounts may be pooled (ie, the details of the beneficial owners are only known to the nominee company) or designated (ie, individual owners are identified on the register, along with the nominee).

Open-Ended Investment Company (OEIC)

Open-ended mutual funds that may have several sub funds and different share classes.

Offer Price

The price at which securities (or units in a collective investment fund) are sold to the investor.

Offshore Funds

Collective investment funds run outside the UK. Usually minimal regulatory oversight (and investor protection) and lower tax regime than the UK, EU or US.

Open-Ended Funds

For example, OEICs and unit trusts (mutual funds in the US).

Cash inflows from new investors increase the NAV of the fund and new units are created.

Redemptions (outflows) from the fund cause the NAV to shrink. Investors' units are re-purchased and may be cancelled.

Open Offer

Offer to shareholder where they can apply to increase the allocation made to them, but offer to buy the rights not taken up by others.

Open Outcry

Trades are conducted on the floor of the exchange, eg, New York Stock Exchange and some derivative exchanges. Largely replaced by electronic trading.

Option

A security that confers the right to buy or sell an underlying asset at a pre-determined strike (or exercise) price on or by a certain date. Options can be bought and sold to profit from the move in price of the option itself.

Ordinary Shares

Shares which confer full voting and dividend rights to the owner.

Out-Of-The-Money

An option or warrant that is not worth exercising at the current price of the underlying asset; the option has time value only.

Over-the-Counter (OTC)

Unregulated markets for dealing in assets or securities.

Overweight

A larger investment in a stock/sector/region than the relevant benchmark weighting.

Packaged Product

A life policy, unit trust or OEIC, ITC saving scheme, stakeholder pension or personal pension

Par

The nominal (or face) value of a security. Fixed income securities are usually redeemed at par.

It is generally illegal for a company to issue its shares at a discount to par.

Partly Paid

Investors in a new issue may be requested to pay the full purchase price in instalments and the shares will trade in partly paid form until they are fully paid.

Passive

Investment approach to match returns with the index/benchmark (see **Index Tracking**).

P/E Ratio

The ratio of the market price of a share to the annual earnings per share.

Perpetual Subordinated Unsecured Loan Stock

An example is a permanent interest bearing share (PIBS) issued by a building society It ranks after all other creditors and is irredeemable. Hence it has the highest credit risk of the liabilities of the issuing institution and it also has a high market risk because of its high duration.

Physical Delivery

Delivery of securities (or certificates evidencing ownership rights) to the buyer's custodian.

Placing

A new issue may be placed with a small number of institutions, thus reducing the costs.

Plain Vanilla or **Vanilla Swap**

A swap which has a very basic structure in which the counterparties to the trade exchange a fixed rate for a floating rate, and the notional principal amount is the same over the life of the swap.

Pooled Funds

Large funds in which several investors have an interest. Life companies usually refer to managed funds.

Portfolio

Group of assets to meet the needs of a specific investor.

Posting

Administration term used to describe transfer of an entry from the journal to the ledger.

Preference Shares

Fixed income shares which pay a fixed dividend (which is quoted as a net percentage of par). Preference dividends must be paid before ordinary dividends, but the dividend may be passed. Preference shareholders rank above ordinary shareholders if the company is wound up.

Premium

For example, the share price of an investment trust may be above the NAV, and is said to be at a premium.

Also, the price paid to buy an option.

Primary Market

The market for newly issued securities.

Private Equity

Unquoted shares in a company. May never have been listed on the Stock Exchange or may have been issued to raise capital in a buy-out (eg, MBO).

Programme Trade

Computer driven trades that are driven by price limits.

Prospectus

Legal document accompanying the issue of shares in a share class by a company or investment fund. Contains information such as details of investment objectives and charges.

Provisional Allotment Letter

See **Renounceable Documents**.

Proxy Votes

The means by which the beneficial owner instructs their representative to vote at a shareholder meeting.

Prudential Regulation Authority (PRA)

Established as an operationally independent part of the Bank of England for the prudential regulation of deposit takers (ie, banks, building societies, credit unions), insurers and systemically important investment firms.

Pump and Dump

A form of fraud that involves artificially inflating the price of an owned stock through false and misleading positive statements, in order to sell the cheaply purchased stock at a higher price. Once the operators of the scheme 'dump' their overvalued shares, the price falls and investors lose their money. Stocks that are the subject of pump-and-dump schemes are sometimes called 'chop stocks'.

Put Option

The right to sell the underlying asset at the strike price.

Put-Through

Also known as an agency cross, when a broker matches a buyer and seller of a security. In such cases each party obtains a price advantage.

Qualifying Policy

A UK life policy that allows the proceeds to be paid tax-free, provided certain HMRC rules are followed.

Qualitative Analysis

Determining the value of an investment by examining non-numeric characteristics, eg, people, products etc.

Quantitative Analysis ('Quant')

Use of mathematical techniques to make investment decisions.

Quartile Ranking

Relative ranking of a fund against its peer group in a league table that is divided into four quartiles.

Real Assets

Investments that are tangible, eg property or commodities. The prices are expected to keep pace with inflation.

Real Rate of Return

Nominal return adjusted for inflation.

Redemption

Cash taken out of an open-ended fund.

Redemption Date (Maturity)

The end of a fixed period, when the nominal value of a redeemable security will be repaid to the investor.

Registered Stock

Stock is registered in the name of the owner (or the nominee). This is the most common form of issue in the US and UK.

Renounceable Documents

Negotiable bearer securities:

- **Allotment Letter** – issued to successful applications in a new issue.
- **Provisional Allotment Letter** – sent to the existing shareholders in the case of a rights issue.
- **Renounceable Certificate** – sent to shareholder in the case of a capitalisation.
- **Split Receipt** – replaces the above during the initial dealing period.

Each includes instructions to either register the securities in the holder's name or sell the rights.

Repo

A repurchase agreement. An agreement to sell securities and buy back (repurchase) at a later date.

Residence

There is no statutory definition of residence. It is where a person lives. A person may have more than one residence or no residence at all. In the UK, a person is generally deemed resident for tax purposes if he is physically present in the UK for six months within a tax year, or makes habitual and substantial visits to the UK.

Retail Prices Index (RPI)

Measure of cost of living (inflation) in the UK.

Retained Earnings

The part of a company's profit that is not paid away as a dividend. Used to produce future earnings.

Return on Equity (ROE)

Company earnings divided by net asset value.

Reverse Yield Gap

Is the excess of the gross redemption yield of long-dated Gilts, minus the dividend yield of equities (FTSE All-Share index). It was the norm from 1959 till 2008 in the UK, because the growth rate expectation for equities exceeded the equity risk premium. Since 2008, gilt yields have fallen so sharply that they are now less than the yield on equities.

Rights Issue

A new issue of shares offered to existing shareholders in proportion to their existing holdings. Usually offered at a discount to entice take-up that causes the existing shares to fall in value to the theoretical ex-rights price.

Risk

See **Standard Deviation**.

Roll Up Fund

Also known as non-distributor funds. Income is not distributed but is accumulated, tax-free, apart from withholding tax but on remittance gains are subject to income tax in the hands of the investor.

Running Yield

The annual income payable on a bond, or on income funds, as a percentage of the price. Also known as the 'flat' or 'income' yield.

Scheme Particulars

Document providing detailed information about a unit trust. Details include charges, types of units, payment dates, equalisation process, investment restrictions etc.

Scrip Issue

Issue of free shares to current shareholders. Often used instead of a cash dividend (scrip dividend alternative).

Secondary Market

A market in which existing securities are traded.

Securities

Rights to payment of regular income or a share in the profits of a corporation. Negotiable (ie, may be market-traded or OTC).

Segregated Portfolios

Separate portfolios with ownership of securities separately identified.

Self-Invested Pension Plan (SIPP)

Has a single member. Aimed at individuals wishing to benefit from a greater range of direct and fund investments. Often effected by higher-paid self-employed professionals.

Settlement

The delivery or receipt of securities in exchange for payment.

Sharpe Ratio

A measure of the excess return earned on a portfolio, per unit of absolute risk (standard deviation).

Shares

Form of security that represents a shareholder's stake in a company (see **Equities** and **Preference Shares**).

Short Selling

Selling more of an asset than the investor owns in order to make a profit once the price falls.

This is usually not permitted for authorised funds and pension funds, but may be a strategy of hedge funds. The fund will need to borrow stock to cover a short position.

Short-Dated Gilts

Gilts with time to maturity of less than five years (Financial Times) or seven years (Bank of England).

Sinking Fund

Provision for repayment of the capital, either by gradually establishing a counterpart fund, or by using the annual provision to buy in through the market or by ballot. This will reduce the market risk (ie, reduce the duration) and the default risk of the bond.

Small Self-Administered Schemes (SSASs)

Company pensions for up to 12 members.

Société Investissement à Capital Variable (SICAV)

An open-ended collective investment fund. Usually operated under the UCITS Directive. Sells units in the fund to the public. Operates on a single (mid) pricing basis.

Sortino Ratio

A ratio developed by Frank Sortino, to differentiate between good and bad volatility in the Sharpe ratio.

Speculate

To engage in the buying or selling of an asset, in order to profit by a change in the market price.

Split

Company splits one share into several, with a corresponding reduction in the share price and the par value.

Spot

Spot price or spot rate is the current prevailing price/rate. This would apply to deals for standard settlement, ie not a forward.

Spread

The difference between the bid and offer prices.

Stag

A person who buys and rapidly sells shares when initially offered in order to make a quick profit; a short-term speculator.

Stamp Duty

Purchase Tax on UK shares. Gilts and AIM stocks are exempt. Currently 0.5%. SDRT (Stamp Duty Reserve Tax) payable on non-physical securities.

Standard Deviation

A measure of absolute volatility. It is the measure of the square root of the variance of returns from the mean. The higher the figure, the greater the volatility (ie, risk).

Statement of Investment Principles (SIP)

A written statement of the principles governing investment decisions. Legally required for stakeholder and occupational pensions.

Stock

Shares (Common Stock in the US). However, UK corporate bonds and government securities may also be described as stock. In this workbook the term 'stock' is generally used in the US sense to mean ordinary shares, or equity.

Stock Exchange

An organisation (either owned by the members or operated as a corporate body) that supervises and runs the market in securities. Ensures compliance with things such as listing rules and corporate governance.

Stock Exchange Automatic Quote (SEAQ)

SEAQ is a quote driven scheme where market makers make two-way prices. It is a quotation system, not an automatic dealing system, unlike SETS. It is largely restricted to fixed interest and less liquid AIM shares.

Stock Exchange Electronic Trading System (SETS)

Anonymous electronic order matching system of the London Stock Exchange.

Stock Lending

An agreement to 'lend' securities. Title of ownership is transferred to the counterparty and the borrower of the stock pays a fee to the lender. Voting rights transfer to the borrower, but any income is usually repaid to the lender.

Strategic Asset Allocation

The choice of assets to be held in a client portfolio and the limits set on the weightings by the client.

Separate Trading in Registered Interest & Principal Securities (STRIPs)

STRIPs are created when a government security is stripped into its component parts (coupons + principal). Each part is sold as a separate zero coupon security (see below).

Structured Product

Anything using derivatives, whether they are call and put options, futures, zero coupon bonds or swaps, to enhance, leverage, protect or guarantee an investment return.

Tactical Asset Allocation (TAA)

The weightings (holdings) of each asset class and market relative to the benchmark. Used to produce superior returns over the chosen time period.

Tail

The amount of government stock sold in an auction below the average price. The larger the tail, the wider the spread of accepted bids.

Tap Stocks

Government stock that may be issued in small amounts after the initial issue.

Tender

A method of setting prices for new issues. Potential investors are asked to tender an amount and price.

Tick

Financial markets move in different size price increments, and the minimum price movement is known as a tick. Futures markets often have specific tick sizes, but stock markets have a tick size of 0.01. Tick sizes and tick values are part of the contract specifications for all financial markets.

Top Down

Investment strategy that relies on decisions about asset classes, markets and industry sectors before stock selection.

Top-Slice

Sell part of a holding to reduce its weight in a portfolio. Also used in establishing taxable gain for non-qualifying life assurance.

Tracker Funds

Funds that seek to produce returns in line with an underlying benchmark (usually a stock index). The manager does not take active bets. The fund may buy stocks or track using quantitative techniques or derivatives.

Tracking Error

The volatility of returns of a fund relative to its benchmark.

Trash and Cash

Deliberately spreading false bear stories in order to depress the share price, and using the opportunity to buy cheaply.

Treasury Stock

Treasuries. Government fixed income securities.

Treasury Bills

Short-dated securities issued by the Central Bank, to finance government expenditure.

Treynor Ratio

A measure of the extra return earned by a portfolio, relative to the systematic risk taken, versus other portfolios.

Trial Balance

List of all ledger accounts. Credits and debits equal each other out.

Trust

A means of holding assets (legally owned by trustees) on behalf of underlying beneficial owners. Investment portfolios within a trust may be professionally managed eg charitable trust, unit trust etc. Governed by Trustee Act 2000.

Trustee

An individual or a group of people or independent institution responsible for the management of the trust, as defined by the trust deed. The trustees have the power to veto any investment they feel does not adhere to the trust deed.

UCITS Directive

A European Directive governing Undertakings For Collective Investment Schemes.

UCITS funds are authorised by the local regulator and subject to investment and borrowing restrictions. They can be marketed throughout the EEA.

Umbrella Fund

A single authorised scheme with any number of sub-funds. Investors (shareholders) may switch (transfer) from one share class to another.

Undated Gilts

Gilts without any redemption date or yield, eg, War Loan.

Underweight

A lower investment in a stock/sector/region than the relevant benchmark weighting.

Underwriter

A firm that agrees to underwrite a new issue, for a fee, thereby guaranteeing the securities will be sold.

Unfranked Income

Income on which no withholding-tax has been deducted. The investor may have a tax liability.

Unit-Linked Policy

A policy where returns are directly linked to the underlying assets. Units are purchased with premiums and are valued on a daily basis. They can be purchased in a variety of life assurance funds.

Unit Trust

An open-ended fund, diversifying investments to spread the risk to the investors. Investors buy units directly from the fund manager.

Authorised unit trusts are subject to FCA investment regulations. Unauthorised funds are not so restricted but cannot be marketed to members of the public.

Unlisted/Unquoted Securities

A security that is not listed on a Stock Exchange and is traded OTC, eg, eurobonds, ADRs, AIM shares and private equity.

Valuation Point

Time when open-ended retail mutual funds are valued, and the unit price is calculated.

Value at Risk (VaR)

An estimate of the maximum expected loss, over a specified period within a given degree of confidence.

Venture Capital

New capital injected into a company to pay for further developments, research and development (R&D) or to improve the balance sheet.

Volatility

See **Standard Deviation**.

Warrants

Long-dated options warrants give the holder the right to buy/sell a specified quantity of a particular stock, or any other asset, at a fixed price on or before a specified date.

Weighting

Percentage holding of a security in a portfolio, relative to the percentage (weight) in the underlying benchmark. Underweight means the portfolio holds a smaller percentage than that in the benchmark. Overweight portfolios hold a higher percentage.

Withholding Tax

Tax deducted from investment income that is paid to foreign investors. May be offset against the investor's domestic tax liability.

With-Profit Policy

A policy in which the policyholder has the right to amounts above the basic sum assured or death benefit, principally as the result of profits made on the investment of a fund.

WM

Independent performance measurement service. Offers pension funds and private client services.

Yield (on fixed interest stock)

The income yield on a fixed interest security is the annual gross interest payment (coupon) on £100 nominal divided by the price. See also Gross Redemption Yield.

Yield Gap

The spread (difference) between Gilt and equity yields (see **Reverse Yield Gap**).

Zero Coupon Security

A security that is issued at a discount to par (face value), and usually redeemed for full face value. May offer tax advantages by utilising CGT rates and allowance rather than income tax.

Abbreviations

ABI	Association of British Insurers
ACD	Authorised Corporate Director
ADR	American Depositary Receipt
AER	Annual Equivalent Rate
AFM	Alternative Fund Manager
AGM	Annual general meeting
AIC	Association of Investment Companies
AIM	Alternative Investment Market
ALM	Asset-Liability Management
AMC	Annual Management Charge
AMF	Annual Management Fee
AP	Approved Person
APP	Appropriate Personal Pension
APR	Annual Percentage Rate
ARTP	Additional Rate Taxpayer
AVC	Additional Voluntary Contribution
BCE	Benefit Crystallisation Event
BES	Business Expansion Scheme
BPR	Business Property Relief
BRTP	Basic Rate Taxpayer
BSP	Basic State Pension
BVLP	Bolsa de Valores de Lisboa e Porto (Portuguese Stock Exchange)
CAD	Capital Adequacy Directive Cash against Delivery
CAPM	Capital Asset Pricing Model
CAP	Chargeable Accounting Period
CAPS	Combined Actuarial Performance Service
CBOT	Chicago Board of Trade
CCP	Central Counterparty
CD	Certificate of Deposit
CF	Controlled Function
CFD	Contract for Difference
CGT	Capital Gains Tax
CHAPS	Clearing House Automated Payment System
CIC	Critical Illness Cover
CIS	Collective Investment Schemes
CJA	Criminal Justice Act
CLT	Chargeable Lifetime Transfer
CMA	Cash Memorandum Account
CME	Chicago Mercantile Exchange
COBS	Conduct of Business Sourcebook
CP	Commercial Paper
CPI	Consumer Prices Index
CRD	Capital Requirements Directive
CSRC	China Securities Regulatory Commission
CTF	Child Trust Fund
DBS	Disclosure and Barring Service
DJIA	Dow Jones Industrial Average
DMA	Direct Market Access
DMO	Debt Management Office
Dow	Dow Jones Industrial Average
DR	Depositary Receipt
DTA	Decreasing Term Assurance
DVP	Delivery versus Payment
EAR	Effective Annual Rate
EEA	European Economic Area
EIS	Enterprise Investment Scheme
EMH	Efficient Markets Hypothesis
EMU	European Monetary Union
EPA	Enduring Powers of Attorney
ETC	Electronic Trade Confirmation
ETC	Exchange-Traded Commodity
ETF	Exchange-Traded Fund

EU	European Union		ICVC	Investment Company with Variable Capital
EV	Enterprise Value		IDB	Inter-Dealer Broker
FAS	Financial Assistance Schemes		IFA	Independent Financial Advisors
FCA	Financial Conduct Authority		IHT	Inheritance Tax
FIB	Family Income Benefit		IOB	International Order Book
FPC	Financial Policy Committee		IMF	International Monetary Fund
FOS	Financial Ombudsman Service		IPI	Income Protection Insurance
FRA	Forward Interest Rate Agreements		IPO	Initial Public Offering
FSA	Financial Services Authority (regulator until April 2013)		IRS	International Retail Service
FSAP	Financial Services Action Plan		ISA	Individual Savings Account
FSAVC	Free Standing Additional Voluntary Contribution		ISD	Investment Services Directive
FSCS	Financial Services Compensation Scheme		ITEPA	Income Tax (Earnings and Pensions) Act
FSMA	Financial Services and Markets Act 2000 (as amended)		ITTOIA	Income Tax (Trading & Other Income) Act
FSMT	Financial Services and Markets Tribunal		JMLSG	Joint Money Laundering Steering Group
FTSE	Financial Times Stock Exchange		JPX	Japan Exchange Group
FUM	Funds Under Management		KFI	Key Facts Illustration
GAD	Government Actuary's Department		KIID	Key Investor Information Document
GARP	Growth At a Reasonable Price		KYC	Know Your Customer
GDP	Gross Domestic Product		LDI	Liability Driven Investment
GDR	Global Depositary Receipt		LEL	Lower Earnings Limit
GEIS	Global Equity Index Series		LET	Low Earnings Threshold
GEMM	Gilt-Edged Market Maker		LIBID	London inter-bank bid rate
GIPS	Global Investment Performance Standards		LIBOR	London Inter-Bank Offered Rate
GRY	Gross Redemption Yield		LIFFE	London International Financial Futures and Options Exchange
HMRC	Her Majesty's Revenue & Customs		LPA	Lasting Power of Attorney
HMT	Her Majesty's Treasury		LPI	Limited Price Indexation
HRTP	Higher Rate Taxpayer		LSE	London Stock Exchange
IA	Investment Association		MCA	Married Couple Allowance
ICE	Intercontinental Exchange		MAS	Money Advice Service
			MFR	Minimum Funding Requirement

MI	Management Information		**OTC**	Over-The-Counter
MiFID	Markets in Financial Instruments Directive		**PAYE**	Pay As You Earn
MIR	Minimum Income Requirement		**PCB**	Pensions Compensation Board
ML	Money Laundering		**PCIAM**	Private Client Investment Advice & Management
MLRO	Money Laundering Reporting Officer		**PCRC**	Performance Category Review Committee
MNT	Member Nominated Trustees		**PEP**	Personal Equity Plan
MPT	Modern Portfolio Theory		**P/E ratio**	Price/earnings ratio
MQS	Minimum Quote Size		**PET**	Potentially Exempt Transfer
MSCI	Morgan Stanley Capital International indices		**PHI**	Permanent Health Insurance
MTF	Multilateral Trading Facility		**PIBS**	Permanent Interest Bearing Share
MVR	Market Value Reduction		**plc**	Public limited company
MWR	Money-Weighted Rate of Return		**PMI**	Private Medical Insurance
NAO	National Audit Officer		**POAT**	Pre-Owned Assets Tax
NASDAQ	National Association of Securities Dealers Automatic Quote		**POTAM**	Panel on Takeovers and Mergers
NAV	Net Asset Value		**PPF**	Pension Protection Fund
NEST	National Employment Savings Trust		**PPP**	Personal Pension Plan
NHS	National Health Service		**PRA**	Prudential Regulation Authority
NIC	National insurance contributions		**PSBs**	Perpetual subordinated bonds
NMS	Normal Market Size		**PSNCR**	Public Sector Net Cash Requirement
NOMAD	Nominated Adviser		**QE**	Quantitative Easing
NRB	Nil-Rate Band		**QIS**	Qualified Investor Schemes
NSC	National Savings Certificate		**QSR**	Quick Succession Relief
NS&I	National Savings & Investments		**RAC**	Retirement Annuity Contract
NURS	Non-UCITS Retail Schemes		**RIE**	Recognised Investment Exchange
NYSE	New York Stock Exchange		**RCH**	Recognised Clearing House
OEIC	Open-Ended Investment Company		**RDC**	Regulatory Decisions Committee
OMO	Open Market Option		**RDR**	Retail Distribution Review
OPRA	Occupational Pensions Regulatory Authority		**REIT**	Real Estate Investment Trust
OPS	Occupational Pension Schemes		**RNS**	Regulatory News Service
ORBs	Order book for Retail Bonds		**ROE**	Return on Equity
			ROCE	Return on Capital Employed
			RPI	Retail Price Index

RUR	Register Update Requests
S&P	Standard and Poor's
S2P	State Second Pension
SAYE	Save as you earn
SDRT	Stamp Duty Reserve Tax
SEAQ	Stock Exchange Automated Quotation system
SERPS	State Earnings Related Pension Scheme
SET	Secondary Earnings Threshold
SETS	Stock Exchange Electronic Trading Service
SETSqx	Stock Exchange Electronic Trading Service – quotes and crosses
SICAV	Société d'Investissement à Capital Variable
SIF	Significant Influence Function
SIP	Statement of Investment Principles
SIPP	Self-Invested Pension Plan
SML	Security Market Line
SMP	Statutory Maternity Pay
SPA	State Pension Age
SPAN	Standard Portfolio Analysis and Risk
SPLAB	Single Premium Life Assurance Bond
SRI	Socially Responsible Investment
SRT	Statutory Residence Test
SSAS	Small Self-Administered Scheme
SSE	Shanghai Stock Exchange
SSE	Single Settlement Engine
SSP	Statutory Sick Pay
STP	Straight Through Processing
STRIPS	Separate Trading in Registered Interest & Principal Securities
STT	Sufficient Ties Test
TAA	Tactical Asset Allocation

TCF	Treating Customers Fairly
TER	Total Expense Ratio
TERP	Theoretical ex-rights price
TMT	Technology, Media and Telecom
TP	Taxpayer
TPR	The Pensions Regulator
TWR	Time-Weighted Rate of Return
UCITS	Undertaking for Collective Investments in Transferable Securities
UFPLS	Uncrystalised Funds Pension Lump Sum
UKLA	UK Listing Authority
VaR	Value at Risk
VAT	Value Added Tax
VCT	Venture Capital Trust
WMA	Wealth Management Association (previously APCIMS)
XD	Ex-Dividend
XR	Ex-Rights

Useful Websites

Barclays Capital	barcap.com
DMO	www.gov.uk/government/organisations/uk-debt-management-office
FCA	fca.org.uk
FCA	fshandbook.info/FS/html/FCA – for the Handbook
HMRC	www.gov.uk/government/organisations/hm-revenue-customs
IMA	investmentuk.org
JMLSG	www.jmlsg.org.uk
NS&I	nsandi.com
PRA	bankofengland.co.uk/pra

Syllabus Learning Map

Aims

The aims of this paper are to:

1. Develop a broad understanding of the principles of private client investment within the context of the current regulatory environment.
2. Identify the investment requirements of clients from the relevant information available.
3. Select suitable products available to meet the clients' needs.
4. Demonstrate the ability to communicate conclusions to a client in an appropriate manner.
5. Ensure that students develop the skills to maintain their competence and knowledge.

Assessment Structure

A three-hour paper divided into three sections:

Section A: Ten compulsory short answer questions. This section will carry 40% of the marks.

Section B: Three essays of which students will be expected to answer one. In this section, students are expected to show depth of knowledge on a particular topic and be able to discuss all aspects of the subject in question. This section will carry 20% of the marks.

Section C: One compulsory structured question comprising a number of parts, based on a case study. The students' ability to give investment advice will be tested. This section will carry 40% of the marks.

Tax tables, RPI figures and Market Makers' Gilts lists will be provided.

Reading List

At the end of this syllabus we have supplied a reading list. Candidates attempting this examination are strongly advised to relate their reading to practitioner experience. Candidates who read more widely and can draw on this broader context fare better in higher, post graduate level examinations of this nature, where both breadth and depth are required.

Section One

Financial Advice within a Regulated Environment

Learning Outcome:

Candidates will be able to assess the implications of the UK legal and regulatory framework as they apply to the provision of private client investment advice.

Assessment Criteria:

Candidates can:

- Interpret the regulatory environment, supervision and rules governing private client advice and management in the UK
- Summarise the fiduciary responsibility towards customers and their legal right to recourse
- Assess the regulatory requirements of the main investment trading and settlement mechanisms within the UK and overseas
- Determine how the factors above govern and influence the business processes and practice of private client advice and management

Learning Objectives:

1.   The Legal and Regulatory Framework

1. Understand the main provisions of the FSMA 2000 and associated secondary legislation and assess their implications for the business operations of the private client adviser.
2. Understand the aims of the European Financial Services Action Plan, and evaluate the effects of MiFID and CRD on the business systems and controls of the private client adviser.
3. Understand the role, regulatory objectives and functions of the Financial Conduct Authority (FCA) and Prudential Regulation Authority (PRA) and how they affect the control structures of firms.
4. Relate the FCA's Principles and Conduct of Business rules to the processes of advising clients, managing investments, and reporting to customers.
5. Apply the rules on 'treating customers fairly' and 'client's best interest' to the process of advising clients.
6. Know the extent of an investment adviser's duty to disclose material information about a recommended investment.
7. Identify 'conflicts of interest' and their potential impact on clients and business operations, and understand the compliance requirements that exist to prevent such occurrences.
8. Understand the fiduciary responsibilities of intermediaries, the rights of aggrieved customers and the rules for handling complaints.
9. Understand the principal measures to combat financial crime (insider dealing, market abuse, money laundering) and evaluate their impact on the firm, the private client adviser and the process of advising and managing private client investments.

Section Two

Investment Taxation

Learning Outcome:

Candidates will be able to assess the impact of taxation on the evaluation of investments and the provision of investment advice.

Assessment Criteria:

Candidates can:

- Summarise the basic structure of the UK tax system.
- Determine the impact of the main taxes (on income and capital) that may be charged to individuals.
- Determine the impact of domicile and residence on an individual's liability to UK tax.
- Assess the impact of taxation on the investment decision-making process, and the need to tailor an appropriate strategy according to the needs of the client and the range of strategies available.

Note: All references to taxation refer to taxes applicable in the United Kingdom. Tax tables will be provided in the examination where necessary.

Learning Objectives:

A.   Income Tax

1. Understand the role of HMRC and the structure of the UK self-assessment tax system.
2. Understand when and how income tax is applied to earnings, interest and dividends and, in some cases, capital gains.
3. Be able to calculate simple tax computations.
4. Apply the main rules relating to allowable deductions, Personal Allowances and reliefs, marriage and civil partnerships and their breakdown, and the tax liabilities of minors.
5. Understand the tax treatment of different kinds of investments and the taxation of income arising on overseas investments.
6. Evaluate the tax efficiency of an investment asset within the wider context of suitability for an individual customer.

B.   Capital Gains Tax

7. Understand the principles of capital gains tax, and when and how it arises.
8. Understand the main CGT exemptions and reliefs available including main residence, exempt assets and exemption limits applicable for individuals, trusts and estates.
9. Understand the main disposal rules for CGT, including special rules that apply to disposals on death and between spouses/civil partners.

10. Know the calculations applicable to assets purchased prior to and post–31 March 1982.
11. Be able to calculate taxable gains on an individual's net gains for a fiscal year.
12. Understand due dates for paying CGT and the use of CGT deferral.

C.   Inheritance Tax

13. Understand the liability to IHT, and the effects on IHT liability of chargeable lifetime transfers and transfers on death.
14. Understand IHT exemptions and reliefs, excluded assets, potentially exempt transfers, and gifts with reservation.
15. Understand the rules governing the administration of estates, grant of probate and registration of probate.
16. Be able to value assets for probate and lifetime transfers.
17. Be able to calculate IHT liability based on a straightforward example.
18. Understand the relationship between the valuation of assets for CGT purposes, and valuation of assets for IHT-related chargeable lifetime and estate transfers.

D.   Offshore Tax

19. Understand the tax treatment of onshore and offshore funds.
20. Evaluate the suitability of an offshore investment for a UK-domiciled individual.

Section Three

Financial Markets

Learning Outcome:

Candidates will be able to evaluate the relevance of market-related factors that can influence investment decisions, processes and advice.

Assessment Criteria:

Candidates can:

- Differentiate between the key features of the main UK and overseas markets (including fixed income and equity) and specify the purpose and methods of trading, settlement, registration and holding of assets.
- Assess and justify the political, economic and practical risks, costs and benefits of trading or investing in a particular market.
- Assess the suitability and appropriateness of trading or investing in certain markets to help meet the investment objectives of a private customer.
- Explain the purposes of and requirements of issuing contract notes and the operation of nominee companies.

Learning Objectives:

A.   World Financial Markets

1. Understand the relative size of world equity markets and predominant asset sectors within each market.
2. Know the key features of the global government and corporate bond markets.
3. Understand the relative benefits, risks and costs of investing in developed and emerging markets.
4. Understand and differentiate between exchange-traded, over-the-counter and alternative markets.
5. Apply the principles of asset and liability matching when managing investments in different currencies.
6. Understand how indices are constructed, and the purposes and limitations in using them.

B.   UK Markets

7. Understand the main organisations and processes for transacting, clearing, settling and safekeeping domestic financial securities.
8. Know the methods by which domestic securities are issued and brought to market.
9. Be aware of the purposes and requirements for issuing contract notes.
10. Understand the applicability of VAT, stamp duty and stamp duty reserve tax to transactions in financial securities.
11. Understand the purposes and operation of nominee companies.

Section Four

Trusts and Trustees

Learning Outcome:

Candidates will be able to understand the principles and key features of Trusts and the law governing their creation and management.

Assessment Criteria:

*   Compare the main types of trusts available under UK law, their key features and taxation considerations.
*   Explain the benefits, limitations and requirements to achieve charitable status.
*   Evaluate the taxation implications of different scenarios involving trusts.
*   Evaluate the merits of using a trust as a means to achieve a specific client objective.

Learning Objectives:

A. Trusts and Trust Legislation

1. Know the key features of trusts – arrangement, participants, types, documentation.
2. Know the different types of trust and what each is designed to achieve.
3. Understand the key provisions of the Trustee Act 2000 and how these relate to the investment powers of trustees and the trust deed.

B. Taxation of Trusts

4. Understand the concept of a chargeable lifetime transfer and be able to assess the IHT consequences of different scenarios relating to interest in possession.
5. Know the requirements for charitable status, how charities are taxed, and the purpose and rules of Gift Aid.

Section Five

Financial Instruments and Products

Learning Outcome:

Candidates will understand the different types of investment asset classes, financial instruments, products and schemes available in the UK.

Assessment Criteria:

Candidates can:

- Differentiate between the investment asset classes, financial instruments, products and schemes that are available in the UK in terms of key features, potential risk and reward, pricing & market availability, and any special taxation, redemption and penalty features that may apply.

Learning Objectives:

To be able to understand, analyse and evaluate:

A. Bank and Building Society Savings Accounts

1. The different types of bank and building society accounts.
2. The advantages and disadvantages of cash investments.
3. The Deposit Protection Scheme.

B.   National Savings & Investments (NS&I)

4. The characteristics of different NS & I investments.
5. Their suitability for different tax status investors.
6. The terms and penalties for early surrender.

C.   Government Debt

7. Types of securities issued by central government and local authorities.
8. Features and redemption terms of fixed, floating rate and index-linked bonds.
9. Strips and strippable bonds.
10. Redemption dates and the use of sinking funds.
11. Calculation of accrued interest.
12. The tax efficiency of comparative stocks.
13. Break-even inflation rates.
14. The calculation and interpretation of flat yield and redemption yield.
15. The features and determinates of the yield curve.
16. Duration and its determinants.
17. Modified duration, its determinants and usefulness as a measure to price volatility.
18. Methods of trading government debt including relative merits and disadvantages.
19. Reasons for investing in government debt.

D.   Corporate Debt

20. Features and redemption terms of different types of corporate debt.
21. Structure and relevance of credit ratings in the evaluation process.
22. Convertible bonds, and the effect of conversions on a company and its securities.
23. Capital and interest cover.
24. Security and borrowing powers.
25. Building Society PIBS and Perpetual Subordinated Bonds.

E.   Corporate Equity

26. Features of ordinary shares and types of dividend.
27. Features of cumulative, non-cumulative, participating, convertible and redeemable preference shares.
28. Shareholders' voting rights and their responsibilities.
29. Capitalisation and rights issues, buy backs and their effects.
30. Risks and rewards of equity.
31. Beta values.
32. Analytical measures of equity valuation, and their relative merits and uses.
33. Measures of dividend yield, dividend cover, earnings yield, price-earnings ratio, and price book ratio.
34. Relevance of the reverse yield gap.

F.   Financial Derivatives

35. Features of UK traded options and covered warrants on individual securities and indices.
36. Terms and timescales of different kinds of traded options and warrants.

37. Valuation and quotation of traded options and warrants.
38. The effect of and treatment of scrip issues, rights and dividends in the underlying security.
39. Features of UK company warrants.
40. Features of financial futures on equity indices.
41. Relevance of cost of carry and fair value.
42. Operation and relevance of margin in the clearing and settlement process.
43. Features of contracts for difference (CFDs).

G.   Unit Trusts and OEICs

44. Similarities and differences.
45. Types of fund, pricing, charging structures, separation of management and ownership, dealing and settlement, tax treatment.

H.   Exchange-Traded Funds

46. Features, including types of fund, pricing, charging structures, dealing and settlement, tax treatment.
47. Comparison with other types of fund.

I.   Investment Trusts

48. Similarities with and differences from other types of fund.
49. Differences between conventional and split-level investment trusts.
50. Concepts of 'B/C' shares and warrants, zero and stepped preference.
51. Real estate investment trusts (REITs).
52. Determinants and relevance of net asset value discounts and premiums.

J.   ISAs

53. Key features of ISAs.
54. Differences between cash and stocks and shares ISAs.

K.   Child Trust Funds

55. Key features and types, including contribution limits.

L.   Private Equity Schemes

56. Characteristics of Enterprise Investment Schemes, Venture Capital Trusts and AIM investments, including contribution limits, tax relief and suitability considerations .

M. Life Assurance and Protection Products

57. Purposes, key features and relative merits of life assurance products – term, whole-life, endowment; regular premium policies and single premium bonds; with/without profits, unit-linked; guaranteed income and growth; annuities.
58. Income, capital gains and inheritance tax implications of investing in life assurance products.
59. Purposes, key features and relative merits of protection products: income protection insurance (IPI), critical illness cover (CIC) and private medical insurance (PMI).

N. Pension Provision and Eligibility

60. State pension scheme including SERPS and S2P.
61. Occupational pension schemes, including the relative merits and disadvantages of defined benefit and defined contribution schemes.
62. Relevance of the Pensions Acts 1995 and 2004 in protecting members of occupational schemes including redress and compensation.
63. Pension simplification, including annual and lifetime limits.
64. Personal pension schemes, stakeholder pensions and eligible forms of retirement benefits.
65. Pension solutions for higher earners – key features and operation of self-invested and self-directed schemes.
66. Impact of employer, income and lifestyle changes on pension provision.

Section Six

Principles of Financial Advice

Learning Outcome:

Candidates will be able to recommend suitable investment products for individual customers.

Assessment Criteria:

Candidates can:

- Integrate fiduciary, ethical and regulatory responsibilities with technical proficiency when conducting customer fact finds.
- Prepare a client profile in line with 'Know Your Customer' principles, showing a clear relationship between the information elicited and the formulation of appropriate customer-led objectives and constraints.
- Identify, analyse and select suitable investments in order to construct a portfolio tailored to meet the agreed objectives of an individual customer.
- Recommend investment suggestions in a non-misleading and balanced way, setting out both the potential merits and disadvantages of an investment and its net effect on a customer's investment portfolio.

Learning Objectives:

A.   Establish Client Objectives and Constraints

1.   Understand risk and return objectives and how to construct a risk-return profile.
2.   Identify the major types of investment risk, and where and how they typically arise.
3.   Explain the impact of inflation, deflation, taxation and charges on investment returns.
4.   Understand the importance of timescale in relation to risk and the time value of money.
5.   Understand the essential features and purpose of a customer profile, particularly the customer's personal details, income, assets, liabilities, expectations, risk tolerance and existing investment provision.
6.   Understand the regulatory requirements regarding the need for and content of client agreement documentation and related communication.
7.   Understand and be able to address customer concerns about confidentiality and security, data protection, fees, periodic reporting and customer communications.

B.   Design an Investment Strategy

8.   Understand the key features and risk-reward profile of the main investment approaches, including passive/active, buy/hold, momentum, core/satellite, value, growth, direct, indirect, ethical/SRI, lifestyle, hedge and structured fund approaches.
9.   Determine a suitable investment strategy with regard to preferred investment approach, time horizon, income, growth, balance, tax position, costs, market and sector diversification and expected risk and return.
10. Analyse the means to implementing that policy, including short–term liquidity, available investments, choice between UK and overseas markets and direct and indirect routes.
11. Specify or recommend appropriate portfolio components, taking into account overall suitability, cost and ease of implementation and maintenance.

Section Seven

Portfolio Performance and Review

Learning Outcome:

Candidates will be able to evaluate investment performance and review portfolio requirements in response to market movements and customer requirements.

Assessment Criteria:

Candidates can:

- Apply appropriate indices and benchmarks to the comparative analysis of investment performance.
- Evaluate and periodically review portfolio composition in order to continually maintain adherence to client objectives.

Learning Objectives:

A.   Portfolio Performance Measurement

1. Understand the principles of time weighted and money weighted rates of return.
2. Understand the principles of risk including volatility, standard deviation, alpha and portfolio risk.
3. Know the main stock market indices and how they operate.
4. Understand the key features of indices published by FTSE and WMA.
5. Apply appropriate indices and benchmarks to the comparative analysis of investment performance.
6. Evaluate and periodically review portfolio composition in order to continually maintain adherence to client objectives.

CISI Chartered MCSI Membership can work for you...

Studying for a CISI qualification is hard work and we're sure you're putting in plenty of hours, but don't lose sight of your goal!

This is just the first step in your career; there is much more to achieve!

The securities and investments industry attracts ambitious and driven individuals. You're probably one yourself and that's great, but on the other hand you're almost certainly surrounded by lots of other people with similar ambitions.

So how can you stay one step ahead during these uncertain times?

Entry Criteria for Chartered MCSI Membership

As an ACSI and MCSI candidate, you can upgrade your membership status to Chartered MCSI. There are a number of ways of gaining the CISI Chartered MCSI membership.

A straightforward route requires candidates to have:
- a minimum of one year's ACSI or MCSI membership;
- passed a full Diploma; Certificate in Private Client Investment Advice & Management or Masters in Wealth Management award;
- passed the IntegrityMatters with an A grade; and
- successfully logged and certified 12 months' CPD under the CISI's CPD Scheme.

Alternatively, experienced-based candidates are required to have:
- a minimum of one year's ACSI membership;
- passed the IntegrityMatters with an A grade; and
- successfully logged and certified six years' CPD under the CISI's CPD Scheme.

Joining Fee:	Current Grade of Membership	Grade of Chartership	Upgrade Cost
	ACSI	Chartered MCSI	£75.00
	MCSI	Chartered MCSI	£30.00

By belonging to a Chartered professional body, members will benefit from enhanced status in the industry and the wider community. Members will be part of an organisation which holds the respect of government and industry, and can communicate with the public on a whole new level. There will be little doubt in consumers' minds that chartered members of the CISI are highly regarded and qualified professionals and as a consequence will be required to act as such.

The Chartered MCSI designation will provide you with full access to all member benefits, including Professional Refresher where there are currently over 60 modules available on subjects including Behavioural Finance, Cybercrime and Conduct Risk. CISI TV is also available to members, allowing you to catch up on the latest CISI events, whilst earning valuable CPD hours.

Revision Express Interactive

You've bought the workbook... now test your knowledge before your exam.

Revision Express Interactive is an engaging online study tool to be used in conjunction with CISI workbooks. It contains exercises and revision questions.

Key Features of Revision Express Interactive:
- Examination-focused – the content of Revision Express Interactive covers the key points of the syllabus
- Questions throughout to reaffirm understanding of the subject
- Special end-of-module practice exam to reflect as closely as possible the standard you will experience in your exam (please note, however, they are not the CISI exam questions themselves)
- Interactive exercises throughout
- Extensive glossary of terms
- Useful associated website links
- Allows you to study whenever you like

IMPORTANT: The questions contained in Revision Express Interactive elearning products are designed as aids to revision, and should not be seen in any way as mock exams.

Price per elearning module: £35
Price when purchased with the CISI workbook: £100 (normal price: £110)

To purchase Revision Express Interactive:

call our Customer Support Centre on:
+44 20 7645 0777

or visit CISI Online Bookshop at:
cisi.org/bookshop

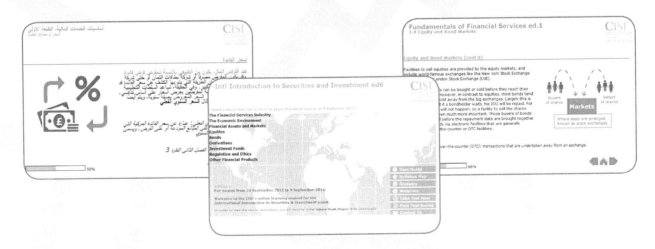

For more information on our elearning products, contact our Customer Support Centre on +44 20 7645 0777, or visit our website at cisi.org/study

Professional Refresher

Self-testing elearning modules to refresh your knowledge, meet regulatory and firm requirements, and earn CPD hours.

Professional Refresher is a training solution to help you remain up-to-date with industry developments, maintain regulatory compliance and demonstrate continuing learning.

This popular online learning tool allows self-administered refresher testing on a variety of topics, including the latest regulatory changes.

There are currently over 70 modules available which address UK and international issues. Modules are reviewed by practitioners frequently and new topics are added to the suite on a regular basis.

Benefits to firms:
- Learning and tests can form part of business T&C programme
- Learning and tests kept up-to-date and accurate by the CISI
- Relevant and useful – devised by industry practitioners
- Access to individual results available as part of management overview facility, 'Super User'
- Records of staff training can be produced for internal use and external audits
- Cost-effective – no additional charge for CISI members
- Available to non-members

Benefits to individuals:
- Comprehensive selection of topics across industry sectors
- Modules are frequently reviewed and updated by industry experts
- New topics introduced regularly
- Free for members
- Successfully passed modules are recorded in your CPD log as Active Learning
- Counts as structured learning for RDR purposes
- On completion of a module, a certificate can be printed out for your own records

The full suite of Professional Refresher modules is free to CISI members or £250 for non-members. Modules are also available individually. To view a full list of Professional Refresher modules visit:

cisi.org/refresher

If you or your firm would like to find out more contact our Client Relationship Management team:

+ 44 20 7645 0670
crm@cisi.org

For more information on our elearning products, contact our Customer Support Centre on +44 20 7645 0777, or visit our website at cisi.org/study

Professional Refresher

Top 5

SCORM COMPLIANT

Integrity & Ethics
- High Level View
- Ethical Behaviour
- An Ethical Approach
- Compliance vs Ethics

Anti-Money Laundering
- Introduction to Money Laundering
- UK Legislation and Regulation
- Money Laundering Regulations 2007
- Proceeds of Crime Act 2002
- Terrorist Financing
- Suspicious Activity Reporting
- Money Laundering Reporting Officer
- Sanctions

Financial Crime
- What Is Financial Crime?
- Insider Dealing and Market Abuse Introduction, Legislation, Offences and Rules
- Money Laundering Legislation, Regulations, Financial Sanctions and Reporting Requirements
- Money Laundering and the Role of the MLRO

Information Security and Data Protection
- Information Security: The Key Issues
- Latest Cybercrime Developments
- The Lessons From High-Profile Cases
- Key Identity Issues: Know Your Customer
- Implementing the Data Protection Act 1998
- The Next Decade: Predictions For The Future

UK Bribery Act
- Background to the Act
- The Offences
- What the Offences Cover
- When Has an Offence Been Committed?
- The Defences Against Charges of Bribery
- The Penalties

Conduct Rules
- Application and Overview
- Individual Conduct Rules – FCA & PRA
- Senior Management Conduct Rules
- Obligations on Firms

Pensions Advice
- Advice or Guidance?
- Advice During Accumulation
- Defined Contribution Pension Freedoms
- Transfers and Decumulation
- Problems with Accessing New Freedoms

Retirement Planning
- Pensions and Provisions
- Money In
- Money Out

Financial Planning (An introduction)
- Related Activities
- The Financial Plan
- Cash Flow Planning and Modelling
- Behavioural Finance and Financial Planning
- Risk
- The Regulatory Framework
- The Future Landscape

Senior Managers and Certification Regime
- Definitions
- Obligations
- Certification
- Conduct Rules
- Scope of the Rules
- Conclusion and Future Developments

Operations

Best Execution
- What Is Best Execution?
- Achieving Best Execution
- Order Execution Policies
- Information to Clients & Client Consent
- Monitoring, the Rules, and Instructions
- Best Execution for Specific Types of Firms

Approved Persons Regime
- The Basis of the Regime
- Fitness and Propriety
- The Controlled Functions
- Principles for Approved Persons
- The Code of Practice for Approved Persons

Corporate Actions
- Corporate Structure and Finance
- Life Cycle of an Event
- Mandatory Events
- Voluntary Events

Wealth

Client Assets and Client Money
- Protecting Client Assets and Client Money
- Ring-Fencing Client Assets and Client Money
- Due Diligence of Custodians
- Reconciliations
- Records and Accounts
- CASS Oversight

Investment Principles and Risk
- Diversification
- Factfind and Risk Profiling
- Investment Management
- Modern Portfolio Theory and Investing Styles
- Direct and Indirect Investments
- Socially Responsible Investment
- Collective Investments
- Investment Trusts
- Dealing in Debt Securities and Equities

Banking Standards
- Introduction and Background
- Strengthening Individual Accountability
- Reforming Corporate Governance
- Securing Better Outcomes for Consumers
- Enhancing Financial Stability

Suitability of Client Investments
- Assessing Suitability
- Risk Profiling
- Establishing Risk Appetite
- Obtaining Customer Information
- Suitable Questions and Answers
- Making Suitable Investment Selections
- Guidance, Reports and Record Keeping

International

Foreign Account Tax Compliance Act (FATCA)
- Foreign Financial Institutions
- Due Diligence Requirements
- Reporting
- Compliance

MiFID II
- The Organisations Covered by MiFID
- The Products Subject to MiFID's Guidelines
- The Origins of MiFID II
- The Products Covered by MiFID II
- Levels 1, 2, and 3 Implementation

UCITS
- The Original UCITS Directive
- UCITS III
- UCITS IV
- Non-UCITS Funds
- Future Developments

cisi.org/refresher

Feedback to the CISI

Have you found this workbook to be a valuable aid to your studies? We would like your views, so please email us at learningresources@cisi.org with any thoughts, ideas or comments.

Accredited Training Partners

Support for examination students studying for the Chartered Institute for Securities & Investment (CISI) Qualifications is provided by several Accredited Training Partners (ATPs), including Fitch Learning and BPP. The CISI's ATPs offer a range of face-to-face training courses, distance learning programmes, their own learning resources and study packs which have been accredited by the CISI. The CISI works in close collaboration with its ATPs to ensure they are kept informed of changes to CISI examinations so they can build them into their own courses and study packs.

CISI Workbook Specialists Wanted

Workbook Authors

Experienced freelance authors with finance experience, and who have published work in their area of specialism, are sought. Responsibilities include:
- Updating workbooks in line with new syllabuses and any industry developments
- Ensuring that the syllabus is fully covered

Workbook Reviewers

Individuals with a high-level knowledge of the subject area are sought. Responsibilities include:
- Highlighting any inconsistencies against the syllabus
- Assessing the author's interpretation of the workbook

Workbook Technical Reviewers

Technical reviewers provide a detailed review of the workbook and bring the review comments to the panel. Responsibilities include:
- Cross-checking the workbook against the syllabus
- Ensuring sufficient coverage of each learning objective

Workbook Proofreaders

Proofreaders are needed to proof workbooks both grammatically and also in terms of the format and layout. Responsibilities include:
- Checking for spelling and grammar mistakes
- Checking for formatting inconsistencies

If you are interested in becoming a CISI external specialist call:
+44 20 7645 0609

or email:
externalspecialists@cisi.org

For bookings, orders, membership and general enquiries please contact our Customer Support Centr on +44 20 7645 0777, or visit our website at cisi.org